THE HUMAN RIGHTS OF ANTI-TERRORISM

The Human Rights of Anti-terrorism

Nicole LaViolette & Craig Forcese
EDITORS

The Human Rights of Anti-terrorism
© Irwin Law Inc., 2008

Published in 2008 by

Irwin Law Inc.
14 Duncan Street
Suite 206
Toronto, Ontario
M5H 3G8

www.irwinlaw.com

ISBN-13: 978-155221-153-3

Library and Archives Canada Cataloguing in Publication

The human rights of anti-terrorism / Nicole LaViolette & Craig Forcese, editors.

Includes the Ottawa principles on anti-terrorism and human rights, and papers written by participants at the conference, The Human Rights of Anti-terrorism: a Colloquium, held at the University of Ottawa, Jun. 15, 2006.
Includes bibliographical references and index.
ISBN 978-1-55221-153-3

1. Human rights—Congresses. 2. Terrorism—Prevention—Congresses. I. Forcese, Craig II. LaViolette, Nicole III. Human Rights of Anti-terrorism: a Colloquium (2006 : University of Ottawa) IV. Title: Ottawa principles on anti-terrorism and human rights.

K3240.H82 2008   341.4'8   C2008-902943-7

The publisher acknowledges the financial support of the Government of Canada through the Book Publishing Industry Development Program (BPIDP) for its publishing activities.

We acknowledge the assistance of the OMDC Book Fund, an initiative of Ontario Media Development Corporation.

Printed and bound in Canada.

1 2 3 4 5   12 11 10 09 08

Table of Contents

Foreword

Since the adoption of the *Universal Declaration of Human Rights* in 1948, significant work has been done to secure fundamental civil and political rights for all. Nevertheless, human rights activists, international lawyers, and scholars have witnessed the expansion of anti-terrorism policies with considerable alarm and apprehension. Many have voiced concerns that both terrorist acts and the measures adopted to counter such criminal behaviour are threatening hard-fought human rights gains at the international and domestic levels. The issues addressed in *The Human Rights of Anti-terrorism* are therefore of pressing and considerable interest to anyone working in the field of human rights.

The Human Rights Research and Education Centre was first approached to assist with the organization of the June 2006 colloquium. This gathering gave birth to the *Ottawa Principles on Anti-terrorism and Human Rights*. The international workshop was of significant interest to the centre as it furthered a central part of our mandate, namely, to foster discussions of the linkages among human rights, international humanitarian law, governance, legal reform, and development. The gathering brought together highly regarded scholars and thinkers from across Canada and around the world to grapple with the interrelationship among anti-terrorism, human rights, and international humanitarian law. The discussions were insightful, challenging, and difficult as the balance between respecting fundamental rights and protecting national security is a difficult one to strike. It is tremendously significant that participants were able to find sufficient consensus to draft the *Ottawa*

Principles. It will be more significant to see grassroots activists, international lawyers, and policy-makers start using the *Ottawa Principles* to influence the development of anti-terrorist policies. It is our hope that the publication of this book will contribute to making this happen.

The Human Rights of Anti-terrorism is also a unique project in that it not only contributes to the advancement of international legal norms and principles applicable to human rights and anti-terrorism, but also to scholarly work in this field. The chapters in the book not only supplement and explain the foundations of the *Ottawa Principles*, but also constitute timely explorations of some of the most important human rights issues facing the international community today. By publishing the scholarly research presented at the colloquium, the editors have ensured that the *Ottawa Principles* are centrally situated in the theoretical and practical debates that surround anti-terrorism policies. More importantly, the scholarly chapters demonstrate that the *Ottawa Principles* are the starting point to further discussions. Many authors who contributed chapters to the book challenge readers to critically examine the *Ottawa Principles* to ensure that the balance struck between human rights and anti-terrorism is the one that will achieve respect for fundamental human dignity, while at the same time protecting human life from the threat of terrorism.

The Human Rights Research and Education Centre is privileged to have supported the project and the publication of this book. The innovative approach adopted in *The Human Rights of Anti-terrorism* is long overdue and most welcome.

Marie-Claude Roberge
Director, Human Rights Research and Education Centre
October 2007

Preface

The attacks on the World Trade Center on September 11, 2001 initiated very rapid and profound changes in how states collaborate with each other to pursue efforts against international terrorism. Given the unprecedented scale and scope of the measures taken by states at all levels—multilateral, regional, bilateral, and national—to react to this threat, it became rapidly clear that research and collective thinking was necessary to explore how such measures interacted with the international human rights law obligations that rest upon states. It was also important that this dialogue be articulated around all human rights (i.e., civil, political, economic, social, and cultural rights).

As a non-partisan Canadian institution with a mandate hard-wired into the *International Bill of Human Rights*, Rights & Democracy is mandated to devise and implement international cooperation programs in the field of human rights and democratic development abroad, and also to foster and support research, education, and discourse regarding international human rights law in Canada. Rights & Democracy therefore participated actively in this collective dialogue on the interplay between international human rights and anti-terrorism internationally and in Canada. Among other activities, Rights & Democracy held a seminar in Ottawa in early 2002 on "Promoting Human Rights and Democracy in the Context of Terrorism" and was a regular participant in the hearings held by the Senate and House of Commons regarding our own Canadian anti-terrorism legislation. Throughout its work, Rights & Democracy was a consistent advocate of a principled and practical approach to factoring international human rights law into the anti-terrorism debate, both in Canada and abroad.

Given this, it was therefore natural for Rights & Democracy to support the organization of a colloquium in June 2006 in Ottawa on the topic of human rights and anti-terrorism, and to further support the publication of the outcomes of the very rich discussions that occurred during this event in the form of the present book. In addition to the extremely high quality of the individual articles that are contained in this book, the 2006 colloquium produced the *Ottawa Principles on Anti-terrorism and Human Rights*. While having benefited from previous international initiatives, the *Ottawa Principles* certainly constitute a landmark document which precisely combines the principled and pragmatic approach to human rights and terrorism that is needed in the international and domestic legal orders. There is no doubt in my mind that the present book constitutes a necessary and extremely useful read for scholars and practitioners who develop and apply policies and legislation in this area.

Finally, I would be sorry to leave without emphasis the truly excellent work and sound intellectual leadership of the editors, professors Craig Forcese and Nicole LaViolette, as well as the support of the University of Ottawa and its Faculty of Law in this book.

Lloyd Lipsett
Senior Assistant to the President
Rights & Democracy

Acknowledgments

This book is the work product of the conference entitled "The Human Rights of Anti-terrorism: A Colloquium," held at the Faculty of Law, University of Ottawa, in June 2006. The project is the result of a collaboration and partnership by many individuals and organizations whose contributions must be underlined and acknowledged.

First, the colloquium and book would not have taken place without the generous financial contribution of several institutions. We would like to thank the Social Sciences and Research Council of Canada, Rights and Democracy, the University of Ottawa, including the Faculty of Law, and the Human Rights Research and Education Centre for the financial support they extended to this endeavour.

The colloquium came together because of the tireless work and invaluable contributions of the following members of the steering committee: Craig Forcese, Nicole LaViolette, Graham Mayeda, Alex Neve, David Paciocco, Roch Tassé, and Lorne Waldman. Several law students helped both with the colloquium and the book project: Pam Anderson, Colleen Bauman, Peter Dostal, Ardiana Hallaci, Jordan Lamontagne, Koren Marriott, and Ambrese Montagu.

The colloquium generated both the *Ottawa Principles* and the chapters for this book. We would like to thank the colloquium participants for their patient efforts in helping draft the *Ottawa Principles*; the many colloquium observers for their thoughtful interventions; and the authors for the quality of the chapters in this book. All deserve to be congratulated for their contributions to this collective product. We would also like to thank Jean-Jacques Goulet for translating the *Ottawa Principles* into French and the Centre de traduction et de documentation juridiques for their work editing the French language version.

Let us also express our appreciation for the support this project received from our publisher, Irwin Law. We would like to thank Jeff Miller for his enthusiasm for this project; the anonymous book reviewer for his or her comments and time; and Dan Wiley for his editing and proofreading work.

Finally, the editors would like to thank each other for what has been a tremendously productive, enriching, and friendly collaboration. We hope that the *Ottawa Principles* and this book will contribute to the efforts of many around the world to secure the human rights of everyone during these most challenging times for democracy and civil liberties.

Nicole LaViolette and Craig Forcese

Introduction

Nicole LaViolette & Craig Forcese

A. INTRODUCTION

The Roman jurist Cicero once said that "during war, the laws are silent" (*silent enim leges inter arma*[1]). Commenting in 2006 on this maxim, Aharon Barak, then president of the Israeli Supreme Court, wrote that such "sayings are regrettable .... It is when the cannons roar that we especially need the laws .... Every struggle of the state—against terrorism or any other enemy—is conducted according to rules and law. There is always law which the state must comply with. There are no 'black holes.'"[2] At the same time, history suggests there may be many circumstances in which the rule of law applies superficially, in a manner that gives a gloss of legitimacy to dubious uses of state power. David Dyzenhaus has labelled these phenomena "gray holes,"[3] and in the campaign against terrorism, they are commonplace. Not least, conventional

---

1   Jon R. Stone, ed., *The Routledge Dictionary of Latin Quotations* (Florence, KY: Routledge, 2005) 112.

2   *Public Committee against Torture in Israel v. The Government of Israel* (2006), HCJ 769/02 (Israeli S.C.) at para. 61.

3   David Dyzenhaus, *The Constitution of Law: Legality in a Time of Emergency* (Cambridge: Cambridge University Press, 2006).

understandings of human and civil rights have altered in sometimes dramatic ways in the last half decade.

It is now trite to observe that the events of September 11, 2001 galvanized world leaders and ensured a dramatic improvement in international cooperation in the fight against terrorism. In recognition of the grave threat terrorism poses to individuals' lives and national security around the world, the majority of the world's nations have taken various military, political, and legal actions to curb the spread of terrorism. Such measures include actions to take terrorists into custody, to freeze terrorist assets, or to provide military forces to combat the threat of terrorism. States have increasingly acted in concert to find and implement international, regional, and local solutions to the challenge of terrorism.

Finding a human rights-based approach to fighting terrorism has been less obvious. In the hope of pursuing perpetrators of terrorist acts, legislatures and executives have been tempted to overlook basic principles of human rights and the rule of law. Yet, in doing so, states risk undermining the very democratic values they are defending. In November 2002, then UN Secretary-General Kofi Annan noted that the September 11, 2001 terrorist attacks presented the international community with a profound dilemma: "We face a nearly unsolvable conflict between two imperatives of modern life—protecting the traditional civil liberties of our citizens and, at the same time, ensuring their safety from terrorist attacks with catastrophic consequences."[4] The concerns raised by the Secretary-General have been echoed frequently since Annan first voiced them. In June 2003, UN special rapporteurs and independent experts adopted a joint statement on terrorism and human rights at their annual meeting in Geneva.[5] In it, they expressed their "unequivocal condemnation of terrorism," but then voiced "profound concern at the multiplication of policies, legislation and practices increasingly being adopted by many countries in the name of the fight against terrorism which affect negatively the enjoyment of virtually all human rights—civil, cultural, economic, political and social." The United Nations Security Council has

---

4   UN, Press Release, (21 November 2002) SG/SM/8518, online: www.un.org/News/Press/docs/2002/SGSM8518.doc.htm.

5   Commission on Human Rights, *Joint Statement by Participants at the Tenth Annual Meeting of Special Rapporteurs/Representatives, Independent Experts and Chairpersons of Working Groups of the Special Procedures of the Commission on Human Rights and of the Advisory Services Programme*, Annex 1, UN Doc. E/CN.4/2004/4 (2003) 22.

also indicated that "States must ensure that any measure taken to combat terrorism comply with all their obligations under international law, and should adopt such measures in accordance with international law, in particular international human rights, refugee, and humanitarian law."[6]

Despite the calls for a human rights-based approach to anti-terrorism, questions remain, however, as to how exactly international human rights are to be reconciled with the anti-terrorism imperatives of the state. What precisely do human rights principles demand of states in relation to anti-terrorism? In the event of conflict between these principles and a legitimate anti-terrorism concern, how should the two be reconciled? How are states held to account in weighing anti-terrorism interests against human rights? The answers to these questions matter to many people, both those whose rights are realized only in a state able to ward off threats to national security and those whose rights have been violated in the name of anti-terrorism.

The Human Rights of Anti-terrorism attempts to critically address these questions. As editors, we decided that the best way to achieve this objective was to give the collection a twofold purpose. First, the book constitutes a mechanism by which we can further disseminate the final version of the *Ottawa Principles on Anti-terrorism and Human Rights*.[7] The *Ottawa Principles* are the collective work product of deliberations held by experts at a June 2006 international colloquium. Second, the chapters of the collection provide readers with substantive critiques of topics related to the principles, and human rights and anti-terrorism more generally. These papers have an academic tone and were written by colloquium participants with professional and scholarly interests in human rights and counter-terrorism policies. Taken together, both sections of the book share a common foundation; namely, the principle that in the global struggle against terrorism, states cannot compromise on core democratic values. As described below, the colloquium, and the *Ottawa Principles* and scholarly papers the gathering generated, all seek to find the right balance between human rights protection and effective security measures.

---

6   *Security Council Resolution 1456*, SC Res. 1456, UN SCOR, 2003, S/RES/1456 at para. 6.

7   See the *Ottawa Principles on Anti-terrorism and Human Rights* at Part One of this book [*Ottawa Principles*, the principles].

B. THE COLLOQUIUM

The idea for an international colloquium on the question of human rights and anti-terrorism first came from Lorne Waldman, a prominent Canadian immigration lawyer. Waldman spent several years representing Maher Arar, a Canadian who was detained by U.S. officials as a terrorism suspect and flown to Syria, where he was tortured and forced to make a false confession.[8] At a human rights conference in Toronto in 2005,[9] Waldman expressed frustration at the absence of serious debates on the place of human rights in the global struggle against terrorism.

Waldman's call for a colloquium was taken up by a small steering committee that developed a list of people who we believed would make substantial and vital contributions to such a gathering. Myriad names came to mind: UN personnel and officials, scholars, lawyers, members of governmental or non-governmental organizations, current and former politicians. In the end, thirty-five international experts participated in the event, which was held from 15–17 June 2006, in Ottawa, Canada.[10] These persons participated in their individual capacities, and not as representatives of the various institutions with which they are affiliated.

The colloquium format consisted of several panel presentations, and plenary and break-up discussions among the invited experts. The main goal of the three-day workshop was the finalization of a specific document, the *Ottawa Principles on Anti-terrorism and Human Rights*, which was designed to articulate precise standards in almost a dozen different areas of counter-terrorism and human rights. While the colloquium focused on finalizing the draft principles, several participants were also tasked with presenting their research and analyzes on anti-terrorism and human rights during the panel presentations. Finally, as this was not a conventional conference, but rather a workshop involving both formal panel presentations and informal discussions, we created places for over

---

8 See Canada, Commission of Inquiry into the Actions of Canadian Officials in Relation to Maher Arar, *Report of the Events Relating to Maher Arar: Analysis and Recommendations* (Ottawa: Public Works and Government Services Canada, 2006) [*Arar Report*].

9 "Raoul Wallenberg Day International Human Rights Symposium," York University, Toronto, Canada, 17–18 January 2005.

10 For more information on the colloquium, see online: www.commonlaw.uottawa. ca/index.php?option=com_content&task=view&id=1371&contact_id=38&lang=en.

thirty additional individuals to observe the various panel presentations during the first two days of the colloquium.

C. THE *OTTAWA PRINCIPLES ON ANTI-TERRORISM AND HUMAN RIGHTS*

The final version of the *Ottawa Principles on Anti-terrorism and Human Rights* was developed from the following: several preliminary drafts prepared by a number of pre-workshop working groups; intensive drafting sessions at the workshop, both in break-out and plenary sessions; and post-workshop communications during the balance of the summer of 2006. The English language version was finalized in October 2006 and translated into French, in order to have the principles published in at least two of the official United Nations' languages. Readers will find both versions included in the book.

It is important to note that the *Ottawa Principles* benefited from previous international initiatives. First, we modelled our initiative on the *Johannesburg Principles on National Security, Freedom of Expression and Access to Information.*[11] Crafted by experts assembled at an event in South Africa, the *Johannesburg Principles* provide guidelines on how national security concepts interrelate with open governments. They have since been endorsed by the UN Special Rapporteur on freedom of opinion and expression.[12] They have also been invoked by the UN Commission on Human Rights in the preamble of many of its resolutions[13] and cited with

---

11 Commission on Human Rights, *Johannesburg Principles on National Security, Freedom of Expression and Access to Information*, UN ESCOR, 52d Sess., Item 8, Annex, UN Doc. E/CN.4/1996/39 (1996) [*Johannesburg Principles*].

12 See Commission on Human Rights, *Promotion and Protection of the Right to Freedom of Opinion and Expression, Report of the Special Rapporteur, Mr. Abid Hussain, Pursuant to Commission on Human Rights Resolution 1993/45*, UN ESCOR, 52d Sess.,, UN Doc. E/CN.4/1996/39 at para. 154:

> the Special Rapporteur recommends that the Commission on Human Rights endorse the Johannesburg Principles on National Security, Freedom of Expression and Access to Information, which are contained in the annex to the present report and which the Special Rapporteur considers give useful guidance for protecting adequately the right to freedom of opinion, expression and information.

13 See, for example, Commission on Human Rights, *The Right to Freedom of Opinion and Expression*, ESC Res. 2003/42, UN ESCOR, 2003, Supp. No. 3, UN Doc. E/2003/23-

approval by the House of Lords, the United Kingdom's highest court, in a leading case.[14] Just as the *Johannesburg Principles on National Security, Freedom of Expression and Access to Information* have helped shape international discussions on the topic they address, so we hope the *Ottawa Principles* will evolve in a similar manner.

Second, the *Ottawa Principles* build on the work of non-governmental organizations in developing guidelines in several critical areas implicated by human rights and anti-terrorism. For instance, in June 2004, lawyers meeting at the International Commission of Jurists' (ICJ) biennial conference in Berlin adopted a *Declaration on Upholding Human Rights and the Rule of Law in Combating Terrorism.*[15] The *Berlin Declaration*

E/CN.4/2003/135, 157; Commission on Human Rights, *The Right to Freedom of Opinion and Expression*, ESC Res. 2002/48, UN ESCOR, 2002, Supp. No. 3, UN Doc. E/2002/23-E/CN.4/2002/200, 206; Commission on Human Rights, *The Right to Freedom of Opinion and Expression*, ESC Res. 2001/47, UN ESCOR, 2001, Supp. No. 3, UN Doc. E/2001/23-E/CN.4/2001/167, 209; Commission on Human Rights, *The Right to Freedom of Opinion and Expression*, ESC Res. 2000/38, UN ESCOR, 2000, Supp. No. 3, UN Doc. E/2000/23-E/CN.4/2000/167, 180; and Commission on Human Rights, *The Right to Freedom of Opinion and Expression*, ESC Res. 1999/36, UN ESCOR, 1999, Supp. No. 3, UN Doc. E/CN.4/1999/167-E/1999/23, all of which state: "Recalling the *Johannesburg Principles on National Security, Freedom of Expression and Access to Information* adopted by a group of experts meeting in South Africa on 1 October 1995 (E/CN.4/1996/39, Annex)." See also Commission on Human Rights, *The Right to Freedom of Opinion and Expression*, ESC Res. 1998/42, UN ESCOR, 1998, Supp. No. 3, UN Doc. E/CN.4/1998/177-E/1998/23; and Commission on Human Rights, *The Right to Freedom of Opinion and Expression*, ESC Res. 1997/27, UN ESCOR, 1997, Supp. No. 3, UN Doc. E /CN.4/1997/150-E/1997/23, both of which state: "Taking note of the *Johannesburg Principles on National Security, Freedom of Expression and Access to Information* adopted by a group of experts meeting in South Africa on 1 October 1995 (E/CN.4/1996/39, Annex)."

14   *Secretary of State for the Home Department v. Rehman*, [2003] 1 AC 153 at 181, Slynn L.J. referring to the *Johannesburg Principles* and then indicating that

> [i]t seems to me that the appellant is entitled to say that "the interests of national security" cannot be used to justify any reason the Secretary of State has for wishing to deport an individual from the United Kingdom. There must be some possibility of risk or danger to the security or well-being of the nation which the Secretary of State considers makes it desirable for the public good that the individual should be deported.

[2001] H.L.J. No. 47 at para. 15, [2001] UKHL 47, [2001] 3 W.L.R. 877.

15   International Commission of Jurists, *The Berlin Declaration: The ICJ Declaration on Upholding Human Rights and the Rule of Law in Combating Terrorism* (Geneva: ICJ, 2004) online: www.icj.org/IMG/pdf/Berlin_Declaration.pdf [*Berlin Declararion*].

highlights the serious challenges to the rule of law brought about by counter-terrorism measures and reaffirms the most fundamental human rights violated by some of those measures. The ICJ has since tasked several eminent jurists to pursue the goals of the *Berlin Declaration* by holding national hearings around the world with a view to releasing detailed recommendations.[16] The *Ottawa Principles* also articulate how the rule of law can be respected in addressing terrorism, but they do so in a more comprehensive, precise, and detailed form than has been achieved in any other forum to date. Indeed, the *Ottawa Principles* were submitted to the ICJ Eminent Jurists Panel on Terrorism, Counter Terrorism and Human Rights at their national hearings in Canada in April 2007. The principles will be similarly communicated to the international community through various UN and other international organization special rapporteurs and directly to governments and non-governmental organizations. In this way, it is hoped that the *Ottawa Principles* will continue to shape further initiatives in the field.

Colloquium participants opted to draft a set of principles with little commentary or annotations. It is important, therefore, to make several supplemental comments about the scope and content of the principles. First, colloquium participants sought to ground the guidelines in universally accepted human rights obligations. Thus, in several sections, the *Ottawa Principles* are limited in their ambition as they are meant to distil rules that exist at present in international law. This is particularly true in the sections on fair trial rights, use of force, and torture. In some other policy areas, this constraint posed some challenges. While there has been a considerable expansion of international human rights norms since the end of World War II, there remain obvious gaps, and international law does not always address matters the framers of the *Ottawa Principles* viewed as important in their task. There is, for example, little or no formal international law on review and oversight of security intelligence agencies *per se*. For this reason, the *Ottawa Principles* are also aspirational, proposing standards drawn from the best practices of states or urging principled positions.

Second, the *Ottawa Principles* focus on human rights issues that have been most implicated by questions of counter-terrorism. As will be underlined later in a review of the chapters included in the book,

---

16   See online: www.icj.org/news.php3?id_article=3503&lang=en.

the principles could be expanded in future iterations to cover additional areas of governmental activity. The *Ottawa Principles* should, therefore, be viewed as a foundation for further iterations, rather than a final pronouncement on the relationship between anti-terrorism policies and human rights obligations. We encourage further critical thinking about the *Ottawa Principles* themselves, and more generally, the ways in which states can effectively counter terrorism while safeguarding fundamental human rights.

D. THE CHAPTERS OF THIS BOOK

Through the other chapters in this book, we seek to stimulate critical thinking on human rights and counter-terrorism policies. As editors, we believed it was important to support the *Ottawa Principles* with a full and rigorous analysis of the many issues touched upon at the colloquium and the in final workshop document. Therefore, the articles in this collection examine the relationship between human rights and anti-terrorism from different angles and through a variety of lenses. Not all contributors agree with one another about the appropriate treatment of human rights in counter-terrorism policies, but all take on the challenge of finding a human rights-based approach to fighting terrorism.

We have grouped the papers into two main parts. The first set of chapters debate the scope, content, and implementation of the *Ottawa Principles*, and as such, serve as a form of commentary on the principles. The second group of chapters suggest issues that future iterations of the *Ottawa Principles* should explore in order for a reconciliation of human rights and anti-terrorism to be complete. In both parts, authors engage with the *Ottawa Principles* through critical analyses, more detailed examinations of the issues, or thoughtful suggestions on how unforeseen issues may tip the future scales of the human rights and anti-terrorism balance.

As with many other standard works on terrorism, this collection starts off with papers devoted to the seemingly interminable attempt to define terrorism. Both Kent Roach and Cathleen Powell, in their respective chapters, tackle the maddeningly complex task of defining terrorism and, by doing so, illuminate the difficulties that exist in that particular task. As both Roach and Powell note, past attempts to work out a general definition of terrorism have been controversial, and no consensual definition has emerged either at the international level or the national level. Yet, both authors make a convincing argument (not shared by all colloquium participants) that defining terrorism is an elemental step in restraining excess in counter-terrorism.

For Kent Roach, the urgency arises from the increasing number of new anti-terrorism laws being enacted throughout the world. In the absence of any international guidance, many of these new laws contain broad definitions of terrorism that are ill-suited, in Roach's view, to enforcement through the criminal law. Moreover, the broad definitions of terrorism threaten to capture forms of protest and civil disobedience that are generally protected by human rights norms. While Roach advocates the adoption of a definition, he does suggest that the definition of terrorism not stray far from ordinary principles of criminal law. Given that the harm caused by terrorist acts usually involves the murder and maiming of civilians, there is no need to broaden the scope of anti-terrorism laws much beyond the well-honed boundaries of criminal law.

Cathleen Powell also argues that a definition is necessary, but she posits that counter-terrorism laws may need a specific framework beyond existing criminal laws. Key to her argument is the need to subject anti-terrorism policies to effective legal control. For this to be done, Powell argues that a definition of terrorism at both the international and national levels must be found. Her main concern is to craft a definition that will effectively constrain state and executive power. In her chapter, Powell outlines an anti-terrorism regime inspired by international humanitarian law, as she asserts that the criminal law is not in itself an adequate response to terrorism.

In both the Roach and Powell chapters, readers will gain a valuable glimpse of the divergent viewpoints present not only at the Ottawa colloquium, but more generally in scholarly and policy debates about the definition of terrorism. At the same time, Roach and Powell also effectively illustrate a point on which there was agreement at the colloquium: developing an effective international strategy to combat terrorism while respecting human rights obligations requires agreement on what we are dealing with. What both their contributions underline is that the journey towards a definition of terrorism may be an end in itself. No one can yet agree on the destination, but the process of debating the issue increases our understanding of terrorism, and the ways in which human rights must configure in all counter-terrorism policies.

Like Powell, Craig Forcese is interested in the relationship between anti-terrorism and international humanitarian law. However, Forcese focuses on the legality of military responses to terrorism, and the ambiguities in the current state of the law. Such an analysis is not only timely, but also necessary as states increasingly favour recourse to military force over criminal investigation and prosecution. In 2001, the United Nations Security Council adopted Resolution 1373, which obliges all states to criminalize terrorist activities. Yet, it is also true that, since the events of September 11, 2001, terrorist acts are increasingly viewed as armed attacks within the laws of war rather than as criminal acts. Commentators have argued that terrorism, although not a recent phenomenon, is overlooked in traditional international law relating to the use of force. The system of collective security established by the UN *Charter*[17] contemplates armed conflict between states and does not anticipate the existence of international terrorists and the now sophisticated ways in which they operate. According to Forcese, the *Ottawa Principles* counter these assertions by adopting a conventional interpretation of the scope of both the *jus ad bellum* (use of force) and *jus in bello* (methods of war) in relation to anti-terrorism. Forcese's contribution challenges this narrow focus, arguing that the *Ottawa Principles* inadequately restate existing international law without addressing its ambiguities, including in the area of self-defence, the relationship between international humanitarian law and human rights law, and the deployment of military force outside situations of armed conflict.

While it is true that many counter-terrorism measures have increasingly become militarized, many states have also turned to administrative laws to combat terrorism. The *Ottawa Principles* include several normative statements intended to capture the full range of administrative measures adopted by states in recent years to counter terrorism. The latter include the expansion of indefinite administrative detentions, the adoption of financial regulations aimed at stopping the flow of funds to terrorist groups, and the creation of national security watch-lists of various sorts. In his contribution, Lorne Waldman analyzes the immigration context to assess specific administrative measures adopted to counter terrorism.

---

17   *Charter of the United Nations*, 26 June 1945, 59 Stat. 1031, T.S. 993, 3 Bevans 1153, (entered into force 24 October 1945) [UN *Charter*].

Of specific concern to Waldman is the ways in which immigration procedures, like the "security certificates" in Canada, may be based on secret evidence, and may be applied in circumstances where the affected parties never have a chance to know or respond to the allegations made against them. Throughout his chapter, Waldman acknowledges the importance of confidentiality in the national security area, but he also reflects on the very challenge that guided the drafting of the *Ottawa Principles*, namely the extent to which anti-terrorism policies can be reconciled with fundamental human rights. In Waldman's paper, this means asking: To what extent is secret evidence compatible with democratic values? He suggests that secrecy and confidentiality are contrary to administrative law principles such as fairness, transparency, accountability, and due process. Conscious of the need to strike the proper balance between national security and the rights of individuals targeted by immigration procedures, Waldman examines alternative models that he contends more adequately ensure procedural fairness, and establish more just and legitimate administrative decision-making.

In his contribution to the volume, Gar Pardy examines the current state of international law in relation to diplomatic and consular protection. The limited scope and effectiveness of consular protection has been the subject of recent debates and disputes, but Pardy is interested in the specific issues that arise when nationals are detained in other countries in connection with terrorism-related activities. In Canada, the Commission of Inquiry into the Actions of Canadian Officials in Relation to Maher Arar concluded that "terrorism" cases often present special challenges. The inquiry found that "detainees are more likely to be subjected to different and harsher treatment" in addition to being more vulnerable to intrusions on their individual liberties and human rights.[18] Pardy is well-versed in the challenges of extending a country's protection to an individual caught up in a terrorism-related investigation abroad: he served as Director General for Consular Services at the Canadian Department for Foreign Affairs and International Trade when Maher Arar, a Canadian and Syrian national, was detained in the United States as a terrorist suspect and removed against his will to Syria, where he was subjected to torture. Pardy is concerned with the limited protection international law currently provides to individuals like Maher Arar.

---

18   *Arar Report*, vol. III, above note 8 at 349–50.

In his chapter, Pardy outlines a proposal for a new multilateral treaty to provide additional protection for persons encountering difficulties in countries of second or non-citizenship.

The suppression of information on national security grounds also played a significant role in the Arar Inquiry process in Canada. For instance, when the final report was released in September 2006, the public had access to an edited version rather than the full report provided to the Government of Canada, with all of the national security materials intact. States are increasing terrorism investigations and information gathering activities in support of national security, yet it is also true that in many states, regulations and practices on access to information contain a mixture of authoritarian and democratic elements. David Paciocco makes a convincing case that international law requires states to demonstrate that the suppression of information on national security grounds is truly necessary. In effect, Paciocco outlines the legal foundation for principles on access to information contained in both the *Ottawa Principles* and the *Johannesburg Principles*.[19] Both instruments outline an obligation for states to avoid restricting access to information unless the government can demonstrate that the restriction is prescribed by law and is necessary in a democratic society to protect a legitimate national security interest. Paciocco argues the balance between access to information and national security depends on the operation of the principles of presumed access, which places the burden on states to prove necessity before suppressing information. He finds support for this proposition in both international and customary international law, and he demonstrates how one state, Canada, has failed to respect the principle of presumed access in its domestic laws and regulations.

The maintenance of national security is considered a vital duty of the state. By ensuring national security, a government is able to protect the fundamental values of a liberal democratic state, namely: the rule of law, democracy, and human rights. In addition, security services, and the intelligence they gather, constitute important tools in a state's struggle against terrorism. At the same time, misconduct by security agencies frequently results in violations of human rights. In the final chapter in this part of the book, Andrea Wright outlines how the establishment of accountable and transparent security sector agencies remains chal-

---

19   *Johannesburg Principles*, above note 11.

lenging for many states. Her contribution explores the extent to which security services, which require secrecy and flexibility to ensure effectiveness, can and should be subjected to civilian monitoring, oversight, and investigation. Wright's piece is particularly valuable as she provides rationales and modes of practical application for the aspirational guidelines found in the *Ottawa Principles* in relation to security agencies. In effect, Wright designs a democratic blueprint by which states can legitimize security intelligence activities.

The final three chapters are grouped together as they attempt to go beyond the *Ottawa Principles* by providing thoughtful critiques of the issues not adequately addressed in that instrument. All three authors urge readers to view the *Ottawa Principles* as a document providing an incomplete picture of the relationship between anti-terrorism and human rights, and indeed of counter-terrorism more generally. The chapters in this part by Victor Ramraj, Graham Mayeda, and François Larocque rightly see the *Ottawa Principles* as a work in progress; in their contributions, they begin the process of debate and reflection, which all the experts involved in the drafting of the *Ottawa Principles* have welcomed.

Victor Ramraj argues that human rights are not the only mechanism for restraining state power. Ramraj suggests that, while the *Ottawa Principles* are a sophisticated attempt to reconcile national security imperatives with human rights principles, other strategies might play an equally important role in restraining state power and reducing the incidence of terrorism. He rightly states that the *Ottawa Principles* rest on an assumption that law is the best answer to contemporary problems of terrorism. In his view it is time to consider how social, political, economic, cultural, and institutional strategies may effectively reduce the incidence of terrorism, thereby reducing the need to focus on human rights as a way to restrain state power.

Graham Mayeda is also concerned with the issue of deterrence and prevention, but specifically in the context of development assistance policies. In his contribution, Mayeda highlights how the *Ottawa Principles*, and debates more generally about human rights and anti-terrorism, overlook the impact of counter-terrorism policies on a state's approach to development. Mayeda outlines how states have increasingly used their development assistance programs to protect their national security interests while at the same time failing to take a progressive view of how social and economic policies might contribute to the prevention of acts of terrorism. Mayeda critiques the *Ottawa Principles* for their focus on policies and laws that apply once a person is suspected of having committed a terrorist act. He is concerned that state activities to prevent terrorism, which are often channelled through development policies, are not scrutinized to assess the extent to which development policies respect the full range of human rights, including social and economic rights. He concludes his chapter with specific principles that could be added to the Ottawa instrument to ensure that the social and economic dimensions of anti-terrorism policies are considered as important as civil and political rights.

It is certainly true that the *Ottawa Principles* are primarily concerned with the way anti-terrorism policies respect the civil and political liberties of suspected terrorists. Similar to Mayeda, François Larocque is concerned that this narrow focus has excluded the fundamental rights of the survivors and victims of terrorism. Larocque comments that few would dispute that individual victims of terrorism and their families deserve some form of reparation, yet there has been conspicuously little debate on the nature or scope of such reparation. In his chapter, Larocque examines the right of victims of terrorism to obtain a civil remedy in Canadian courts and the procedural obstacles to such redress posed by the doctrine of state immunity. Larocque's contribution is timely and informative as the question of using the civil litigation system to deter terrorist acts, and to provide victims of terrorism with redress and remedies, is increasingly attracting the attention of scholars and victims themselves. For instance, Debra Strauss has argued that civil litigation in the United States could help dismantle the business holdings of terrorist groups in the same way lawsuits were used to undermine the infrastructure of hate groups.[20] Other authors have highlighted how civil actions can meet goals of deterrence.[21] For example, in the United States, where anti-terrorism legislation provides a private right to a cause of action, a lawsuit by more than 600 family members, firefighters, and rescue work-

---

20 Debra M. Strauss, "Enlisting the U.S. Courts in a New Front: Dismantling the International Business Holdings of Terrorist Groups through Federal Statutory and Common-Law Suits" (2005) 38 Vand. J. Transnat'l L. 679.

21 "Introduction" in John Norton Moore, ed., *Civil Litigation against Terrorism* (Durham, NC: Caroline Academic Press, 2004).

ers affected by the September 11, 2001 attacks has been filed.[22] Larocque contributes to these debates by suggesting ways that the civil justice system could be strengthened to serve an important function for victims and survivors of terrorism.

E. CONCLUSION

It is our belief that the chapters in this volume, and the *Ottawa Principles* themselves, constitute an important contribution to discussions on the topic of human rights and counter-terrorism. At their core, the principles underscore the real limitations imposed by law and principles of legality on the steps states take in responding to the terrorism menace. These are shackles on state action that will seem unacceptable to some observers. However, the framers of the *Ottawa Principles* would likely all concur with the observation by President Aharon Barak, delivered in a decision in which the Israeli Supreme Court declared illegal some forms of extreme interrogation. In that case, the Court acknowledged that these curbs on state action would make the task of the security services more difficult. It then observed that

> This is the destiny of democracy, as not all means are acceptable to it, and not all practices employed by its enemies are open before it. Although a democracy must often fight with one hand tied behind its back, it nonetheless has the upper hand. Preserving the rule of law and recognition of an individual's liberty constitutes an important component in its understanding of security. At the end of the day, they strengthen its spirit and its strength and allow it to overcome its difficulties.[23]

In the final analysis, the human rights constraints found in documents like the *Ottawa Principles* are exactly the precepts that create societies worth securing in the first place.

---

22 "$116 Trillion Lawsuit Filed By 9/11 Families" CNN (16 August 2002), online: http://archives.cnn.com/2002/LAW/08/15/attacks.suit.

23 *Public Committee against Torture in Israel v. The Government of Israel* (1999), HCJ 5100/94 at para. 39.

The Ottawa Principles on Anti-terrorism and Human Rights

The Ottawa Principles on Anti-terrorism and Human Rights[*]

INTRODUCTION

In June 2006, experts on human rights and terrorism met in their individual capacities at the Faculty of Law, University of Ottawa, Ottawa, Canada to develop the following Principles on Anti-terrorism and Human Rights. They shared a common view that the preservation of human rights—not least the right to life—is the central motivator of anti-terrorism. They also believed that human rights constitute an elemental and immutable constraint on how anti-terrorism is conducted. The struggle for collective security must not be an assault on the individual's life, liberty and security of the person. This document is the product of their deliberations.

---

[*]   Available online at http://aix1.uottawa.ca/~cforcese/hrat/principles.pdf.

Les Principes d'Ottawa relatifs à la lutte au terrorisme et aux droits de l'homme[*]

INTRODUCTION

En juin 2006, des spécialistes des droits de l'homme et de la lutte au terrorisme se sont réunis, à titre individuel, à la faculté de droit de l'Université d'Ottawa, à Ottawa, Canada pour élaborer les Principes suivants relatifs à la lutte au terrorisme et aux droits de l'homme. Ils ont tous partagé le point de vue voulant que la protection des droits de l'homme et, au premier chef, le droit à la vie, constitue l'élément moteur de la lutte au terrorisme. Ils ont également estimé que les droits de l'homme restreignent de façon essentielle et immuable la manière dont la lutte au terrorisme est menée. La lutte pour la sécurité collective ne doit pas constituer une atteinte à la vie, à la liberté et à la sécurité des personnes. Ce document est le fruit de leurs délibérations.

---

[*]   Disponible en ligne à http://aix1.uottawa.ca/~cforcese/hrat/principles.pdf.

Part 1: General Principle on Anti-terrorism and Human Rights

Principle 1.1: Right to non-discrimination and respect for the rule of law

1.1.1   All persons are equal before the law and are entitled without any discrimination to the equal protection of the law.

1.1.2   All measures taken by states to fight terrorism must respect human rights and the rule of law, while excluding any form of arbitrariness as well as any discriminatory or racist treatment, and must be subject to appropriate supervision.

1.1.3   State activities to prevent, investigate or prosecute acts of terrorism must not involve discrimination based on race, color, sex, sexual orientation, language, religion, political or other opinion, national or social origin, nationality, property, birth, immigration status, or other status.

1.1.4   In particular, state activities to prevent, investigate or prosecute acts of terrorism must not subject particular groups to increased scrutiny or differential treatment on the basis of their status or personal characteristics. State officials must not use race, ethnicity, or other personal characteristics as the basis for stopping, searching, detaining, or in other ways restricting the rights and freedoms of affected individuals, except in relation to a specific suspect description, relevant to a particular offence, place and time.

Partie 1 : Principe général relatif à la lutte au terrorisme et aux droits de l'homme

Principe 1.1 : Droit à la non-discrimination et respect de la primauté du droit

1.1.1 Toutes les personnes sont égales devant la loi et ont droit, sans aucune discrimination, à une égale protection de la loi.

1.1.2 Toutes les mesures prises par les États pour combattre le terrorisme doivent respecter les droits de l'homme et la primauté du droit, exclure toute forme d'arbitraire de même que tout traitement discriminatoire ou raciste, et être assujetties à un contrôle adéquat.

1.1.3 Les activités d'un État visant à prévenir les actes terroristes, à enquêter sur de tels actes ou à poursuivre des terroristes devant les tribunaux ne doivent comporter aucune discrimination fondée sur la race, la couleur, le sexe, l'orientation sexuelle, la langue, la religion, les opinions politiques ou autres, l'origine nationale ou sociale, la nationalité, la fortune, la naissance, le statut d'immigrant, ou tout autre statut.

1.1.4 En particulier, les activités d'un État visant à prévenir les actes terroristes, à enquêter sur de tels actes ou à poursuivre des terroristes devant les tribunaux ne doivent pas assujettir des groupes en particulier à une surveillance plus soutenue ou à un traitement différent en fonction de leur statut ou de leurs caractéristiques personnelles. Les représentants de l'État ne doivent pas se fonder sur la race, l'ethnicité ou d'autres caractéristiques personnelles pour interpeller, fouiller, détenir des personnes ou autrement restreindre les droits et libertés de personnes, à moins qu'on ne leur ait fourni le signalement d'un suspect en particulier en ce qui concerne à une infraction particulière commise à une date et dans un lieu qu'on aura précisés.

Part 2: Anti-terrorism, Human Rights and the Criminal Law

Principle 2.1: Application of principles of criminal law and procedure; enactment of specific terrorism offences

2.1.1 States should use the existing criminal law to respond to terrorism and, in doing so, states have a continuing obligation to ensure that their criminal justice systems embody the highest standards of procedural and substantive fairness. These standards include principles of legality, non-retroactivity, non-discrimination, proportionality, proof of individual fault and responsibility, and the presumption of innocence.

2.1.2 States should only enact specific terrorism offences and procedures to the extent strictly necessary because of demonstrable inadequacies in existing criminal law and procedures. Terrorist offences should be defined domestically to respect the principle of legality by including a narrow and precise definition of terrorism that should be no broader than: "any action intended to cause death or serious harm to civilians with the purpose of intimidating a population or compelling a government or political or international organization to do, or abstain from doing, an act." Definitions of terrorism should recognize that state actors can also commit terrorist offences.

Commentary

In many countries, existing criminal law adequately addresses terrorist acts and omissions. The danger of creating new criminal law provisions to respond to terrorism is that they will be redundant, vague and overbroad. As well, they have the potential to unduly complicate the application of the criminal law and to undermine important criminal law principles and democratic values. Moreover, whether terrorism is addressed through an expansive interpretation of the ordinary criminal law, or whether it is addressed through a legislative scheme specifically aimed at terrorist acts, we have seen throughout history that these responses will seep into the ordinary criminal law and become generalized in their application.

There is also the risk that, contrary to the principle of restraint in using the criminal law power, states may amend their general criminal law provisions to provide for the aggressive prosecution of inchoate acts, or the creation of broad financing and association-based offences

Partie 2 : Lutte au terrorisme, droits de l'homme et droit pénal

Principe 2.1 : Application des principes de droit pénal et de procédure pénale; promulgation d'infractions précises de terrorisme

2.1.1 Les États doivent appliquer le droit pénal en vigueur pour combattre le terrorisme et, ce faisant, les États doivent respecter en tout temps leur obligation de voir à ce que leurs systèmes de justice de droit pénal appliquent les standards d'équité procédurale et substantielle les plus élevés. Ces standards comprennent notamment les principes de légalité, de non-rétroactivité, de non-discrimination, de proportionnalité, de preuve de la faute et de la responsabilité individuelles ainsi que celui de la présomption d'innocence.

2.1.2 Les États ne doivent pas promulguer d'infractions ni de procédures précises de terrorisme que dans la mesure strictement nécessaire et lorsqu'il est démontrable que le droit pénal et la procédure pénale existants contiennent des carences. Un État doit définir les infractions de terrorisme de sorte à respecter le principe de légalité en employant une définition étroite et précise du terrorisme dont la portée se limiterait à ce qui suit : «toute action menée avec l'intention de provoquer la mort ou d'infliger de graves sévices corporels à des civils dans le but d'intimider une population ou encore d'induire un gouvernement ou une organisation internationale à poser un geste, ou à s'en abstenir». Les définitions de terrorisme doivent également reconnaître que des représentants de l'État peuvent aussi commettre des infractions de terrorisme.

Commentaire

Dans un grand nombre de pays, le droit pénal traite convenablement des actes terroristes et des omissions. Lorsque l'on créé de nouvelles dispositions de droit pénal pour contrer le terrorisme, on court le risque que ces dispositions soient redondantes, vagues et trop larges. Ces dispositions risquent également de compliquer indûment l'application du droit pénal et de saper d'importants principes de droit pénal et d'importantes valeurs démocratiques. De plus, que l'on prenne des mesures antiterroristes en donnant une interprétation large aux dispositions usuelles de droit pénal ou en adoptant un régime de dispositions visant tout particulièrement les actes de terrorisme, l'histoire nous démontre que ces réponses s'infiltreront dans le droit pénal usuel et qu'elles deviendront d'usage courant.

so that those states will have the tools they believe are required to address the risk of terrorist attack. This can cause the net of criminal law to be cast too widely. States should therefore use the utmost care and restraint in creating or amending offences because of perceived inadequacy in existing criminal law. Any new criminal law initiatives taken in response to the threat of terrorist attack should respect the highest standards of procedural and substantive fairness, and avoid the pitfalls identified above.

Recognizing that some states have or will enact provisions aimed specifically at terrorist acts, those provisions must be confined to the purposes for which they are intended. Where terms such as "terrorism" are employed, they should be defined so as to satisfy the principle of legality. The definition should avoid making motive an element of offences, and in particular religious or political motive. If religious or political motive were to be included in the definition, this could unduly restrict political and religious expression and make evidence about the accused's political and religious beliefs admissible regardless of its prejudicial effects on the trier of fact.

Nevertheless, terrorism can be distinguished from ordinary crime by requiring that terrorist acts be committed with the intent to intimidate a population or compel a governmental, political or international organization to behave in a certain manner. This purpose element is important, because without it, the definition of terrorism could cast the net too wide. Finally, the definition of terrorism in the domestic criminal law should be such that terrorism can apply to both state actors as well as non-state actors, since states, like individuals, can commit terrorist acts.

2.1.3 Offences involving terrorism should require that the state prove beyond a reasonable doubt that the defendant intended to cause the specified harm.

2.1.4 Any person accused, arrested or detained in relation to the commission of a terrorist offence has, at a minimum, the following rights:

a) the right not to be arbitrarily detained or imprisoned;

b) the right to be presumed innocent;

c) the right to be promptly informed, in a language that the person can understand, of the reason for arrest or detention and the right to a translator when one is required to understand and participate in the hearings;

Il y a également le risque que les États passent outre au principe de retenue dont ils doivent faire preuve lorsqu'ils appliquent leurs pouvoirs en droit pénal et modifient leurs dispositions générales de droit pénal pour favoriser une judiciarisation agressive d'actes inchoatifs ou créer des infractions de financement ou d'association avec des terroristes ayant une large portée, dans le but de se doter de moyens qu'ils estiment nécessaires pour affronter le risque d'attaques terroristes. Les dispositions de droit pénal pourraient alors être d'une portée exagérée. Les États doivent donc faire preuve d'un soin et d'une retenue extrêmes lorsqu'ils créent ou modifient des infractions parce qu'ils ont perçu une carence dans le droit pénal existant. Toute initiative en droit pénal qui répond à une menace d'attaque terroriste doit respecter les plus hauts standards d'équité procédurale et substantielle et éviter les écueils mentionnés ci-dessus.

Nous reconnaissons que certains États ont déjà entériné ou entérineront des dispositions législatives concernant particulièrement les actes terroristes; il est donc nécessaire que ces dispositions ne servent qu'aux fins auxquelles elles sont destinées. Lorsque des termes comme « terrorisme » sont utilisés, ils doivent être définis de sorte à satisfaire au principe de légalité. La définition doit éviter de considérer le motif, notamment les motifs d'ordre religieux ou politique, comme un élément des infractions. Si les motifs d'ordre religieux ou politique étaient inclus dans la définition, cela restreindrait indûment l'expression religieuse et politique, et la preuve relative aux croyances politiques et religieuses de l'accusé serait admissible, sans égard aux effets préjudiciables qu'elle pourrait avoir sur le juge des faits.

Il est toutefois possible d'établir une distinction entre le terrorisme et une infraction criminelle courante en exigeant que les actes terroristes aient été perpétrés avec l'intention d'intimider une population ou de forcer un État ou une organisation internationale à se comporter d'une façon donnée. Ce volet de l'intention a son importance, car en son absence la définition du terrorisme aurait une trop grande portée. Enfin, le libellé de la définition de terrorisme dans le droit pénal interne doit être tel qu'il puisse s'appliquer aussi bien aux acteurs étatiques qu'aux acteurs non étatiques, étant donné que les États, tout comme les personnes, peuvent commettre des actes terroristes.

d) the right to be informed without delay of the offence charged;

e) the right to prompt access to legal counsel of choice and to be informed of this right;

f) the right to have the lawfulness of detention determined as soon as possible;

g) the right to pre-trial release unless the state has just cause to deny such release;

h) the right not to have adverse inferences drawn from pre-trial silence;

i) the right to a fair public trial within a reasonable time before an independent, impartial and regularly constituted tribunal;

j) the right to full disclosure of the state's case and to adequate time to prepare a defence;

k) the right not to be a witness in proceedings against oneself;

l) the right to examine prosecution witnesses and call defence witnesses;

m) the right to appeal the decision of the tribunal; and

n) the right not to be tried again for an offence following either an acquittal or finding of guilt and punishment.

2.1.5 Secret detention centres for persons suspected, charged or convicted of terrorist offences should be prohibited under international law and states that have secret detention centres should be subject to sanction. The international community must declare all secret detention centres illegal. Detainees should be held in places that are publicly recognized and there must be proper registration of the names of detainees and places of detention.

2.1.6 When releasing a person whom the state has arrested and detained in relation to the commission of a terrorist act, the state must use the means that are least restrictive of rights while consistent with the protection of the public and must in no case limit rights in a manner inconsistent with international human rights law.

Commentary

Conditions imposed on persons released from arrest of detention should limit rights only on credible public safety grounds. Further, in no circumstance should they limit rights in a manner not anticipated by the *International Covenant on Civil and Political Rights* (ICCPR), including the requirement that permissible derogations from that instrument be justi-

2.1.3 Les infractions impliquant le terrorisme doivent comporter l'obligation pour l'État de prouver hors de tout doute raisonnable que l'accusé avait l'intention de causer le préjudice qu'il est censé avoir voulu causer.

2.1.4 Toute personne inculpée, appréhendée ou détenue en relation avec la perpétration d'une infraction de terrorisme doit pouvoir invoquer, à tout le moins, les droits suivants :

a) le droit à la protection contre la détention ou l'emprisonnement arbitraires;

b) le droit d'être présumée innocente;

c) le droit d'être informée dans les plus brefs délais, et dans une langue qu'elle comprend, des motifs de l'arrestation ou de la détention et le droit à un interprète lorsqu'il devient nécessaire d'y recourir pour comprendre les débats et y participer;

d) le droit d'être informée sans délai de l'infraction dont elle est accusée;

e) le droit d'accès, dans les plus brefs délais, à un avocat et d'être informée de ce droit;

f) le droit à ce que la légalité de la détention soit établie dans les meilleurs délais possible;

g) le droit à une mise en liberté avant le procès, sauf si l'État a un motif valable de refuser une telle libération;

h) le droit à ce qu'aucune inférence défavorable ne soit tirée de son silence avant procès;

i) le droit à un procès public et équitable devant un tribunal indépendant, impartial et dûment constitué;

j) le droit à la divulgation complète du dossier de l'État et à un délai raisonnable pour préparer une défense;

k) le droit de ne pas témoigner dans sa propre cause;

l) le droit de contre-interroger les témoins de la poursuite et d'assigner ses propres témoins en défense;

m) le droit d'en appeler de la décision du tribunal; et,

n) le droit de ne pas subir un nouveau procès pour une infraction dont elle a été acquittée ou déclarée coupable et punie.

2.1.5 Le droit international doit interdire les centres secrets de détention pour les personnes soupçonnées, accusées ou reconnues coupables d'infractions de terrorisme et doit sanctionner les États qui y recourent. La communauté internationale doit proclamer l'il-

fied by a *bona fide* threat to the life of the nation as set out in a formal statement to that effect. Specific attention must be drawn to the absolutely non-derogable nature of some ICCPR rights. These non-derogable rights may never be abridged as part of conditions on release from detention.

2.1.7   The state must disclose all relevant evidence in its possession to a person accused of committing a terrorist act so as to ensure that the defendant can prepare a full and effective defence, and to ensure that the defendant has a fair trial.

2.1.8   An exception to Principle 2.1.7 is permissible if the state can demonstrate that non-disclosure is necessary to protect national security. To justify non-disclosure, the state must:

a) permit defence counsel with the appropriate security clearance and undertakings with respect to non-disclosure to review the evidence; or

b) permit an independent advocate with the appropriate security clearance and undertakings with respect to non-disclosure to review the evidence and challenge it; and

c) either way, demonstrate to a tribunal in an adversarial process that:

i.   the refusal to disclose the evidence is a proportionate limit on the accused's right to disclosure that is necessary to protect the legitimate national security interests of the state, including the safety of sources and the exchange of information between states; and

ii. the refusal to disclose is consistent with a fair trial. If a fair trial is not possible because the defendant has not received sufficient disclosure, the appropriate response will be the termination of the proceedings.

Principle 2.2: Application of human rights standards

2.2.1   Any measures, criminal, quasi-criminal, or otherwise, taken by or on behalf of a state to prevent terrorism, must comply with international human rights standards.

2.2.2   Expression may only be subject to criminal sanction on grounds of terrorism if it constitutes incitement of terrorism (as described in Principle 2.1.2) with the intent and likelihood that a terrorist of-

légalité de tels centres secrets de détention. Les détenus doivent être incarcérés dans des endroits qui sont connus du public et, de plus, leur identité et le lieu de leur détention doivent être consignés de façon appropriée.

2.1.6 Lors de la mise en liberté d'une personne qu'il a appréhendée et détenue en relation avec la perpétration d'un acte terroriste, l'État doit prendre les mesures qui n'enfreignent les droits de cette personne que dans la plus stricte mesure tout en assurant la protection du public, et, en aucun cas, l'État ne doit prendre des mesures qui restreignent les droits de la personne d'une façon qui va à l'encontre des lois internationales relatives aux droits de l'homme.

Commentaire

Les conditions imposées aux personnes mises en liberté ne doivent pas restreindre leurs droits que pour des motifs crédibles liés à la sécurité publique. De plus, ces conditions ne doivent, en aucune circonstance, restreindre les droits de la personne d'une manière non prévue par le *Pacte international relatif aux droits civils et politiques* (PIRDCP) et ne pas respecter l'exigence selon laquelle les dérogations à cet instrument doivent être justifiées par une crainte raisonnable d'une menace envers la vie de la nation, telle qu'énoncée dans une déclaration officielle à cet effet. On doit porter une attention toute particulière au fait que certains des droits prévus dans le PIRDCP sont de natures absolument inviolables. Ces droits inviolables ne peuvent être brimés lorsqu'on impose des conditions à une mise en liberté.

2.1.7 Pour qu'une personne accusée d'avoir commis un acte terroriste puisse préparer une défense pleine et entière et avoir un procès équitable, l'État doit lui divulguer toute la preuve pertinente en sa possession.

2.1.8 Il peut être fait exception au Principe 2.1.7, si l'État démontre qu'il est nécessaire de ne pas divulguer une certaine preuve pour protéger la sécurité nationale. Pour justifier un refus de divulgation, l'État doit :

a) soit autoriser l'avocat de la défense, qui est titulaire de l'attestation de sécurité appropriée et qui a pris l'engagement de ne pas divulguer la preuve, à examiner la preuve; ou

fence will be committed. In particular, publication of information issued by, or about, groups that have been labelled as terrorist, or by or about any of their members, should not be criminalized. Attempts to justify terrorist acts in writing or speech should also not be criminalized.

Principle 2.3: Departures from ordinary criminal law principles and human rights standards

2.3.1 Any departures from ordinary principles of criminal law and procedure or derogable international human rights standards must be strictly necessary to prevent the identified harm and be rationally connected to the achievement of this goal; they should infringe the rights of those subject to the law as little as possible; and their effectiveness should be weighed against the degree of rights infringement that they permit. Any such departures must also be reviewable on this basis by a regularly constituted court or tribunal.

2.3.2 Any law enacted to deal with a threat from terrorism, war, invasion, general insurrection, disorder, natural disaster or other public emergency:

    a) must only apply prospectively;

    b) must be subject to strict and express time limits that are determined in accordance with the principles of necessity and proportionality; and

    c) must not indemnify the state or any person in respect of an unlawful act.

Principle 2.4: States of emergency and derogations

2.4.1 Any state of emergency must be prescribed by the law of the state and officially declared. A state of emergency must be understood as an exceptional measure to which resort may be made only in situations of a genuine threat to the life of the nation, its independence or its security. In proclaiming a state of emergency, a state must articulate in detail the nature of the threat, as well as the scope of any derogation taken and the reason(s) for which this derogation is deemed necessary.

2.4.2 A declaration of a state of emergency will be effective only if:

    a) it applies prospectively;

b) soit autoriser un avocat indépendant, qui est titulaire de l'attestation de sécurité appropriée et qui a pris l'engagement de ne pas divulguer la preuve, à examiner et à contester la preuve; et

c) dans les deux cas, établir devant un tribunal, dans le cadre d'un processus contradictoire que :

    i. le refus de divulguer la preuve constitue une restriction proportionnelle au droit de l'accusé à la divulgation et est nécessaire pour protéger les intérêts légitimes de l'État en matière de sécurité nationale, notamment la sécurité des sources et le partage d'information entre États; et

    ii. le refus de divulguer la preuve est conforme aux règles d'un procès équitable. Si la tenue d'un procès équitable devenait impossible parce que l'accusé n'a pas bénéficié d'une divulgation suffisante, l'arrêt des procédures s'avérerait alors le remède approprié.

Principe 2.2 : Application des normes relatives aux droits de l'homme

2.2.1 Toute mesure pénale, quasi pénale ou autre prise par un État ou en son nom, pour contrer le terrorisme, doit respecter les normes internationales relatives aux droits de l'homme.

2.2.2 L'expression ne peut faire l'objet de sanction pénale pour motifs de terrorisme que si elle constitue une incitation au terrorisme (selon la description dans le Principe 2.1.2) dans l'intention qu'une infraction de terrorisme soit commise et qu'une infraction de terrorisme sera vraisemblablement commise. Tout particulièrement, ni la publication d'informations par ou concernant des groupes qui ont été étiquetés comme des groupes terroristes, ni la publication d'information sur ou concernant les membres de tels groupes ne doivent constituer une infraction. Le fait de tenter de justifier, par des écrits ou en paroles, des actes terroristes ne doit également pas constituer une infraction.

Principe 2.3 : Dérogations aux principes usuels en droit pénal et aux normes en matière des droits de l'homme

2.3.1 Toute dérogation aux principes usuels et à la procédure usuelle en droit pénal ou aux normes internationales relatives aux droits de l'homme doit s'avérer absolument nécessaire pour éviter le préjudice identifié et doit logiquement avoir un lien avec l'atteinte de cet objectif; de plus, elle doit porter le moins possible atteinte aux

b) it is subject to strict and express time limits that are determined in accordance with the principles of necessity and proportionality; and

c) it is subject to legislative ratification as soon as practicable after it has been proclaimed.

2.4.3 Renewal of a declaration of a state of emergency must be:

a) preceded by a public debate in a democratically-elected assembly; and

b) adopted by a greater majority of a democratically-elected assembly than was required to ratify the initial declaration of a state of emergency.

2.4.4 If a state declares a state of emergency, any law that the state enacts in consequence of this declaration must meet the following conditions:

a) the law must only apply prospectively;

b) the law must be subject to strict and express time limits that are determined in accordance with the principles of necessity and proportionality;

c) the law must be strictly necessary to achieve the legitimate aim of the state in declaring the state of emergency;

d) the law must be consistent with the state's obligations under international law applicable to states of emergency;

e) the law must not indemnify the state or any person in respect of an unlawful act;

f) the law must be made public promptly after enactment; and

g) the law must only infringe rights in a way that is strictly necessary and proportional to the harm to be avoided.

2.4.5 The declaration of a state of emergency must be capable of being challenged before an independent and impartial tribunal, which will determine:

a) the validity of a declaration of a state of emergency;

b) the necessity of extending a declaration of a state of emergency; or

c) the validity of any law enacted or action taken in consequence of the declaration.

2.4.6 In enacting a law in consequence of a declaration of a state of emergency, derogations from the human rights guaranteed by the *International Covenant on Civil and Political Rights* (ICCPR) must

droits de ceux qui sont assujettis à la loi; et son efficacité doit être soupesée par rapport à l'importance de la violation des droits qu'elle permet. De telles dérogations doivent également pouvoir être examinées, en fonction de ces principes, par une cour de justice ou un tribunal dûment constitué.

2.3.2 Toute loi adoptée en vue de contrer une menace provenant du terrorisme, d'une guerre, d'une invasion, d'une insurrection générale, d'un désordre interne, d'une catastrophe naturelle ou d'une autre situation d'urgence :

   a) doit seulement s'appliquer que pour le futur;

   b) doit être assujettie à des limites de temps rigoureuses et définies, elles-mêmes établies en conformité avec les principes de nécessité et de proportionnalité; et

   c) ne doit pas procurer réparation à un État ou à une personne pour un acte illégal.

Principe 2.4 : États d'urgence et dérogations

2.4.1 L'état d'urgence doit être prescrit dans une loi de l'État et proclamé officiellement. On doit considérer l'état d'urgence comme une mesure d'exception à laquelle on ne doit recourir qu'en situation de menace réelle à la vie de la nation, à son indépendance ou à sa sécurité. Lorsque l'état d'urgence est proclamé, un État doit expliquer la nature de la menace de façon détaillée, l'étendue de toute dérogation prévue autorisée et les raisons pour lesquelles une dérogation est présumée nécessaire.

2.4.2 Une déclaration d'état d'urgence n'entre en vigueur que si :

   a) elle ne s'applique que pour le futur;

   b) elle est assujettie à des limites de temps rigoureuses et spécifiques, elles-mêmes établies selon les principes de nécessité et de proportionnalité; et

   c) elle doit faire l'objet d'une ratification législative dès que possible après sa proclamation.

2.4.3 Le renouvellement d'une déclaration d'état d'urgence doit être :

   a) précédé d'un débat public au sein d'une assemblée démocratiquement élue; et

   b) adopté à une plus grande majorité d'une assemblée démocratiquement élue que celle exigée pour ratifier la déclaration d'urgence initiale.

comply with Article 4 of that convention, and in particular, may not extend to the following rights:

a) life;

b) security of the person, including:

    i. freedom from torture or cruel, inhuman or degrading treatment or punishment, and freedom from medical or scientific experimentation to which the person has not freely consented;

    ii. freedom from slavery;

    iii. freedom from servitude;

c) the right not to be discriminated against, at the very least, on the basis of:

    i. race;

    ii. ethnicity;

    iii. place of origin;

    iv. citizenship status; or

    v. religion;

d) freedom of thought, conscience and religion. This right includes freedom to have, to adopt or to refuse a religion or belief of a person's choice, and freedom, either individually or in community with others and in public or private, to manifest this religion or belief in worship, observance, practice and teaching. Freedom to manifest one's religion or beliefs must only be subject to such limitations as are prescribed by law and are necessary to protect public safety, order, health, or morals or the fundamental rights and freedoms of others;

e) the right not to be found guilty of any criminal offence on account of any act or omission which did not constitute a criminal offence under national or international law at the time it was committed;

f) the right to be protected against arbitrary deprivations of liberty;

g) the right to a fair trial, including the presumption of innocence and *habeas corpus/recurso de amparo*;

h) the right to the judicial guarantees essential for the protection of non-derogable rights.

2.4.4 Si l'État a déclaré l'état d'urgence, toute loi qui en découle doit satisfaire aux conditions suivantes :
   a) elle ne doit s'appliquer que pour le futur;
   b) elle doit être assujettie à des limites de temps rigoureuses et définies, elles-mêmes établies selon les principes de nécessité et de proportionnalité;
   c) elle doit s'avérer d'une nécessité absolue pour atteindre l'objectif légitime visé par l'État quand il a proclamé l'état d'urgence;
   d) elle doit respecter les obligations d'un État en vertu des normes de droit international s'appliquant aux états d'urgence;
   e) elle ne doit pas procurer réparation à un État ou à une personne pour un acte illégal;
   f) elle doit être rendue publique aussitôt après son adoption; et
   g) elle ne doit porter atteinte aux droits que dans la mesure strictement nécessaire et proportionnelle au dommage contre lequel on veut se prémunir.

2.4.5 La déclaration d'état d'urgence doit pouvoir être contestée devant un tribunal indépendant et impartial qui devra se prononcer sur :
   a) la validité de la déclaration d'état d'urgence;
   b) la nécessité de prolonger la déclaration d'état d'urgence; et
   c) la validité de toute loi adoptée ou de toute mesure prise suite à la déclaration d'état d'urgence.

2.4.6 Lors de l'adoption d'une loi à la suite d'une déclaration d'état d'urgence, les dérogations aux droits de l'homme garantis par le *Pacte international relatif aux droits civils et politiques* (PIRDCP) doivent respecter les dispositions de l'article 4 de cet instrument, et plus particulièrement, elles ne doivent pas s'appliquer aux droits suivants :
   a) le droit à la vie;
   b) le droit à l'intégrité et à la sécurité de la personne humaine, notamment :
      i.   l'interdiction de recourir à la torture et à autre peine ou traitement cruel, inhumain ou dégradant, et l'interdiction d'expérience médicale ou scientifique à laquelle la personne n'a pas librement consenti;
      ii. l'interdiction de l'esclavage;
      iii. l'interdiction de l'asservissement.

Commentary

Additional state obligations may be non-derogable if they are needed to protect the non-derogable rights listed above. The United Nations Human Rights Committee used this reasoning to extend protection to certain procedural rights in its General Comment 29 on States of Emergency (Article 4) of the *International Covenant on Civil and Political Rights* (UN Doc. CCPR/C/21/Rev.1/Add.11 (2001)).

c) le droit de ne pas faire l'objet de discrimination, à tout le moins, en raison de :
   i. la race;
   ii. l'ethnicité;
   iii. le lieu d'origine;
   iv. le statut de citoyenneté;
   v. la religion;

d) le droit à la liberté de pensée, de conscience et de religion. Ce droit implique la liberté pour une personne de choisir, de pratiquer, ou de refuser une religion ou une conviction et la liberté, exercée soit individuellement, soit collectivement, en public ou en privée, d'afficher cette religion ou conviction par le culte, l'accomplissement de rites, les pratiques et l'enseignement. La liberté d'afficher sa religion ou ses convictions ne doit être assujettie qu'aux seules restrictions imposées par la loi et qui s'avèrent nécessaires à la protection de la sécurité, de l'ordre, de la santé, de la moralité publique, des droits fondamentaux et des libertés d'autrui;

e) le droit de ne pas être condamné pour une infraction pénale suite à un acte ou une omission qui ne constitue pas un acte délictueux en vertu du droit national ou international au moment où elle est commise;

f) le droit à la protection contre la privation arbitraire de liberté;

g) le droit à un procès équitable, notamment à la présomption d'innocence et à l'*habeas corpus/recurso de amparo*;

h) le droit aux garanties judiciaires essentielles à la protection des droits auxquels on ne peut déroger.

Commentaire
Les États peuvent être astreints à des obligations additionnelles auxquelles on ne peut déroger, dans la mesure où elles s'avèrent nécessaires à la protection des droits auxquels on ne peut déroger mentionnés ci-dessus. C'est le raisonnement qu'a adopté le Comité des droits de l'homme de l'ONU afin de procurer une protection aux droits relatifs à la procédure, tel que rapporté dans son Commentaire général 29 relatif aux états d'urgence (article 4) du *Pacte international relatif aux droits civils et politiques* (UN Doc. CCPR/C/21/Rev.1/Add.11 (2001)).

Part 3: Anti-terrorism, Human Rights and the Use of Force

Principle 3.1: Exceptional nature of the use of military force

3.1   As a general rule, terrorist acts are criminal acts subject to ap-.plicable domestic, transnational and/or international criminal law enforcement measures. The international use of armed force by states in response to terrorist acts is only permissible in accordance with international law regulating such use of force.

Principle 3.2: International rules on the use of force continue to apply

3.2.1 Anti-terrorism goals do not change the international rules on the use of force by one state against another or within the territory of another: use of military force must comply with the requirements of the United Nations Charter in being either explicitly authorized by the UN Security Council or a *bona fide* exercise of collective or individual self-defence within the constraints of Article 51.

3.2.2 Self-defence justifies the use of force against a state or within the territory of that state only in response to an act of terrorism that:
   a) rises to the level of an "armed attack" within the meaning of international law;
   b) has already occurred or is evidently about to occur; and
   c) is properly attributable, as a matter of international law, to the state against which the act of self-defence is directed.

3.2.3 The force used in self-defence must be necessary and proportionate in accordance with international law.

3.2.4 In accordance with Article 51 of the UN Charter, all uses of force in self-defence must be immediately reported to the UN Security Council and may continue only until the Security Council has taken measures necessary to maintain international peace and security.

3.2.5 "Pre-emptive self-defence"—the use of force in response to a feared security threat that is not evidently about to occur—is a violation of international law and is not a legitimate basis for use of military force.

Partie 3 : Lutte au terrorisme, droits de l'homme et recours à la force

Principe 3.1 : Caractère exceptionnel du recours aux forces militaires

3.1.1   Règle générale, les actes terroristes sont des actes criminels qui sont assujettis aux dispositions pertinentes de mise en application du droit pénal national, transnational ou international. Au plan international, les États ne peuvent recourir aux forces armées pour contrer des actes de terrorisme qu'en conformité avec le droit international réglementant un tel usage des forces armées.

Principe 3.2 : Les règles du droit international concernant l'usage de la force continuent à s'appliquer

3.2.1   Des objectifs liés à la lutte au terrorisme ne modifient en rien les règles internationales sur le recours à la force par un État à l'encontre d'un autre État, ou sur le territoire d'un autre État. Ainsi, le recours à la force militaire doit se conformer aux formalités de la Charte des Nations Unies : il doit être expressément autorisé par le Conseil de Sécurité de l'ONU ou il doit constituer l'exercice *bona fide* du droit individuel ou collectif de légitime défense à l'intérieur des limites de l'article 51.

3.2.2   La légitime défense justifie le recours à la force à l'encontre d'un État ou sur le territoire d'un État seulement en réponse à un acte terroriste qui :

   a) atteint les proportions d'une « agression armée » au sens du droit international;

   b) est déjà survenu ou est manifestement sur le point de survenir;

   c) est légitimement attribuable, en droit international, à l'État à l'encontre duquel le geste de légitime défense est dirigé.

3.2.3   La force utilisée en légitime défense doit s'avérer nécessaire et proportionnelle selon les critères du droit international.

3.2.4   Conformément à l'article 51 de la Charte des N.-U., toutes les utilisations de la force en légitime défense doivent être immédiatement signalées au Conseil de Sécurité des N.-U, et elles peuvent continuer de s'appliquer seulement jusqu'à ce que le Conseil de Sécurité ait pris les mesures nécessaires pour maintenir la paix et la sécurité internationale.

Principle 3.3: International humanitarian law and human rights law

3.3.1   In any situation of armed conflict, applicable customary and treaty-based international humanitarian law is to be observed by the combatants.

3.3.2   In a situation of armed conflict, international human rights obligations remain in force except where recognized international derogation provisions such as Article 4 of the ICCPR apply. International human rights and international humanitarian law are complementary and mutually reinforcing, and should be interpreted in light of each other.

3.2.5 Les «attaques préemptives», soit le recours à la force en réponse à une menace à la sécurité appréhendée n'offrant aucune preuve quant à l'imminence de sa survenance, contreviennent au droit international et ne confèrent aucune légitimité au recours à des forces armées.

Principe 3.3: Droit international humanitaire et droit international des droits de l'homme

3.3.1 En situation de conflit armé, les combattants doivent observer les dispositions pertinentes du droit international humanitaire issues tant du droit coutumier que de celui des traités.

3.3.2 En situation de conflit armé, les obligations relatives aux droits de l'homme en droit international demeurent en vigueur, sauf en cas d'application de dispositions dérogatoires internationales reconnues comme celles de l'article 4 du PIRDCP. Les droits internationaux de l'homme et le droit international humanitaire sont complémentaires et supplétifs, et doivent, en conséquence, s'interpréter à la lumière l'un de l'autre.

Part 4: Prevention of and Responses to the Use of Torture

Principle 4.1: The absolute prohibition against torture and cruel, inhuman or degrading treatment or punishment

4.1.1   No person, including those suspected or convicted of terrorist related offences, shall be subjected to torture or to cruel, inhuman or degrading treatment or punishment.

4.1.2   Principle 4.1.1 is a peremptory norm of international law (*jus cogens*). No circumstances whatsoever, including a state of war, a threat of war, a threat to national security, an emergency threatening the life of the nation, internal political instability or any other public emergency, may be invoked by a state as a justification for torture or cruel, inhuman or degrading treatment or punishment.

Principle 4.2: Obligations to respect and ensure the right to be free from torture and cruel, inhuman or degrading treatment or punishment

4.2.1   States shall take all necessary effective legislative, administrative, judicial or other measures to prevent torture and cruel, inhuman or degrading treatment or punishment. Without limitation, these shall include the establishment of a system of regular visits undertaken by international and national independent bodies to all places where people are deprived of their liberty, in order to prevent torture and cruel, inhuman or degrading treatment or punishment.

4.2.2   States shall prohibit by law torture and cruel, inhuman or degrading treatment or punishment and make any violations of such prohibitions subject to appropriate sanctions, including criminal penalties.

4.2.3   States shall ensure that complaints and reports of torture or cruel, inhuman or degrading treatment or punishment are promptly, effectively and impartially investigated. States shall ensure, including through cooperation with other states, that persons against whom there is sufficient evidence of having committed torture or cruel, inhuman or degrading treatment or punishment are prosecuted.

4.2.4   States shall take all necessary steps to ensure that they do not aid or assist in the commission of torture or cruel, inhuman or degrading treatment or punishment.

Partie 4 : Prévention de la torture et réponses à l'usage de la torture

Principe 4.1 : Interdiction absolue de la torture ou des peines et traitements cruels, inhumains ou dégradants

4.1.1 Nul, notamment les personnes soupçonnées ou trouvées coupables d'infractions liées au terrorisme, ne sera soumis à la torture ou à des peines ou traitements cruels, inhumains ou dégradants.

4.1.2 Le Principe 4.1.1 constitue une norme impérative de droit international (*jus cogens*). Aucune circonstance, quelle qu'elle soit, notamment un état de guerre, une menace de guerre ou à la sécurité nationale, une urgence mettant en péril la vie de la nation ou la stabilité politique intérieure et toute autre situation d'urgence ne peut être invoquée par un État pour justifier la torture ou les peines ou traitements cruels, inhumains ou dégradants.

Principe 4.2: Obligations de garantir le droit à la protection contre la torture ou les peines ou traitements cruels, inhumains ou dégradants et de veiller à la protection de ce droit

4.2.1 Les États prennent toutes les mesures législatives, administratives, judiciaires ou autres qui sont nécessaires et efficaces pour prévenir la torture et les peines ou traitements cruels, inhumains ou dégradants. Sans restreindre la généralité de ce qui précède, ces mesures comprennent l'implantation d'un système de visites régulières par des organisations nationales et internationales indépendantes de tous les endroits où des personnes sont privées de leur liberté pour prévenir la torture et les peines ou traitements cruels, inhumains ou dégradants.

4.2.2 Les États adoptent des lois qui interdisent la torture et les peines ou traitements cruels, inhumains ou dégradants et qui prescrivent que tout manquement à cette interdiction est passible de sanctions appropriées, notamment de sanctions pénales.

4.2.3 Les États s'assurent de mener une enquête rapide, efficace et impartiale sur les plaintes au sujet de la torture ou de peines ou traitements cruels, inhumains ou dégradants et sur les rapports en faisant état. Les États s'assurent, notamment en coopérant avec d'autres États, que les personnes à l'égard desquelles il existe des preuves suffisantes qu'elles ont torturé des personnes ou qu'elles

4.2.5 No state shall transfer any person, or aid or assist another state to transfer any person—no matter what his or her status or suspected crime—to another state where there are grounds for believing that the individual would be in danger of being subjected to torture or to cruel, inhuman or degrading treatment or punishment in that state.

4.2.6 States may only transfer persons to other states pursuant to a legal process that accords with internationally recognized standards of legality and fairness. Without limitation, such processes must include the opportunity for individuals to interpose claims against transfer on the basis that they fear torture or cruel, inhuman or degrading treatment or punishment upon transfer and an opportunity for effective, independent and impartial review of the decision to transfer.

4.2.7 Diplomatic assurances against torture and other cruel, inhuman or degrading treatment or punishment shall not be relied upon to effect transfers. Such assurances do not provide an effective safeguard against such abuse and they are legally insufficient to overcome the transferring state's obligation to refrain from transferring an individual to a known risk.

Principle 4.3: Statements, evidence and information obtained under torture

4.3.1 States shall ensure that statements, evidence or other information obtained by torture or cruel, inhuman or degrading treatment or punishment cannot be used in any judicial, administrative or other proceedings, other than for the purpose of establishing the occurrence of the act of torture or cruel, inhuman or degrading treatment or punishment.

4.3.2 Information, data, or intelligence that has been obtained through torture or cruel, inhuman or degrading treatment or punishment may not be used as a basis for:
   a) the deprivation of liberty;
   b) the transfer, through any means, of an individual from the custody of one state to another;
   c) the designation of an individual as a person of interest, a security threat or a terrorist or by any other description purporting to link that individual to terrorist activities; or

ont imposé à des personnes des peines ou traitements cruels, inhumains ou dégradants sont poursuivies devant les tribunaux.

4.2.4 Les États prennent toutes les mesures nécessaires pour s'assurer
qu'ils n'aident pas à la perpétration d'actes de torture ou à l'imposition de peines ou traitements cruels, inhumains ou dégradants.

4.2.5 Nul État ne transfère une personne, ni n'aide un autre État à transférer une personne, quel que soit son statut ou le crime qu'elle est
soupçonnée d'avoir commis, vers un autre État, s'il existe des motifs de croire que cette personne serait en danger de se voir soumise à la torture ou de se voir imposer des peines ou traitements
cruels, inhumains ou dégradants dans cet État.

4.2.6 Les États ne peuvent transférer des personnes vers d'autres États
que dans le cadre d'un processus juridique qui respecte les normes
de légalité et de justice internationalement reconnues. Sans limi-
ter la généralité de ce qui précède, un tel processus doit comprendre : premièrement, la possibilité pour les personnes de faire valoir
des arguments à l'encontre du transfert au motif qu'elles craignent,
de ce fait, d'être soumises à la torture ou de se voir imposer des
peines ou traitements cruels, inhumains ou dégradants et, deuxiè-
mement, la possibilité pour ces personnes d'obtenir une révision
efficace, indépendante et impartiale de la décision de transférer.

4.2.7 Nul État n'autorise le transfert d'une personne sur la base de garanties diplomatiques qui excluent la possibilité de torture ou de peines
et de traitements cruels, inhumains et dégradants. Ces garanties ne
fournissent pas de protection adéquate à l'encontre de ces mauvais
traitements et, sur le plan juridique, elles sont insuffisantes pour
libérer un État de son obligation de s'abstenir de transférer une personne vers un endroit où il est su qu'elle court un risque.

Principe 4.3 : Déclarations, preuves et informations obtenues sous l'effet de la torture

4.3.1 Les États veillent à ce que les déclarations, preuves et autres informations obtenues sous l'effet de la torture ou par suite de l'imposition de peines ou de traitements cruels, inhumains ou dégradants
ne puissent être utilisées dans le cadre d'instances judiciaires,
administratives ou autres, sauf s'il s'agit d'établir la commission
d'un acte de torture ou l'imposition d'une peine ou de traitements
cruels, inhumains ou dégradants.

d) the deprivation of any other internationally protected human right.

Principle 4.4: Remedies and reparations

4.4.1 Each state shall ensure that victims of torture or cruel, inhuman or degrading treatment or punishment have equal and effective access to a judicial remedy and have an enforceable right to full and effective reparations, including the following:

a) restitution;
b) compensation;
c) rehabilitation;
d) satisfaction; and
e) guarantees of non-repetition.

Reparations should be proportional to the gravity of the violations and the harm suffered.

4.4.2 States and their courts shall not apply or develop legal doctrine, including doctrines of judicial deference, that fail to give effect to the duty to ensure the right to be free from torture or cruel, inhuman or degrading treatment or punishment, including such doctrines as "act of state," "political questions," "non-justiciability," "comity," "state secrecy," "national security confidentiality" and the like.

4.4.3 A state that has engaged in, participated in, aided, assisted, been complicit in, or acquiesced to torture or cruel, inhuman or degrading treatment or punishment committed abroad must provide an enforceable right to compensation in its own courts against itself, its officials and any persons, including corporate actors and foreign state officials, with whom the state has been involved.

4.4.4 Each state has, at the very least, the international legal jurisdiction to provide access to its courts for purposes of adjudicating compensation claims for torture or cruel, inhuman or degrading treatment or punishment wherever it occurs in the world.

4.4.5 In view of the *jus cogens* nature of the duty to ensure the right to be free from torture and cruel, inhuman or degrading treatment or punishment, states and states' courts should modify or develop the law on state immunity so as not to grant immunity to foreign states or persons who are or were officials of a foreign state from

4.3.2 Les informations, les données ou les renseignements obtenus sous l'effet de la torture ou par suite de l'imposition de peines ou de traitements cruels, inhumains ou dégradants ne peuvent motiver :

a) la privation de liberté;

b) le transfert, de quelque façon que ce soit, d'une personne d'un État qui a la garde à un autre État;

c) la désignation d'une personne comme personne d'intérêt, une menace à la sécurité ou terroriste ou, encore, de tout autres manières visant à établir un lien entre cette personne et des activités terroristes; ou

d) la privation de tout autre droit de l'homme jouissant d'une protection internationale.

Principe 4.4 : Recours et réparations

4.4.1 Chaque État veille à ce que les victimes de torture, de peines ou de traitements cruels, inhumains ou dégradants bénéficient d'un accès égal et utile au recours judiciaire et jouissent du plein exercice de leur droit à une réparation pleine et entière, notamment :

a) à la restitution;

b) à la compensation;

c) à la réhabilitation;

d) à la satisfaction; et

e) à des garanties de non-répétition.

Les indemnisations doivent s'établir en proportion de la gravité des violations et du préjudice subi.

4.4.2 Les États et leurs tribunaux n'appliquent ni ne formulent de théories juridiques, notamment des théories de retenue judiciaire, qui feraient échec au devoir d'assurer la protection du droit de ne pas être soumis à la torture ou aux peines et aux traitements cruels, inhumains ou dégradants et notamment des théories comme celles de l'« acte d'État », des « questions politiques », de la « non-judiciarisation », de la « courtoisie internationale », du « secret d'État », de la « confidentialité liée à la sécurité nationale » et ainsi de suite.

4.4.3 Un État qui a commis un acte de torture ou imposé des peines ou des traitements cruels, inhumains ou dégradants à l'étranger, a participé à, a donné son appui à, ou a prêté assistance à un acte de torture ou à l'imposition de peines ou de traitements cruels, inhumains ou dégradants à l'étranger, a été complice d'un acte de

adjudicative jurisdiction over compensation claims for torture or cruel, inhuman or degrading treatment or punishment.

torture ou de l'imposition de peines ou de traitements cruels, inhumains ou dégradants à l'étranger, ou a approuvé un acte de torture ou l'imposition de peines ou de traitements cruels, inhumains ou dégradants à l'étranger doit accorder un recours en réparation exécutoire devant ses propres tribunaux contre lui-même, ses fonctionnaires et toute personne, notamment les représentants d'entreprises et les fonctionnaires d'États étrangers, auprès desquelles l'État est intervenu.

4.4.4 Tout État possède, à tout le moins, la compétence juridique internationale d'accorder un accès à ses tribunaux, aux fins d'adjudication des recours en réparation pour des actes de torture et l'imposition de peines et de traitements cruels, inhumains ou dégradants où que ce soit dans le monde.

4.4.5 Étant donné le caractère *jus cogens* du devoir de garantir le droit de ne pas être soumis à la torture et aux peines ou traitements cruels, inhumains ou dégradants, les États et leurs tribunaux doivent modifier et interpréter la loi sur l'immunité des États de sorte à ne pas accorder à des États étrangers ou à des personnes qui sont ou ont été des fonctionnaires d'un État étranger une immunité contre la compétence juridictionnelle en matière de demande de réparation alléguant la torture ou des peines ou traitements cruels, inhumains ou dégradants.

Part 5: Administrative and *De Facto* Detention and Other Practices

Principle 5.1: Administrative and *de facto* deprivation of liberty

5.1.1   Persons deprived of their liberty by a state are entitled, without delay, to a procedure that allows them, at a minimum and in accordance with due process guarantees under international human rights law, to challenge the legal basis for their detention and have an opportunity to have their detention independently reviewed by an independent and impartial court of law.

5.1.2   Every state with effective control over an individual deprived of his or her liberty must:

a)   ensure access by independent monitoring bodies to all detainees and places where persons are deprived of their liberty;

b)   ensure that the monitoring bodies have confidential access to the detainees;

c)   register all persons it detains; this registration must contain full details on the circumstances of the detention, the identity of the detainee, and information about any release or transfer of the detainee; and

d)   ensure that all facilities where individuals are deprived of their liberty meet internationally recognized principles for the treatment of prisoners and/or detainees.

5.1.3   Administrative measures must not be used to deprive an individual of his or her liberty without a proceeding that recognizes the individual's legal personality and complies with international human rights standards regarding due process. At a minimum, these procedures must comply with the following:

a)   the burden of proof on a balance of probabilities must always rest with the state;

b)   the person must have a right to effective independent counsel;

c)   the person must have a right to access to family members, consular officials (where the person is a foreign national) and to his or her counsel;

d)   the acts that lead to the administrative proceeding must be attributable to the person who is the subject of the proceeding;

Partie 5 : Détention administrative, détention de fait et autres pratiques

Principe 5.1 : Perte de liberté administrative et de fait

5.1.1 Les personnes privées de leur liberté par un État ont droit sans délai à une instance qui leur permet, à tout le moins et conformément aux garanties d'application régulière de la loi que prescrit le droit international des droits de l'homme, de contester le fondement juridique de leur détention et elles peuvent, sans délai, demander à un tribunal indépendant et impartial d'effectuer un examen indépendant de leur détention.

5.1.2 L'État qui a le contrôle effectif d'une personne privée de sa liberté doit :

a) veiller à ce que les organismes indépendants de surveillance aient accès à tous les détenus et à tous les endroits où des personnes sont privées de leur liberté;

b) veiller à ce que les organismes de surveillance aient un accès confidentiel aux détenus;

c) inscrire toute personne qu'il détient; cette inscription doit contenir les circonstances détaillées de la détention, l'identité du détenu et les informations relatives à la libération ou au transfert du détenu; et

d) veiller à ce que les installations où des personnes sont privées de leur liberté répondent aux principes reconnus internationalement relatifs au traitement des prisonniers ou des détenus.

5.1.3 L'on ne peut utiliser de mesures administratives pour priver une personne de sa liberté sans que soit tenue une instance dans le cadre de laquelle on reconnaît la personnalité juridique de la personne et qui satisfait aux normes du droit international des droits de l'homme en matière d'application régulière de la loi. Ces instances doivent, à tout le moins, respecter les critères suivants :

a) le fardeau de la preuve selon la prépondérance des probabilités doit toujours incomber à l'État;

b) la personne doit avoir droit d'être représentée de façon utile par un avocat indépendant;

c) la personne doit avoir un droit d'accès aux membres de sa famille, aux fonctionnaires consulaires (si la personne est un ressortissant étranger) et à son avocat;

e) the individual must be provided with sufficient information to be able to know and meet the case against him or her;

f) the proceeding must comply with principles of non-discrimination;

g) in an immigration context, there must be a principle of presumptive release. Where detention is to secure removal, it cannot exceed a reasonable time and may only be effected where strictly necessary; and

h) the deprivation of liberty must be for a reasonable period of time.

Principle 5.2: Enforced disappearances

5.2.1 States must not subject a person to enforced disappearance, nor assist nor aid in such an act. Enforced disappearance is a crime under international law and persons responsible for, or complicit in, the commission or attempted commission of enforced disappearance should be brought to justice.

5.2.2 States responsible for enforced disappearance must provide to victims a full and effective remedy and reparation, in accordance with international standards.

5.2.3 No state shall transfer a person to another state where there are substantial grounds for believing that he or she would be in danger of being subjected to enforced disappearance.

5.2.4 Enforced disappearance includes holding persons in secret, unacknowledged or inaccessible detention.

Principle 5.3: Transfer, immigration remedies and due process

5.3.1 Compliance with international legal obligations to prosecute or extradite individuals engaged or suspected of engaging in terrorist activities must be the preferred method of dealing with such individuals.

5.3.2 In circumstances where immigration remedies are pursued in relation to terrorism concerns, procedures must comply with international principles of non-discrimination and due process of law and:

a) the burden of proof on a balance of probabilities must always rest with the state;

b) sanctions should be strictly limited to cases where individual responsibility is established; and

d) les actes qui ont donné ouverture à l'instance administrative doivent être attribuables à la personne qui fait l'objet de l'instance;

e) des informations suffisantes doivent être fournies à la personne pour lui permettre de prendre connaissance de la cause et de se défendre;

f) l'instance doit respecter les principes de non-discrimination;

g) en matière d'immigration, le principe de date prévue pour la libération doit s'appliquer. Si la détention est aux fins d'expulsion, elle ne peut s'exercer que pour une période de temps raisonnable et ne doit s'exercer qu'en cas de stricte nécessité; et

h) la privation de liberté ne doit prévaloir que pour une période de temps raisonnable.

Principe 5.2 : Disparitions forcées

5.2.1 Les États ne doivent assujettir personne à une disparition forcée, ni la favoriser ou y prêter son assistance. La disparition forcée constitue un crime en vertu du droit international et les personnes responsables d'avoir commis ce crime, qui ont tenté de le commettre, ou qui en ont été complices doivent faire face à la justice.

5.2.2 Les États responsables de disparition forcée doivent procurer aux victimes un recours utile et une réparation complète conformément aux normes internationales.

5.2.3 Nul État ne doit transférer une personne à un autre État s'il y existe des motifs sérieux de croire qu'elle serait en danger d'être soumise à une disparition forcée.

5.2.4 La disparition forcée inclut le fait de détenir des personnes au secret, de ne pas reconnaître que des personnes sont détenues et de refuser tout accès aux personnes détenues.

Principe 5.3 : Transfert, recours en matière d'immigration et application régulière de la loi

5.3.1 Respecter les obligations juridiques internationales selon lesquelles les personnes qui commettent des activités terroristes ou sont soupçonnées de les avoir commis doivent faire l'objet de poursuite devant les tribunaux ou d'une extradition doit être la méthode préférée de contrer les activités de ces personnes.

5.3.2 Lorsque des recours en immigration sont intentés en relation avec des situations liées au terrorisme, ces procédures doivent se

    c) consistent with penal principles of law, states must enact measures that provide fair and transparent procedures for recognizing rehabilitation in the immigration context.

5.3.3 More generally, any state effecting the transfer of a detainee to the jurisdiction or effective control of another state may only effect this in accordance with international due process norms and is under a continuing obligation to ensure that the receiving state respects international standards in respect of detention, including those set out above.

Principle 5.4: National and regional security lists

5.4.1 States should not create security lists except where there is a pressing and substantial security reason for doing so. Moreover, security lists should only include the names of persons or groups that present a real, substantial and established danger to the national security of the state or the international or regional collectivity creating the list. States must not adopt listings, made by other countries or entities, that do not meet this test, or use security lists for reasons not related to national security.

5.4.2 States should avoid using the terms "terrorist" or "terrorism" as a criterion for listing because of the definitional problems associated with the terms, but if they do, those terms must be precisely and narrowly defined by law (see Principle 2.1.2 above), so that they do not capture legitimate political activity, expression, association or insurgency.

5.4.3 The precise national security criteria for listing, and the consequences of listing, must be clearly prescribed by law and not subject to discretion.

5.4.4 The standard of proof for making a listing should be clear and convincing proof and, where criminalization is a consequence, the criminal standard of proof—beyond a reasonable doubt—should apply.

5.4.5 States must ensure that no evidence which may have been obtained through torture may be used to support a listing.

5.4.6 Due to the serious consequences of listing an individual or group, including infringements of constitutional and international human rights, affected parties must be afforded, at a minimum: a right to reasonable notice of the intent to list; a right to know the allega-

conformer aux principes internationaux de non-discrimination et d'application régulière de la loi et, de plus :

a) le fardeau de la preuve selon la prépondérance des probabilités doit toujours incomber à l'État;

b) des sanctions ne doivent être imposées que dans les cas où une responsabilité personnelle est établie;

c) conformément aux principes de droit pénal, les États doivent adopter des dispositions instaurant des procédures justes et transparentes pour reconnaître la réhabilitation dans le contexte de l'immigration.

5.3.3 De façon plus générale, l'État qui procède au transfert d'un détenu sous la compétence d'un autre État, ou qui le place sous le contrôle effectif d'un autre État, ne peut le faire qu'en conformité avec les normes internationales en matière d'application régulière de la loi et il demeure astreint à respecter l'obligation de veiller à ce que l'État qui accueille la personne respecte les normes internationales relatives à la détention, notamment celles formulées ci-dessus.

Principe 5.4 : Listes de sécurité nationales et régionales

5.4.1 Sauf pour des raisons impérieuses et primordiales de sécurité, les États ne doivent pas établir de listes de sécurité. Qui plus est, ces listes ne doivent pas se composer que des noms de personnes ou de groupes qui représentent un danger réel, important et avéré envers la sécurité nationale de l'État ou de la collectivité internationale ou régionale qui créent la liste. Les États ne doivent pas adopter de listes élaborées par d'autres pays ou entités et qui ne répondent pas à ces critères, pas plus qu'ils ne doivent avoir recours aux listes de sécurité pour des raisons qui ne sont pas liées à la sécurité nationale.

5.4.2 Les États doivent éviter l'utilisation des termes « terroriste » et « terrorisme » comme critère d'inscription sur une liste, en raison des difficultés que pose leur définition. Si les États utilisent tout de même ces termes, ils doivent être définis par une loi qui leur attribue un sens étroit et précis (voir le Principe 2.1.2 ci-dessus) de façon à ce qu'ils ne comprennent pas l'activité politique, l'expression, l'association ou l'insurrection exercées légitimement.

5.4.3 Le critère spécifique lié à la sécurité nationale en ce qui concerne la création d'une liste, de même que les conséquences de l'inscrip-

tions and evidence offered in support of the listing; and a right to respond, including the right to call evidence and witnesses. Parties should also be afforded a right to a *de novo* appeal before an impartial judicial body with power to grant relief.

5.4.7   Each listing by a state should be reviewed on a yearly basis. States should also provide a mechanism by which individuals and groups may periodically seek delisting and call new evidence in support of their case. There should be automatic delisting after a reasonable period of time, subject to renewal through the same processes used in the initial listing.

5.4.8   The criteria states adopt for listing groups must also take into account the scope and degree of activity within the group which threatens national security. Where only certain individuals within a group are engaged in violent activity targeting civilians, the individuals and not the group should be listed.

5.4.9   If the legislative branch of government is called upon to ratify a state's listings, that ratification must take place on a case-by-case basis.

Commentary

Since the events of September 11, 2001, states have created a large number of security lists intended for a variety of purposes and using a variety of methodologies. Such lists include proscription lists, domestic and border watch lists, no fly lists, asset freezing lists, known terrorist lists, and lists of "potential" terrorists produced by highly questionable data mining programs. In most cases no due process is afforded to the affected individual or group before the listing takes place and no or minimal recourse is available to challenge the listing. These practices violate existing constitutional guarantees, human rights treaty obligations, criminal process rights and administrative law principles regarding due process.

Notably, the consequences of listing an individual as a security threat, terrorist, or terrorist supporter will almost invariably be the devastation of his or her livelihood and reputation, and the consequences of listing a group will be its destruction or criminalization (and a consequent infringement of its members' rights to association and expression). In these circumstances, due process protections are essential.

tion sur une liste doivent être clairement établis par la loi sans qu'aucune discrétion y soit associée.

5.4.4 Une preuve explicite et convaincante doit constituer la norme en matière de preuve pour la création des listes et, là où une criminalisation en découle, la norme de preuve pénale—hors de tout doute raisonnable—doit alors s'appliquer.

5.4.5 Les États doivent veiller à ce qu'aucune preuve qui a peut-être été obtenue sous l'effet de la torture ne puisse être utilisée pour la création de listes.

5.4.6 En raison des sérieuses conséquences affectant les personnes ou les groupes inscrits sur une liste, notamment les atteintes aux droits constitutionnels et aux droits internationaux de l'homme, les parties visées doivent, à tout le moins, pouvoir invoquer le droit : à un avis raisonnable de l'intention de les inscrire sur une liste; de connaître les allégations et la preuve présentée à l'appui de leur inscription sur une liste; de se défendre, notamment de produire des preuves et de convoquer des témoins. Les parties doivent également pouvoir bénéficier d'un droit d'appel *de novo* devant une entité judiciaire dotée du pouvoir de décréter des mesures de redressement.

5.4.7 Chaque inscription sur une liste par un État doit être examinée annuellement. Les États doivent aussi établir un processus permettant aux personnes et aux groupes de tenter périodiquement d'obtenir le retrait de leur inscription sur une liste et de présenter de nouvelles preuves à l'appui de leur cause. Un retrait automatique de l'inscription doit s'opérer après une période de temps raisonnable, sous réserve du renouvellement des inscriptions selon le même processus que lors de la création de la liste initiale.

5.4.8 Les critères que les États appliquent pour inscrire des groupes sur une liste doivent également prendre en considération l'envergure des activités et le niveau d'activités régnant à l'intérieur du groupe qui menace la sécurité nationale. Si seulement certaines personnes dans le groupe sont impliquées dans des activités violentes ciblant des civils, les personnes, et non les groupes, doivent être inscrites sur les listes.

5.4.9 Dans la mesure où il est demandé au pouvoir législatif d'un gouvernement de ratifier les listes dressées par un État, cette ratification ne s'effectue qu'au cas par cas.

Principle 5.5: Listing pursuant to UN Security Council Resolution 1267

5.5.1 States should call on the UN Security Council to adopt as quickly as possible a fair and clear procedure to govern the listing and delisting of individuals and groups pursuant to Security Council Resolution 1267.

5.5.2 The procedure must stipulate the standard of proof required to list an individual or group. Given the serious consequences of listing for the party, the standard of proof should be higher than a balance of probabilities. The UN Security Council must also develop guidelines or jurisprudence regarding the weight to be given different kinds of evidence and must stipulate that no evidence which may have been obtained through torture can be used to support a listing.

5.5.3 States must respect and meet the standard of proof stipulated by the procedure when asking the 1267 Committee to list an individual or group, and must not seek listing for illegitimate reasons. States should be liable under their domestic law for negligently, maliciously or fraudulently seeking the UN listing of individuals and groups.

5.5.4 The procedure adopted must provide affected parties with a right to reasonable notice of the intent to list, a right to know the allegations and evidence offered in support of the listing, a right to respond, including the right to call evidence and witnesses, and a right to a *de novo* appeal before an impartial judicial or quasi judicial body with power to grant relief.

5.5.5 The procedure should include: yearly reviews of each listing; a mechanism by which individuals and organizations may periodically seek delisting and call new evidence in support of their case; and automatic delisting after a reasonable period of time, subject to renewal through the same processes used in the initial listing.

5.5.6 The procedure adopted must also ensure that listed individuals who have their assets frozen are not deprived of their livelihood by allowing specific exceptions or arrangements to be made by the Security Council, or the state freezing the assets, on humanitarian grounds.

Commentaire

Depuis les événements du 11 septembre 2001, les États ont dressé, en utilisant une grande variété de méthodes, une pléthore de listes de sécurité dont l'utilisation revêt une foule de variantes. On retrouve parmi celles-ci des listes de proscription, de surveillance interne et frontalière, d'interdiction de voyager par avion, de gel d'actif, de terroristes reconnus et de terroristes en devenir, toutes ces listes ayant été créées à l'aide de logiciels d'exploration de données fort discutables. Dans la plupart des cas, les personnes ou les groupes visés ne bénéficient d'aucune application régulière de la loi avant que les listes ne soient créées et, une fois que les listes sont dressées, ils ne disposent soit, d'aucun recours utile, soit uniquement d'un recours de portée très limitée pour contester leur inscription sur les listes. Ces pratiques violent les garanties constitutionnelles existantes, les obligations relatives aux droits de l'homme découlant de traités, les droits associés au respect du processus judiciaire et les principes de droit administratif en matière d'application régulière de la loi.

Il convient de souligner que l'inscription d'une personne sur une liste comme menace à la sécurité, comme terroriste ou comme partisane du terrorisme la privera presque invariablement de tout moyen de subsistance et ruinera presque invariablement sa réputation, alors que, d'autre part, les groupes aussi inscrits risquent quant à eux de disparaître et d'être criminalisés (et les droits d'association et d'expression des membres de tels groupes risquent d'être enfreints). En pareilles circonstances, les protections de l'application régulière de la loi s'avèrent essentielles.

Principe 5.5 : Création de listes conformément à la résolution 1267 du Conseil de sécurité de l'ONU

5.5.1   Les États doivent en appeler au Conseil de sécurité de l'ONU le presser d'adopter dans les plus brefs délais une procédure juste et explicite régissant l'inscription de personnes et de groupes sur une liste et la désinscription de personnes et de groupes d'une liste, conformément à la résolution 1267 du Conseil de sécurité.

5.5.2   La procédure doit énoncer la norme de preuve requise pour l'inscription d'un individu ou d'un groupe sur une liste. Compte tenu de la gravité des conséquences pour la partie de l'inscription sur une liste, la norme de preuve doit surpasser celle de la prépondérance des probabilités. Le Conseil de sécurité de l'ONU doit également

5.5.7 The procedure should provide redress in the form of monetary compensation and other remedies to individuals and groups who have been wrongly listed.

5.5.8 Until a procedure, like that described above, is adopted by the Security Council, states have a duty to assist their citizens and residents in seeking delisting from the 1267 list. This duty includes helping the individual, or individuals belonging to a group, to ascertain the allegations made, and the evidence used in support of, the listing and appealing to the Security Council and the foreign state, if any, that put forward the listing.

5.5.9 No person should be detained as a result of listing on a United Nations or a domestic list of terrorists or terrorist groups.

Commentary

UN Security Council Resolution 1267 (as amended) provides for the listing of "members of the Al-Qaeda organization and the Taliban and other individuals, groups, undertakings and entities associated with them." The resolution calls on states to freeze the assets of, and prevent arms sales to, listed entities, as well as to deny listed individuals entry to, and transit through, their territory. In its 2005 World Summit Outcome document, the General Assembly called for the development of "fair and clear procedures" in respect of the 1267 list, and the 1267 Committee is currently examining a number of proposed reforms. In administering the 1267 list, the Security Council is bound by the UN Charter and international customary law, including customary human rights norms. Due process is a principle of international customary law and the prohibition on torture is a customary human rights norm.

élaborer des lignes directrices ou de la jurisprudence traitant du poids relatif attribuable à des preuves de nature différente et prescrire qu'aucune preuve qui a peut-être été obtenue sous l'effet de la torture ne puisse être utilisée à l'appui de l'inscription du nom d'une personne ou d'un groupe sur une liste.

5.5.3 Les États doivent satisfaire à la norme de preuve prescrite par la procédure lorsqu'ils demandent au Comité créé conformément à la résolution 1267 d'inscrire une personne ou un groupe sur une liste, et les États ne doivent jamais demander d'inscription pour des motifs illégitimes. Les États doivent supporter en vertu de leur droit interne la responsabilité de toute démarche négligente, malicieuse ou frauduleuse en vue d'obtenir l'inscription du nom d'une personne ou d'un groupe sur une liste.

5.5.4 La procédure adoptée doit garantir aux parties visées le droit : à un avis raisonnable de l'intention de les inscrire sur une liste; de connaître les allégations et la preuve présentée à l'appui de leur inscription sur une liste; de se défendre, notamment de produire des preuves et de convoquer des témoins. Les parties doivent également pouvoir bénéficier d'un droit d'appel *de novo* devant une entité judiciaire dotée du pouvoir de décréter des mesures de redressement.

5.5.5 La procédure doit prévoir : la revue annuelle de chaque liste; un processus permettant aux personnes et aux groupes de tenter périodiquement d'obtenir le retrait de leur inscription sur une liste et de présenter de nouvelles preuves à l'appui de leur cause; un retrait automatique de l'inscription après une période de temps raisonnable, sous réserve du renouvellement des inscriptions selon le même processus que lors de la création de la liste initiale.

5.5.6 La procédure adoptée doit également veiller à ce que les personnes inscrites sur une liste et dont l'actif a été gelé ne soient pas privées de tout moyen de subsistance en autorisant le Conseil de sécurité ou l'État ayant procédé au gel à convenir, pour des motifs humanitaires, de mesures spécifiques d'exception ou d'accommodements.

5.5.7 La procédure doit aussi prévoir une réparation aux personnes et groupes ayant été injustement inscrits sur une liste sous forme de compensation monétaire ou d'autres mesures de redressement.

5.5.8 D'ici l'adoption par le Conseil de sécurité d'une procédure similaire à celle décrite ci-dessus, les États ont l'obligation de soutenir leurs citoyens et leurs résidents dans leurs démarches visant leur désinscription d'une liste créée conformément à la résolution 1267. Les États doivent notamment aider les personnes et les membres d'un groupe à s'assurer de la véracité des allégations formulées et de la preuve présentée à l'appui de leur inscription sur la liste et à interjeter appel devant le Conseil de sécurité et, le cas échéant, devant l'État étranger responsable de l'inscription de la personne sur la liste.

5.5.9 Nul ne doit être détenu en raison de la mention de son nom sur une liste de terroristes ou de groupes de terroristes émanant soit des Nations Unies, soit d'un État.

Commentaire
La résolution 1267 du Conseil de sécurité de l'ONU (tel que modifiée) établit la liste des «membres de l'organisation Al-Qaeda et des taliban, autres personnes, groupes, entreprises et entités qui leur sont associés.» La résolution enjoint aux États de geler les actifs des entités mentionnées dans la liste, d'empêcher que des armes leur soient vendues et de refuser aux personnes inscrites sur la liste l'accès à leur territoire ainsi que tout transit par celui-ci. Dans son Document final sur le sommet mondial 2005, l'Assemblée générale demande la mise au point de «procédures justes et explicites» en ce qui concerne la liste établie conformément à la résolution 1267 et le Comité créé conformément à la résolution 1267 se penche présentement sur un certain nombre de propositions de réformes. Quand il gère la liste établie conformément à la résolution 1267, le Conseil de sécurité est lié par la Charte de l'ONU, le droit coutumier international, notamment les règles coutumières du droit de l'homme. Le principe de l'application régulière de la loi est un principe du droit coutumier international, et la prohibition de torture est une des règles coutumières du droit de l'homme.

Part 6: Anti-terrorism and Consular and Diplomatic Protection

Principle 6.1: Consular protection

6.1.1   A foreign state must:

a) advise foreign persons, upon being imprisoned, placed in custody or detained, of their right to be in contact with the consular authorities of the state of nationality. Should the person request such contact then the foreign state shall notify, without delay, the consular post of the state of nationality;

b) make arrangements for initial and ongoing contact between the person imprisoned, placed in custody or detained and the consular officials of the state of nationality;

c) ensure that all communications between the consular authorities of the state of nationality and the person imprisoned, in custody or detained are confidential and conducted in private. Officials of the foreign state will not attend meetings between the consular authorities of the state of nationality and the person imprisoned, in custody or detained unless invited to do so by the consular authorities of the state of nationality; and

d) permit the state of nationality to provide assistance and support to the person imprisoned, in custody or detained in accordance with Paragraph (a) above.

6.1.2   At the request of a national imprisoned or detained by a foreign state, the state of nationality should:

a) contact in person, in writing and by electronic devices its nationals who have been imprisoned, held in custody or detained within 24 hours of the deprivation of their liberty;

b) maintain contact, in person, in writing and by electronic devices, with its nationals who have been imprisoned, held in custody or detained on a basis to be determined by the state of nationality;

c) communicate in private with persons imprisoned, held in custody or detained and obtain confidentiality for all written and electronic communications;

d) on a regular basis provide persons in prison, in custody or in detention with appropriate personal articles and material including those relating to leisure, intellectual and academic pursuits, hygiene, diet, and medical and dental treatment;

Partie 6 : Lutte au terrorisme, protection consulaire et protection diplomatique

Principe 6.1 : Protection consulaire

6.1.1 Un État étranger doit :

a) informer les étrangers, dès l'instant où ils sont emprisonnés, placés en détention ou détenus, de leur droit de communiquer avec les autorités consulaires de l'État dont ils ont la nationalité. Si l'étranger requiert une telle communication, l'État étranger doit alors notifier, sans délai, le poste consulaire de l'État dont l'étranger a la nationalité;

b) prendre des dispositions en vue de la communication initiale et celles qui suivront entre l'étranger emprisonné, placé en détention ou détenu et les fonctionnaires consulaires de l'État dont l'étranger a la nationalité;

c) veiller à ce que toutes les communications entre l'étranger emprisonné, placé en détention ou détenu et les autorités consulaires de l'État dont l'étranger a la nationalité soient confidentielles et s'échangent en privé. À moins d'y avoir été invités par les autorités consulaires de l'État dont l'étranger a la nationalité, les fonctionnaires de l'État étranger ne peuvent assister aux réunions entre l'étranger emprisonné, placé en détention ou détenu et les autorités consulaires de l'État dont l'étranger la nationalité; et

d) autoriser l'État dont le ressortissant étranger a la nationalité à porter aide et assistance à la personne emprisonnée, gardée ou détenue, conformément au sous-paragraphe (a) ci-dessus.

6.1.2 À la demande d'un ressortissant emprisonné ou détenu par un État étranger, l'État dont le ressortissant a la nationalité doit :

a) communiquer en personne, par écrit ou par voie électronique avec ses ressortissants au plus tard dans les 24 heures suivant le moment où ils ont été privés de leur liberté;

b) demeurer en contact, en personne, par écrit ou par voie électronique avec ses ressortissants emprisonnés, placés en détention ou détenus selon la fréquence qu'il détermine lui-même;

c) communiquer en privé avec les personnes emprisonnées, placées en détention ou détenues et obtenir que toutes les communications écrites ou électroniques soient confidentielles;

e) obtain information from appropriate officials of the foreign state on the reasons for the imprisonment, custody or detention of its nationals and the legal or regulatory process to which they will be subjected;

f) arrange for visits by family and friends to persons imprisoned, in custody or detained;

g) arrange for legal, forensic and investigatory assistance, as appropriate, to the person imprisoned, in custody or detained; and

h) maintain regular contact with family members of detained persons and keep them fully informed.

Principle 6.2: Diplomatic protection

6.2   Diplomatic protection consists of resort to diplomatic action or other means of peaceful settlement by a state adopting in its own right the cause of its national in respect of an injury to that national arising from an internationally wrongful act of another state. It includes (but is not limited to) the following:

a) representations by the injured person's state to the foreign state at various levels up to and including heads of state and government;

b) provision of written information, both interpretative and factual;

c) appeals to appropriate members of the legislative branch of government;

d) appeals to the judicial organs of the foreign state;

e) appeals to other bodies of the foreign state as may be appropriate;

f) representations to appropriate international bodies and agencies; and

g) legal action against the foreign state before an international agency, tribunal or court.

Principle 6.3: Nationality

6.3.1 The state that exercises consular or diplomatic protection is a state of nationality. A state of nationality means a state whose nationality the protected individual has acquired by birth, descent, succession of states, naturalization or in any other manner not inconsistent with international law.

d) procurer régulièrement aux personnes emprisonnées, placées en détention ou détenues les accessoires et effets personnels nécessaires, notamment ceux requis pour la détente, les activités intellectuelles, l'hygiène, le régime, les soins dentaires et médicaux;

e) obtenir de l'information des fonctionnaires en autorité de l'État étranger sur les motifs de l'emprisonnement, de la garde ou de la détention de leur ressortissant ainsi que sur le processus judiciaire ou réglementaire auquel il sera assujetti;

f) faire des démarches pour que des membres de la famille et des amis puissent visiter les personnes emprisonnées, gardées ou détenues;

g) faire en sorte que les personnes emprisonnées, gardées ou détenues puissent, selon leurs besoins, obtenir des services juridiques, médico-légaux et ceux d'enquêteurs; et

h) communiquer régulièrement avec les membres de la famille des personnes détenues et les tenir complètement informés.

Principe 6.2 : Protection diplomatique

6.2 La protection diplomatique s'entend du recours à une intervention diplomatique ou à toute autre méthode de règlement pacifique des différends utilisée par un État qui épouse la cause de son ressortissant qui a subi un préjudice par suite de l'acte fautif d'un autre État. La protection diplomatique comprend notamment ce qui suit :

a) des représentations par l'État dont la personne qui a subi un préjudice a la nationalité à différents niveaux de l'État étranger jusqu'à et incluant les chefs de l'État et du gouvernement;

b) la fourniture d'information tant interprétative que factuelle;

c) des appels auprès des membres indiqués du pouvoir législatif du gouvernement;

d) des appels devant les tribunaux de l'État étranger;

e) le cas échéant, des appels devant d'autres organismes de l'État étranger;

f) des représentations à des organismes et agences internationaux; et

g) des procédures judiciaires contre l'État étranger devant un organisme, un tribunal ou une cour internationaux.

6.3.2 Any state of which a dual or multiple national is a national may exercise consular or diplomatic protection in respect of that national against a state of which that individual is not a national.

6.3.3 A state of nationality may exercise consular or diplomatic protection in respect of a person against a foreign state of which that person is also a national provided that the person has the predominant nationality of the claimant state. In determining "predominant nationality," states should consider:

a) habitual residence;

b) state of passport used and/or issuance of visa by the foreign state;

c) the amount of time spent in each country of nationality;

d) date of naturalization (i.e., the length of the period spent as a national of the protecting state before the claim or representation arose);

e) place, curricula and language of education;

f) employment and financial interests including bank accounts, and social security insurance;

g) place of family life;

h) family ties in each country; and

i) language used by immediate family.

6.3.4 In the event states of nationality are unable to agree on the predominant nationality of a claimant for consular or diplomatic protection, then the matter should be referred to a mutually agreed third party for resolution.

6.3.5 States are encouraged to enter into bilateral agreements in order to resolve conflicts of nationality between their respective citizens.

Principle 6.4: Exception to nationality

6.4   Any state may exercise consular or diplomatic protection in relation to persons injured by a violation of international norms with *erga omnes* status.

Principle 6.5: Obligation to extend consular and diplomatic protection

6.5.1 States should extend consular and diplomatic protection to their nationals. When there is reason to believe that a national is being mistreated by a foreign state in violation of *jus cogens* norms,

Principe 6.3 : Nationalité

6.3.1 L'État qui offre une protection consulaire ou diplomatique est un État dont une personne a la nationalité. Un tel État s'entend d'un État dont une personne a acquis la nationalité par naissance, hérédité, succession d'États, naturalisation ou de tout autres manières qui n'est pas incompatible avec le droit international.

6.3.2 Un État dont un ressortissant a la double ou une multiple nationalité peut accorder une protection consulaire ou diplomatique à ce ressortissant à l'encontre d'un État dont il n'est pas un ressortissant.

6.3.3 Un État peut accorder une protection consulaire ou diplomatique à une personne à l'encontre d'un État étranger dont cette personne est également le ressortissant à la condition que la nationalité prédominante de la personne soit celle de l'État revendicateur. Pour établir la «nationalité prédominante», les États doivent prendre en considération :

a) le lieu habituel de résidence;

b) l'état du passeport en usage ou la délivrance d'un visa par l'État étranger;

c) la durée des séjours dans chacun des pays dont la personne a la nationalité;

d) la date de naturalisation (c.-à-d., le laps de temps écoulé en tant que ressortissant du pays protecteur avant la survenance de la réclamation ou représentation);

e) le lieu, le cursus et la langue d'enseignement;

f) le travail et les intérêts financiers, notamment les comptes bancaires et la sécurité sociale;

g) l'environnement de vie familiale;

h) les liens familiaux dans chaque pays; et

i) la langue des proches.

6.3.4 Si les États ne peuvent s'entendre sur la nationalité prédominante du demandeur de protection consulaire ou diplomatique, le règlement du différend doit alors être soumis à une tierce partie choisie d'un commun accord.

6.3.5 On incite les États à conclure des ententes bilatérales pour résoudre les différends portant sur la nationalité de leurs citoyens respectifs.

including the prohibition against torture, states have an even greater responsibility to extend consular or diplomatic protection at the request of the national being imprisoned or detained by the foreign state or at the request of his or her family members.

6.5.2 States should draw up an additional optional protocol to the Vienna Convention on Consular Relations aimed at providing detailed rules concerning consular and diplomatic protection.

Principe 6.4 : Exception à la nationalité

6.4   Un État peut accorder une protection consulaire ou diplomatique aux personnes qui ont subi un préjudice par suite d'une violation de normes internationales *erga omnes*.

Principe 6.5 : Obligation d'accorder la protection consulaire et diplomatique

6.5.1   Les États doivent accorder une protection consulaire et diplomatique à leurs ressortissants. Lorsqu'il existe des raisons de croire qu'un État étranger inflige de mauvais traitements à un ressortissant en violation de normes *jus cogens*, notamment l'interdiction de soumettre une personne à la torture, si le ressortissant emprisonné ou détenu par un État étranger ou les membres de sa famille en font la demande, les États assument une plus grande responsabilité encore d'accorder une protection consulaire ou diplomatique à leur ressortissant.

6.5.2   Les États doivent établir un protocole optionnel supplémentaire à la Convention de Vienne sur les relations consulaires dans le but d'introduire des directives détaillées concernant la protection consulaire ou diplomatique.

Part 7: Anti-terrorism, Human Rights and Information Disclosure

PART 7A: RIGHTS OF ACCESS, POSSESSION AND COMMUNICATION

Principle 7.1: Securing access to information

7.1   Subject to the justifiable limitations listed below, everyone has the right to obtain information from a state in accordance with Principles 12–14 of the *Johannesburg Principles on National Security, Freedom of Expression and Access to Information* and to possess and to impart that information to anyone, orally, in writing, or through any other medium of his or her choice, including information considered by a state to relate to the protection of national security or public safety from terrorist threat. Principles 12–14 of the *Johannesburg Principles* provide:

> *Principle 12: Narrow Designation of Security Exemption*
> A state may not categorically deny access to all information related to national security, but must designate in law only those specific and narrow categories of information that it is necessary to withhold in order to protect a legitimate national security interest.

> *Principle 13: Public Interest in Disclosure*
> In all laws and decisions concerning the right to obtain information, the public interest in knowing the information shall be a primary consideration.

> *Principle 14: Right to Independent Review of Denial of Information*
> The state is obliged to adopt appropriate measures to give effect to the right to obtain information. These measures shall require the authorities, if they deny a request for information, to specify their reasons for doing so in writing and as soon as reasonably possible, and shall provide for a right of review of the merits and the validity of the denial by an independent authority, including some form of judicial review of the legality of the denial. The reviewing authority must have the right to examine the information withheld.

Partie 7 : Lutte au terrorisme, droits de l'homme et divulgation d'information

PARTIE 7A : DROITS D'ACCÈS, POSSESSION ET COMMUNICATION

Principe 7.1 : Assurer l'accès à l'information

7.1   Sous réserve des restrictions justifiables dont la liste apparaît ci-dessous, quiconque a le droit d'obtenir des informations d'un État conformément aux Principes 12 à 14 énoncés dans les *Principes de Johannesburg relatifs à la sécurité nationale, à la liberté d'expression et à l'accès à l'information,* de posséder et de dévoiler cette information, notamment l'information qui, selon les États, concerne la protection de la sécurité nationale ou de la sécurité du public contre la menace terroriste, à quiconque verbalement, par écrit ou par l'intermédiaire de tout autre médium de son choix. Les Principes 12 à 14 des *Principes de Johannesburg* stipulent :

> *Principe 12 : Définition étroite de l'exception de sécurité*
> Un État ne peut pas systématiquement refuser l'accès à toute information concernant la sécurité nationale, mais doit préciser dans la loi les catégories précises et étroites d'information qu'il est nécessaire de ne pas divulguer pour protéger un intérêt légitime de sécurité nationale.

> *Principe 13 : Intérêt public de la divulgation*
> Dans toutes les lois et décisions concernant le droit d'obtenir l'information, l'intérêt public de connaître cette information doit être une préoccupation primordiale.

> *Principe 14 : Le droit à un contrôle indépendant du refus de donner l'information*
> L'État est obligé d'adopter les mesures appropriées pour mettre en vigueur le droit d'obtenir l'information. Ces mesures doivent exiger que les autorités, si elles refusent de satisfaire une demande d'information, précisent le plus tôt raisonnablement possible les raisons du refus; et ces mesures doivent prévoir un droit de contrôle des raisons et de la validité du refus par une autorité indépendante, notamment une sorte de recours judiciaire de la légalité du refus. L'autorité de contrôle doit avoir le droit d'examiner l'information non divulguée.

Principle 7.2: Released information

7.2   Subject to the justifiable limitations listed below, everyone has the right to receive, possess, and impart to anyone orally, in writing or through any other medium of his or her choice, any terrorism-related information that is released by a person who obtained the information by virtue of government service, either with or without government approval.

Principle 7.3: Disclosure of information and open proceedings

7.3.1   Subject to the justifiable limitations listed below (and in immigration or refugee cases, subject to the consent of the applicant), all proceedings brought by a state that threaten to infringe or deny the life, liberty, or human rights of anyone shall be open to the public, and publication bans or related orders shall not be made.

7.3.2   Subject to the justifiable limitations listed below and to Principle 2.1.8 (in criminal matters), everyone whose life, liberty, or human rights are put at risk in a proceeding brought by a state on anti-terrorism grounds has the right: (a) to effective means to challenge the credibility, reliability or accuracy of any information relied upon by the state in those proceedings; and (b) to the disclosure and use of any information known to, or in the possession of, the state that could reasonably assist in defending against the state's case.

PART 7B: GENERAL PRINCIPLES ON JUSTIFIABLE LIMITS AND ANTI-TERRORISM

Principle 7.4: General principles on justifiable limits and anti-terrorism

7.4.1   Subject to the more specific rule for criminal matters found in Principle 2.1.8, to limit or deny the rights provided for in Principles 7.1–7.3 using justifications related to anti-terrorism, a state must demonstrate before a tribunal that has powers of full and effective scrutiny that the restriction:

a)   is prescribed by a law that is accessible, unambiguous, drawn narrowly and with precision so as to enable individuals to foresee whether a particular action is unlawful, and which provides adequate safeguards against abuse, including prompt and effective judicial scrutiny of the validity of the restriction by an independent court or tribunal;

Principe 7.2 : Information divulguée

7.2   Sous réserve des restrictions justifiables dont la liste apparaît ci-dessous, quiconque a le droit de recevoir, de posséder et de dévoiler à quiconque verbalement, par écrit ou par l'intermédiaire de tout autre médium de son choix, toute information concernant le terrorisme divulguée par une personne qui l'a obtenue grâce à des services gouvernementaux, avec ou sans l'approbation du gouvernement.

Principe 7.3 : Divulgation d'information et instances publiques

7.3.1   Sous réserve des restrictions justifiables dont la liste apparaît ci-dessous (et, sous réserve du consentement du requérant, dans les cas d'immigration ou de revendication du statut de réfugié), le public doit pouvoir assister à toutes les instances intentées par un État qui risquent d'enfreindre ou de nier le droit à la vie, le droit à la liberté ou les droits de l'homme de quiconque, et aucune interdiction de publication ni autre ordonnance de semblable nature ne doivent être rendues.

7.3.2   Sous réserve des restrictions justifiables dont la liste apparaît ci-dessous et du Principe 2.1.8 (en matière pénale), quiconque voit sa vie, sa liberté ou ses droits de l'homme mis en péril dans des instances reliées à la lutte au terrorisme et intentées par un État jouit du droit : (a) d'accès aux ressources nécessaires pour contester la crédibilité, la fiabilité ou l'exactitude de toute information sur lesquelles l'État s'appuie dans le cadre de ces procédures; et (b) à la divulgation et à l'utilisation de toute information connue par l'État ou en sa possession et qui pourrait raisonnablement servir à contrer les prétentions de l'État.

PARTIE 7B : PRINCIPES GÉNÉRAUX RELATIFS AUX RESTRICTIONS JUSTIFIABLES ET À LA LUTTE AU TERRORISME

Principe 7.4 : Principes généraux relatifs aux restrictions justifiables et à la lutte au terrorisme

7.4.1   Sous réserve de la règle plus précise en matière pénale énoncée au Principe 2.1.8, pour restreindre de nier les droits énoncés dans les Principes 7.1 à 7.3 en invoquant des justifications concernant la lutte au terrorisme, un État doit démontrer à un tribunal doté de pleins pouvoirs d'examen que la restriction :

b) is necessary in a free and democratic society to protect against a serious threat to a legitimate national security or public safety interest;

c) poses a rational means of protecting national security or public safety interests and is proportional to the specific risks that disclosure would present, and the benefit achieved for national or public security interests outweighs the damage done by denying access to information; and

d) is compatible with democratic principles.

7.4.2 Restrictions on access to government information, or penalties or consequences relating to unauthorized access to government information, can be justified as necessary in the interests of preventing terrorist acts only if they relate to national security interests as defined in Principle 2 of the *Johannesburg Principles*, or to the public safety interests in protecting against the reasonable apprehension of serious bodily harm or substantial damage to property. Principle 2 of the *Johannesburg Principles* provides:

a) A restriction sought to be justified on the ground of national security is not legitimate unless its genuine purpose and demonstrable effect is to protect a country's existence or its territorial integrity against the use or threat of force, or its capacity to respond to the use or threat of force, whether from an external source, such as a military threat, or an internal source, such as incitement to violent overthrow of the government.

b) In particular, a restriction sought to be justified on the ground of national security is not legitimate if its genuine purpose or demonstrable effect is to protect a government from embarrassment or exposure of wrongdoing, or to conceal information about the functioning of its public institutions, or to entrench a particular ideology, or to suppress industrial unrest.

7.4.3 Justifiable limitations on obtaining information shall be based on the contents of the information alone and not on its class or the manner by which it was acquired.

Principle 7.5: Disclosure of information policies

7.5 Everyone has the right to obtain agreements, guidelines and policy statements regarding information-sharing among states, sub-

a) est prescrite par une loi qui peut être consultée, qui est sans équivoque et qui est rédigée avec rigueur et précision et qui offre une protection adéquate contre les abus, notamment un recours à un examen judiciaire rapide et utile portant sur la validité de la restriction par un tribunal indépendant;

b) est nécessaire dans une société libre et démocratique pour protéger contre une menace sérieuse envers un intérêt légitime de sécurité nationale ou de sécurité publique;

c) créé un processus logique de protection des intérêts de sécurité nationale et de sécurité du public tout en étant proportionnelle aux risques que la divulgation représente, et que le bénéfice qu'en tire la sécurité nationale et la sécurité du public l'emporte sur le préjudice causé par le refus de donner accès à l'information; et

d) s'accorde avec les principes de démocratie.

7.4.2 Les restrictions concernant l'accès à l'information gouvernementale, ou les pénalités et les conséquences concernant un accès non autorisé à l'information gouvernementale peuvent être justifiées comme étant nécessaires à la prévention d'actes terroristes seulement si elles concernent des intérêts de sécurité nationale tel que définis au Principe 2 des *Principes de Johannesburg* ou des intérêts de sécurité publique dans la protection contre une crainte raisonnable de sérieuses blessures corporelles ou de dommages considérables à des biens. Le Principe 2 des *Principes de Johannesburg* stipule que :

a) Une restriction qu'un gouvernement tenterait de justifier par des raisons de sécurité nationale n'est pas légitime à moins que son véritable but et son effet démontrable ne soient de protéger l'existence d'un pays ou son intégrité territoriale contre l'usage ou la menace d'usage de la force que cela vienne de l'extérieur, comme une menace militaire, ou de l'intérieur, telle l'incitation au renversement d'un gouvernement.

b) En particulier, une restriction qu'un gouvernement tenterait de justifier par des raisons de sécurité nationale n'est pas légitime si son véritable but et son effet démontrable sont de protéger des intérêts ne concernant pas la sécurité nationale, comme de protéger un gouvernement de l'embarras ou de la découverte de ses fautes, ou pour dissimuler des informations sur le fonc-

ject to the justifiable exceptions above. Confidentiality rules that apply to information-sharing agreements between states may not take precedence over the right of citizens to access information from their governments.

Principle 7.6: Penalties

7.6.1   No person may be punished on national security or public safety grounds for the receipt or possession of information from whatever source obtained if: (1) the receipt, possession or disclosure of that information does not actually harm and is not likely to harm a legitimate national security or public safety interest; or (2) the public interest in knowing the information outweighs the harm from disclosure.

7.6.2   No person may be punished on national security or public safety grounds for disclosing information that he or she learned by virtue of government service if the public interest in knowing the information outweighs the harm from disclosure.

7.6.3   Protection of national security or public safety may not be used as a reason to compel a journalist to reveal a confidential source.

Principle 7.7: Appeal rights

7.7   Any decisions concerning the suppression of information, including the sanctioning of those who receive, possess or impart such information, whether arrived at in open court or not, should be subject to appeal.

tionnement des institutions publiques, ou pour imposer une certaine idéologie, ou pour réprimer des troubles sociaux.

7.4.3 Les restrictions justifiables sur l'obtention d'information sont fondées seulement se fonder sur le contenu de l'information, et non sur sa catégorie ou la façon dont elle a été obtenue.

Principe 7.5 : Divulgation des politiques d'information

7.5 Sous réserve des exceptions justifiables mentionnées ci-dessus, quiconque a le droit d'obtenir les ententes, les directives et les énoncés de politique concernant le partage d'information entre États. Les règles de confidentialité s'appliquant aux ententes de partage d'information entre États ne peuvent pas avoir préséance sur le droit d'accès des citoyens aux informations émanant de leurs gouvernements.

Principe 7.6 : Pénalités

7.6.1 Nul ne doit se voir pénalisé pour des motifs liés à la sécurité nationale ou à la sécurité du public pour la réception ou la possession d'information obtenue de quelque source que ce soit si : (1) la réception, la possession ou la divulgation de cette information ne cause vraiment aucun préjudice ou n'est pas susceptible de nuire à un intérêt légitime de sécurité nationale ou de sécurité du public; ou (2) l'intérêt du public de connaître l'information l'emporte sur le tort résultant de la divulgation de l'information.

7.6.2 Nul ne doit se voir pénalisé pour des motifs liés à la sécurité nationale ou à la sécurité du public pour la divulgation d'informations acquises grâce aux services gouvernementaux, si l'intérêt du public de connaître l'information l'emporte sur le tort résultant de la divulgation de l'information.

7.6.3 La protection de la sécurité nationale ou de la sécurité du public ne peut constituer une raison valable pour contraindre un journaliste à dévoiler une source confidentielle.

Principe 7.7 : Droits d'appel

7.7 Il doit être possible d'interjeter appel de toutes les décisions concernant la suppression d'information, notamment celles qui sanctionnent ceux qui reçoivent, possèdent ou divulguent telle information, qu'elles aient été rendues lors d'une audience publique ou non.

Part 8: Anti-terrorism, Human Rights and the Use and Exchange of Information and Intelligence

Principle 8.1: General principles on information, privacy and intelligence

8.1.1   Everyone has the right to protection of personal information concerning him- or herself. This includes the right to:

  a) know what information is held about him- or herself, subject to justifiable limitations applied *mutatis mutandis* from Principle 7.4;

  b) be notified as soon as possible, consistent with justifiable limitations applied *mutatis mutandis* from Principle 7.4, that information has been collected;

  c) have personal information corrected or deleted; and

  d) compensation from states or private entities where injury arises from the misuse of information.

8.1.2   Unless there are credible grounds to believe that information, data or intelligence is accurate and reliable and that it has not been obtained either by torture or cruel, inhuman or degrading treatment or punishment, that information, data or intelligence may not be used as a basis for:

  a) the deprivation of liberty;

  b) the transfer, through any means, of an individual from the custody of one state to another;

  c) the designation of an individual as a person of interest, a security threat or a terrorist or by any other description purporting to link that individual to terrorist activities; or

  d) the deprivation of any other internationally protected human rights.

Principle 8.2: The collection and use of personal data by states

8.2.1   Personal information must be obtained by lawful means and processed in accordance with statutory rules and procedures that safeguard the rights set out above.

8.2.2   All state agencies involved in the collection and storage of personal information must ensure that:

  a) data are protected against unauthorized access, use or disclosure;

Partie 8 : Lutte au terrorisme, droits de l'homme, utilisation et partage d'informations et de renseignements

Principe 8.1 : Principes généraux relatifs à l'information, à la protection de la vie privée et au renseignement

8.1.1 Quiconque a droit à la protection des renseignements personnels le concernant, et notamment le droit :

a) sous réserve de l'application *mutatis mutandis* des restrictions justifiables visées au Principe 7.4, de savoir quels renseignements personnels sont détenus à son égard;

b) conformément aux restrictions justifiables visées au Principe 7.4, d'être avisé dès que des renseignements personnels sont recueillis;

c) de faire corriger ou enlever des renseignements personnels à son sujet; et

d) d'obtenir une réparation d'États ou d'entités privées pour le préjudice subi par suite d'une utilisation inadéquate des renseignements personnels.

8.1.2 À moins qu'il existe des motifs plausibles de croire que les informations, les données ou les renseignements sont exacts et fiables et qu'ils n'ont pas été obtenus sous l'effet de la torture, ni à la suite de l'imposition de peines ou de traitements cruels, inhumains ou dégradants, ces informations, données ou renseignements ne peuvent justifier :

a) la perte de liberté;

b) le transfert d'une personne, par quelque moyen que ce soit, de la garde d'un État à un autre;

c) la désignation d'une personne comme personne d'intérêt, menace à la sécurité ou terroriste ou de toute autre manière qui laisse supposer que cette personne a des liens avec des activités terroristes;

d) la perte de tout autre droit de l'homme internationalement reconnu.

Principe 8.2 : La collecte et l'utilisation de renseignements personnels par l'État

8.2.1 Les renseignements personnels doivent être recueillis en toute légalité et être traités selon les règles et procédures prévues par la loi qui assurent la sauvegarde des droits exposés ci-dessus.

b) data are only used in connection with the purpose for which they were collected; and

c) data are only held for as long as necessary and are destroyed thereafter.

8.2.3 States should ensure that their privacy laws prevent private companies from being forced to disclose personal data to state agencies in the absence of an order to do so from an independent judicial authority. Private companies should only be compelled by states to retain personal data for law enforcement purposes on a case-by-case basis subject to an order from an independent judicial authority. Mandatory "data retention" regimes should be repealed and prohibited. "Data mining" and other practices that involve the processing of large amounts of personal data in the absence of specific criminal investigations should also be prohibited.

8.2.4 All states should establish independent data protection supervisory bodies with the power to adjudicate individual complaints and conduct audits of public and private entities.

8.2.5 All state agents involved in intelligence collection and information-sharing must receive ongoing and up-to-date training concerning human rights obligations and data protection rules.

Principle 8.3: Exchanges of personal data between states

8.3.1 States must ensure that their receipt, dissemination and use of any information, data, or intelligence to and from other states does not result in the violation of human rights.

8.3.2 States should only share information on a case-by-case basis and only where there are reasonable grounds for believing that it is accurate and reliable. Prior to the exchange of data the sending state must ensure that the receiving state will treat the information to an adequate level of data protection. Bulk transfers of personal information must be prohibited.

8.3.3 States sharing information have an obligation to correct information once they learn of its unreliability. State agencies and/or private companies involved must be subject to shared, joint and several liability where errors or abuses occur.

8.3.4 Confidentiality rules that apply to information-sharing agreements between states may not be used as grounds to deny indi-

8.2.2 Tous les organismes gouvernementaux qui recueillent des renseignements personnels doivent s'assurer que les données :

a) sont protégées contre un accès, une utilisation ou une divulgation non autorisée;

b) ne sont utilisées que pour le motif pour lequel elles ont été recueillies;

c) ne sont conservées que pour la période qui s'avère nécessaire et, par la suite, détruites.

8.2.3 Les États doivent s'assurer que leur législation concernant le respect de la vie privée empêche que les compagnies privées soient contraintes de divulguer des renseignements personnels à des organismes gouvernementaux, sauf si une autorité judiciaire indépendante l'ordonne. Les États ne doivent contraindre les compagnies privées à conserver des renseignements personnels à des fins d'exécution de la loi qu'au cas par cas et suivant une ordonnance émanant d'une autorité judiciaire indépendante. Les systèmes de rétention obligatoire des données doivent être abrogés et interdits. L'extraction de connaissances à partir de données et autres méthodes de traitement de renseignements personnels en vrac, sans qu'aucune enquête criminelle particulière n'y soit associée, doit également être interdite.

8.2.4 Tous les États doivent se doter d'organismes indépendants supervisant la protection des données et leur conférer les pouvoirs de se prononcer sur les plaintes de particuliers et de procéder à une vérification d'entités publiques et privées.

8.2.5 Tous les représentants de l'État qui interviennent dans la collecte et les ententes de partage d'information doivent recevoir une formation continue et actualisée en matière d'obligations relatives aux droits de l'homme et aux règles de protection des données.

Principe 8.3 : Les échanges de renseignements personnels entre États

8.3.1 Les États doivent s'assurer que ni la réception d'informations, de données ou de renseignements d'autres États, ni le partage d'informations, de données ou de renseignements avec d'autres États et que ni la diffusion ni l'utilisation de ces informations, de ces données ou de ces renseignements ne donnent lieu à des violations des droits de l'homme.

vidual data protection rights or take precedence over the right of citizens to access information from their governments.

8.3.5 All international agreements authorizing the exchange of personal information should be agreed to at ministerial level and subject to parliamentary scrutiny. Such agreements must also be subject to regular examination by an independent review body.

8.3.6 All international agreements and practices authorizing the exchange of personal information must be reviewed in order to ensure their compliance with human rights law and data protection standards. Adequate safeguards must be introduced where necessary.

8.3.7 The UN member states should develop and adopt an international instrument affirming privacy and data protection as fundamental human rights and laying down minimum standards for protection in accordance with these principles.

8.3.2 Les États ne doivent partager de l'information qu'au cas par cas et seulement s'il existe des motifs raisonnables de croire que l'information est exacte et fiable. Avant de partager de l'information, l'État qui la transmet s'assure que l'État qui la reçoit la protégera à un niveau approprié de protection des données. Les transferts en vrac de renseignements personnels doivent être interdits.

8.3.3 Les États qui partagent de l'information ont l'obligation de la corriger une fois qu'ils apprennent qu'elle n'est pas fiable. Les organismes gouvernementaux et les sociétés privées concernés doivent être assujettis à un régime de responsabilité partagée, conjointe et solidaire en cas d'erreurs ou d'abus.

8.3.4 Les règles de confidentialité régissant les ententes d'échange d'informations entre États ne peuvent être invoquées pour dénier les droits individuels à la protection des données et ne peuvent avoir préséance sur le droit d'accès des citoyens aux informations sous le contrôle de leurs gouvernements.

8.3.5 Toutes les ententes internationales permettant l'échange d'information doivent être conclues à l'échelon ministériel, être assujetties à un examen parlementaire ainsi qu'à un examen périodique par une commission indépendante d'examen.

8.3.6 Toutes les ententes et pratiques internationales permettant l'échange de renseignements personnels doivent être examinées pour s'assurer qu'elles respectent la législation sur les droits de l'homme et les normes de protection des données; le cas échéant, on doit mettre en place des mesures de protection adéquates.

8.3.7 Les États membres de l'ONU doivent mettre au point et adopter un instrument international confirmant que le respect à la vie privée et la protection des données constituent des droits de l'homme fondamentaux et instaurant des normes minimales de protection qui soient conformes à ces principes.

Part 9: Oversight, Review and Control of Security Intelligence Agencies

Principle 9.1: Monitoring regime for security intelligence activities

9.1.1 States must ensure that security intelligence activities, including law enforcement activities related to national security, are subject to a multifaceted regime of safeguards and scrutiny, which should include:

a) clear statutory and internal controls;

b) oversight and accountability by the executive branch of government;

c) review by an independent body;

d) review by a body of the legislative branch of government;

e) judicial scrutiny;

f) human rights, data protection, freedom of information, financial audit and whistleblower protection instruments; and

g) free and independent civil society institutions, including the media and advocacy groups.

9.1.2 The objective of this monitoring regime should be to ensure:

a) the propriety of security intelligence activities;

b) the effectiveness of security intelligence activities;

c) maximal transparency of security intelligence activities;

d) the legitimacy of security intelligence activities; and

e) the accountability of the government and security intelligence agencies for their activities.

9.1.3 These principles apply to all security intelligence activities, whether carried out by specialized security intelligence agencies, other governmental or public agencies, non-state actors or foreign actors on behalf of, or for the use of, the state or its agencies. The regime of safeguards and scrutiny may vary according to the risks posed by the activity or combination of activities in question. Law enforcement activities related to national security should in particular be subject to specialized safeguards and scrutiny.

9.1.4 States must ensure that the joint or integrated conduct of security intelligence activities by state actors, foreign actors and non-state actors does not undermine these principles or diminish the protections afforded by a state's monitoring regime.

Partie 9 : Surveillance, examen et contrôle des organismes du renseignement de sécurité

Principe 9.1 : Mesures de contrôle des activités des organismes du renseignement de sécurité

9.1.1 Les États doivent s'assurer que les activités du renseignement de sécurité, notamment les activités de mise en application de la loi liées à la sécurité nationale, sont assujetties à un système de mesures de protection et d'examen à multiples volets qui doit comporter :

a) des contrôles prévus par la loi et internes qui sont précis;

b) une surveillance par l'organe exécutif du gouvernement et une obligation de rendre compte à cet organe;

c) un examen par un organisme indépendant;

d) un examen par un organisme de l'organe législatif du gouvernement;

e) un examen judiciaire;

f) des instruments assurant le respect des droits de l'homme, la protection des données, la liberté de l'information, la vérification financière ainsi que la protection des dénonciateurs; et

g) des institutions civiles libres et indépendantes, notamment les médias et les groupes de revendication.

9.1.2 Ce système de suivi doit viser à assurer :

a) le caractère adéquat des activités du renseignement de sécurité;

b) l'efficacité des activités du renseignement de sécurité;

c) la transparence maximale des activités du renseignement de sécurité;

d) la légitimité des activités du renseignement de sécurité;

e) l'imputabilité du gouvernement et des organismes du renseignement de sécurité pour leurs activités.

9.1.3 Ces principes s'appliquent à toutes les activités du renseignement de sécurité, qu'elles soient menées par les organismes spécialisés du renseignement ou d'autres organismes gouvernementaux ou publics, des acteurs non étatiques ou étrangers agissant pour le compte de l'État, de ses organismes ou à leur intention. Ce système de mesures de protection et d'examen peut varier en fonction du risque résultant des activités en question ou de leur combinaison. Les activités de mise en application de la loi liées à la sécurité nationale doivent, en particulier, faire l'objet de mesures de protection et d'examen spécialisés.

9.1.5   In principle, the powers and resources available to independent agencies that review national security activities should be commensurate with the national security activities being reviewed.

Principle 9.2: Oversight and accountability by the executive branch of government

9.2.1   The executive branch of government must be accountable for the effectiveness and propriety of security intelligence activities. It must oversee these activities by directing them and scrutinizing them on an ongoing basis.

9.2.2   There must be safeguards against impropriety by the executive branch in its oversight of security intelligence activities.

Principle 9.3: Review by an independent body

9.3.1   Security intelligence activities must be reviewed by a body that is independent of government and the agencies that it reviews.

9.3.2   The review body must at minimum be charged with auditing and reviewing the propriety of the security intelligence activities.

9.3.3   The review body must at minimum be empowered to:

    a)   review and investigate, where and how it sees fit, the activities and policies of the agencies within its purview;

    b)   compel any information, including all levels of secure information, from any person;

    c)   investigate and resolve complaints, including ensuring effective access, representations and remedies for complainants;

    d)   make public reports of its findings and recommendations; and

    e)   take all reasonable steps to protect the confidentiality of information that is subject to national security confidentiality.

Principle 9.4: Scrutiny by a body of the legislative branch

9.4   Security intelligence activities should be scrutinized by a body of members of the legislative branch, independent from the executive branch, with power to compel any information, including all levels of secure information, from any person.

Principle 9.5: Scrutiny and control by the judicial branch

9.5   States must ensure that independent, impartial and regularly constituted tribunals play a role in the scrutiny and control of intrusive powers.

9.1.4 Les États doivent s'assurer que la conduite conjointe ou intégrée des activités du renseignement de sécurité par des acteurs étatiques, des acteurs étrangers ou des acteurs non étatiques ne sapent pas ces principes ou ne diminuent pas les protections intégrées dans le système de suivi de l'État.

9.1.5 Les pouvoirs et les ressources mis à la disposition des organismes indépendants chargés de l'examen des activités liées à la sécurité nationale doivent, en principe, être à la hauteur des activités examinées.

Principe 9.2 : Surveillance et imputabilité de l'organe exécutif du gouvernement

9.2.1 L'organe exécutif du gouvernement doit rendre compte du caractère efficace et adéquat des activités du renseignement de sécurité. Il doit superviser ces activités en les orientant et en les examinant de façon constante.

9.2.2 Des mesures de protection à l'encontre d'un acte irrégulier de l'organe exécutif du gouvernement posé dans l'exercice de sa surveillance des activités du renseignement de sécurité doivent être mises en place.

Principe 9.3 : Examen par un organisme indépendant

9.3.1 Les activités du renseignement de sécurité doivent être examinées par un organisme indépendant du gouvernement et des organismes qu'il examine.

9.3.2 Le mandat confié à l'organisme doit, à tout le moins, comprendre la vérification et l'examen du caractère adéquat des activités du renseignement de sécurité.

9.3.3 L'organisme d'examen doit, à tout le moins, être habilité à :

   a) revoir les activités et lignes de conduite des institutions qui sont de son ressort et mener des enquêtes à leur égard, au moment et à l'endroit qu'il jugera opportuns;

   b) contraindre quiconque à fournir de l'information quelle que soit la cote de sécurité dont elle fait l'objet;

   c) instruire et résoudre les plaintes, en assurant notamment aux plaignants un accès, un droit de représentation et des recours utiles;

   d) publier des rapports sur ses conclusions et ses recommandations;

Principle 9.6: Role of other instruments and institutions

9.6.1 States must ensure that security intelligence activities are subject to human rights, data protection, freedom of information, financial audit and whistleblower protection instruments.

9.6.2 States must ensure the freedom and independence of civil society institutions that play a role in scrutinizing security intelligence activities, including the media and advocacy groups.

e) prendre toutes les mesures raisonnables pour protéger la confidentialité des informations faisant l'objet de la confidentialité liée à la sécurité nationale.

Principe 9.4 : Examen par un organisme du pouvoir législatif

9.4 Les activités du renseignement et sécurité doivent être examinées par un organisme formé de membres du pouvoir législatif, indépendant du pouvoir exécutif et investi du pouvoir de contraindre quiconque à fournir de l'information quelle que soit la cote de sécurité dont elle fait l'objet.

Principe 9.5 : Examen et contrôle par le pouvoir judiciaire

9.5 Les États doivent s'assurer que des tribunaux indépendants, impartiaux et dûment constitués jouent un rôle dans l'examen et le contrôle des pouvoirs d'intrusion.

Principe 9.6 : Rôle d'autres instruments et institutions

9.6.1 Les États doivent s'assurer que les activités du renseignement de sécurité sont assujetties aux droits de l'homme, à la protection des données, à la liberté de l'information, à la vérification financière et aux instruments qui protègent les délateurs.

9.6.2 Les États doivent assurer la liberté et l'indépendance des institutions civiles, notamment les médias et les groupes de revendication, qui jouent un rôle dans l'examen des activités du renseignement de sécurité.

Part 10: Anti-terrorism, Human Rights and the Role of the United Nations Security Council

Principle 10.1: UN Charter is binding

10.1   The UN Security Council is bound by the UN Charter to act in accordance with the purposes and principles of the Charter, including human rights.

Principle 10.2: *Jus cogens* human rights

10.2   The UN Security Council may not limit or derogate from human rights that are of a *jus cogens* character, including the right not to be subject to torture.

Partie 10: Lutte au terrorisme, droits de l'homme et rôle du Conseil de sécurité des Nations Unies

Principe 10.1 : La Charte de l'ONU est exécutoire

10.1   Le Conseil de sécurité de l'ONU a, aux termes de la Charte des Nations Unies, l'obligation d'agir conformément aux objectifs et aux principes de la Charte, notamment aux droits de l'homme.

Principe 10.2 : Les droits de l'homme ayant atteint le seuil de *jus cogens*

10.2   Le Conseil de sécurité de l'ONU ne peut restreindre les droits de l'homme, notamment celui de ne pas subir la torture, ayant atteint le seuil de *jus cogens*, ni y déroger.

Commentary: Debating the Scope, Content, and Implementation of the *Ottawa Principles*

Defining Terrorism:
The Need for a Restrained Definition

Kent Roach

A. INTRODUCTION

One of the more difficult issues discussed in the meetings leading to the *Ottawa Principles on Anti-terrorism and Human Rights*[1] was whether they should address or endorse any definition of terrorism. The fact that the group that met in Ottawa spent considerable time on this issue and had difficulty reaching agreement on it should not be surprising. It is well known that a general definition of terrorism has so far eluded international agreement. Instead, the existing conventions on terrorism focus on specific forms of terrorism such as hijackings, bombings, and most recently nuclear terrorism.

However difficult the task of defining terrorism may be, it is neverthe-less an urgent necessity to agree on a restrained definition of terrorism that is based on basic criminal law principles. New anti-terrorism laws are being enacted throughout the world[2] and many of these laws contain unnecessarily broad definitions of terrorism with terms and mandates

---

1   See the *Ottawa Principles on Anti-terrorism and Human Rights* at Part One in this book [*Ottawa Principles*].

2   See, generally, the country reports submitted to the UN Security Council, Counter-Terrorism Committee, *Reports Submitted by Member States Pursuant to Resolution 1373 (2001)*, online: www.un.org/sc/ctc/countryreports.shtml. See also Victor

that are better suited to the collection of security intelligence than the enforcement of the criminal law. A restrained and precise definition of terrorism that focuses on intentional acts of violence could respond to many, albeit not all, legitimate concerns that anti-terrorism efforts will infringe human rights. A precise definition of terrorism that concentrates on the murder and maiming of civilians could become a unifying point that focuses on the worst forms of terrorism, while also providing maximal protection for dissent and protest. It should also provide the most firm and broad foundation for denouncing and condemning the type of terrorism seen on September 11 and afterwards in Bali, Madrid, London, and elsewhere.

Failure to agree on a definition of terrorism is a luxury that can no longer be afforded in the present context of increased anti-terrorism laws and activities. Over one half of all states now have a general definition of terrorism in their domestic laws and these definitions suffer from a lack of international guidance on the meaning of terrorism.[3] The absence of a precise and restrained definition of terrorism has allowed many states to define the term in an overly broad manner that raises concerns that some forms of protest and civil disobedience will be caught within the definition of terrorism and be subject to the special powers, procedures, and penalties that many states reserve for crimes of terrorism. The United Nations Security Council is particularly complicit in this endeavour because

---

Ramraj, Michael Hor, & Kent Roach, eds., *Global Anti-Terrorism Law and Policy* (Cambridge: Cambridge University Press, 2005).

3   As Ben Saul argues, a legal definition of terrorism could help provide a restrained alternative to the use of war and extra legal measures.

Set against the vain hope of pounding terrorists into oblivion through war, the criminal law offers the promise of restraint: individual rather than collective responsibility; a presumption of innocence; no detention without charge; proof of guilt beyond a reasonable doubt; due process; the right to prepare and present an adequate defence; independent adjudication; and rational and proportionate punishment . . . . In the absence of any "law of terrorism" in public international law, it is not sufficient to leave the definition of terrorism to individual governments, as the Security Council has done. Definition . . . could normatively express and articulate the wrongfulness of terrorism . . . and restrain excessive national counter-terrorism responses . . . . In the absence of definition, a lingering "conceptual chaos" . . . privileges those in the hegemonic position to define and interpret "terrorism" and to erratically brand it upon their enemies.

Ben Saul, *Defining Terrorism in International Law* (Oxford: Oxford University Press, 2006) at 316–17 and 320.

in its Resolution 1373,[4] it required all states to establish serious criminal offences for terrorism and enact laws prohibiting the financing of terrorist acts without providing guidance on the definition of terrorism. The Security Council's attempt in its Resolution 1566[5] to provide a working definition of terrorism came too late, as many states had already responded to Resolution 1373 by enacting overbroad definitions of terrorism.

Although it may practically be too late to repeal many overbroad definitions of terrorism that have been enacted since 9/11, matters could become worse as states begin to respond to Security Council Resolution 1624,[6] which calls on states to prohibit, by law, incitement to terrorist acts, again without defining what constitutes a terrorist act, or incitement for that matter. Although not enacted under the binding provisions of Chapter VII, this new resolution follows the dangerous pattern set by Resolution 1373, which calls on states to enact laws against terrorism without defining what constitutes terrorism.[7] The Security Council, eager to assert leadership over other matters of anti-terrorism law and policy, has left the issue of a comprehensive definition to the General Assembly, which so far has been unable to reach an agreement. The result of the critical lacunae in Security Council Resolutions 1373 and 1624 is that each nation has been allowed to devise its own definition of terrorism and, now, its own definition of incitement of terrorism. As will be discussed below, many states have opted for very broad definitions of terrorism that could include some forms of protest and civil disobedience and go well beyond what was required to respond to the evil of lethal mass terrorism against civilians. New incitement laws threaten to aggravate the excessive breadth of existing definitions of terrorism by focusing on speech.

B. THE SUFFICIENCY OF THE CRIMINAL LAW

Principle 2 of the *Ottawa Principles* expresses a distinct preference for using the existing criminal law as a means to respond to terrorism. The

---

4   *Security Council Resolution 1373*, 2001 SC Res. 1373, UN SCOR, S/RES/1373 [Resolution 1373].

5   *Security Council Resolution 1566*, 2004 SC Res. 1540, UN SCOR, S/RES/1566 [Resolution 1566].

6   *Security Council Resolution 1624*, 2005 SC Res. 1624, UN SCOR, S/RES/1624 [Resolution 1624].

7   Resolution 1373, above note 4.

criminal law is the principled starting point for dealing with terrorism and even when countries add to or amend their criminal laws in order to deal with terrorism, they should not stray far from the basic principles of criminal law.

Immediately after 9/11, I wrote that "what the September 11 terrorists did was a crime long before they boarded the doomed aircraft. The existing law related to assisting, attempting, counselling and conspiring to commit criminal offences is very broad."[8] These comments were made in the distinct context of Canadian criminal law. Section 465 of the *Criminal Code of Canada*[9] provides a general offence of conspiracy that applies to agreements to commit crimes such as murder and includes agreements in Canada to commit crimes outside Canada and agreements outside Canada to commit crimes in Canada. The accused must be proven to intend to agree and intend to commit the crime. At the same time, conspiracy law does not require a contractual agreement and the law recognizes that a conspiracy can still exist even though "there may be changes in methods of operation, personnel or victims without bringing the conspiracy to an end."[10] Although the prosecution will be held to particulars placed in an indictment, the indictment can be worded quite broadly.[11]

The American law of conspiracy is even broader than the Canadian law and the United States Supreme Court has concluded that "the law rightly gives room for allowing the conviction of those discovered upon showing sufficiently the essential nature of the plan and their connections with it, without requiring evidence of knowledge of all of its details or the participation of others."[12] Although sophisticated cell-based terrorism presents challenges for the criminal law, conspiracy law was used in the United States to convict a number of people involved in the 1993 bombing of the World Trade Center. After 9/11, Zacarias Moussaoui was convicted of six counts of conspiracy including conspiracy to murder.

---

8 Kent Roach, "The New Terrorism Offences and the Criminal Law" in Ronald Daniels, Patrick Macklem, & Kent Roach, eds., *The Security of Freedom: Essays on Canada's Anti-terrorism Bill* (Toronto: University of Toronto Press, 2001) 151.

9 R.S.C. 1985, c. C-46 [*Criminal Code*].

10 *R. v. Cotroni* (1979), 45 C.C.C. (2d) 1 at 17 (S.C.C.).

11 *R. v. Saunders* (1990), 56 C.C.C. (3d) 220 (S.C.C.).

12 *Blumenthal v. United States*, 322 U.S. 539 at 551 (1947). See also *Pinkerton v. United States*, 328 U.S. 640 (1946).

In addition to the general law of conspiracy, Canada has a general law of attempt that applies to every person who, with intent to commit the offence, has done an act beyond mere preparation to commit an offence.[13] The Supreme Court of Canada has held that an accused with a clear intent to commit a crime could be guilty of an attempted crime even though the commission of the completed crime could only occur a considerable time in the future.[14] Although many new crimes of terrorism can be seen as attempts by the legislature to make various acts of preparation for terrorism separate crimes, the ability of courts to interpret the distinction between non-culpable acts of preparation and culpable acts that go beyond preparation should not be ignored.

Canadian criminal law also has a general offence of counselling an offence that is not committed.[15] Counselling is defined to include soliciting, procuring, or inciting an offence. A recent decision of the Supreme Court has expanded this offence by defining it to include actively inducing or advocating the commission of an offence when the accused either intends that the offence be committed, or is aware of a risk that the offence counselled will be committed.[16] Thus, the Canadian crime of incitement carries a lower fault requirement than the Canadian offence of attempts or conspiracy, which are united in their insistence that the prosecutor prove an intent to complete the crime. It is questionable whether incitement law should be expanded in such a manner. In any event, these three general crimes allow intervention long before completed acts of terrorism. They also allow the state's case to focus on the intended crime, such as murder. In many ways, these crimes are better at denouncing terrorism than the many broad new terrorism offences created by Canada's *Anti-terrorism Act*[17] that was enacted in response to Resolution 1373. The older offences of conspiring, attempting, and counselling murder allow terrorists to be punished and denounced on the basis of their intent to commit the most serious crime known to man: murder.

---

13   *Criminal Code*, above note 9, s. 24.
14   *R. v. Deutsch* (1986), 27 C.C.C. (3d) 385 (S.C.C.).
15   *Criminal Code*, above note 9, s. 464.
16   *R. v. Hamilton* (2005), 198 C.C.C. (3d) 1 (S.C.C.).
17   S.C. 2001, c. 41 [*Anti-terrorism Act*].

Although the Canadian criminal law, and undoubtedly that of many other countries, was sufficiently robust to respond to apprehended acts of terrorism, this is not true of the criminal law of all countries. The *Penal Code of Indonesia*, for example, has no general offences of conspiracy or incitement. Article 53 of the code defines attempted crime in the following fashion:

> Attempt to commit a crime is punishable if the intention of the offender has revealed itself by a commencement of the performance and the performance is not completed only because of circumstances independent of his will.[18]

The above formulation is very restrictive, and would apply only if the crime was underway but frustrated by some intervening action independent of the accused. Even in the United Kingdom, courts have held that an accused found with an imitation firearm and a disguise was not guilty of attempted robbery because he had not yet entered the place he was intending to rob.[19]

The determination of the adequacy of the criminal law to deal with apprehended acts of terrorism depends on the particular state of the law in each country. In some countries, new offences based on intentional preparation or agreements to commit acts of terrorism are necessary in the absence of a wholesale reform of the criminal law. Wholesale reforms of the criminal law may be driven and rushed by concerns about terrorism and result in broad and sweeping offences that will apply to all crimes and not just those related to terrorism. In some cases, narrowly focused and restrained laws against terrorism may be preferable to wholesale expansion of the criminal law.

Regardless of whether terrorism offences are justified in any particular country, in many countries they have already been enacted. Any offence, or indeed any new police power, that contains the word "terrorism" or "terrorist activities" requires that the legislator attempt to define those words given the requirements for precision and legality in the law. Once there is a law specifically targeting terrorism, a definition is a necessity that cannot be avoided.

---

18 *Penal Code of Indonesia*, Article 53.
19 *R. v. Campbell* (1991), 93 Cr. App. R. 350. See also *R. v. Geddes*, [1996] Crim. L.R. 894 (C.A.).

C. RETAINING THE BASICS OF A CRIMINAL LAW APPROACH

In cases in which the existing criminal law is not sufficient to deal with apprehended acts of terrorism, and in cases where countries have, for other reasons, introduced new terrorism offences, it is important to retain as much as possible the virtues of the criminal law approach to terrorism. These virtues include the general requirement in criminal law for proof of fault, including requirements that the accused intend or have knowledge in relation to the prohibited act, at least for the most serious offences. Another virtue of the criminal law is its requirement that a specific culpable act be established and that a person's actions not be criminalized simply on the basis of the person's status or associations. The requirement of some intentional act is essential to ensure that the innocent are not punished on the basis of their associations or status.

Justice Dennis O'Connor's conclusions in his report on the activities of Canadian officials in relation to Maher Arar underline the importance, even at the investigative stage, of focusing on criminality. He found that Canadian officials passed on unfair and inaccurate information about Mr. Arar, a Syrian-born Canadian citizen who was apprehended by American officials as he was returning to Canada and removed to Syria where he was tortured as well as detained for almost a year. The unfair information was based not on the actions of Mr. Arar, but rather on his associations with others who were the target of a national security investigation. In other words, the focus was on Mr. Arar's perceived associations and status and not on his actions or intent.[20]

One of the dangers of overbroad anti-terrorism laws is that they may blur important distinctions between law enforcement and security intelligence, and between admissible evidence of wrongdoing and intelligence about a person's associations and expressive activities. Both the act and fault requirements of the criminal law help ensure that anti-terrorism law focuses on criminal wrongdoing. The act and fault requirement justify punishment of the offender and send a denunciatory message to society about the particular crime. The requirement for a culpable act and fault can protect the innocent.

---

20 Canada, Commission of Inquiry into the Actions of Canadian Officials in Relation to Maher Arar, *Report of the Events Relating to Maher Arar: Analysis and Recommendations* (Ottawa: Public Works and Government Services Canada, 2006) at 13–14, 312–15, and 335–37 [*Arar Report*].

D. POLITICAL AND RELIGIOUS MOTIVES FOR ACTS OF TERRORISM

A particular strength of the criminal law is its attitude towards motive. In general, the criminal law does not require proof of motive as an essential element of a crime, nor does it consider a motive as an excuse or justification for the commission of the crime. In order to avoid any impression that anti-terrorism efforts are directed against Islam or any other religion, it is best to focus not on the offender's motive, but whether they intentionally committed a culpable act. From the perspective of public safety, it should not matter why someone explodes a bomb or hijacks a plane.

In *R. v. Khawaja*,[21] a trial judge in Canada held that the requirement for proof of political or religious motive with respect to crimes of terrorism, added to Canada's *Criminal Code*[22] by the 2001 *Anti-terrorism Act*,[23] constituted an unjustified violation of freedom of expression, religion, and association. Justice Rutherford concluded "that the focus on the essential ingredient of political, religious or ideological motive will chill freedom protected speech, religion, thought, belief, expression and association, and therefore, democratic life; and will promote fear and suspicion of targeted political or religious groups, and will result in racial or ethnic profiling by governmental authorities at many levels."[24] Once he concluded that the political and religious motive requirement violated section 2 of the *Charter*,[25] Justice Rutherford then found that the government had failed to justify the limitation as a reasonable limit on those rights under section 1 of the *Charter*. Although he expressed some concern about such a legislative objective, he concluded that if the purpose of the provision was "to sharpen the Canadian criminal law's focus on existing crimes committed for political, religious or ideological object-

---

21   [2006] O.J. No. 4245 (S.C.J.) [*Khawaja*].

22   Above note 9.

23   Above note 17.

24   Above note 21 at para. 73. Elsewhere he similarly concludes that the political or religious motive requirement will have "chilling" effects on the expression of religious and political beliefs and will "focus investigative and prosecutorial scrutiny on the political, religious and ideological beliefs, opinions and expressions of persons both in Canada and abroad," *ibid.* at para. 58.

25   *Canadian Charter of Rights and Freedoms*, Part I of the *Constitution Act, 1982*, being Schedule B to the *Canada Act 1982* (U.K.), 1982, c. 11, s. 2 [*Charter*].

ives or causes,"[26] this could have been done simply by recognizing such motives as aggravating factors at sentencing. On the other hand, if the purpose of the impugned law was to prevent terrorism, then this purpose could be satisfied without requiring proof of political or religious motive. He noted that the United Nations, the United States, and a number of European countries have defined terrorism without a political or religious motive requirement, as did the Supreme Court of Canada in *Suresh v. Canada (Minister of Citizenship and Immigration)*[27] when it read in a definition of terrorism taken from international law to an otherwise undefined reference to terrorism in immigration law. In short, Justice Rutherford considered two possible objectives for justifying the political or religious motive requirement: (1) the desire to punish politically or religiously motivated crimes; and (2) the desire to combat terrorism. In both cases, he concluded that less rights-invasive alternatives existed and that the limit the political or religious motive requirement placed on fundamental freedoms was not proportionate and had not been justified.

Although Justice Rutherford made no reference to the findings of the Arar Commission in his judgment, the *Arar Report* constituted part of the social backdrop of the decision. Justice O'Connor, in the first *Arar Report*, commented:

> Although this may change in the future, anti-terrorism investigations at present focus largely on members of the Muslim and Arab communities. There is therefore an increased risk of racial, religious or ethnic profiling, in the sense that the race, religion or ethnicity of individuals may expose them to investigation. Profiling in this sense would be at odds with the need for equal application of the law without discrimination and with Canada's embrace of multiculturalism.[28]

Justice O'Connor added to these normative concerns about discrimination another, very practical concern: "perceptions, whether founded or not, can have a serious impact on the level of co-operation members of communities give investigators."[29] In his second report, Justice O'Connor discussed the political and religious motive requirement

---

26 Above note 21 at para. 75.
27 [2002] 1 S.C.R. 3 [*Suresh*].
28 *Arar Report*, above note 20 at 356.
29 *Ibid.* at 357.

as one of the factors that merited increased review of the RCMP's national security activities. Although designed to place an extra burden of proof on the state, the political or religious motive requirement could also contribute to a process in which investigators may "lean towards increased inquiry and investigation based on religious and political beliefs. This could raise concerns about profiling in addition to the concerns about privacy and freedom of religion and expression."[30] The political and religious motive provision required police to collect evidence about a terrorist suspect's religion and politics, and the *Arar Report* illustrates how the police could use this information to make inaccurate and unfair assumptions about people such as Maher Arar and his wife Monia Mazigh.[31] The removal of the political and religious motive requirement is, of course, no guarantee that profiling or unfairness will not occur, but it is a step in the right direction.

The striking down of the political or religious motive requirement in *Khawaja*, and its omission in other definitions of terrorism, could also benefit those accused of terrorism offences. If there is no requirement for proof of political or religious motive, the trial judge will no longer be required as a matter of law to admit evidence about the accused's religious and political views into the trial. Evidence of political and religious motive can distract and prolong a trial: turning it quite literally into a religious or political trial. There have been terrorism trials in other countries where both sides have called competing expert evidence on the meaning of a prayer or the writings of a religious scholar found in the possession of the accused.[32]

The striking down of the political and religious motive requirement does not, however, guarantee that the prosecutor or the accused will

---

30 Canada, Commission of Inquiry into the Actions of Canadian Officials in Relation to Maher Arar, *A New Review Mechanism for the RCMP's National Security Activities* (Ottawa: Public Works and Government Services, 2006) at 438. The author served on the research advisory committee with respect to this report.

31 The Arar Commission found that the RCMP wrongly passed on inaccurate information to American officials designating Mr. Arar and his wife as "Islamic Extremist individuals suspected of being linked to the al-Qaeda terrorist movement": *Arar Report*, above note 20 at 13. At the same time, Justice O'Connor did not conclude that the RCMP had engaged in racial profiling when it included Mr. Arar as a person of interest in its investigation, *ibid.* at 18.

32 Amy Waldman, "Prophetic Justice" *The Atlantic Monthly* (October 2006) at 82*ff.*

not seek to introduce evidence relating to political or religious motive. Motive is generally admissible evidence, albeit subject to the trial judge's discretion to balance its probative value against its prejudicial effect. In a conspiracy to commit murder trial in relation to the 1985 Canadian-based bombing of an Air India flight that killed 329 people in what was, before 9/11, the most deadly act of aviation terrorism, the trial judge determined that the probative value of the motive evidence outweighed its prejudicial effect and allowed the Crown to introduce evidence of the accused's motives to commit acts of terrorism directed at the state of India.[33] In his judgment acquitting the two accused, however, the trial judge found that the motive evidence was not helpful because so many Sikhs at the time had similar motives.[34] Concerns are being raised that a number of American trials, in which trial judges have admitted evidence about the religious motives of the accused, are being distracted and consumed with evidence from competing experts about the meaning of various prayers, scholarly works, and other aspects of the Islamic faith.[35]

Many will argue, however, that it is not realistic to expect that evidence about religious or political motive will not be collected and admitted in terrorism trials. They can argue with some justification that the distinction between motive and intent can be illusive. Some commentators argue that the inclusion of political and religious motive is necessary to distinguish private from public violence and to respond to the phenomena of terrorism, which is in fact often driven by political and religious motives and extremism.[36]

In my view, it is possible to distinguish terrorism from other crimes without reliance on a political or religious motive requirement. Many definitions of terrorism require that the accused act with the intent to intimidate the public and/or compel governments or international organizations to act. This allows a kidnapping of a public official in an attempt to change governmental policy to be distinguished from a kidnapping of a child of a wealthy family in an attempt to collect money. Some might argue that such requirements of intimidation of the public or compulsion of governments constitute *de facto* motive requirements.

---

33 *R. v. Malik and Bagri*, 2002 BCSC 823 at paras. 49–55.
34 *R. v. Malik and Bagri*, 2005 BCSC 350 at para. 1238.
35 Waldman, above note 32 at 82*ff.*
36 See, for example, Saul, above note 3 at 38–45.

Nevertheless, in my view, intimidation and compulsion requirements differ in important respects from political and religious motive requirements. An accused's political or religious beliefs, the prayers that he or she says and the holy texts that he or she reads, lie at the core of the freedoms of expression and religion. In contrast, beliefs that relate to the attempt to intimidate the public or compel governments or other people to act exist more on the periphery of protected freedoms. A religious and political motive requirement authorizes state inquiries into the deepest convictions and beliefs of the accused. Although state inquiry into an accused's intent to intimidate a population or to compel actions could also involve inquiry into political or religious beliefs, the expression and thought affected by such a requirement are deserving of less constitutional protection than religious or political thought that is not directed at intimidation or compulsion.

It is important to preserve as much of the traditional criminal law as possible in order to maximize its denunciatory effects in condemning and punishing terrorism. One of the great dangers of terrorism is that it will goad and scare liberal democracies into changing their fundamental, defining rules. As much as possible, we should retain our traditional principles and rules in the face of terrorism. It is particularly important to maintain the traditional approach, that motive does not constitute an essential element of a criminal offence, if we are to rely on the equally traditional rule, that no motive excuses crime.[37] If motive cannot be a shield for the accused, it should also not be a sword for the state.

The focus in terrorism prosecutions should be on violence and preparations to commit violence and not on the accused's religious and political views. Such conclusions are supported by both normative and practical concerns. There are normative arguments that the political and religious motive requirement should be removed in order to protect

---

37 For a recent decision that rejected an argument that the *Convention for the Protection of Human Rights and Fundamental Freedoms*, 4 November 1950, 213 U.N.T.S. 221; Eur. T.S. 5, was violated when British anti-terrorism laws were applied to acts of preparation for terrorism against the government of Libya and Colonel Gaddafi, see *R v. F*, [2007] EWCA Crim. 243. The Court of Appeal in that case relied on the traditional idea that "Terrorism is terrorism, whatever the motives of the perpetrators," at para. 27. As will be discussed below, however, British anti-terrorism law is not consistent in this respect because it also makes political and religious motive an essential element of the definition of terrorism.

the accused and others from discrimination on the basis that they are members of an unpopular religious group, or that they express unpopular religious or political views.[38] The idea that terrorism trials will inevitably be political or religious trials may have some force from a historical, political science, or sociological perspective but it is contrary to the logic of the criminal law, which suggests that motive neither excuses nor constitutes intentional crime.

There are also powerful practical objections to the political and religious motive requirement. A focus on the accused's religion and politics can prolong and distract trials. It could also create harmful and counterproductive impressions that the accused are being prosecuted for their political or religious beliefs. The motive requirement could also provide an accused with a possible platform to politicize the trial process by offering extensive evidence about the true meaning of often ambiguous religious and political beliefs. The controversial political or religious motive requirement unnecessarily sacrifices attempts to gain the broadest possible consensus about the illegitimacy of terrorism because a number of states seem to interpret reference to political and religious mo-

---

38 Ronald Dworkin has been particularly consistent and courageous in retaining his focus on equal rights in the post-9/11 era. See Ronald Dworkin, "The Threat to Patriotism" (2002) 49 New York Times Book Review 3. Another way of addressing the normative questions would be to follow John Rawls: ask whether a person, behind a veil of ignorance, who did not know whether he or she would be Muslim, would select a *criminal code* that would require proof of political or religious motive or one that would not require such proof. Given present attitudes towards Muslims, the answer is obvious: John Rawls, *A Theory of Justice* (Cambridge, MA: Belknap Press of Harvard University Press, 1971). This line of inquiry is followed by Michael Plaxton, but rejected on the basis that the liberalism of Rawls and Dworkin is controversial. Michael Plaxton, "Irruptions of Motive in the War on Terror" (2007) 11 Can. Crim. L. Rev. 233. This may be so, but it is not clear that there is a viable alternative to such political liberalism. One possible alternative is a theory of militant democracy that denounces political and religious views that do not accord with liberal democracy. For my reservations about that theory, see Kent Roach, "Anti-terrorism and Militant Democracy" in András Sajó, ed., *Militant Democracy* (Utrecht: Eleven International, 2004). In a possible nod to militant democracy, Justice Rutherford, in *Khawaja*, above note 21, considered that the purpose of the political or religious motive requirement could be to denounce crimes committed with such motives, but concluded that this objective could be more proportionately pursued by considering political or religious motives to be aggravating factors at sentencing.

tive as a western attempt to target Islam and movements for national self-determination.[39]

Although acts of terrorism are frequently committed for political or religious reasons, many people may have similar beliefs but not act on them by committing crimes. Conversely, the bombing and killing of civilian targets should not be exempted from the label of terrorism in cases where we do not know what motivated the accused or in cases where the motive related to factors that are not easily included in vague references to political or religious motive.[40] Focusing on motive may contribute to the dangerous process discussed above in which the distinction between intelligence that identifies risks of political or religious violence is blurred with evidence relating to culpable acts by identified individuals to plan or prepare to commit such acts.

---

39 A number of Arab states, as well as Indonesia, do not include political or religious motive requirements in their main definitions of terrorism. Lynn Welchman, "Rocks, Hard Places and Human Rights: Anti-terrorism Law and Policy in Arab States" in Ramraj *et al.*, eds., above note 2 at 581. The *Arab Convention on the Suppression of Terrorism*, 22 April 1998 (English translations available online: www.fidh. org/intgouv/ua/articles/1998/convantiterroo4a.htm) and the *Convention of the Organization of the Islamic Conference on Combating International Terrorism*, 1 July 1999 (online: www.oic-un.org/26icfm/c.html) both do not include religious or political motive requirements in their main definitions of terrorism. At the same time, these conventions both have exemptions for liberation struggles against foreign occupation but these exemptions do not apply to struggles against member states. Both the exemption and its limitations allow political and religious factors to shape the scope of terrorism covered by the two conventions. I thank my colleague Ed Morgan for bringing this point to my attention. My point is not that the definition of terrorism used by Islamic states or organizations should necessarily be followed, but that the western countries should seek the broadest possible consensus on a definition of terrorism. Best efforts at comprehensive international definitions of terrorism, like the definition of terrorism found in Indonesia, do not include religious or political motive requirements.

40 South African anti-terrorism law, for example, has added philosophical motive to the Australian, British, and Canadian reference to political, religious, or ideological objectives, perhaps due to concerns that anarchist or nihilistic terrorism would not be included in the former: *Protection of Constitutional Democracy Against Terrorist and Related Activities Act 2004*, No. 33 of 2004, s. 1. See Kent Roach, "A Comparison of South African and Canadian Anti-terrorism Legislation" (2005) 18 South African Journal of Criminal Justice 127 at 138–39.

E. SECURITY COUNCIL RESOLUTION 1373

In the immediate aftermath of 9/11, many countries enacted new anti-terrorism laws. Resolution 1373[41] of the United Nations Security Council played a crucial role in this worldwide expansion of anti-terrorism law as this resolution enacted, under Chapter VII of the United Nations *Charter*,[42] a call on all states to criminalize the willful provision or collection of funds for terrorism and to "ensure that, in addition to any other measures against them, such terrorist acts are established as serious criminal offences in domestic laws and regulations and that the punishment duly reflect the seriousness of such terrorist acts."[43] The striking feature of the resolution is that, while it called on states to criminalize terrorism and terrorist financing, it did not attempt to define terrorism.

Principle 10 of the *Ottawa Principles* rightly calls attention to the role that the Security Council has played in anti-terrorism efforts and calls on the Security Council to be bound by the UN *Charter* and customary human rights. I would go further, however, and argue that when the Security Council is effectively legislating and demanding legislation for the world under Chapter VII, that it should respect principles of legality that are implicit in Articles 9 and 15 of the *International Covenant on Civil and Political Rights*.[44] These principles should require a definition of terrorism as the basis for convicting a person of a serious criminal offence and depriving them of liberty. Although the Security Council was, without a doubt, responding to the political difficulties in finding a consensual definition of terrorism when it did not define terrorism in Resolution 1373, the effect was to allow all 192 members to define terrorism in their own way. Left to their own devices, member states could enact over-broad definitions of terrorism, including definitions that would allow for the criminalization of dissent and protest.

---

41 Above note 4.
42 *Charter of the United Nations*, 26 June 1945, 59 Stat. 1031, T.S. 993, 3 Bevans 1153 (entered into force 24 October 1945) [UN *Charter*].
43 Above note 4.
44 19 December 1966, 999 U.N.T.S. 171, Can. T.S. 1976 No. 47, 6 I.L.M. 368.

F. THE GENERAL DEFINITION OF TERRORISM IN THE 1999 *INTERNATIONAL CONVENTION ON THE SUPPRESSION OF TERRORISM FINANCING*

Much of Resolution 1373 revolves around the financing of terrorism. This focus reflects the fact that the *International Convention for the Suppression of Financing of Terrorism*[45] was, at the time, the most recent international convention on terrorism and the United Nations, at the time of 9/11, had an established mechanism to attempt to freeze the assets of bin Laden and the Taliban. I have argued elsewhere that this focus on financing was questionable given the low cost of many lethal acts of terrorism and the inefficacy of laws against terrorism-financing in preventing even relatively expensive acts of terrorism such as 9/11.[46]

Regardless of whether the focus on the financing of terrorism was appropriate, there is a bitter irony in the fact that the Security Council, in Resolution 1373, placed such an emphasis on the 1999 *Financing Convention*, while at the same time ignoring the general definition of terrorism *found in that very* convention. Article 2(1)(b) of the *Financing Convention* defines terrorism as an

> act intended to cause death or serious bodily injury to a civilian, or to any other person not taking an active part in the hostilities in a situation of armed conflict, when the purpose of such act, by its nature or context, is to intimidate a population, or to compel a government or an international organization to do or to abstain from doing any act.[47]

This definition of terrorism would have been particularly appropriate for the United Nations to have sanctioned in Resolution 1373 because it captures the horrific nature of the terrorist acts of September 11, 2001 that

---

45 10 January 2000, 39 I.L.M. 270, 2002 Can. T.S. 9 [*Financing Convention*].

46 Kent Roach, "Sources and Trends in Post 9/11 Anti-terrorism Laws" in Benjamin Goold & Liora Lazarus, eds., *Security and Human Rights* (Oxford: Hart, 2007).

47 Above note 45, Article 2(1)(b). One potential omission from this definition is hostage-taking. This was included in the subsequent Resolution 1566, above note 5, that defined terrorism as "criminal acts, including against civilians, committed with the intent to cause death or serious bodily injury or taking of hostages, with the purpose to provoke a state of terror . . . intimidate a population or compel a government or international organization to do or abstain from doing an act." This definition will be discussed below.

resulted in the intentional murder of almost three thousand civilians. Many overbroad definitions of terrorism enacted in post-9/11 anti-terrorism laws could have been avoided had the Security Council included the above definition of terrorism as part of Resolution 1373. In 2002, the Supreme Court of Canada recognized that the above definition "catches the essence of what the world understands as terrorism," and used it as a precise and restrained definition for a legislatively undefined reference to terrorism in Canadian immigration legislation.[48] Unfortunately, however, the Security Council did not champion this definition of terrorism in Resolution 1373 despite the extensive reliance that it placed on other parts of the *Financing Convention*.

G. POST-9/11 DEFINITIONS OF TERRORISM

Without any guidance from the United Nations Security Council in Resolution 1373 about the appropriate definition of terrorism, many countries, particularly in the Commonwealth, turned to the British *Terrorism Act 2000*[49] for guidance in defining terrorism in the new anti-terrorism laws. This was unfortunate in my view because the British definition was very broad and went well beyond the intentional murder and maiming of civilians that was the focus of the neglected general definition in the *Financing Convention*. Section 1(1) of the *Terrorism Act 2000* distinguishes terrorism from other crimes by providing that the proscribed harms be "designed to influence the government or to intimidate the public or a section of a public; and the use or threat is made for the purpose of advancing a political, religious or ideological cause."[50] The law also defines governments and the public to include those from a foreign country and, in 2006, this definition was amended to include attempts to influence international organizations.[51]

A requirement that a terrorist action attempt to compel governments or international organizations or intimidate the public would have followed the orientation in the general definition of terrorism in

---

48 *Suresh*, above note 27 at para. 98.
49 *Terrorism Act 2000* (U.K.), 2000, c. 11.
50 *Ibid.* s. 1(1).
51 *Terrorism Act 2006* (U.K.), 2006, c. 11, s. 34.

the *Financing Convention* and is a quite common method used in domestic and international laws to distinguish terrorism from other crimes.[52] The British law, however, substitutes the broader concept of influencing governments for the more coercive concept of compelling governments. The appropriate focus in a criminal law approach to terrorism should be on violence as opposed to political influence or motivation. The requirement that governments be compelled rather than influenced better captures the focus on violence and is contained in the suggested definition of terrorism in principle 2.1.2 of the *Ottawa Principles*.

The British definition was particularly influential in requiring as an essential element of the definition of terrorist acts that they be committed for the purpose of advancing a political, religious, or ideological cause. This motive requirement was followed in a number of countries including Australia, Canada, and South Africa, but interestingly enough not in the United States or Indonesia.[53] The origin of Britain's requirement that terrorism be committed for political, religious, or ideological motives is interesting and, given the American rejection of such a requirement, somewhat ironic. Lord Lloyd, in his 1996 review of British anti-terrorism legislation, expressed concerns that the existing definition might not catch some forms of terrorism and expressed approval for the following working definition of terrorism used by the Federal Bureau of Investigation in the United States:

---

52   Although he is otherwise supportive of the political or religious motive requirement for definitions of terrorism, Ben Saul acknowledges that

> the common element in the Hostages, Rome, UN Personnel and Terrorist Financing Treaties is . . . the requirement that the prohibited physical acts be committed to intimidate or compel another to do or refrain from doing any act. The motive of the acts—in the sense of motive as the end, purpose or object of an act—is coercion of specified targets. In contrast proof of motive in another juridical sense—as an emotion prompting an act (such as political or private motives) is not required . . . . This approach avoids the difficulty of having to identify and prove the motives underlying violence to secure a conviction.

> Ben Saul, above note 3 at 138.

53   See Kent Roach, "The Post 9/11 Migration of the *Terrorism Act, 2000*" in Sujit Choudhry, ed., *The Migration of Constitutional Ideas* (Cambridge: Cambridge University Press, 2006).

The use of serious violence against persons or property, or the threat to use such violence, to intimidate or coerce a government, the public or any section of the public, in order to promote political, social or ideological objectives.[54]

As Professor Clive Walker notes, however, the FBI's definition of terrorism was used "for jurisdictional, budgetary and other administrative purposes" and not "as a legal term of art of which liberty depends."[55] Because the United States has no domestic security intelligence agency, the FBI collects security intelligence as well as evidence. The codification of the FBI's definition of terrorism into the British law creates a danger of blurring the distinction between law enforcement, which has traditionally focused on culpable acts regardless of their motive, and security intelligence, which is more concerned with potential risks and threats. In any event, it should be noted that the definition of terrorism in American law, both before and after 9/11, was less vague than the FBI's working definition and it makes no reference to political or religious motives, factors likely to attract critical scrutiny under the First Amendment of the *United States Bill of Rights*.[56]

Under the United Kingdom's *Terrorism Act 2000*, politically or religiously motivated actions or threats of actions designed to influence any government or intimidate the public will constitute a terrorist activity if it:

1) involves serious violence against a person;
2) involves serious damage to property;
3) endangers a person's life, other than the person committing the action;
4) creates a serious risk to public health or safety;
5) is designed seriously to interfere with or seriously disrupt an electronic system.[57]

These prohibited acts are broadly defined in an attempt to include modern forms of terrorism, such as the use of biological or chemical poisons or disruptions of computer systems. At the same time, the British law

---

54 U.K., "Report of the Lord Lloyd Inquiry into Legislation against Terrorism," Cm. 3420 (1996) at para. 5.22.

55 Clive Walker, *Blackstone's Guide to the Anti-terrorism Legislation* (Oxford: Oxford University Press, 2002) at 21.

56 U.S. Const. amend. I.

57 Above note 49, s. 1(2).

overshoots the mark when it defines all politically motivated serious damage to property as terrorism, or when it defines political actions such as a general strike as terrorism because it endangers life, public health, or safety. My point is not that such actions should be immune from the law, but only that they should not be treated as acts of terrorism. Events such as 9/11 and the Madrid and London bombings underline that the terrorism problem is the murder and maiming of civilians, not property damage or disruptions of electronic systems.

The reference to serious interference with electronic systems was expanded in many subsequent Commonwealth laws to include interference with a broad range of essential public and private services. Canada included such a definition and expanded it even further by including attempts to compel "persons," as well as governments or international organizations, to act.[58] These expansions of the definition raised legitimate concerns among many civil society groups that new anti-terrorism laws could be used against various forms of civil disobedience and protests that would disrupt essential services. Canada and some other governments responded to these concerns with exemptions for certain forms of protest and dissent, and Canada also responded to criticisms of the political and religious motive requirement with a provision that states that the expression of political and religious belief would not, in itself, constitute a terrorist activity.[59] These amendments narrowed the British definition, but much of this debate, and some of civil society resistance to new anti-terrorism laws, might have been avoided had legislatures focused on the more restrained definition of terrorism provided in Article 2 of the *Financing Convention*.[60] If the focus was on intentional killing and causing serious bodily harm, few civil society groups would have felt potentially targeted by anti-terrorism laws and resisted them on that basis.

H. THE SECURITY COUNCIL'S BELATED WORKING DEFINITION OF TERRORISM IN RESOLUTION 1566

Three years after it called on all states to ensure that acts of terrorism were treated as serious crimes, in 2004 the Security Council finally

---

58 *Criminal Code*, above note 9, s. 83.01.
59 *Ibid.*, s. 83.01(1.1).
60 Above note 45, Article 2.

provided some guidance about how states should define terrorism. Unfortunately, this guidance came too late to influence the new legislation that was adopted in many countries in the immediate aftermath of 9/11. The Security Council's working definition was also not expressed in a binding form, as was Resolution 1373.

Resolution 1566, adopted by the Security Council on 8 October 2004, states that the Security Council:

> Recalls that criminal acts, including against civilians, committed with the intent to cause death or serious bodily injury, or taking of hostages, with the purpose to provoke a state of terror in the general public or in a group of persons or particular persons, intimidate a population or compel a government or an international organization to do or to abstain from doing any act, which constitute offences within the scope of and as defined in the international conventions and protocols relating to terrorism, are under no circumstances justifiable by considerations of a political, philosophical, ideological, racial, ethnic, religious or other similar nature, and calls upon all States to prevent such acts, and if not prevented, to ensure that such acts are punished by penalties consistent with their grave nature.[61]

This working definition adopts the traditional criminal law principle that no motive, including philosophical as well as political and religious motives, can excuse intentional crimes. It is consistent in declaring that such motives cannot excuse or constitute an essential element of crimes of terrorism. The working definition also defines terrorism more narrowly than the domestic definitions reviewed above because it focuses on intentional causing of death or serious bodily injury or taking of hostages and does not include property damage or the disruption of electronic systems or essential services. At the same time, its reference to provoking a state of terror is vague and circular because of the failure to define terror.

I. SECURITY COUNCIL RESOLUTION 1624

Security Council Resolution 1624, adopted on 14 September 2005,[62] calls upon all states to take steps to prevent incitement to commit terrorist

---

61 Resolution 1566, above note 5.
62 Above note 6.

acts. The resolution, which does not have binding force under Chapter VII, declares that states have "obligations under international law to counter incitement of terrorist acts motivated by extremism and intolerance and to prevent the subversion of educational, cultural and religious institutions by terrorists and their supporters." Like Resolution 1373, this new resolution makes no attempt to define what constitutes a terrorist act. This raises the danger that overbroad definitions of terrorism will be made even broader by criminalizing speech that incites terrorism. For example, if terrorism is defined to include politically motivated serious property damage, then the incitement of a crowd to commit such damage could be prohibited under the incitement laws called for in Resolution 1373.[63] The dangers of Resolution 1624 are also increased by its lack of a definition of incitement. On some definitions, incitement could occur regardless of the probability of the incited act occurring. Indeed, many criminal law offences of incitement may apply even if the person incited or counselled to commit an offence has no intention whatsoever of committing an offence. Thus, one of the paradigmatic crimes found in incitement law is when the accused unsuccessfully tries to solicit or recruit an undercover officer or informer to commit a crime.

Incitement in the context of large public gatherings may, in some countries, require some degree of probability that the act incited will actually occur.[64] The *Ottawa Principles* favour this more restrictive and libertarian approach. Principle 2.2.2 provides:

> Expression may only be subject to criminal sanction on grounds of terrorism if it constitutes incitement of terrorism (as described in principle 2.1.2) with the intent and likelihood that a terrorist offence will be committed. In particular, publication of information issued by, or about, groups that have been labelled as terrorist, or by or about any of their members, should not be criminalized. Attempts to justify terrorist acts in writing or speech should also not be criminalized.[65]

This principle attempts to link any new incitement offence to the more restrictive definition of terrorism that is outlined in principle 2.1.2[66] and

---

63 Resolution 1373, above note 4.
64 *Brandenburg v. Ohio*, 395 U.S. 444 (1969).
65 *Ottawa Principles*, above note 1, principle 2.2.2.
66 *Ibid.*, principle 2.1.2.

that generally defines terrorism as follows: intentional killing or causing of serious bodily harm in order to intimidate a population or compel a government or an international organization to act. In addition,
this principle also suggests that incitement should only be prohibited
if there is a "likelihood" that a terrorist offence will be committed as a
result of the incitement. In these ways, the *Ottawa Principles* attempt to
restrain laws against the incitement of terrorism that will emerge from
Resolution 1624.

A recent report by the Counter-Terrorism Committee (CTC) outlines
how sixty-nine nations, including many that do not have a tradition of
respecting freedom of expression, have already reported back to the
CTC on their implementation of Resolution 1624.[67] The report notes
that some states have raised concerns in their reports about respecting
freedom of expression, and that countries differ with respect to whether
there should be a crime of incitement in the absence of some probability
that incitement will lead to the commission of an act of terrorism. The
Resolution 1624 process unfortunately may be repeating the mistakes
of the Resolution 1373 process by failing to define crucial terms, in this
case both what constitutes incitement and what constitutes terrorism.
The failure to define such terms in a restrained manner provides space,
and indeed cover, for member states to take actions in the name of combating terrorism that unnecessarily infringe rights.

In some respects, however, the Resolution 1624 process is potentially more rights-sensitive than the Resolution 1373 process both because Resolution 1624 itself contains reference to the need for states
to respect international human rights[68] and because the CTC has taken
some preliminary steps to build regard for human rights into its mandate. Despite this, however, the CTC's initial report on compliance with
Resolution 1624 is disappointing. It fails to conclude that any state has
engaged in an unreasonable or disproportionate restriction of freedom
of expression contrary to international human rights law. This recent
report suggests that the CTC is still not yet comfortable in criticizing
states for violating human rights in their anti-terrorism efforts or in tak-

---

67 Security Council, Counter-Terrorism Committee, *Report of the Counter-Terrorism
    Committee to the Security Council on the Implementation of Resolution 1624 (2005)*,
    UN SCOR, 2006, UN Doc. S/2006/737 at para. 9.
68 Resolution 1624, above note 6 at para. 4.

ing a position on which anti-terrorism measures are or are not consistent with human rights.

The new focus on speech that incites terrorism, combined with
broad definitions of terrorism, presents a new danger that anti-terrorism efforts will unnecessarily collide with human rights. Resolution 1624
raises the danger that states will focus limited anti-terrorism efforts not
on those who would prepare, plan, and commit heinous acts of violence,
but on those who engage in high-profile speech that advocates politically or religiously motivated violence, property destruction, or disruption of essential services. It opens the possibility that those who defend
or advocate acts of violence in far away lands will be prosecuted domestically for inciting terrorism. It also continues the trend of blurring
the distinct realms of law enforcement and security intelligence. Those
who publicly praise or advocate acts of terrorism should be watched by
security intelligence agencies, but not necessarily charged by the police
with violating criminal laws.

Laws that target speech associated with terrorism should be subject
to rigorous proportionality analysis of the type contemplated in principle 2.3.1 of the *Ottawa Principles*. This principle provides:

> Any departures from ordinary principles of criminal law and procedure
> or derogable international human rights standards must be strictly ne-
> cessary to prevent the identified harm and be rationally connected to
> the achievement of this goal; they should infringe the rights of those
> subject to the law as little as possible; and their effectiveness should be
> weighed against the degree of rights infringement that they permit. Any
> such departures must also be reviewable on this basis by a regularly
> constituted court or tribunal.[69]

Applied to the context of speech prohibitions, this proportionality analysis will require states to identify the harm that they intend to prevent. Here, it will be important to distinguish between the harm of hate
speech against identifiable minorities and the harm of terrorism.

Former Justice Minister of Canada Irwin Cotler has argued that
the "anti-hate principle" should be one of the building blocks of mod-

---

69 *Ottawa Principles*, above note 1, principle 2.3.1.

ern national security policies.[70] In my view, however, there is a danger in conflating the distinct justification for laws against hate speech and terrorism. Criminal laws against hate speech can be seen as a response to the harm that is caused to minorities by such speech and as social condemnation of such speech.[71] The connection between hate speech, or speech that encourages or praises acts of terrorism, and actual acts of terrorism, however, is much less clear. Moreover, there are other, less drastic measures than the use of the criminal sanction, such as condemnation and rebuttal of the speech.[72]

It may be difficult to justify the restriction of speech that advocates or justifies terrorism as a proportionate restriction on freedom of expression that is necessary to stop terrorism.[73] There is a fundamental difference between speech and violence, but unfortunately this distinction may be lost if the next trend in anti-terrorism law is the prosecution of speech associated with terrorism. It is far from clear that prosecuting speech is rationally connected with the prevention of terrorism given the many causes of terrorism. Even if courts assumed that there was a rational connection, there is a wide range of less rights-invasive measures, including prosecutions under existing offences relating to inciting murder and other serious crimes. There are also other, less drastic alternatives including condemnation of speech that advocates terrorism. Finally, the danger that prosecution of speech associated with terrorism may result in more publicity and sympathy for extremists cannot be ignored, especially when compared to the unclear benefits of such speech prosecutions in preventing terrorism.

Already the effects of Resolution 1624 are being felt in some parts of the world. In 2005, Australia enacted new laws that prohibit some forms of incitement to terrorism as sedition and that allow organizations that

---

70 Irwin Cotler, "Terrorism, Security and Rights: The Dilemmas of Democracies" (2002) 14 N.J.C.L. 13.

71 *R. v. Keegstra*, [1990] 3 S.C.R. 697.

72 For arguments that Canada should not follow the British lead and enact new offences against the encouragement of terrorism, see Kent Roach, "Ten Ways to Improve Canadian Anti-terrorism Law" (2005) 51 Crim. L.Q. 102.

73 For further arguments that the new British offences are a disproportionate restriction on freedom of expression see Kent Roach, "Must We Trade Rights for Security?" (2006) 27 Cardozo L. Rev. 2151 at 2179–84.

advocate terrorism to be prohibited as terrorist groups.[74] A particularly problematic feature of the new Australian law is the ability of the Governor in Council to list a group on the basis that it advocates a terrorist act. The expansive definition of advocating a terrorist act includes (1) directly or indirectly counselling or urging the doing of a terrorist act; or (2) directly or indirectly providing instructions on the doing of a terrorist act and most broadly directly praising

> the doing of a terrorist act in circumstances where there is a risk that such praise might have the effect of leading a person (regardless of his or her age or any mental impairment) . . . to engage in a terrorist act.[75]

Britain's *Terrorism Act 2006* contains controversial new offences against speech and publications that directly or indirectly encourage terrorism. The law deems that indirect encouragement includes:

> Every statement which a) glorifies the commission or preparation (whether in the past, in the future or generally of [terrorist] acts or offences and b) is a statement from which those members of the public could reasonably be expected to infer that what is being glorified is being glorified as conduct that should be emulated in existing circumstances.[76]

Both the new British and Australian laws build on existing broad definitions of terrorism and the British law states explicitly that it is irrelevant to guilt "whether any person is in fact encouraged or induced by the statement to commit, prepare or instigate"[77] any act of terrorism.

The new trend of prosecuting speech that is associated with terrorism is one that needs to be approached with caution with respect to its effects on Muslim minorities. One danger is the potential divisiveness of prosecutions based on speech that, for example, sympathizes with acts of terrorism in foreign lands. Although such speech should be rebutted and deplored, it does not constitute as direct a threat to national security and public safety as the provision of physical or financial support

---

74 *Anti-Terrorism Act (No. 2), 2005*, No. 144 of 2005, Sch. 1 and 7.

75 *Criminal Code Act, 1995*, No. 12 of 1995, s. 102.1 (1A)(c), as amended by the *Anti-Terrorism Act (No. 2), 2005, ibid.*

76 Above note 51, s. 1(3).

77 *Ibid.*, s. 1(5).

for such terrorism or as plots or assistance for actual acts of terrorism. Prosecuting a person in Canada for saying that he or she supports acts of terrorism in the Middle East, Afghanistan, or Chechyna may create an impression that the war against terrorism is a war against Islam. If anti-terrorism policy is to become the grounds for societal consensus on what Will Kymlicka has called "certain 'non-negotiable' principles,"[78] it is best to focus on acts of assistance and commission of violence as opposed to speech that praises or condones terrorism.

Resolution 1624 also calls on states "to continue dialogue and broaden understanding among civilizations, in an effort to prevent the indiscriminate targeting of different religions and cultures." Unfortunately, the targeting of what is considered by state officials to be "extremist" speech that incites terrorism could inhibit intercultural dialogue, particularly if groups believe that some in their community have been unfairly stigmatized as supporting terrorism, or fear that this may occur. The criminalization of speech is a problematic anti-terrorism strategy both because it burdens freedom of expression and because criminal prosecutions of such speech may be counterproductive.

Finally, Resolution 1624 repeats the problem seen in Resolution 1373 in calling for states to take action against terrorism without defining terrorism. Resolution 1373 helped produce many new anti-terrorism laws with overbroad definitions of terrorism. Now Resolution 1624 threatens to aggravate this overbreadth by calling on states to enact laws criminalizing those that incite terrorism. Resolution 1624 appears to be agnostic about how states define either terrorism or incitement. In turn, the CTC does not seem overly concerned that broad definitions of both terms might threaten human rights, while not substantially assisting in the prevention of terrorism.

J. THE PROPOSED DEFINITION OF TERRORISM IN THE *OTTAWA PRINCIPLES*

In *Suresh*, the Supreme Court of Canada recognized the difficulty of defining terrorism. It commented that

---

78 Will Kymlicka, *Finding Our Way: Rethinking Ethnocultural Relations in Canada* (Toronto: Oxford University Press, 1998) at 23.

one searches in vain for an authoritative definition of "terrorism." The Immigration Act does not define the term. Further, there is no single definition that is accepted internationally. The absence of an authoritative definition means that, at least at the margins, "the term is open to politicized manipulation, conjecture, and polemical interpretation" . . . . Perhaps the most striking example of the politicized nature of the term is that Nelson Mandela's African National Congress was, during the apartheid era, routinely labelled a terrorist organization, not only by the South African government but by much of the international community.[79]

After recognizing the difficulties of defining terrorism, the Court came up with its own definition of terrorism, which it then read into the undefined reference to terrorism in Canada's immigration law. It concluded that,

> following the *International Convention for the Suppression of the Financing of Terrorism*, that "terrorism" in s. 19 of the Act includes any "act intended to cause death or serious bodily injury to a civilian, or to any other person not taking an active part in the hostilities in a situation of armed conflict, when the purpose of such act, by its nature or context, is to intimidate a population, or to compel a government or an international organization to do or to abstain from doing any act." This definition catches the essence of what the world understands by "terrorism." Particular cases on the fringes of terrorist activity will inevitably provoke disagreement.[80]

This definition of terrorism is considerably narrower than the definition of terrorism found in Canada's *Anti-terrorism Act*[81] or other similar laws inspired by the British *Terrorism Act 2000*.[82]

The *Suresh* definition focuses on acts intended to cause death or serious bodily harm to civilians, as opposed to the more ambiguous concepts of endangering a person's life or causing a serious risk to health and safety, and broader harms relating to property damage or disruption of essential services. It refers only to the concept of intimidating a population or compelling governments or international organizations

---

79 *Suresh*, above note 27 at paras. 94–95.
80 *Ibid.* at para. 98.
81 Above note 17.
82 Above note 49.

without resort to nebulous concepts of threatening security (including economic security) found in Canada's *Anti-terrorism Act*,[83] or the broad concept of "influencing governments" found in Britain's *Terrorism Act 2000*.[84] This restrained definition of terrorism minimizes the chances that Aboriginal protesters, anti-globalization protesters, and the animal rights movement will be investigated or charged as terrorist suspects. A minimal definition of terrorism that focuses on death and injury to humans can be defended on both the normative basis that it minimizes targeting dissent and on the practical basis that it guards against the misallocation of scarce investigative resources on dissenters.

The *Suresh* definition, taken from the general definition of terrorism in the *Financing Convention*, is also noteworthy because, unlike definitions based on the *Terrorism Act 2000*, it does not require proof of political or religious motive. As suggested above, this avoids singling out the political or religious aspects of terrorism and focuses on the violence. The danger of the political and religious motive requirement is only increased by the new post-Resolution 1624 emphasis on speech. The danger is that extreme religious and political speech may be defined as incitement of terrorism, in part on the basis of definitions of terrorism, which stress the religious or political motives for acts, and in part on the basis of definitions of terrorism that apply to foreign lands that may be in a state of war or rebellion.

The omission of political or religious motive as a defining feature of terrorism, however, raises concerns ·about whether terrorist activities could be adequately distinguished from other forms of crime.[85] The danger is that terrorism defined without regard to political or religious motive may be difficult to distinguish from other forms of crime, particularly organized crime. A partial answer to this concern, however, is found in the narrower focus in the *Suresh* definition on intentional killing and causing serious bodily harm. A fuller answer is found in the requirement that such acts be done either to intimidate a population or to compel a government or international organization to act. Serious or-

---

83   Above note 17.

84   Above note 49.

85   Stanley Cohen, "Safeguards in and Justifications for Canada's New *Anti-terrorism Act*" (2002) 14 N.J.C.L. 99 at 121–22; Stanley Cohen, "Policing Security: The Divide between Crime and Terror" (2004) 15 N.J.C.L. 405.

ganized crime should not generally be directed at governments or international organizations or designed to intimidate the population. Should organized crime ever have such ambitions, however, there seems to be no principled reason to exclude it from the definition of terrorism just because it was not motivated by political or religious objectives.

The general definition of terrorism contained in the *Financing Convention* and endorsed by the Supreme Court in *Suresh* provides the most restrained and defensible definition of terrorism of which I am aware.[86] Although some who participated in the formation of the *Ottawa Principles* were reluctant to endorse this or any definition of terrorism, my own view is that, at this point of history, agreement on a precise and restrained definition of terrorism is a practical necessity. Anti-terrorism law is here to stay and it cannot be wished away. The task then is to define the ambit of terrorism law in a way that addresses the worst form of terrorism while protecting human rights.

As the *Ottawa Principles* rightly recognize, a definition of terrorism is a requirement of legality whenever the legislator creates crimes based on terrorism or gives the state special powers to investigate or prevent terrorism. The Security Council of the United Nations has encouraged states to enact such crimes and, most recently, is now encouraging states to enact laws that prohibit incitement of terrorism. It is extremely regrettable, however, that the Security Council did not endorse a restrained definition of terrorism until 2004,[87] after many states had already enacted new laws with overbroad definitions of terrorism.

---

86 Saul, above note 3 at 261, criticizes the Supreme Court of Canada, however, for overestimating the degree of international consensus behind the definition on the basis that "agreement on the generic definition in the 1999 Terrorist Financing Convention was reached only because the definition triggered financing offences, and not any broader criminal liability or other serious legal disability." Nevertheless, the *Financing Convention* definition is more restrained than the Security Council's working definition in Resolution 1566, examined above, or general definitions of terrorism in the treaties of regional organizations or best efforts to define terrorism in international treaty law: Saul, *ibid.*, c. 3.

87 See Resolution 1566, above note 5.

K. CONCLUSION

The closer that the definition of terrorism is to the basics of laws against murder and intentional injury that are accepted throughout the world, the less controversial anti-terrorism laws should be. Overbroad definitions of terrorism are deficient not only from the perspective of protecting human rights, but also from the perspective of condemning terrorism. Overbroad terrorism laws that target the destruction of property or the disruption of essential services create an impression in civil society that those targeted as terrorists could include those involved in protest or civil disobedience. Overbroad terrorism laws that include religious and motive requirements and focus on speech play into dangerous ideas that the focus in anti-terrorism efforts is on religious or political beliefs, as opposed to violence against civilians. The events of 9/11, and subsequent acts of terrorism, however, suggest that the acts of terrorism of which the world is rightly concerned about do not involve activities that are on the margins of possible definitions of terrorism. Rather, acts of terrorism involve the intentional murder and maiming of civilians and this should be the essence of any definition of terrorism.

Defining Terrorism: Why and How

Cathleen Powell[1]

A. INTRODUCTION

There was an underlying conflict between two main approaches at the 2006 Ottawa Colloquium on the Human Rights of Anti-terrorism. On the one hand, some participants wanted to redress the abuses of the anti-terrorism regime by denying it the status of a separate legal regime and forcing governments to comply with the "normal" legal procedures in the range of anti-terrorism areas under discussion. On the other hand, some participants wanted to codify and constrain current government practice against terrorism, recognizing the existing anti-terrorism programs of governments and incorporating them into a legal regime that sets human rights-based limits on the measures that a government can take in defence of security. The goals of these two approaches are not mutually exclusive and it was often possible to find common ground.

1 Part of this article is an adaptation of part of an earlier article: C.H. Powell & Garth Abraham, "Terrorism and International Humanitarian Law" (2006) 1 African Yearbook on International Humanitarian Law 118–47. I am grateful to Garth Abraham, and to the editors of the African Yearbook, for permission to reprint part of this article. Thank you, too, to Grant Tungay and Simon van Dugteren for their research support, and Salim Nakhjavani and Jewel Amoah for their comments on earlier drafts.

However, some fundamentally different premises underlie the two approaches, and several of the colloquium discussions brought these differences into sharp relief.

One extremely controversial issue was that of definition. Some participants vehemently rejected defining terrorism at all. In their view, the existing criminal law dealt adequately with any crimes that might form part of terrorist acts, and anti-terrorism regimes created by governments were at best redundant and at worst a shield for the misuse of power to abuse individual rights. A definition of terrorism would validate this abuse by forming the basis of a separate legal regime and acknowledging the qualitative difference between terrorism and other crimes.

In this chapter, I will argue that a definition of terrorism is necessary, both in the international sphere and within domestic legal systems. In doing so, I proceed from three main premises: first, that terrorism is a phenomenon that may require special rules and special processes, particularly as it is one of the crimes for which the emphasis must be on prevention rather than prosecution; second, that there is already in existence a substantial anti-terrorism program at both the international and the domestic levels; and, third, that this program is heavily dominated by the executive branch of government. From these premises, I will argue that the rule of law requires that the anti-terrorism program needs to be brought into a legal framework and subjected to legal control. For this to be done effectively, terrorism must be defined and the anti-terrorism program placed on a secure and determinate legal foundation.

The main body of the paper is devoted to the problem of definition at an international level. Section B describes the current international regime against terrorism and analyzes the existing attempts at definition. It reveals that the current practice of states is either not to define terrorism or to define it in an indeterminate manner. This section focuses on the problems that have dogged definition and suggests an approach which has the capacity both to ensure reliable cooperation against terrorism and to create an effective constraint on state, and executive, power.

Section C will examine the extent to which the theoretical framework suggested for international law can be transposed to the domestic level, identifying the factors that make it necessary to adapt the definition in a domestic context. Although the definition should take a slightly different form at the domestic level, it is still needed as a means to facilitate a working system against terrorism, to constrain the anti-terrorism regime already existing in most states, and to bring anti-terrorism under the rule of law.

B. THE INTERNATIONAL ANTI-TERRORISM REGIME

1) The Existing Anti-terrorism Regime

This regime is grounded in a wide-ranging United Nations Security Council (Security Council) program and a number of international treaties. Over the past decade, the Security Council has taken both legislative[2] and executive measures against terrorism in the course of more than forty resolutions (Security Council Resolutions), and it has built up an extensive bureaucracy to monitor and administer state compliance with the obligations that the resolutions impose.

Some of the general, substantive obligations have been imposed on states through Chapter VII of the *Charter of the United Nations*,[3] which renders them binding.[4] These obligations include the following: not to provide any kind of support to terrorist groups, to prevent terrorist acts

---

2   In "The Security Council Starts Legislating" (2002) 96 A.J.I.L. 901, Paul Szasz analyzes the first of these "legislative" measures against terrorism, namely, *Security Council Resolution 1373*: SC Res. 1373, UN SCOR, 2001, S/RES/1373 [Resolution 1373], and explains why Resolution 1373 constitutes a fundamental shift towards a new legislative function by the Security Council. For discussion of the legislative power of the UN Security Council, see Szasz, "The Security Council Starts Legislating," *ibid.* at 901–2; S. Talmon, "The Security Council as World Legislature" (2005) 99 A.J.I.L. 175; R. Lavalle, "A Novel, If Awkward, Exercise in International Law-making: Security Council Resolution 1540 (2004)" (2004) 51 Nethl. Int'l L. Rev. 411; A. Marschik, "The Security Council as World Legislator? Theory, Practice and Consequences of an Expanding World Power," IILJ Working Paper 2005/18, online: www.iilj.org/publications/documents/2005.18Marschik.pdf; E. Rosand, "The Security Council as 'Global Legislator': *Ultra Vires* or Ultra Innovative?" (2005) 28 Fordham Int'l L.J. 542; and C.H. Powell, "The Legislative Authority of the United Nations Security Council" in Benjamin Goold & Liora Lazarus, eds., *Security and Human Rights* (Oxford: Hart, 2007).

3   *Charter of the United Nations*, 26 June 1945, 59 Stat. 1031, T.S. 993, 3 Bevans 1153 (entered into force 24 October 1945) [UN *Charter*].

4   Under Chapter VII of the UN *Charter*, the Security Council has the power to issue binding measures, which all states bear a legal obligation to implement. See Articles 25, 39, 42, and 103 of the UN *Charter*, *ibid.*

through early warning systems and mutual assistance in investigation and prosecution, to establish and prosecute a range of terrorist offences within domestic criminal justice systems, and to suppress recruitment to terrorist groups.[5] Other general, substantive obligations have been phrased as recommendations. These include, most recently, those in *Security Council Resolution 1624*, which "calls on" states to criminalize the incitement to terrorism,[6] and resolutions calling on states to sign international conventions against terrorism.[7] Both the binding decisions and the recommendations of the Security Council have been very effective, as Rosand notes:

> Partly as a result of Resolution 1373, and the work of its offspring, the Counter-Terrorism Committee ("CTC"), almost every country has taken steps to enhance its counter-terrorism machinery, whether in the form of adopting anti-terrorism legislation, strengthening border controls, becoming party to international treaties related to terrorism, or becoming proactive in denying safe haven to terrorists and their supporters.[8]

In addition, the council has created mechanisms to designate certain persons and organizations as terrorist, and it mandates and coordinates a range of sanctions against these entities and other targets on an ongoing basis.[9] Four committees of the Security Council monitor and support the implementation of the anti-terrorism program at the domestic level: the "1267 Committee";[10] the Counter-Terrorism Committee;[11] the "1566 Working Group";[12] and the "1540 Committee," set up to monitor

5 Articles 1(a), 2(a) & (b) of Resolution 1373, above note 2

6 See *Security Council Resolution 1624*, SC Res. 1624, UN SCOR, 2005, S/RES/1624 [Resolution 1624].

7 *Ibid*. See also *Security Council Resolution 1566*, SC Res. 1566, UN SCOR, 2004, S/RES/1566 [Resolution 1566]; *Security Council Resolution 1456*, SC Res. 1456, UN SCOR, 2003, S/RES/1456 [Resolution 1456]; and Resolution 1373, above note 2.

8 Rosand, above note 2 at 548–49 (footnotes omitted).

9 These two categories of measures are discussed below.

10 Set up by *Security Council Resolution 1267*, SC Res. 1267, UN SCOR, 1999, 1999, S/RES/1267 [Resolution 1267]. See the website of the Committee, online: www.un.org/Docs/sc/committees/1267Template.htm.

11 Set up by Resolution 1373, above note 2. See the website of the Committee, online: www.un.org/sc/ctc/.

12 Set up by Resolution 1566, above note 7. See the website of the Committee, online: www.un.org/Docs/sc/committees/1566Template.htm.

compliance with the Security Council Resolution on weapons of mass destruction.[13]

The 1267 Committee, initially established to monitor the compliance of states with a range of sanctions imposed against Al-Qaeda and the Taliban, has had its mandate extended by later resolutions.[14] It administers one of the most controversial of the Security Council's anti-terrorism mechanisms: the so-called "listing" system. Under this mechanism, the committee designates a person or organization as linked to Al-Qaeda or the Taliban once one or more states have submitted the name of this person or organization, the name has been circulated to other states, and no objection has been received within forty-eight hours. The delisting procedure, on the other hand, requires negotiation between the government that wants to remove the name and the original, "designating" government.[15] Chapter VII of the UN *Charter* obliges states to impose a range of sanctions on listed individuals and entities: states have to freeze their financial assets, deny them entry into and transit through their territories, and prevent them from selling and supplying military equipment, whether such sales and supplies are carried out from their territories or even by their nationals outside their territories.[16]

The Counter-Terrorism Committee was set up by *Security Council Resolution 1373* of 2001 to monitor compliance with a range of general obligations set out in the resolutions. Since September 2005, it has also

---

13 Set up by *Security Council Resolution 1540*, SC Res. 1540, UN SCOR, 2004, S/RES/1540 [Resolution 1540]. See the website of the Committee, online: http:// disarmament2.un.org/Committee1540.

14 See for example, *Security Council Resolution 1363*, SC Res. 1363, UN SCOR, 2001, S/RES/1363; *Security Council Resolution 1390*, UN SCOR, 2002, S/RES/1390 [Resolution 1390]; and *Security Council Resolution 1526*, SC Res. 1526, UN SCOR, 2004, S/RES/1526.

15 The delisting procedure was added only after Sweden challenged the listing of three of its nationals. See B. Kingsbury, N. Krisch, & R. Stewart, "The Emergence of Global Administrative Law" (2005) 68 Law & Contemp. Probs. 15 at 19 and 21 and the authorities listed there; P. Gutherie, "Security Council Sanctions and the Protection of Individual Rights" (2004) 60 N.Y.U. Annual Survey of American Law 491 at 511–13.

16 Paragraphs 2(a)–(c) of Resolution 1390, above note 14; reaffirmed by *Security Council Resolution 1455*, SC Res. 1455, UN SCOR 2003, S/RES/1455; and Resolution 1456, above note 7.

monitored compliance with Resolution 1624.[17] Apart from requiring, evaluating, and publicizing reports from member states of the UN on their compliance with the Security Council Resolutions, the Counter-Terrorism Committee advises states, facilitating the drafting and passing of legislation that is required by the resolutions.[18] Among other measures, it provides a list of best practices,[19] which includes models for domestic anti-terrorism legislation.[20]

The most recent committee in the Security Council system is the 1566 Working Group, which is meant to deal with terrorist groups not falling within the purview of the 1267 Committee. It is tasked with examining "practical measures to be imposed upon individuals, groups or entities involved in or associated with terrorist activities, other than those designated by the Al-Qaeda/Taliban Sanctions Committee" and "the possibility of establishing an international fund to compensate victims of terrorist acts and their families."[21]

The treaty regime runs parallel to the Security Council program and has been given a significant boost by the support of the council.[22] Although a number of international conventions are routinely touted as "anti-terrorism" conventions,[23] only three deal directly and express-

---

17 See above note 6 and the accompanying text.

18 See Rosand, above note 2 at 582.

19 See Security Council, Counter-Terrorism Committee, *Directory of International Best Practices, Codes and Standards for the Implementation of Security Council Resolution 1373 (2001)*, online: www.un.org/sc/ctc/bestpractices.shtml.

20 Available online: www.unodc.org/pdf/crime/terrorism/explanatory_english2.pdf.

21 See the website of the 1566 Working Group, above note 12.

22 See Rosand, above note 2 and accompanying text.

23 The full collection is set out in the UN website on its actions against terrorism: online: http://untreaty.un.org/English/Terrorism.asp. The international anti-terrorism treaties that do not use the term "terrorism" include: the *Convention on the Prevention and Punishment of Crimes against Internationally Protected Persons, including Diplomatic Agents*, 14 December 1973, 1035 U.N.T.S. 167, 13 I.L.M. 41; the *International Convention against the Taking of Hostages*, 17 December 1979, 1316 U.N.T.S. 205; the *Convention on Offences and Certain Other Acts Committed on Board Aircraft*, 14 September 1963, 704 U.N.T.S. 219; the *Convention for the Suppression of Unlawful Seizure of Aircraft*, 16 December 1970, 860 U.N.T.S. 105; the *Convention for the Suppression of Unlawful Acts against the Safety of Civil Aviation*, 23 September 1971, 974 U.N.T.S. 178; the *Convention on the Physical Protection of Nuclear Material*, 3 March 1980, 1456 U.N.T.S. 124; the *Protocol on the Suppression of Unlawful Acts of Violence at Airports Serving International Civil Aviation, supplementary to the Convention for the Sup-*

ly with the phenomenon, namely, the *International Convention for the Suppression of the Financing of Terrorism* of 9 December 1999,[24] the *International Convention for the Suppression of Terrorist Bombings* of 15 December 1997,[25] and the *International Convention for the Suppression of Acts of Nuclear Terrorism* of 13 April 2005.[26] A range of regional conventions have also been set up to enhance co-operation against terrorism on a regional basis: the *Arab Convention on the Suppression of Terrorism* of 22 April 1998,[27] the *Convention of the Organization of the Islamic Conference on Combating International Terrorism* of 1 July 1999,[28] the *European Convention on the Suppression of Terrorism*,[29] the *OAS Convention to Prevent and Punish Acts of Terrorism Taking the Form of Crimes against Persons and Related Extortion that are of International Significance*,[30] the *OAU Convention on the Prevention and Combating of Terrorism* of 14 July 1999,[31] the *SAARC Regional Convention on Suppression of Terrorism* of 4 November 1987,[32] and the *Treaty on Cooperation among States Members of the Commonwealth of Independent States in Combating Terrorism*, done at Minsk on 4 June 1999.[33]

---

pression of Unlawful Acts against the Safety of Civil Aviation, 24 February 1988, 1589 U.N.T.S. 474; the *Convention for the Suppression of Unlawful Acts against the Safety of Maritime Navigation*, 10 March 1988, 1678 U.N.T.S. 221; the *Protocol for the Suppression of Unlawful Acts against the Safety of Fixed Platforms Located on the Continental Shelf*, 10 March 1988, 1678 U.N.T.S. 304; and the *Convention on the Marking of Plastic Explosives for the Purpose of Detection*, 1 March 1991, 30 I.L.M. 726.

24 10 January 2000, 39 I.L.M. 270, 2002 Can. T.S. 9 [*Financing Convention*].

25 12 January 1998, 37 I.L.M. 251 [*Bombing Convention*].

26 7 July 2007, UN Doc. A/59/766 [*Nuclear Terrorism Convention*].

27 [*Arab Convention*]. English translations of this treaty are available online: www.fidh. org/intgouv/ua/articles/1998/convantiterro04a.htm and www.ciaonet.org/cbr/ cbr00/video/cbr_ctd/cbr_ctd_27.html.

28 Online: www.oic-un.org/26icfm/c.html.

29 27 January 1977, 1137 U.N.T.S. 93, Eur. T.S. No. 90 [*European Convention*].

30 2 February 1971, 1438 U.N.T.S. 195.

31 Online: http://untreaty.un.org/English/Terrorism/oau_e.pdf.

32 [*SAARC Convention*], online: http://untreaty.un.org/English/Terrorism/Conv18. pdf.

33 Online: http://untreaty.un.org/English/Terrorism/csi_e.pdf. The description of the treaty regime which follows below is based on the international, and not the regional, treaty provisions.

The anti-terrorism treaty regime revolves around two main phases. In the first phase, a wide range of measures attempt to prevent terrorism.[34] These measures include the surveillance of suspects[35] and the monitoring, freezing, and even permanent seizure of their assets.[36] In the monitoring of assets, neither states nor individuals may refuse to provide information on the basis of bank secrecy.[37]

The second phase concerns the prosecution and extradition of terrorists. Terrorism is considered to be a particularly grave offence, for which punishment must be harsh.[38] The conventions require signatories to create a range of specific crimes and provide expressly for wide accomplice and attempt liability.[39] States must either prosecute or extradite persons accused of terrorism or organized crime.[40] They may not refuse to extradite, or to assist in other stages of the criminal process, on the basis that the offence is politically motivated or fiscal in nature.[41]

The conventions aim to set up a mechanism of close co-operation between states: they require an early warning system against terrorist

---

34 See *Financing Convention*, above note 24, Article 18 and *Bombing Convention*, above note 25, Article 15(a).

35 *Financing Convention*, *ibid.*, Article 18(3).

36 *Ibid.*, Article 8.

37 *Ibid.*, Article 12(2).

38 See Article 4(b) of both the *Financing Convention*, above note 24, and the *Bombing Convention*, above note 25 and Article 5(b) of the *Nuclear Terrorism Convention*, above note 26.

39 See *Financing Convention*, above note 24, Article 2; *Bombing Convention*, above note 25, Article 2(3); and *Nuclear Terrorism Convention*, above note 26, Articles 2 and 5.

40 See *Financing Convention*, above note 24, Article 10 and *Bombing Convention*, above note 25, Article 8.

41 See *Financing Convention*, above note 24, Articles 6, 11, 13, and 14; *Bombing Convention*, above note 25, Articles 5 and 11; *Nuclear Terrorism Convention*, above note 26, Article 15. Note, however, the "persecution" exemptions in Article 12 of the *Bombing Convention*, Article 15 of the *Financing Convention*, and also Article 16 of the *Nuclear Terrorism Convention*. These common articles release states from their obligation to provide mutual legal assistance if the requested state party has "substantial grounds" for believing that the request for extradition or mutual legal assistance with respect to the convention offences "has been made for the purpose of prosecuting or punishing a person on account of that person's race, religion, nationality, ethnic origin or political opinion or that compliance with the request would cause prejudice to that person's position for any of these reasons."

threats[42] and expect states to cooperate with one another to facilitate investigation, prosecution, and extradition of offenders[43] and the confiscation and disposal of assets connected to the treaty crimes.[44]

While many international anti-terrorism treaties insist that their provisions are subject to general international law and human rights law in particular,[45] the anti-terrorism regime nonetheless threatens a range of human rights. It has the potential to allow states to deprive individuals of their property, in such a manner as to threaten both the right to property and the right to be presumed innocent until proven guilty.[46] The worst threat, however, emanates from the various provisions facilitating investigation and prosecution of terrorism, and requiring a broader substantive basis for criminal liability. Together, these provisions have the potential to violate the right to privacy, the right to a fair trial, and a range of freedoms, including freedom and security of the person.[47]

It is the human rights implications of anti-terrorism that lie at the heart of the refusal to recognize the legal validity of a separate, anti-terrorism regime.[48] But this is not a viable solution to the problem. The

---

42 See generally *Financing Convention*, above note 24, Article 18.

43 See *Financing Convention, ibid.*, Article 12; *Bombing Convention*, above note 25, Article 10; and *Nuclear Terrorism Convention*, above note 26, Article 14.

44 See *Financing Convention, ibid.*, Article 8.

45 See the discussion below at note 51 and the accompanying text.

46 Property rights are intimately linked to trial rights in this context. Seizure of property as a preventive measure against crime is often posited not as a punitive measure, but as a civil measure: see A.J. Van der Walt, "Civil Forfeiture of the Instrumentalities and Proceeds of Crime and the Constitutional Property Clause" (2000) 16 S.A.J.H.R. 1–45. This, in turn, can mean that the onus lies with the alleged criminal to show that the property is not linked to criminal activity, thus creating a reverse onus of proof. For a criticism of the "civil" construction of forfeiture, see J. Pretorius & H. Strydom, "The Constitutionality of Civil Forfeiture" (1998) 13 South African Public Law 385.

47 Victor Ramraj discusses the impact of the substantive criminal law on due process in "Freedom of the Person and Principles of Criminal Fault" (2002) 18 S.A.J.H.R. 225.

48 See the description, provided at the beginning of this paper, of the conflict underlying many of the debates at the colloquium. One of the arguments against the recognition of a separate legal anti-terrorism regime was that the creation of such a regime would merely serve to validate governments' claims to extra power against the phenomenon—power that is used to abuse human rights. This argument alerts us to an underlying danger: if the anti-terrorism regime is accorded the status of a separate legal system, it may benefit from the legitimating function of

anti-terrorism regime is undeniably part of international law. While the validity of some of the Security Council resolutions may be open to challenge,[49] the two main international anti-terrorism conventions, as well as the regional conventions, are in force, which means that they impose binding legal obligations on their signatories.[50] Instead of ignoring the anti-terrorism regime, we should be interrogating the relationship of this regime with international human rights law. In this way, we can make use of the fact that the anti-terrorism treaties defer expressly to the international human rights regime,[51] and are worded broadly enough to allow for a range of interpretations.[52] By interpreting the anti-terrorism provisions to comply, as far as possible, with international human rights law, legal scholarship will be able to provide a valuable—and possibly valued—guide to states in their compliance with the international anti-terrorism regime. The alternative pits the ideal and the practice directly against one another, risking a scenario in which human rights lawyers ignore anti-terrorism requirements and governments ignore human rights lawyers.

It is also important to note that, whatever position we adopt on particular aspects of the anti-terrorism regime, the question of definition

---

law, thereby claiming additional authority in any clash between itself and the human rights regime. See also the conclusion in Powell, above note 2.

49   The European Court of First Instance has held that the Security Council is bound by *jus cogens* norms, see *Kadi v. Council of the European Union*, Case T-315/01, Judgment of the Court of First Instance (Second Chamber, extended composition) (21 September 2005) at paras. 220–30, online: http://curia.europa.eu/jurisp/cgi-bin/form.pl?lang=en&Submit=Rechercher&alldocs=alldocs&docj=docj&docop=docop&docor=docor&docjo=docjo&numaff=T-315/01&datefs=&datefe=&nomusuel=&domaine=&mots=&resmax=100. For discussion of other possible challenges to Security Council decisions, see also Kingsbury, Krisch, & Stewart, above note 15 and Powell, *ibid.*

50   *Statute of the International Court of Justice*, 26 June 1945, 59 Stat. 1055, 3 Bevans 1153, Article 38, sets out the sources to which the Court must refer in deciding a legal dispute, the first of which is treaties.

51   See *Financing Convention*, above note 24, Articles 15 and 17 and *Bombing Convention*, above note 25, Articles 12 and 14. See also Article 21 of the *Financing Convention* and Article 19 of the *Bombing Convention*, which subject the conventions to international law, although they do not expressly mention international human rights law.

52   See the discussion in C.H. Powell, "Terrorism and Governance in South Africa and Eastern Africa" in Victor Ramraj, Michael Hor, & Kent Roach, eds., *Global Anti-terrorism Law and Policy* (Cambridge: Cambridge University Press, 2005) 555 at 576*ff.*

should remain separate from our critique of specific human rights infringements. If we are to allow any limitation of human rights at all—and the anti-terrorism regime suggests that this is, to some extent, unavoidable—we must insist that such limitation is contained within as secure a legal framework as possible. The lack of a definition of terrorism and of a set of criteria to identify members of a terrorist group opens a path for an extra-legal exercise of power by the executive branch of government.

The argument, therefore, is that one of the most dangerous features of the anti-terrorism regime is not directly addressed by the international human rights regime, and that is its elevation of the executive above the other two branches of government and, particularly, the judiciary.[53] The first reason that the executive enjoys this privilege is that terrorism is not defined, or is too broadly defined. The resulting uncertainty about what terrorism really is widens the discretion enjoyed by law enforcement agencies in identifying and responding to it.

Executive privilege is also buttressed by other features of both the domestic and international systems. At the international level, these features are fairly invisible and insidious. Thus, for example, the popular notion of state sovereignty suggests that the international community is a purely horizontal arrangement, with no governmental structure. And yet, through the UN *Charter*, the international community has vested considerable executive power in the Security Council. Furthermore, the UN *Charter* imposes almost no express limits on the UN Security Council in its exercise of these powers. In this way, the UN Security Council is able to operate without any judicial oversight or consideration for the rules of natural justice in its listing mechanism, described above, exercising untrammelled power in a manner which would be unthinkable in a domestic constitutional system subject to the rule of law.[54]

---

53 Some rights, by their nature, protect the individual against the executive; for example, the right to a fair trial and freedom from arbitrary deprivation of property. However, international human rights law does not treat the structure of government as a problem in itself. See R. Bellamy, "The Political Form of the Constitution: The Separation of Powers, Rights and Representative Democracy" (1996) 44 Political Studies 436 at 436–37.

54 For legal responses to the "listing" mechanism, see, generally, D. Dyzenhaus, "The Rule of (Administrative) Law in International Law" (2005) 68 Law & Contemp. Probs. 127; E. de Wet & A. Nollkaemper, "Review of Security Council Decisions by National Courts" (2002) 45 German Yearbook of International Law 166, Kingsbury,

Another source of executive influence stems from the fact that the executive is the organ responsible for foreign affairs for each domestic system. The executive forms the interface between states and between international and domestic legal regimes. Thus the process of international cooperation involves the communication between law-enforcement agencies and other members of the executive, with little guidance from the law on what kind of crime they are dealing with when they prosecute and investigate "terrorist" offenders, and little oversight by the judicial branch of government over how they exercise the discretion created by the vagueness of the legal provisions. Through a large part of the process, states have simply to assume both competence and good faith on the part of the executives from other states and the Security Council.

In this way, the Security Council's listing process is in fact an incident of triple executive domination. It allows each state, through its executive, to put forward names for the list, with few procedural controls to protect the entity in question; it restricts any discussion of the listing to an inter-executive interchange; and it is buttressed by the full might of the international "executive" (the Security Council) throughout its operation. It is one of the clearest indications that the anti-terrorism program could move beyond law and become simply an exercise of unfettered executive discretion.

The rule of law requires that bodies which wield power in society are kept within the confines of the law. If the law loses its determinacy—if its terms are vague and overbroad—then it loses its ability to constrain power and becomes simply a means of legitimating the exercise of power. The global community is faced with a functioning anti-terrorism regime, one which, moreover, grants the executive considerable discretion. In order to protect society and the law's function of preventing the arbitrary use of power,[55] we need to bring this anti-terrorism regime into a secure legal framework by defining its terms.

Krisch, & Stewart, above note 15 at 19 and 21n and the authorities listed there; Gutherie, above note 15; C.H. Powell, "Terrorism and the Separation of Powers at the National and International Level" (2000) 18 S.A. J. Crim. Justice 151; and Powell, above note 2.

55 Dyzenhaus, *ibid.* at 162. See also the discussion in Powell, above note 2.

2) Current Definitions of Terrorism

a) State-centred Models of Terrorism

The argument has thus far focused on meeting a specific type of objection to defining terrorism, namely, the objection that a definition of terrorism will work to the disadvantage of the individual and place illegitimate power in the hands of the government. As argued above, a definition works instead to keep the elevated powers of states and their executives within a determinate legal system. Indeed, in this section, I have to meet a completely different type of objection—what we might call the state-centred objection—which will see the specific definition I propose as an attempt to legitimate terrorism and weaken the state. In this section, I argue that a determinate definition is also the only route to an effective system of international cooperation against terrorism.

Terrorism can be seen as politically motivated violence to the extent that it aims to influence how power is exercised over a particular group of people. It does so by attempting either to replace or to coerce the group wielding power, usually the government of a state. Traditionally, international law has reflected little interest in questions concerning the legitimacy of a government, allowing a government that has been in long-term, effective control of a state to speak for the state.[56] Thus, although international law distinguishes between "state" and "government" for some purposes, it equates violence against the *government* with violence against the *state*.[57] Because terrorism is understood as politically motivated violence, many commentators then equate it with violence by non-state actors against state actors. The two principal models for a definition of terrorism—normative and descriptive—both reflect an understanding of the phenomenon that is premised on the state's monopoly over violence. The normative model defines the crime

---

56 There have been some exceptions to this general practice, including the international response to South Africa and Rhodesia. For a discussion of illegitimate governments and the recognition of governments, see B. Roth, *Governmental Illegitimacy in International Law* (Oxford: Oxford University Press, 2000) and S. Talmon, *Recognition of Governments in International Law with Particular Reference to Governments in Exile* (Oxford: Clarendon Press, 1998).

57 Note that the terrorists are generally *not* members of the government under attack, although, in the definition proposed below, governments can carry out terrorist attacks on other governments or non-state actors.

expressly by its political nature. By contrast, the descriptive model simply prohibits a range of violent acts.

The normative definition prohibits political violence while implicitly accepting the state's right of recourse to force. Use of force by the military and the police is generally justified for political reasons, but violence of this kind is considered acceptable because it is exercised by the state.[58] On the other hand, political violence directed against the state is proscribed as terrorism.

The descriptive definition, by ignoring the political element inherent in the crime, and, instead, simply proscribing a range of violent acts, effectively criminalizes all violence beyond a certain limit, thereby outlawing politically motivated violence at this level as well. And, once again, the recourse to force by the military and the police on behalf of the government of a state is excluded from the definition of terrorism.[59]

This "state-centred" approach has persistently dominated any attempt at formulating a definition of terrorism. So, for example, the very first attempt at definition, the 1937 League of Nations definition cited above, defined "acts of terrorism" as "criminal acts *directed against* a *State*."[60] Subsequent attempts remain centred on the state, vacillating between the normative and descriptive approaches.

For most of its history, terrorism has been seen as a range of particular, proscribed acts. Indeed, during the period of decolonization, while conventions were concluded against airplane hijacking and other offences popularly seen as "terrorist" today, the term "terrorism" almost disappeared from international instruments.[61] Later, normative defin-

---

58 Note that I am referring here to the legitimacy of the *recourse* to violence as such, not to the legitimacy of the particular types of violence carried out by the state. In times of armed conflict, international humanitarian law limits the types of violence that the state may use, as does international and domestic human rights law in times of peace. For an analysis of the prohibition of terrorism by both state and non-state actors in times of armed conflict, see Powell & Abraham, above note 1.

59 See *ibid.* for the legal limits on the use of such violence by the state.

60 Article 1(2) of the *League of Nations Convention for the Prevention and Punishment of Terrorism*, LN Doc. C.546(1).M.383(1).1937.V [*League of Nations Convention*], in M. Hudson, ed., *International Legislation*, vol. VII (Dobbs Ferry, NY: Oceana, 1941) 862 at 865 [emphasis added].

61 See the description of international instruments on terrorism in E. McWhinney, "International Terrorism: United Nations Projects for Legal Controls" (1984) 7:2 Terrorism: An International Law Journal 175 at 177–80.

itions referred expressly to the political nature of the offence. Thus, the General Assembly's *Declaration on Measures to Eliminate International Terrorism* referred to "criminal acts intended or calculated to provoke a state of terror in the general public, a group of persons or particular persons for political purposes."[62] Similarly, the *International Convention for the Suppression of the Financing of Terrorism* renders an offence any act

> intended to cause death or serious bodily injury to a civilian, or to any other person not taking part in the hostilities . . . when the purpose of such act . . . is to intimidate a population, or to compel a government or an international organisation to do or to abstain from doing any act.[63]

The current definition in the UN's draft *Comprehensive Convention on International Terrorism* reads:

> Any person commits an offence within the meaning of this Convention if that person, by any means, unlawfully and intentionally, causes:
>
> • Death or serious bodily injury to any person; or
> • Serious damage to public or private property, including a place of public use, a State or government facility, a public transportation system, an infrastructure facility or the environment; or
> • Damage to property, places, facilities, or systems . . . resulting or likely to result in major economic loss,
>
> when the purpose of the conduct, by its nature or context, is to intimidate a population, or to compel a Government or an international organization to do or abstain from doing any act.[64]

This definition has within it elements of both the normative and descriptive approaches. It generally prohibits a range of violent acts while also requiring a particular political purpose. Through this definition and through its saving clauses, the draft convention proposes a strongly state-centred approach to terrorism. The definition itself aims at pro-

---

62   Article 3 of *Declaration on Measures to Eliminate International Terrorism*, GA Res. 49/60, UN GAOR, 49th Sess., Supp. No. 49, UN Doc. A/49/49 (1995) 303.

63   *Financing Convention*, above note 24, Article 2(1)(b).

64   Article 2 of the *Draft Comprehensive Convention on International Terrorism*, annexed to the Report of the Co-ordinator of the Draft Convention, 3 August 2005, online: http://daccessdds.un.org/doc/UNDOC/GEN/No5/460/57/PDF/No546057. pdf?OpenElement.

tecting a government (or other forms of recognized authority) against non-state actors. The saving clauses, set out in Article 20(2) and (3), exempt from the operation of the convention "armed forces . . . as [this term] is understood under international humanitarian law" and "military forces of a State." Both of these terms refer only to state forces,[65] which underscores the general approach in the convention that only non-state actors can commit terrorism.

b) Contradictions of the State-centred Models

Unfortunately, no state-centred definition can provide the international community with the foundation for a legally determinate anti-terrorism regime, or one that remains workable through changing political land-scapes. This is because it is neither legally nor politically tenable to con-fer a monopoly over violence on the state.

There are two related areas of international law that reject the state's claim to a legitimate monopoly on violence. First, human rights law and international criminal law set limits on the violence that a state may it-self carry out, thereby demonstrating that a state's use of violence might well be illegitimate. Second, international law and international practice both allow for recourse to force by non-state actors.

Unlike classical international law, human rights law and parts of international criminal law regulate the relationship between a govern-ment and the people within a state. By doing so, these legal regimes proscribe a range of violent acts to which states could previously resort. The recognition of the category of crimes against humanity attaches criminal consequences to particularly severe forms of violence on the part of the government of the state while the human rights regime pro-hibits lesser forms. So, for example, a government may not torture[66] and

---

65 The term "armed forces" is generally used in the Geneva Conventions with refer-ence to the armed forces of a state party, rather than to rebel forces opposing a state party. See, for example, common Article 4 of the Geneva Conventions of 1949, as well as Articles 12 & 13 of all four Geneva Conventions.

66 See, for example, Article 7(1)(f) of the *Rome Statute of the International Criminal Court*, 17 July 1998, 2187 U.N.T.S. 90, 37 I.L.M. 1002, UN Doc. A/CONF.183/9 (1998) [*Rome Statute*]; and Article 7 of the *International Covenant on Civil and Political Rights*, 19 December 1966, 999 U.N.T.S. 171, Can. T.S. 1976 No. 47, 6 I.L.M. 368 [*ICCPR*]. The *Rome Statute* prohibits torture if it is "committed as part of a wide-spread or systematic attack directed against any civilian population, with knowledge

it may not use coercion against the individual's rights to freedom of assembly, freedom of religion, or freedom of expression.[67]

Perhaps the most significant right, for the purposes of constraint on the state's monopoly on violence, is the right to self-determination. Recognized as a binding norm of international law,[68] which imposes on all states an obligation *erga omnes*,[69] the right to self-determination entitles a people to withdraw from the authority of a state and its government, either completely[70] or to a lesser extent.[71] Where the state denies this right, some commentators and states have argued that the people thus denied their right may resort legally to force in order to realize that right.[72]

---

of the attack." The *ICCPR* prohibits all "torture or . . . cruel, inhuman or degrading treatment or punishment" without attaching a criminal sanction to acts of torture.

67 See Articles 18–19 and 21 of the *ICCPR, ibid.*

68 *Declaration on the Granting of Independence to Colonial Countries and Peoples*, GA Res. 1514 (XV), UN GAOR, 15th Sess., Supp. No. 16, UN Doc. A/4684 (1960) 66; *Declaration on Principles of International Law concerning Friendly Relations and Co-operation among States*, GA Res. 2625 (XXV), UN GAOR, 25th Sess., Supp. No. 28, UN Doc. A/5217 (1970) 121; the *Legal Consequences for States of the Continued Presence of South Africa in Namibia notwithstanding Security Council Resolution 276*, [1970] I.C.J. Rep. 1971; *Western Sahara Case*, [1975] I.C.J. Rep. 12; *East Timor Case*, [1995] I.C.J. Rep. 90.

69 *East Timor Case, ibid.*

70 In the *Western Sahara Case*, above note 68 at para. 57, the Court notes that GA Resolution 1514 (XV), above note 68, allows a people to choose from three options: to emerge as an independent state, to associate with an independent state, and to integrate with an independent state.

71 The impact of the right to self-determination on minority groups is contested. Some writers hold that minority groups do not have a right to self-determination, whereas others suggest that minority groups, while not enjoying a right to secede from their state, are entitled to exercise "internal" self-determination. See Antonio Cassese, *Self-Determination of Peoples* (Cambridge: Cambridge University Press, 1995).

72 Additional Protocol I to the Four Geneva Conventions of 1949 seems to recognize a right to resort to force in such cases by elevating struggles of national liberation, as well as struggles against colonial and racist oppression, to the status of international armed conflict: see Article 1(4) of *Protocol Additional to the Geneva Conventions of 12 August 1949, and relating to the Protection of Victims of International Armed Conflicts (Protocol I)*, 8 June 1977, 1125 U.N.T.S. 3 [Protocol I]. See also E. Chadwick, *Self-Determination, Terrorism and the International Humanitarian Law of Armed Conflict* (The Hague: M. Nijhoff, 1996) 36–41 and the authorities cited at note 13; McWhinney, above note 61 at 181; International Law Association, Committee on Terrorism, 1982, "Fourth Interim Report" (1984) 7 Terrorism: An International

Although it has not been widely argued that a suppressed people might resort to force if its government violates international norms other than the right to self-determination, states have claimed for themselves a mechanism that protects particular individuals from the criminal process of another state if these individuals have engaged in politically motivated violence against that state. This mechanism, the political offence exception, allows a state to refuse to extradite an individual whose extradition is requested by another state if the offence for which the individual is being sought was a politically motivated offence.[73]

The political offence exception is often justified with reference to human rights law, even though the crimes in question might today be considered terrorist.[74] Thus Lord Reid commented in the British case of *Schtraks v. Government of Israel* that "many people then regarded insurgents against continental governments as heroes intolerably provoked by tyranny who ought to have asylum here, although they might have destroyed life and property in the course of their struggles."[75]

It is significant that the political offence exception is a highly flexible and indeterminate mechanism, subject to the political environment and dependent on the relationship between the states concerned. As Colm Campbell notes,

No universally accepted definition of a political offence emerged . . . . What did emerge was a degree of acceptance of the right of each requested state to decide what might constitute a political offence.[76]

In this way, the political offence exception has a second function. Apart from protecting human rights, it can also be seen to express reluctance on the part of states to commit themselves on the unlawfulness of

---

Journal 123 at 125 [ILA Report]; J. Sundberg, "Comments on the Fourth Interim Report of the Committee on International Terrorism" (1984) 7:2 Terrorism: An International Journal 185 at 187–88.

73 See generally C. Van den Wijngaert, *The Political Offence Exception to Extradition* (Deventer, The Netherlands: Kluwer, 1980).

74 C. Campbell, "Extradition to Northern Ireland: Prospects and Problems" (1989) 52:5 Mod. L. Rev. 585 at 586–87. Campbell identifies four main justifications for the political offence exception, two of which focus on the rights of the person to be extradited.

75 [1964] A.C. 556 at 583 (H.L.).

76 Campbell, above note 74 at 586.

violence by non-state actors in the international arena. The mechanism of the exception guards a state's right to "auto-interpret" when other state and non-state actors may use force.[77]

The political offence exception is just one of the ways in which states reserve for themselves a wide discretion to qualify or accept the use of violence.[78] This reluctance becomes apparent in many of the older international instruments against terrorism, which are phrased in such a way as to provide states with a broad discretion in carrying out their obligations under the instruments. Thus the very first instrument attempting to set up an international anti-terrorism regime—the *League of Nations Convention*[79]—allowed each high contracting party to interpret which offences fell within its ambit,[80] what action to take regarding extradition,[81] and what course a prosecution should follow.[82] Over and above these provisions, the convention expressly sets out a political offence exception.[83] Despite this extensive protection of state sovereignty, a protection that, in effect, allowed the state to legitimate acts of violence, the treaty failed to secure enough ratifications to enter into force. The same reluctance is still apparent today, as the UN struggles to formulate a widely accepted Convention on Terrorism.[84] Significantly, the Palestinian conflict is a central sticking point. Some states argue that a people might well have to take up arms against a state in order to protect their

---

77 The term "auto-interpret" was used by the ILA Committee on International Terrorism to describe states' insistence on retaining the right to qualify the use of violence. ILA Report, above note 72 at 124*ff.*

78 Whether the violence is carried out by state actors or non-state actors.

79 See *League of Nations Convention*, above note 60.

80 *Ibid.*, Articles 2 and 19.

81 *Ibid.*, Articles 8–10.

82 *Ibid.*, Articles 17(8), 18, and 19.

83 *Ibid.*, Article 8(4).

84 See UN, Press Release, SG/SM/10242/Rev.2, GA/L/3293/Rev.2, "Secretary-General Disappointed No Agreement Reached in Legal Committee on Comprehensive Terrorism Legislation" (1 December 2005), online: www.un.org/News/Press/docs/2005/sgsm10242.doc.htm. The controversial articles include one on definition, one on the application of the anti-terrorism norms to armed forces, and one on the recognition of the right of resistance against occupation. See UN, *Ad Hoc* Committee on Assembly Resolution 51/210, Press Release, "Finalizing Treaty Requires Agreement on 'Armed Forces,' 'Foreign Occupation' Anti-terrorism Committee Told," 6th Sess., 26th Mtg. (1 February 2002), online: www.un.org/News/Press/docs/2002/L2993.doc.htm. See also Rosand, above note 2 at 549.

inalienable freedoms, and, when this occurs, it is incumbent on the UN to protect political freedom and political participation.[85]

Evidently, while states might interpret political violence directed against themselves by non-state actors as terrorism, states are unwilling to condemn *all* political violence against *other* states as terrorism.[86] Perhaps the most direct example of this attitude is found in the Arab League's definition of terrorism. The *Arab Convention on the Suppression of Terrorism* excludes from the definition of terrorism all cases of struggle against "foreign occupation and aggression for the sake of liberation and self-determination" but adds that "[s]uch cases shall not include any act prejudicing the territorial integrity of any Arab state."[87]

The ambivalence of states towards the use of force by non-state actors has resulted in an indeterminate or selectively enforceable definition of terrorism. Where the definition rested on the political motivation behind the crime, states could decide whether the political cause was acceptable or not. Where the definition omitted the political element, states were free to apply the political offence exception at the point of extradition of the offender. As a result, treaties based on these types of definition had limited practical value during the Cold War. Because the acts they proscribed were generally already criminal within the domestic law of each state,[88] the main advantage of re-criminalizing them was to provide mechanisms for international cooperation through which terrorism could be prevented or prosecuted.[89] Because states cooperated selectively, with an eye to political alliances, the treaties were not able to provide a reliable and secure mechanism for the prosecution of terrorists.

---

85 See *Ad Hoc* Committee on Assembly Resolution 51/210, Press Release, *ibid.*; and "UN seeks definition of terrorism" *BBC News* (26 July 2005), online: news.bbc. co.uk/2/hi/americas/4716957.stm (date of access: 16 October 2006).

86 Some of the more recent anti-terrorism conventions do exclude the political offence exception—see the discussion under section B(2)(c), below in this chapter.

87 Article 2(a) of the *Arab Convention*, above note 27. See further Lynn Welchman, "Rocks, Hard Places and Human Rights: Anti-Terrorism Law and Policy in Arab States" in Ramraj, Hor, & Roach, eds., above note 52 at 589.

88 Redundancy is a common feature of anti-terrorism legislation. See the review of domestic legislation on this point in Victor Ramraj, "Terrorism, Security and Rights: A New Dialogue" (2002) Sing. J.L.S. 1 at 3–6.

89 These include the sharing of intelligence, co-operation in investigations, and extradition of suspected terrorists.

c) The Current Solution

The current solution to the indeterminate nature of the anti-terrorism regime has been achieved not by engaging with the theoretical anomalies of the definition, but instead by strengthening the international consensus against the particular forms of terrorism prevalent today. The anti-terrorism approach that has gained ground since the attacks of September 11, 2001 is strongly state-centred. Changes have been introduced to extradition treaties to exclude the political offence exception for terrorist crimes,[90] so that *all* violent acts beyond a certain threshold become subject to the anti-terrorism regime. Second, terrorism is being treated as a crime that only non-state actors can commit. Finally, many states and writers will not deal with terrorism unless it has international ramifications,[91] deliberately leaving the treatment by a state of its own citizens and residents out of the reckoning. Current thinking therefore tends to legitimize the recourse to violence by the state and delegitimize any such recourse by non-state actors.

This is a very short-term solution. It depends on a tacit, international agreement on a wide range of factors, particularly on the identity of the terrorist, the illegitimacy of any use of violence by the terrorist group, and, most importantly, the automatic legitimacy of the use of force by any state threatened by this terrorist.[92] In effect, then, this solution

---

90 Articles 5 and 11 of the *Bombing Convention*, above note 25; Articles 6 and 14 of the *Financing Convention*, above note 24; and Article 2 of the OAS, 2d Plenary Session, *Inter-American Convention against Terrorism*, 3 June 2002, AG/RES. 1840 (XXXII-O/02) expressly exclude the political offence exception; other international instruments allow for the exclusion of the political offence exception on a bilateral basis. See Article 2 of the *European Convention*, above note 29, and Article 2 of the *SAARC Convention*, above note 32.

91 See Article 3 of both the *Bombing Convention, ibid.*, and the *Financing Convention, ibid.*, and R. Friedlander, "Comment: Unmuzzling the Dogs of War" (1984) 7:2 Terrorism: An International Journal 169.

92 It has even been argued that states are allowed to take measures against terrorists residing outside their own borders. One form of this argument insists that states may use force in self-defence even if the attack to which they are responding was not initiated by another state. For example, Yoram Dinstein has argued that the "war on terror," instigated by the September 11, 2001 attacks, entitles the U.S. to take military action in self-defence against any state in which the terrorists reside. See Yoram Dinstein, "Humanitarian Law on the Conflict in Afghanistan" (2002) 96 American Society of International Law Proceedings 23. Another form of this

demands a consensus not on the definition of terrorism, but, rather, on which political motivations for violence are acceptable and which are not. Such a conception shifts the focus from the act to the actor. Furthermore, by determining the moral value of conduct with reference to the actor, it opens a pathway to the dangerous idea that the very nature of the "good" actor can justify its conduct.

3) A Proposed Definition

The dilemma in which the international community finds itself is that terrorists do not respect national borders. To be effective, an anti-terrorism program therefore relies on international cooperation. However, in order to remain effective, to retain its legitimacy, and to avoid abuses, the anti-terrorism program also needs to be contained within a functioning and workable legal system.

The political nature of the crime of terrorism seems to be both a definitional requirement and the element that renders the definition indeterminate. The question, therefore, is whether a legal regime can be constructed which acknowledges the political element of the crime of terrorism but does not turn on it, thus allowing all states to cooperate within a uniform legal system, independent of their approval of the cause for which the non-state actor is fighting.

a) Lessons from International Humanitarian Law (IHL)
Located within international law, IHL provides us with a body of rules dealing directly with politically motivated violence. This alone should

---

approach claims that states have a right of pre-emptive, and not merely anticipatory, self-defence. This was famously mooted by President George W. Bush in his speech to the 2002 Graduating Class at the United States Military Academy West Point, New York (1 June 2000), online: www.whitehouse.gov/news/releases/2002/06/20020601-3.html. The "Bush Doctrine" has received some academic support. See W. Bradford, "'The Duty to Defend Them': A Natural Law Justification for the Bush Doctrine of Preventive War" (2004) 79 Notre Dame L. Rev. 1365–492; J. Paul, "The Bush Doctrine: Making or Breaking Customary International Law?" (2004) 27 Hastings Int'l & Comp. L. Rev. 457–79; B. Langille, "It's 'Instant Custom': How the Bush Doctrine Became Law after the Terrorist Attacks of September 11, 2001" (2003) 26 B.C. Int'l & Comp. L. Rev. 145–56; J. Cohan, "The Bush Doctrine and the Emerging Norm of Anticipatory Self-defense in Customary International Law" (2003) 15 Pace Int'l L. Rev. 283–357.

make it worth examining in any discussion of terrorism. Furthermore, IHL seems to avoid many of the pitfalls presented by existing responses to terrorism, because IHL rules apply to governments, liberation groups, and rebels. While taking political violence as its subject, IHL also focuses squarely on the *means* by which the conflict is conducted, rather than the justification for the resort to arms itself. Indeed, the justification is of no relevance to the application of IHL.[93]

This is not a proposal to apply IHL to peacetime terrorism, because IHL does not apply outside of a situation of armed conflict. Instead, it is an argument that some of the principles underlying IHL might underpin a peacetime anti-terrorism legal regime. These principles demonstrate a means by which the peacetime anti-terrorism regime can achieve a goal it shares with IHL; that is, the legal control of politically motivated violence. Reasoning by analogy, we should be able to model some of the anti-terrorism norms, particularly the definition of its underlying concepts, on the approach taken by IHL.

The relevance of IHL to the debate on an appropriate response to acts of terrorism was first raised by the ILA Committee on International Terrorism in the mid-1980s. In an interim report published in 1982, the majority of the committee suggested that terrorism should be defined by analogy to IHL. The majority report noted that previous international attempts at definition had either not been accepted by sufficient states or had been "weakened by reservations under which states insisted on their discretion to apply their own municipal laws in their own way to politically motivated violence."[94] The main problem identified by the committee was the unwillingness of states to submit themselves to a binding, supranational system in cases of terrorism. The report claimed, however, that parts of the international legal regime override the uncertainty created by the auto-interpretation of rules by states, referring in particular to the rules of IHL.[95]

The majority report pointed out that IHL contains no political offence exception and even creates an obligation on states to punish acts

---

93 IHL maintains a strict division between the reasons for the recourse to force (*jus ad bellum*) and the rules that apply in a situation of armed conflict (*jus in bello*). See generally M. Sassòli & A. Bouvier, *How Does Law Protect in War?* (Geneva: International Committee of the Red Cross, 2006) 102–8.

94 ILA Report, above note 72.

95 *Ibid.* at 127, para. 11.

which would, in peacetime, be considered terrorist.[96] On this basis, it suggested the development of the "humanitarian law concerned with political violence" in step with IHL:

> There is no reason in theory or practice why states should be willing to concede to politically motivated foreigners a licence to commit atrocities while saddling their own organized forces with the restraints contained in the 1949 Geneva Conventions against committing the same atrocities.[97]

The proposal of the majority report was therefore to define terrorism on the premise that

> No person shall be permitted to escape trial or extradition on the grounds of his political motivation who, if he performed the same acts as a soldier engaged in an international armed conflict, would be subject to trial or extradition.[98]

The minority report rejected any juxtaposition of terrorism and IHL, claiming as the essence of an act of international terrorism the fact that "it is committed during a time of peace"[99] by non-state groups that are not recognized as belligerents.[100] The minority argued that conceptual and legal confusion would occur were the two disciplines in any way meshed together.[101] Implicit in the rejection of the majority definition was the fear that the application of IHL to terrorists would legitimate the use of violence by non-state groups and thereby provide some legitimacy for the non-state terrorist group itself.[102] This fear was to be repeated in written comments on the definition. Dinstein, for example, emphasized that war permits acts that would otherwise be criminal[103] and Friedlander accused the ILA of "upgrading . . . politically motivated

---

96 *Ibid.* at 129 & 130. See also Powell & Abraham, above note 1.

97 ILA Report, *ibid.* at 130.

98 *Ibid.* at 131.

99 *Ibid.*

100 *Ibid.*

101 *Ibid.* at 132.

102 See the comments of C.G. Cyril (at 368), J.A. Frowein (at 370), and S. Sorabjee (at 375) in (1984) 7 Terrorism: An International Journal.

103 Yoram Dinstein, "Comments on the Fourth Interim Report of the ILA Committee on International Terrorism" (1982) 7 Terrorism: An International Journal 163 at 165.

terrorist actors to the status of regular combatants in armed conflicts."[104]
At the time, the ILA debate reached no definite conclusions.

However, the proposal that terrorism be defined with reference to
IHL was to resurface and has gained popularity in recent years in a
proposal to the UN and in domestic jurisprudence.[105] It has also been
revived by the current campaign for a comprehensive anti-terrorism
convention, in which the notion of an IHL-based definition of terrorism
received significant support from Kofi Annan.[106] There is, nonetheless,
still considerable resistance to using IHL as a potential template in the
war on terror.

Before discussing these objections to reasoning from IHL, the following section provides a brief description of what an IHL-based conception of terrorism would entail.

b) An IHL-inspired Anti-terrorism Regime

A definition of terrorism that draws inspiration from IHL would not encompass all violence by non-state actors. While other forms of violence
would remain criminal within the domestic law of the individual state,
the international anti-terrorism regime would identify the point at which
politically motivated violence, perpetrated during peacetime, becomes
terrorism. Once the violence reaches this point,[107] the international
anti-terrorism system would then be triggered—bringing with it full
cooperation in the investigation, extradition, and prosecution of offenders, without resort to the political offence exception. Furthermore, this
system would not be state-centred, in that it would focus on the *type* of

---

104 Friedlander, above note 91 at 169.

105 See the discussion and critique of M. Scharf, "Defining Terrorism as the Peacetime
Equivalent of War Crimes: Problems and Prospects" (2004) 36 Case W. Res. J. Int'l
L. 359 at 374. See also C.L. Lim's analysis of this proposal in "The Question of a
Generic Definition of Terrorism under General International Law" in Ramraj, Hor,
& Roach, eds., above note 52, 37 at 52*ff.*

106 Although the definition proposed in the convention is wider, see above note 52,
the public debate seems to focus on the protection of civilians. See, for example,
"UN seeks definition of terrorism," above note 85; and http://english.aljazeera.
net/NR/exeres/9523F50F-43BF-47B9-86C1-73B596D703ED.htm.

107 See below for a discussion of how this point is to be measured. The three rules
I draw from IHL suggest that we would evaluate the border between "ordinary"
politically motivated violence by reference to both the intensity and the nature of
the act.

violence perpetrated, ignoring both the nature of the perpetrator and the nature of the political cause being espoused. Thus, it would be possible for states as well as non-state actors to perpetrate acts of terrorism.

The rules and principles of IHL that would help to flesh out a definition of terrorism are those that protect civilians—the people so often targeted in a terrorist attack. The detailed rules of IHL providing for the protection of civilians rest on three main premises: civilians and civilian objects may never be the target of attack;[108] attacks whose primary purpose is to cause terror among civilians are illegal;[109] and *excessive* harm to civilians is prohibited.[110]

In the military context, the harm caused is considered excessive if it is out of proportion to the military objective of the attack. While we cannot speak of a military objective in a peacetime context, the amnesty proceedings of both South Africa and Chile provide precedent for the use of proportionality in determining the legitimacy of politically motivated violence. Both sets of proceedings compared the severity of the violence with the aim behind the attack when deciding whether to grant amnesty to the perpetrators.[111] In this way, IHL rules and principles relating to indiscriminate attacks and excessive civilian damage might be adapted to the peacetime context.

For the most part, an IHL-inspired definition will not detract from the popular or common understanding of terrorism—that of politically motivated attacks on innocent people. However, there are two fundamental differences to the popular or common understanding. First, the IHL-inspired definition will apply equally to *all* actors in the internation-

---

108 J.-M. Henckaerts & L. Doswald-Beck, *Customary International Humanitarian Law*, vol. 1 (Cambridge: Cambridge University Press, 2005) at 3–8.

109 *Ibid.* at 8–11.

110 The principle of proportionality as used in IHL does not allow for the direct targeting of civilians, but recognizes that civilians might suffer collateral harm when a military target is attacked. See Henckaerts & Doswald-Beck, *ibid.* at 3–8 and 46–50, and the discussion below at note 133.

111 A. Pedain, "Was Amnesty a Lottery? An Empirical Study of the Decisions of the Truth and Reconciliation Commission's Committee on Amnesty" (2004) 121 S.A.L.J. 785. Pedain, however, argues that the actual practice of the South African Amnesty Committee focused less on the question of proportionality and more on the political motivation behind the violence.

al sphere, whether state or non-state. Second, this definition, by focusing on the protection of civilians, does not protect military personnel or
installations from attack.

On the one hand, the proposed definition may alarm states and
commentators because it applies equally to state and non-state actors
and refuses to accord special protection to the military interests of the
state.[112] On the other hand, it appears almost too obvious to mention
in that it so clearly covers the main examples of terrorist activity. It is
therefore worth establishing that, obvious or not, terrorism as defined
by analogy to IHL is *not* comprehensively prohibited by current codifi-
cations of international criminal law.

There are two main bodies of treaty and custom, IHL itself and the
prohibition on crimes against humanity, which might be expected to
deal with terrorism as defined in this paper. However, these two bodies provide little assistance in prohibiting or prosecuting many instances of terrorism. IHL itself may not be applicable in its own right. This
is because the proposed definition of terrorism deals exclusively with
peacetime acts of terrorism, with the result that IHL, the legal regime
governing armed conflict, has no direct application.[113] Furthermore, even
if there is, in fact, a situation of armed conflict, IHL may not be applied
because the state in question might not be prepared to recognize the
situation as one of armed conflict. The prohibition on crimes against
humanity might be expected to be more helpful, as it applies outside
of a situation of armed conflict. However, particularly as codified in the
Rome Statute,[114] the prohibition on crimes against humanity leaves several loopholes through which terrorists could fall. Article 7 of the *Rome
Statute* defines crimes against humanity as any of a list of acts "when
committed as part of a widespread or systematic attack directed against
any civilian population." The requirement of a "widespread" or "systematic" attack in itself seems to exclude a single act of terrorism, or even

---

112 This point is discussed in more detail below at note 120, but it must be noted that
     an IHL-based conception of terrorism does not render attacks on the military and
     its installations legal, because it does not equate terrorism with armed conflict.
     The IHL-based definition merely removes this particular form of violence from the
     purview of an international anti-terrorism program.

113 See Powell & Abraham, above note 1, for a discussion of how IHL prohibits acts of
     terrorism during times of armed conflict.

114 *Rome Statute*, above note 66.

a series of random attacks."[115] Furthermore, paragraph 2(a) of the *Rome Statute* narrows the notion of "attack" even further by stipulating that it means "a course of conduct . . . pursuant to or in furtherance of a State or organizational policy to commit such attack."[116] While this aspect of the *Rome Statute* seems to conflict with customary international law[117] and its interpretation is open to question, there is a possibility that some terrorist offences will not meet the threshold of crimes against humanity in the *Rome Statute*.

c) Obstacles to an IHL-based Definition of terrorism

The central common problem is the fear that reference to, or use of, IHL will legitimate the cause of the terrorists/insurgents. Over and above this objection there are also practical barriers. States may fear that submission to a binding legal regime on terrorism will constrain them to the extent that they cannot counter the terrorist threat successfully.[118] At the same time, states may argue that the anti-terrorism regime will have no effect on their opponents—terrorists, by their very

---

115 W.A. Schabas, *An Introduction to the International Criminal Court* (Cambridge: Cambridge University Press, 2004) at 36. Note that the wording of Article 7(2)(a) (1984) suggests that the attack must have both widespread and systematic aspects.

116 See the critique of Article 7 in A. Cassese, P. Gaeta, & J. Jones, eds., *The Rome Statute of the International Criminal Court: A Commentary* (Oxford: Oxford University Press, 2002) at 375–77. The authors note that the "Elements of Crimes" document goes even further by requiring that the state or organization actively promote or encourage the attack.

117 See, for example, the finding in the case of *Prosecutor v. Kunarac*, IT-96-23 & IT-96-23/1-A (12 June 2002) (ICTY, Appeals Chamber).

118 See, for example, one of Michael Scharf's objections to a "war crimes-based" definition of terrorism:

> Even if they are ultimately denied POW status, under the Geneva Conventions the al Qaeda detainees are still entitled to fundamental guarantees of humane treatment and may not be tortured or degraded. In contrast, if the members of al Qaeda were deemed common criminals not subject to the protections of the laws of war, the United States would actually have more leeway in how it treats al Qaeda members that are captured and detained outside of its borders.

Scharf, above note 105 at 373. It goes without saying that any attempt to interpret the status of detainees in such a way as to allow for torture and degradation runs counter to human rights law. See principles 2.2–2.4 and part 4 of the *Ottawa Principles on Anti-terrorism and Human Rights*, at Part One of this book [*Ottawa Principles*].

nature, ignore the rules (indeed, one of the most common justifications voiced by states for their refusal to respect existing law in the area of terrorism is that the terrorists have no respect for legal norms).[119] Thus, an objection to an IHL-inspired anti-terrorist regime is that, without reciprocity, there is no incentive for states to commit to the program. Finally, the IHL-inspired definition offers less protection than do current definitions, as it does not condemn attacks on the government and the military as terrorist *per se*.[120]

It is, of course, the purpose of an anti-terrorism program to ensure effective co-operation among states in identifying threats and finding and prosecuting offenders. But this highly practical purpose can be achieved only if the anti-terrorism program is reliable and determinate, and if anti-terrorism operations do not need to be negotiated on a case-by-case basis with friendly states. It is therefore the ideological under-pinning of the traditional approach to terrorism that actually frustrates the primary, practical purpose of an international anti-terrorism regime. When states insist that the definition of terrorism affirm their right to violence while stripping the non-state actor of all legitimacy, they are expecting the anti-terrorism regime to fulfill a second function, which is psychological and political in nature. By doing so, they are demanding a value judgment which is legally indeterminate and cannot be provided in advance. States have never committed themselves to a permanent position on the legitimacy of violent resistance to the government of other states. What states can do, however, is accept that politically mo-tivated violence may not cross certain boundaries and agree to cooper-ate in preventing such attacks and prosecuting their perpetrators.

An IHL-based conception of terrorism will not force states to accept as lawful violence against their own institutions and military objects car-ried out by non-state actors. The proposed definition does not equate terrorism with armed conflict[121] and therefore does not give non-state

---

119 One of the most famous examples of such a claim is provided by President George W. Bush's speech to the 2002 graduating class at the United States Military Acad-emy West Point, above note 92.

120 Thus, Scharf complains that "terrorist attacks" on military, police or government buildings, navy vessels, and military aircraft "would not be regarded as criminal": above note 105 at 371.

121 This seems to be the main difference between the definition proposed here and that criticized by Scharf, above note 105. Scharf sees as implicit in the treatment

actors a right to attack government or military objectives. What it does instead is to remove that particular form of violence from the purview of an international anti-terrorism program. The proposal is that such forms of violence should fall into a different category of illegal conduct, to be dealt with by the victim state and its allies in terms of their domestic law or bi- and multilateral agreements. The international anti-terrorism regime, by contrast, should be globally applicable. It should be tailored specifically to those crimes that threaten international interests, rather than the interests of a specific state or group of states.

Finally, the objection to the lack of reciprocity can be met in two ways. First, it is clear that, unless states are prepared to respect the humanity they accuse terrorists of desecrating, they will lose their moral claim to win the war on terror. In this way, it is the very lack of reciprocity that allows states to continue their battle against terrorist groups. Second, on a practical level, states have nothing to lose by submitting to the anti-terrorism regime. The reciprocity of this regime operates not between the state and the terrorist, but between the state and other states in their sharing of information, their extradition arrangements, and other forms of mutual assistance. The more confidence that states have in each other's respect for the legal system, the more effective the cooperation will be.

C. THE DOMESTIC ANTI-TERRORISM REGIME

Before this conception of terrorism can be transferred to the domestic sphere, it must meet three human rights-based objections.

First, it may once again be argued that the normal criminal law is sufficient to deal with the phenomenon. The main elements of a terrorist offence, as defined above, killing and assault, are already crimes within each domestic system and they can be investigated and prosecuted as such. While some domestic systems may achieve an anti-terrorism regime without express reference to terrorism, there is a risk in such an

---

of terrorism as "peacetime" war crimes: (1) that the laws of war are being applied outside of a situation of armed conflict (or that an incident of terrorism in itself creates the situation of armed conflict); and (2) that the "terrorists" gain combatant status, can rely on the defence of superior orders, etc. However, the definition proposed here does not import IHL into peacetime.

approach. This is that any concessions that need to be made effectively to combat terrorism can seep into the criminal legal system as a whole. However, it would in any event be counterproductive to ignore the fact that most states already have an anti-terrorism regime.[122]

Furthermore, these regimes generally privilege the executive to the point where it may become unaccountable. While it is beyond the scope of this paper to examine executive dominance at the domestic level in any great detail, the following brief remarks should provide some impression of the scope of the problem.

The problem of domestic executive dominance permeates the discourse on anti-terrorism measures. It is clear that one of the underlying aims of the *Ottawa Principles* was to protect the individual from arbitrary state, particularly executive, action.[123] The dangers that the principles try to address are also clear from just a few examples of anti-terrorism legislation. Overall, the effect of the legislation is to increase executive discretion, insulate the executive from judicial or legislative control, and protect the executive from the consequences of its own decisions. The first notable feature is, of course, the extremely wide definition of terrorism and related offences, easing the task of the prosecutor in a criminal trial[124] but, more importantly, allowing police and investigators more scope in the pre-trial phase. The second feature is the enhanced powers of investigation and prevention granted to the relevant executive authorities where terrorism is suspected.[125] Third, some states vest in their executives the power to decide when persons or organizations

---

122 See above note 8 and the accompanying text above.

123 This aim is a *leitmotiv* of the whole document, but is particularly important to parts 5 and 9.

124 Particularly where terrorism becomes a negligence-based offence. See Kent Roach's criticism of South Africa's legislation in K. Roach, "A Comparison of South African and Canadian Anti-terrorism Legislation" (2005) 18 South African Journal of Criminal Justice 127 at 140–44.

125 Legislation in the United States of America, Australia, Canada, and South Africa provides examples of heightened executive powers in the pre-trial phase through use of a variety of mechanisms including investigative hearings, preventive detention, and enhanced powers of the investigating authorities when terrorism is suspected. See Roach, *ibid.*; W. Banks, "United States Responses to September 11" in Ramraj, Hor, & Roach, eds., above note 52; G. Williams, "The Rule of Law and the Regulation of Terrorism in Australia and New Zealand" in Ramraj, Hor, & Roach, eds., *ibid.*; and K. Roach, "Canada's Response to Terrorism" in Ramraj, Hor, & Roach, eds., *ibid.*

are terrorists,[126] and many delegate this decision to the international "executive" (the Security Council) by giving effect to its listing process.[127] Finally, some states expressly indemnify their executives against any claims resulting from their actions against terrorism.[128]

As in the international arena, the most practical and legally coherent response to the existing domestic anti-terrorism regime would be to put it on a secure legal footing. In addition, because the domestic regime is largely tailored towards international cooperation, the conception of terrorism in the domestic and international spheres should correspond as closely as possible.[129]

The second possible objection is that the international definition proposed in this chapter might be seen to be too broad, as it ostensibly covers any attacks on civilians. The international law definition is, however, confined to very serious crimes, both through its proportionality requirement and through the analogy to war crimes, which are the more serious violations of IHL.[130] As discussed below, the proportionality requirement may not be applicable in the domestic setting. The *Ottawa Principles* have instead restricted the concept to its core incidents by excluding any violence that does not produce death or severe bodily harm.[131] This definition is very similar to that adopted by the Canadian Supreme Court in *Suresh v. Canada (Minister of Citizenship and Immigration)*,[132] with one important addition: the target of the violence includes not only recognized authorities — governments and international organizations — but also non-state political organizations.

---

126 See Powell, above note 52 at 583–84.

127 As they are bound by Chapter VII of the UN *Charter* to give effect to the list produced by the Security Council, almost all states have done so. See UN, *Reports of Member States Pursuant to Paragraph 6 of Resolution 1455 (2003)*, online: www.un.org/Docs/sc/committees/1267/1455reportsEng.htm.

128 Compare the examples of Uganda and Tanzania in Powell, above note 52 at 573.

129 It is worth noting that investigations of genuine terrorist threats are likely to have international ramifications. See the discussion of the global nature of terrorism in Rosand, above note 2 at 548.

130 Henckaerts & Doswald-Beck, above note 108 at 568–74. See also M. Bothe, "War Crimes" in Cassese, Gaeta, & Jones, eds., above note 116 at 381; and P. Gaeta, "The Defence of Superior Orders" (1999) 10 E.J.I.L. 172 at 190, although Gaeta's remarks are limited to the formulation of war crimes in the *Rome Statute*.

131 See principle 2.1.1, above note 118.

132 [2002] 1 S.C.R. 3.

The third objection relates to the inclusion of the political nature of the offence in the definition of terrorism. At the international level, the definition of terrorism is based fundamentally on its political element and it is impossible, without this element, to recognize the possible legitimacy of politically motivated violence. At the domestic level, however, such a conception of terrorism can easily be seen simply to stigmatize opposition to the current government.

This problem alerts us to the fundamentally different context of the domestic setting: within their domestic systems, states cannot realistically be expected to give up their monopoly on violence. Indeed, within constitutional democracies, they have a moral claim to this monopoly as they embody the authority of the citizenry as a whole and have a duty to protect it.[133] This is the reason that states would tend to resist seeing terrorism as the inflicting of *disproportionate* damage on civilians,[134] as the proportionality inquiry would entail some degree of acceptance of the use of violence against themselves. It is also the reason why the reference to terrorism as politically motivated violence in the domestic setting connotes violence against the state by a non-state actor.

We therefore cannot expect the state to surrender the same privileges domestically as it should internationally. But we must be careful to distinguish between two kinds of political violence. The first type is political violence *per se*; that is, violence that has not reached the threshold of terrorism. The second type is political violence that has crossed this threshold; that is, terrorism as defined above. Where the first type of violence is concerned, I have argued that international law requires that both states and non-state actors must be allowed a claim to resort to

---

133 A similar argument was made by the Canadian Supreme Court in *Reference re Secession of Quebec* (1998) 37 I.L.M. 1340, in which it held that Quebec's right to self-determination would entail a right to secede only if Quebec were unable to exercise the rights flowing from self-determination within the constitutional arrangement of Canada.

134 Use of the proportionality criterion should not be misunderstood as condoning attacks on civilians. It is one of the central tenets of IHL that civilians may never be the target of an attack. As used in IHL, the term "disproportionate" describes attacks on military targets that cause collateral civilian damage which is out of proportion to the military advantage anticipated from the attack. See section 3(b) above and above note 110; Article 51 of Protocol I, above note 72; and Powell & Abraham, above note 1 at 123–27.

violence of this nature. At the domestic level, this egalitarian approach is not feasible, and states will continue to criminalize all violence by non-state actors. However, there can be no privileging of the state where the second type of violence, terrorism itself, is concerned. As mentioned above, the *Ottawa Principles* maintain the absolute prohibition against terrorism. By maintaining that non-state bodies can also be victims of the crime, they recognize that states might also be perpetrators.

Given the unequal relationship between the state and the non-state actor in the domestic sphere, there are fundamentally different reasons why the political element of the crime should be maintained in the latter. Perhaps one of the central arguments for retaining this element is that it constitutes another limiting factor which prevents the definition from becoming too broad.

Including the political element in the definition of the offence does, however, create other difficulties as well. That the political element is a contextual element is not a problem in itself, as international crimes frequently include contextual elements within their definitional requirements.[135] However, it may have dangerous consequences to express this element as a *motive* rather than as a *purpose* specific to the terrorist act. As Roach explains

> The political or religious motive requirement will require the police to investigate the politics or religion of suspected terrorists and this may blur the line between policing and security intelligence. It may also encourage the targeting of people as suspects primarily on the basis that they share political and religious beliefs with other suspects or terrorists and this can infringe freedom of expression and religion as well as discriminate on the basis of political and religious belief.[136]

---

135 So, for example, the category of crimes against humanity includes persecutions "on political, racial or religious grounds": Article 6(c) of the *Charter of the Military Tribunal at Nuremburg*, 8 August 1945, 82 U.N.T.S. 284 and Article 7(1)(h) of the *Rome Statute*, above note 66, while genocide is defined as "[a range of criminal] acts committed with intent to destroy, in whole or in part, a national, ethnical, racial or religious group": Article 2, *Convention for the Prevention and Punishment of the Crime of Genocide* of 9 December 1948, 78 U.N.T.S. 277 and Article 6, *Rome Statute, ibid.*, thereby requiring a specific genocidal intent.

136 Roach, above note 124 at 138.

Furthermore, the practical difficulty created by the fact that the prosecution must prove the accused's political or religious motive beyond a reasonable doubt can lead to two further problems. First, the accused's motivation may be impossible to obtain without a confession,[137] which provides an incentive towards unscrupulous handling of suspects to coerce them into confessing.[138] Second, even assuming that the prosecution can establish what the accused's motivation was, the question of whether a particular motivation should be categorized as political, rather than perhaps anti-social or nihilistic, can entail a vexed and lengthy theoretical discussion not ideally suited to the courtroom.[139]

Instead of referring to motive, the *Ottawa Principles* have included the political element in the crime of terrorism by requiring that the purpose behind the offence be to intimidate a population or compel a government or political or international organization to do, or abstain from doing, an act. This purpose is more clearly and restrictively defined than political motivation can be, and expresses the intention behind the specific offence in question, rather than the overall belief system of the perpetrator. In this way, the formulation helps to focus on the act, rather than the actor, which brings the definition at the domestic level in line with the proposal for international law as far as possible.

The final reason for retaining the political element of the crime at the domestic level is that such a definition best expresses what terrorism really is.[140] Together with attacks on civilians, the political element expresses the central understanding of terrorism that it is aimed at a social group or an entire society, and it will strike victims effectively at random within that society. This is possibly one of the most frightening aspects of terrorism: from the victim's perspective, terrorism picks its targets in an unpredictable and arbitrary manner, rendering every mem-

---

137 *Ibid.* at 139.

138 The United Nations Office on Drugs and Crime warns against a requirement of political or religious motive on the basis that "unless a suspected offender confesses, such a subjective motivation could be impossible to prove": UN, Office on Drugs and Crime, *Legislative Guide to the Universal Anti-Terrorism Conventions and Protocol* (New York: United Nations, 2003) at para. 84.

139 Roach, above note 124 at 139.

140 See the discussion in section B(2), above in this chapter, as well as the survey of definitions in S. Tiefenbrun, "A Semiotic Approach to a Legal Definition of Terrorism" (2003) 9 ILSA Journal of International and Comparative Law 357.

ber of society vulnerable. It is impossible for any individual to remove herself from the target group.

D. CONCLUSION

The *Ottawa Principles* insist that states should use the existing criminal law to respond to terrorism wherever possible.[141] This is partly to prevent extra-legal responses such as assassinations, detentions, and military invasions not justified under the UN *Charter*, and partly an attempt to restrain the growth of a separate anti-terrorism regime as far as possible. But the preference for criminal law should not be read as a claim that the criminal law is in itself an adequate response to terrorism.

There are two main dangers in relying exclusively on the criminal law. First, it is inadequate in a practical sense, because it does little to limit the damage created by terrorist incidents when they do occur.[142] The criminal law therefore needs to be supplemented by a range of measures from disciplines such as public health, science, and technology.[143] Second, criminal law, with its strong moral overtones, may encourage a polarized response to terrorism, which suggests that criminal law must be supplemented by an ongoing endeavour to investigate and address the causes of terrorism. Exclusive reference to the criminal law can lead to an unreflective assumption that the state is good and its opponents bad—the very assumption that the definition of terrorism in the international sphere seeks to avoid. The moral high ground claimed by states in the war on terrorism possibly fuels the worst state excesses against suspects because it dehumanizes the opponent and even suggests that he is outside the law altogether.[144]

---

141 See principle 2.1.

142 K. Roach, *September 11: Consequences for Canada* (Montreal: McGill-Queen's University Press, 2003) at 168–74, applying a matrix for preventing and reducing injury from traffic accidents to terrorism. The "Haddon matrix" is set out in W. Haddon, "A Logical Framework for Categorising Highway Safety Phenomena and Activity" (1972) 12 Journal of Trauma 193.

143 See also McWhinney, above note 61 at 180.

144 David Rose cites a sermon by Lieutenant-General William G. Boykin, Deputy Undersecretary of Defense for Intelligence, in which he claimed that terrorists were "demonic," coming from "the principalities of darkness." See David Rose, *Guantanamo: America's War on Human Rights* (London: Faber and Faber, 2004) at 138.

But there are two sides to a polarized debate, and we should resist both of them. It does not help if we unthinkingly swap the moral categories and assume that the state is bad, or that it only ever fabricates a terrorist threat. While it is true that terrorist incidents occur infrequently, and that the threat of terrorism is misused for political purposes, it would be irresponsible of states not to attempt to prevent and contain a phenomenon with a demonstrated capacity to devastate individuals and destabilize society.

A secure anti-terrorism regime, which is both constrained and supported by a determinate legal definition, is the best mechanism to enable law to address the diverging concerns of the anti-terrorism debate.

De-militarizing Counter-Terrorism: Anti-terrorism, Human Rights, and the Use of Force

Craig Forcese[1]

A. INTRODUCTION

One phrase more than any other captures the reaction of the inter-national community to the catastrophic events of September 11, 2001: the "war on terror." A reasonably apt descriptor of the initial post-9/11 assault against the Taliban and Al-Qaeda in Afghanistan, the term has since morphed into a cultural meme, one used to describe the defining preoccupation of international (and much of domestic) relations in the early twenty-first century.

But the war on terror is more than metaphor. The struggle against the tactics of violence employed by Islamic jihadists has been militar-ized since 9/11 to an extent unknown prior to that day. Certainly, states have responded to terrorism by using military force in the past. The Israeli experience is a case in point, as are U.S. air or missile strikes in the wake of the 1986 Berlin discotheque terrorist bombing, the 1993 assassination attempt against former President George H.W. Bush, and the 1998 embassy attacks in East Africa. Compared to the contemporary

1   The author would like to thank the Social Sciences and Humanities and Research Council and the Law Foundation of Ontario for their support of his research. He would also like to thank Koren Marriott, third-year LL.B. student at the University of Ottawa, for her helpful suggestions on this paper.

period, however, these uses of force were modest in both scale and duration. None involved "regime change" or (the rather unique Israeli experience aside) the invasion or occupation of territories. Post-9/11, the latter two strategies have had pride of place among the tactics deployed by the United States and its allies in places like Afghanistan and Iraq.

These military responses—justified sometimes under the rubric of the "Bush Doctrine"—have challenged established legal doctrines on the use of force by states. A rethinking of the rules of international law, the Bush Doctrine is best known for advancing a theory of "pre-emptive" use of military force against feared—as opposed to actual—adversaries. By the time of this writing, the implications of that strategy continue to play out in the streets of Iraq.

Perhaps even more radically, on the evening of September 11, 2001, President George W. Bush announced that, in reacting to the calamities of that day, the United States would "make no distinction between the terrorists who committed the attacks and those who harbor them."[2] This conflation of terrorists with their host states constitutes a reassessment of existing rules of state responsibility and their application in the law of self-defence. If it is a correct assertion of current international law, it significantly lowers the barriers on use of military force in responding to both terrorists and their host states, greatly expanding the *jus ad bellum*.

Critically, anti-terrorism via military force changes the legal playing field. The international criminal law response to terrorism (the preferred approach to the terrorism of the twentieth century) does not pre-empt other, regular rules of international law, such as in the human rights area. However, once military force is employed with sufficient intensity, this regular law gives way to the *jus in bello*, the law applicable to armed conflict. In this *lex specialis*, the absolute bar in international human rights law on taking human life is tempered by International Humanitarian Law (IHL). IHL accepts that combatants in an armed conflict may be targeted with lethal force and even permits collateral casualties among civilians in some circumstances. In sum, life is much cheaper where anti-terrorism is viewed as a military issue and not one of criminal law.

This may be the inevitable reality in the regions where the militarization of anti-terrorism has been most marked: Afghanistan and Iraq.

---

2   George W. Bush, Presidential Address to the Nation on the Terrorist Attacks, 37 Weekly Comp. Pres. Doc. 1301 (11 September 2001).

President Bush announced, however, that the "war" "will not end until every terrorist group of global reach has been found, stopped, and defeated."[3] He placed no geographic limit on this objective. Since this assertion, military force has been deployed occasionally in other states, far removed from the Afghan and Iraqi theatres. In these far-flung places in which a shadowy, potentially inter-generational struggle against Islamist violence is contested, the "war on terror" meme could translate into the dominance of international laws privileging state violence.

These are the concerns that animated the drafting of the use of force portion of the *Ottawa Principles on Anti-terrorism and Human Rights*.[4] I was the original drafter of this section of the *Ottawa Principles*, and a keen proponent of their development. Therefore, I bear disproportionate responsibility for their content. However, with this opportunity for second sober thought, it is time for an unsparing critique of the instrument. The principles assert a conventional, even conservative, view on the *jus ad bellum* use of force rules, denying that anti-terrorism may be invoked to contort or extend established justifications for the deployment of military force. They also urge that *jus in bello* does not entirely exclude human rights principles from its ambit. In each of these respects, the objectives of the principles are commendable. The principles do, however, shy away from truly pronouncing on a series of difficult and controversial issues in the areas of *jus ad bellum* and *jus in bello*. On militarization, the principles may add little to the progressive realization of an anti-terrorism strategy that is sensitive to human rights.

The chapter that follows explores the assertions made in this introduction, and explains the rationale for the language employed in the *Ottawa Principles*. It does so in three parts. The first part briefly examines terrorism as a predominantly criminal act. The second examines how anti-terrorism has affected the *jus ad bellum*. The final part highlights the impact the militarization of anti-terrorism has had on the *jus in bello*, the law guiding state military conduct. The chapter concludes by suggesting several areas that future iterations of the principles might usefully probe more deeply.

---

3   George W. Bush, President's Address Before a Joint Session of the Congress on the United States Response to the Terrorist Attacks of September 11, 37 Weekly Comp. Pres. Doc. 1348 (20 September 2001).

4   See the principles found in Part One of this book [*Ottawa Principles*].

B. TERRORISM AS CRIME

Principle 3.1 of the *Ottawa Principles* asserts a core premise underlying several portions of that document: "As a general rule, terrorist acts are criminal acts subject to applicable domestic, transnational and/or international criminal law enforcement measures." As this passage implies, an act of terrorism is, above all else, a crime. International law is rich with anti-terrorism treaties. At present, there are thirteen multilateral anti-terrorist treaties.[5] All but two of the thirteen multilateral conventions create international criminal offences and oblige state parties to the treaties to criminalize these acts in their domestic penal codes.

However, the great failing of this anti-terrorism criminal law is the absence of an anti-terrorism treaty that defines "terrorism" comprehensively. The thirteen existing treaties are piecemeal in their coverage, barring certain forms of violence and support of terrorism, without denouncing terrorism writ large. This patchwork coverage is no accident.

---

5   *Convention on Offences and Certain Other Acts Committed on Board Aircraft*, 14 September 1963, 704 U.N.T.S. 219 [*Tokyo Convention*]; *Convention for the Suppression of Unlawful Seizure of Aircraft*, 16 December 1970, 860 U.N.T.S. 105 [*Hague Convention*]; *Convention for the Suppression of Unlawful Acts against the Safety of Civil Aviation*, 23 September 1971, 974 U.N.T.S. 178 [*Montreal Convention*]; *Protocol on the Suppression of Unlawful Acts of Violence at Airports Serving International Civil Aviation, supplementary to the Convention for the Suppression of Unlawful Acts Against the Safety of Civil Aviation*, 24 February 1988, 1589 U.N.T.S. 474 [*Montreal Convention Protocol*]; *Convention for the Suppression of Unlawful Acts Against the Safety of Maritime Navigation*, 10 March 1988, 1678 U.N.T.S. 221 [*Maritime Convention*], as amended by 2005 Protocol; *Protocol for the Suppression of Unlawful Acts against the Safety of Fixed Platforms Located on the Continental Shelf*, 10 March 1988, 1678 U.N.T.S. 304 [*Maritime Convention Protocol*], as amended by 2005 Protocol; *Convention on the Prevention and Punishment of Crimes against Internationally Protected Persons, including Diplomatic Agents*, 14 December 1973, 1035 U.N.T.S. 167, 13 I.L.M. 41 [*Protected Person Convention*]; *International Convention for the Suppression of Acts of Nuclear Terrorism*, 7 July 2007, UN Doc. A/59/766 [*Nuclear Terrorism Convention, 2005*]; *International Convention against the Taking of Hostages*, 17 December 1979, 1316 U.N.T.S. 205 [*Hostage Convention*]; *International Convention for the Suppression of Terrorist Bombings*, 12 January 1998, 37 I.L.M. 251 [*Bombing Convention*]; *Convention on the Physical Protection of Nuclear Material*, 3 March 1980, 1456 U.N.T.S. 124 [*Nuclear Material Convention*]; *Convention on the Marking of Plastic Explosives for the Purpose of Detection*, 1 March 1991, 30 I.L.M. 726 [*Plastic Explosives Convention*]; *International Convention for the Suppression of the Financing of Terrorism*, 10 January 2000, 39 I.L.M. 270, 2002 Can. T.S. 9 [*Financing Convention*].

Terrorism is a tactic, monopolized by no single political, religious, or ideological cause. As such, it has attracted derision or support according to the sympathies generated by the cause of those who practise or espouse it. Acts of politically motivated violence undertaken as part of anti-colonial struggles for self-determination, for instance, have been evaluated very differently from similar acts of violence committed in different contexts. It has, therefore, been notoriously difficult to arrive at a shared definition of "terrorism" that is satisfactory to the world community. The adage "one person's terrorist is another person's freedom fighter" is more than cliché; it also appears to be an empirical reality.

The problem of definition persists, even post-9/11. As one scholar has noted, "terrorism is a loaded term that is often used as a politically convenient label by which to deny legitimacy to an adversary while claiming it for oneself."[6] In these circumstances, not everyone is prepared to condemn unequivocally every act of political violence, although the world community now emphatically denounces terrorism in principle. Key international legal instruments like UN *Security Council Resolution 1373* abet this apparent contradiction. Resolution 1373 requires that "terrorist acts are established as serious criminal offences in domestic laws and regulations and that the punishment duly reflects the seriousness of such terrorist acts."[7] It fails, however, to define terrorism or terrorist acts. While the Security Council has provided more definitional guidance since 2001,[8] terrorism remains, in large measure, something adjudged by the eye of the beholder.

---

6   Tal Becker, *Terrorism and the State: Rethinking the Rules of State Responsibility* (Oxford: Hart, 2006) at 85 [Becker].

7   SC Res. 1373, UN SCOR, 2001, S/RES/1373 at para. 2(e) [Resolution 1373].

8   In *Security Council Resolution 1566*, SC Res. 1566, UN SCOR, 2004, S/RES/1566., the Security Council partially corrected its definitional omission by offering up its understanding of terrorism:

> criminal acts, including against civilians, committed with the intent to cause death or serious bodily injury, or taking of hostages, with the purpose to provoke a state of terror in the general public or in a group of persons or particular persons, intimidate a population or compel a government or an international organization to do or to abstain from doing any act, which constitute offences within the scope of and as defined in the international conventions and protocols relating to terrorism [Resolution 1566].

By 2007, it was unclear whether this failure of definition would be cured in the proposed comprehensive international anti-terrorism treaty. It was also uncertain whether the historical focus on criminal law responses to terrorism had been superseded by states' propensity to respond to terrorism with military force, a matter to which this chapter now turns.

C. *JUS AD BELLUM* AND TERRORISM

Terrorism may be a crime, but it is an unusual crime. It is one that is overtly political, and often intended to destabilize the political, social, and/or economic status quo. As such, terrorism is a crime with potential geopolitical consequences. Acts of terrorism have precipitated armed conflict in the past. Two events on either side of the twentieth century underscore this point. In 1914, Archduke Franz Ferdinand of the Austro-Hungarian Empire was assassinated by a terrorist in Sarajevo, ultimately causing the First World War. On September 11, 2001, Islamist terrorists brought down the twin towers of the World Trade Center in New York and damaged the Pentagon in Washington, prompting the subsequent invasion of Afghanistan and creating a climate for the Bush administration's "war on terror" and its doctrine of "pre-emptive self-defence."

Nevertheless, despite terrorism's overtly political dimension, principle 3.1 of the *Ottawa Principles* rejects the view that terrorism is a special event, with its own *jus ad bellum*. It asserts that "[t]he international use of armed force by states in response to terrorist acts is only permissible in accordance with international law regulating such use of force." This view requires amplification because it leaves open questions as to the nature and scope of those international rules regulating force.

1) Core Principles on Use of Force

In classic terms, *jus ad bellum* is the body of rules determining when recourse to military force is permissible. Article 2(4) of the UN *Charter* lies at the core of the modern law on use of force. It specifies that "[a]ll Members shall refrain in their international relations from the threat or use of force against the territorial integrity or political independence of any state, or in any other manner inconsistent with the Purposes of the

United Nations."⁹ The rule also exists as part of customary international law¹⁰ and is widely regarded as a *jus cogens* norm.¹¹

There is occasional debate as to the reach of Article 2(4) and its customary equivalent. Certain jurists urge, for example, that use of force that does not impair the "territorial integrity or political independence of any state" is not prohibited.¹² In practice, however, it is difficult to imagine any non-consensual use of force that does not in some way impair a state's territorial integrity or political independence. The very act of using the force is an assault on a state's sovereign control over affairs within its borders.¹³

---

9 *Charter of the United Nations*, 26 June 1945, 59 Stat. 1031, T.S. 993, 3 Bevans 1153 (entered into force 24 October 1945) [UN *Charter*].

10 *Nicaragua v. United States of America*, [1986] I.C.J. Rep. 14 at para. 187*ff* [*Nicaragua*].

11 A *jus cogens* (or peremptory) norm "is a norm accepted and recognized by the international community of States as a whole as a norm from which no derogation is permitted and which can be modified only by a subsequent norm of general international law having the same character," *Vienna Convention on the Law of Treaties*, 23 May 1969, 1155 U.N.T.S. 331, Article 53. See discussion in Helen Duffy, *The 'War on Terror' and the Framework of International Law* (Cambridge: Cambridge University Press, 2005) at 147.

12 The narrow interpretation of Article 2(4) is sometimes raised to justify "humanitarian intervention". See discussion, for example, in Celeste Poltak, "Humanitarian Intervention: A Contemporary Interpretation of the *Charter of the United Nations*" (2002) 60 U.T. Fac. L. Rev. 1.

13 Support for this strict reading of the prohibition on the use of force is found in the UN General Assembly's influential *Declaration on Principles of International Law concerning Friendly Relations and Co-operation among States*, GA Res. 2625 (XXV), UN GAOR, 25th Sess., Supp. No. 28, UN Doc. A/5217 (1970) at 121. The declaration denounces "armed intervention and all other forms of interference or attempted threats against the personality of the State or against its political, economic and cultural elements, are in violation of international law." While not binding in its own right, the declaration "elaborates the major principles of international law in the UN Charter, particularly on use of force, dispute settlement, nonintervention in domestic affairs, self-determination, duties of cooperation and observance of obligations, and 'sovereign equality.' [I]t has become the international lawyer's favorite example of an authoritative UN resolution." Oscar Schachter, "United Nations Law" (1994) 88 A.J.I.L. 1. Referring in part to this declaration, Schachter has strongly urged a strict reading of the Article 2(4) prohibition. See Oscar Schachter, "The Right of States to Use Armed Force" (1984) 82 Mich. L. Rev. 1620. This approach is consistent with the International Court of Justice's recent ruling in *Case Concerning Armed Activities on the Territory of the Congo (Democratic Republic of the Congo v.*

There are limited exceptions to the prohibition found in Article 2(4). For example, use of force by one state within the territory of another is permissible where the territorial state gives its permission.[14] Beyond this situation, however, military force directed by one state against another state or its territory is permissible in international law in only two circumstances, both expressly anticipated by the UN *Charter*. First, pursuant to Chapter VII of the UN *Charter*, the UN Security Council may legitimize and authorize this use of force. Second, an inherent right to self-defence is also recognized by the UN *Charter*.

This area of international law is clearly oriented towards interstate conflicts. As such, it does not include emphatic, special rules for terrorism cases; that is, rules on force used in response to violence directed at states or their populations by non-state actors. The general principles on the use of military force employed by one state against the territory of another state therefore remain intact. This view is encapsulated in principle 3.2.1 of the *Ottawa Principles*: "[a]nti-terrorism goals do not change the international rules on the use of force by one state against another or within the territory of another: use of military force must comply with the requirements of the United Nations *Charter* in being either explicitly authorized by the UN Security Council or a *bona fide* exercise of collective or individual self-defence within the constraints of Article 51." Both of these sources of authorization are reviewed below.

Uganda), I.C.J. General List No. 116 (19 December 2005) at para. 163*ff* [*Case Concerning Armed Activities*]: The Court further affirms that acts which breach the principle of non-intervention "will also, if they directly or indirectly involve the use of force, constitute a breach of the principle of non-use of force in international relations."

14 See discussion in Davis Brown, "Use of Force against Terrorism after September 11th: State Responsibility, Self-Defense and Other Responses" (2003) 11 Cardozo J. Int'l & Comp. L. 1 at 30. NATO's current deployment in Afghanistan, for example, is done with the agreement of the Afghan government. See, for example, *Afghanistan Compact*, London Conference on Afghanistan (2006) at 3, online: www.fco.gov. uk/servlet/Front?pagename=OpenMarket/Xcelerate/ShowPage&c=Page&cid=113 2599286730 (in which Afghanistan and the "international community" agreed to the presence of the "NATO-led International Security Assistance Force (ISAF) and the US-led Operation Enduring Freedom (OEF)"); *Declaration by the North Atlantic Treaty Organisation and the Islamic Republic of Afghanistan* (6 September 2006), online: www.nato.int/docu/basictxt/b060906e.htm ("Afghanistan recognizes that at present it is unable to fully meet its own security needs and highly appreciates NATO's contribution to providing security and stability in Afghanistan").

a) UN Security Council Practice

The UN Security Council has responsibility in the United Nations system for declaring a threat or breach of international peace and security and authorizing responses to such breaches, including the possible use of force. The council has repeatedly recognized that terrorism may constitute a threat to international peace and security. In Resolution 1526, for instance, the council condemned "in the strongest terms all acts of terrorism irrespective of their motivation, whenever and by whomsoever committed, as one of the most serious threats to peace and security."[15] In practice, the council has issued resolutions requiring states to enhance anti-terrorism cooperation[16] and respond to terrorism with criminal law measures,[17] and has sanctioned specific terrorist or terrorist supporting entities[18] or states that harbour or support terrorists.[19] It has not expressly authorized, however, use of force in response to a terrorist act, even those of 9/11.[20]

---

15 · See, for example, *Security Council Resolution 1526*, SC Res. 1526, UN SCOR, 2004, S/RES/1526: labelling terrorism a threat to international peace and security [Resolution 1526].

16 See, for example, Resolution 1373, above note 7.

17 *Ibid.*, requiring the criminalization of terrorism and particularly terrorist financing.

18 See, for example, *Security Council Resolution 1267*, SC Res. 1267, UN SCOR, 1999, S/RES/1267 against the Taliban.

19 See, for example, *Security Council Resolution 1054*, SC Res. 1054, UN SCOR, 1996, S/RES/1054: sanctions against Sudan for failing to extradite alleged terrorists; *Security Council Resolution 748*, SC Res. 748, UN SCOR, 1992, S/RES/748: sanctions against Libya in relation to the Lockerbie bombings.

20 That said, there is literature suggesting that the language in Resolution 1373, above note 7, reaffirming "the need to combat by all means, in accordance with the *Charter of the United Nations*, threats to international peace and security caused by terrorist acts," and calling upon all states to "cooperate . . . to prevent and suppress terrorist attacks and take action against perpetrators of such acts" constitutes authorization to use force against Al-Qaeda, even if the language used is different from past instances where the council has clearly authorized force. See, for example, discussion in Sean D. Murphy, "Terrorism and the Concept of 'Armed Attack' in Article 51 of the U.N. Charter" (2002) 43 Harv. Int'l L.J. 41 at 44; Michael Byers, "Terrorism, the Use of Force and International Law after 11 September" (2002) 51 I.C.L.Q. 401 at 401–2; Jordan Paust, "Use of Armed Force against Terrorists in Iraq, Afghanistan and Beyond" (2002) 35 Cornell Int'l L.J. 533 at 545.

b) Use of Force in Self-Defence

As a consequence, military action in response to terrorism has usually been justified, where legal justifications are in fact offered up, as self-defence. Article 51 of the UN *Charter* preserves "the inherent right of individual or collective self-defence if an armed attack occurs against a Member of the United Nations, until the Security Council has taken measures necessary to maintain international peace and security." As the invocation of an "inherent right" suggests, the self-defence concept exists also as part of customary international law.[21] The precise relationship between the customary norm and Article 51 is a point of some debate. Certainly, in all cases the act of self-defence must be both proportional and necessary.[22] More contentious is the question of imminence; that is, whether the defending state must actually have suffered the blow of an "armed attack" before responding. The issues of "armed attack," proportionality, necessity, and imminence are discussed in turn below.

i)   Terrorism As an Armed Attack

a.   Armed Attack and Non-State Actors

While Article 51 of the UN *Charter* is silent on this point, an armed attack was once commonly associated with purely state conduct. Thus, in conventional understandings of international law, an act of terrorism *per se* would not be an armed attack justifying Article 51 self-defence. In some measure, this may reflect scale differences: pre-9/11 terrorism caused limited injury, as compared to the typical assault by a state military in an armed conflict. Still, even a minor state military assault would likely be considered an armed attack for self-defence purposes.[23] What generally distinguishes terrorism from an armed attack justifying self-defence, therefore, is not necessarily the scope of the violent act, but

---

21   See *Nicaragua*, above note 10. For a discussion of Article 51 and the persistence of a parallel customary source of the right to self-defence, see Leo Van Den Hole, "Anticipatory Self-Defence Under International Law" (2003) 19 Am. U. Int'l L. Rev. 69.

22   *Nicaragua, ibid.* at para. 176. See also *Case Concerning Oil Platforms (Islamic Republic of Iran v. United States of America)*, I.C.J. General List No. 90 (6 November 2003) at para. 76 [*Oil Platforms Case*].

23   *Oil Platforms Case, ibid.*: for instance, the United States characterized occasional exchanges of missile and gunfire with U.S. forces and the mining of sea lanes, in which American and international shipping travelled over multiple years, allegedly by Iran, as acts of violence constituting an "armed attack."

rather the identity of its perpetrator: terrorism is generally conceived as an act undertaken by non-state actors, while an armed attack is a violent act mounted by a state. Pearl Harbour in 1941, for instance, would constitute an armed attack within the meaning of Article 51. The Madrid bombing of 2004 was an act of terrorism, but certainly not an armed attack. In fact, the International Court of Justice has concluded that acts of violence directed against a state by non-state actors from *within* that state or from a territory occupied by that state cannot generally trigger a right to self-defence under Article 51.[24]

Nevertheless, it was widely accepted even before 9/11 that an act of terrorism may certainly give rise to Article 51 self-defence if the nexus between the terrorist act and another state is sufficiently close. The peril lies in determining the scope of that connection. This issue was engaged by the 1986 response of the United States to the bombing of a Berlin discotheque, which killed two U.S. military personnel and a Turkish civilian. That bombing was greeted enthusiastically by Libya's leader, Colonel Gaddafi. The United States claimed, in addition, conclusive evidence of direct Libyan involvement in the bombing. The net result was air strikes against Libya. In justifying this course of action, the U.S. ambassador to the United Nations argued that the United States acted in self-defence, against Libya's "continued policy of terrorist threats and the use of force, in violation of . . . Article 2(4) of the Charter."[25] This justification failed to sway most of the world's states, a fact illustrated most starkly by a condemnation of the U.S. attacks in a Resolution of the UN General Assembly.[26] A disapproval of the U.S. actions was also proposed in the Security Council, but vetoed by the United States, the United Kingdom, and France.[27] One scholar suggests that the poor reception given to the U.S. self-defence claim stemmed, in part, from a

---

24 *Legal Consequences of the Construction of a Wall in the Occupied Palestinian Territory*, I.C.J. General List No. 131 (9 July 2004), (2004) 43 I.L.M. 1009 at para. 139 [*Israeli Wall Case*].

25 Letter from the Acting Permanent Representative of the United States of America, to the United Nations, Addressed to the President of the Security Council, 14 April 1986, UN SCOR, 41st Sess., UN Doc. S/17990.

26 *Declaration of the Assembly of Heads of State and Government of the Organization of African Unity on aerial and naval military attack against the Socialist Peoples' Libyan Arab Jamahiriya by the Present United States Administration in April 1986*, GA Res. 41/38, UN GAOR, 41st Sess., Supp. No. 53, UN Doc. A/41/53 (1986) 34.

27 UN SCOR, 41st Sess., 2682d mtg., UN Doc. S/PV.2682 (1986) 43.

"perceived lack of evidence tying the West Berlin discotheque bombing and other terrorist activities to Libya."[28]

More recently, U.S. armed responses in Sudan and Afghanistan to the 1998 U.S. embassy bombings in Kenya and Tanzania—again explained by the United States as an act of self-defence[29] —provoked less sweeping criticism. Those states critical of the United States tended to hang their objections on the proportionality and necessity of the U.S. armed response (to the extent they raised legal issues at all).[30] While far from enthusiastic, these more muted reactions in the 1990s to force deployed in response to terrorism suggest an international warming to the notion that the actions of non-state actors could constitute an "armed attack" under Article 51.

In fact, the text of Article 51 does not close the door to violence by non-state actors against a state being viewed as an armed attack,[31] an assessment affirmed by the world reaction to 9/11. Given the shocking scale of the terrorist strike on September 11, 2001, and the fact that it was so evidently directed against the territory of the United States, the international community quickly embraced the view that self-defence against the terrorist perpetrators was warranted, despite their non-state nature. The UN Security Council, for instance, invoked the right to self-defence in condemning the terrorist acts.[32] For its part, the North Atlan-

---

28 Jack M. Beard, "America's New War on Terror: The Case for Self-Defense under International Law" (2002) 25 Harv. J.L. & Pub. Pol'y 559 at 564–65.

29 See Letter to Congressional Leaders Reporting on Military Action against Terrorist Sites in Afghanistan and Sudan, 34 Weekly Comp. Pres. Doc. 1650 (20 August 1998), reported in Sean D. Murphy, "Contemporary Practice of the United States Relating to International Law" (1999) 93 A.J.I.L. 161 at 162–63.

30 See discussion in Becker, above note 6 at 203–4.

31 See, for example, Major Darren C. Huskisson, "The Air Bridge Denial Program and the Shootdown of Civil Aircraft under International Law" (2005) 56 A.F. L. Rev. 109 at 144: "The concept of an armed attack was left deliberately open to the interpretation of Member States and UN Organs, and the wording is broad enough to include the acts of non-State actors as 'armed attacks.'" See also Carsten Stahn, "'Nicaragua is Dead, Long Live Nicaragua'—The Right to Self-defence under Article 51" in Christian Walter et al., Terrorism as a Challenge for National and International Law: Security versus Liberty (Berlin: Springer, 2004) at 830 [Walter et al., eds., Terrorism as a Challenge].

32 Security Council Resolution 1368, SC Res. 1368, UN SCOR, 2001, S/RES/1368 [Resolution 1368]; Resolution 1373, above note 7.

tic Treaty Organisation (NATO) declared that the 9/11 acts satisfied the requirements of an armed attack under Article 5 of the *North Atlantic Treaty*, triggering a collective response from NATO.[33] The Organization of American States arrived at a similar conclusion, invoking Article 3 of the *Inter-American Treaty of Reciprocal Assistance*.[34]

These responses, and the widespread reaction of individual states offering assistance to the United States, support the conclusion that Al-Qaeda's terrorist act on 9/11 reached the level of an armed attack. Under these circumstances, a common (although not unanimous) view is that the armed response to Al-Qaeda was compliant with international law (as it is now understood), so long as other elements of self-defence law, such as proportionality and necessity, were observed.[35]

b.   Armed Attack and State Responsibility

The *Ottawa Principles* suggest, however, a potentially more conservative view. They specify that a state nexus — the attribution of responsibility to a state — is required before force can be deployed against a state or its territory. Thus, principle 3.2.2 specifies that "[s]elf-defence justifies the use of force against a state or within the territory of that state only in response to an act of terrorism that: . . . is properly attributable, as a matter of international law, to the state against which the act of self-defence is directed." Put another way, self-defence is only available where the attack bears the imprimatur, at some level, of another state.

A key question is what sort of connection must exist between the state and the terrorist attacker. By simply requiring that this connection comply with international law, the principles are unhelpfully opaque. It seems plausible, however, that the answer to this question of connection may depend on *who* the target of the exercise of self-defence is. For instance, is the use of force restricted to the assets of the non-state ac-

---

33   NATO, Press Release, "Invocation of Article 5 Confirmed" (2 October 2001).

34   See OAS, Twenty-fourth Meeting of Consultation of Ministers of Foreign Affairs, Terrorist Threat to the Americas, 21 September 2001, OAS Doc. RC.24/Res.1/01. Article 3 reads: "an armed attack by any State against an American State shall be considered as an attack against all the American States and, consequently, each one of the said Contracting Parties undertakes to assist in meeting the attack in the exercise of the inherent right of individual or collective self-defense recognized by Article 51 of the *Charter of the United Nations*."

35   See, for example, Paust, above note 20.

tor on the territory of another state, or does it amount to an assault on the institutions of that state itself?

USE OF FORCE AGAINST STATES

With respect to the latter possibility, international law is reasonably clear. The International Court of Justice (ICJ) has concluded that the existence of a right to self-defence against a state *per se* depends on an armed attack being attributable to the state against whom the act of self-defence is directed.[36] The question of attribution was addressed most clearly by the ICJ in the *Nicaragua* case. There, the Court concluded that "an armed attack must be understood as including not merely action by regular armed forces across an international border, but also the *sending by or on behalf of a State* of armed bands, groups, irregulars or mercenaries, which carry out acts of armed force against another State of such gravity as to amount to (inter alia) an actual armed attack conducted by regular forces, or its substantial involvement therein."[37] The ICJ expressly ruled out "assistance to rebels in the form of the provision of weapons or logistical or other support" as an armed attack.[38]

More recently, in the *Case Concerning Armed Activities*, the International Court of Justice invoked Article 3 (g) of General Assembly Resolution 3314 as the standard for attribution of private violent action to the state. Proposing a definition of aggression, this resolution specifies in Article 3(g) that aggression includes "[t]he sending by or on behalf of a State of armed bands, groups, irregulars or mercenaries, which carry out acts of armed force against another State of such gravity as to amount to the acts listed above, or its substantial involvement therein."[39] The "acts

---

36 *Oil Platforms Case*, above note 22 at para. 55:

> [I]n order to establish that it was legally justified in attacking the Iranian platforms in exercise of the right of individual self-defence, the United States has to show that attacks had been made upon it for which Iran was responsible; and that those attacks were of such a nature as to be qualified as "armed attacks" within the meaning of that expression in Article 51 of the United Nations Charter, and as understood in customary law on the use of force.

37 *Nicaragua*, above note 10 at para. 195.

38 *Ibid.*

39 *Definition of Aggression*, GA Res. 3314 (XXIX), UN GAOR, 29th Sess., Supp. No. 31 (1974). See the *Case Concerning Armed Activities*, above note 13 at para. 146, holding that there was

listed above" include attacks on the territory of a state, its occupation or annexation, bombardment or use of weapons against the territory of a state, attacks on a state's armed forces, and a blockade of a state's ports or coast.

In the 2007 *Crime of Genocide Case*, the Court underscored that attribution rules require "effective control" over a non-state actor by the state: "where an organ of the State gave the instructions or provided the direction pursuant to which the perpetrators of the wrongful act acted or where it exercised effective control over the action during which the wrong was committed."[40]

Read together, therefore, the ICJ appears to take the view that an armed attack may be attributable to a state where a state dispatches the attackers, or gives sufficient direction to, or is in a role of sufficient agency with the non-state perpetrator of the assault. This emphasis on

---

> no satisfactory proof of the involvement in these attacks [on Uganda], direct or indirect, of the Government of the DRC. The attacks did not emanate from armed bands or irregulars sent by the DRC or on behalf of the DRC, within the sense of Article 3(g) of General Assembly resolution 3314 (XXIX) on the definition of aggression, adopted on 14 December 1974.

40 *Application of the Convention on the Prevention and Punishment of the Crime of Genocide (Bosnia and Herzegovina v. Serbia and Montenegro)*, I.C.J. General List No. 91 (26 February 2007) at para. 406 [*Crime of Genocide Case*]. The International Criminal Tribunal for the Former Yugoslavia (ICTY) has proposed a caveat to these rules where the group in question is a military or paramilitary group:

> In order to attribute the acts of a military or paramilitary group to a State, it must be proved that the State wields overall control over the group, not only by equipping and financing the group, but also by coordinating or helping in the general planning of its military activity. Only then can the State be held internationally accountable for any misconduct of the group. However, it is not necessary that, in addition, the State should also issue, either to the head or to members of the group, instructions for the commission of specific acts contrary to international law.

Prosecutor v. Dusko Tadic, decision of the UN International Tribunal for the Prosecution of Persons Responsible for Serious Violations of International Humanitarian Law Committed in the Territory of Former Yugoslavia since 1991, reprinted in (1999) 38 I.L.M. 1518 at para. 131. This position was rejected by the International Court of Justice in the *Crime of Genocide Case* at para. 404*ff*, which reaffirmed its position in *Nicaragua*, above note 10. It remains to be seen which approach other bodies, such as the International Criminal Court, will adopt.

agency is reflected in the current understanding of the law of state re-sponsibility. The International Law Commission's (ILC) draft articles on that topic contain a number of circumstances in which internationally wrongful acts may be attributed to a state. Thus, "[t]he conduct of a person or group of persons shall be considered an act of a State under international law if the person or group of persons is in fact acting on the instructions of, or under the direction or control of, that State in carrying out the conduct."[41] Similarly, attribution may exist where the state acknowledges and adopts the conduct of these non-state actors as its own.[42]

Where attribution rules are not satisfied, it seems unlikely force in self-defence may be directed at targets beyond the terrorist group itself. This was a commonly held view prior to 9/11,[43] and continues to be held by at least some scholars today:

> Harboring terrorists, providing formal or effective amnesty for terrorists
> . . . , otherwise tolerating, acquiescing, encouraging, or inciting terror-
> ists within one's borders, or providing certain other forms of assistance
> to terrorists can implicate state responsibility and justify various pol-
> itical, diplomatic, economic, and juridic sanctions in response . . . . Yet,
> unless the state is organizing, fomenting, directing, or otherwise dir-
> ectly participating in armed attacks by non-state terrorists, the use of
> military force against the state, as opposed to only the non-state terror-
> ists, would be impermissible.[44]

This doctrine sits poorly, however, with state practice post-9/11. If any regime deserved removal, it was the Taliban. Nevertheless, the Taliban has never been tied to the crimes of Al-Qaeda. Al-Qaeda found shelter in the Taliban's Afghanistan, but they were not the Taliban's proxies. As one scholar summarizes, "the United States and its allies never express-ly advanced the argument that the Taliban regime directed or controlled the actions of Al-Qaeda or adopted Al-Qaeda conduct as its own."[45] Yet

---

41   International Law Commission, *Draft Articles on Responsibility of States for Inter-*
      nationally Wrongful Acts, UN GAOR, 56th Sess., Supp. No. 10, UN Doc. A/56/10,
      (2001) 42, Article 8 [ILC draft].

42   *Ibid.*, Article 11.

43   See discussion in Becker, above note 6 at 163*ff.*

44   Paust, above note 20 at 540.

45   Becker, above note 6 at 217.

the international community moved swiftly in supporting massive military action against Afghanistan, culminating in the displacement of the Taliban from government. This fact has led some scholars to conclude that attribution rules for states harbouring terrorists have shifted and that the threshold is (or at least should) be much lower than the agency-type requirements invoked in earlier cases.[46]

There is an evident risk to lowering that threshold for violence directed at states that, while perhaps not complying with their anti-terrorism obligations to not harbour terrorists, do not themselves direct or participate in a terrorist act. More aggressive rules on attribution may serve as a wedge in the unravelling of vital constraints on the exercise of state violence, legalizing wider inter-state wars in response to terrorism. While the threat of catastrophic terrorism looms large in the twenty-first century, the lessons of the twentieth century should not be lost: the body count attributable to wars between states dwarfs that associated with violence by non-state actors. For exactly these reasons, the *Ottawa Principles* should probably be read as rejecting the use of force directed against a state's own institutions, absent the sort of link of agency-style attribution between that state and the actions of the non-state actor.

USE OF FORCE AGAINST TERRORISTS WITHIN A STATE

It is less clear whether the *Ottawa Principles* impose as demanding a test of attribution when force is directed against terrorist assets on the territory of a state, but not at the state's own institutions. Certainly, the principles must be read as rejecting the notion that an act of sufficient violence by a non-state actor—one amounting to an armed attack—automatically entitles the use of force on the territories where these terrorists are located. If it did, then countries around the world in which Al-Qaeda cells are domiciled might appropriately be the *situs* for select missile strikes. In other words, mere presence of terrorists should not suffice to render a state's territories vulnerable to attack.

However, it may also be unsustainable, given the scale of violence non-state actors are evidently now able and prepared to wield, to limit self-defence against terrorist bases and camps to circumstances where the link between the terrorists and states rises to an agency-like level. An obvious intermediate position is to regard the connection between

---

46 See, for example, *ibid.*: a strong defender of this view; Stahn, above note 31 at 838*ff*.

state and terrorist as robust enough to justify military force against (strictly) the latter where the state fails manifestly to fulfill its anti-terrorism obligations.

In this last respect, Security Council resolutions have compounded state treaty obligations to cooperate in anti-terrorism efforts. Pre-9/11 resolutions, such as Resolution 1269, "called upon" states to "cooperate with each other, particularly through bilateral and multilateral agreements and arrangements, to prevent and suppress terrorist acts, protect their nationals and other persons against terrorist attacks and bring to justice the perpetrators of such acts," and to "exchange information in accordance with international and domestic law, and cooperate on administrative and judicial matters in order to prevent the commission of terrorist acts."[47] After 9/11, this hortatory language gave way to binding legal dictates. Thus, in Resolution 1373, the council decided that all states must, *inter alia*, "[t]ake the necessary steps to prevent the commission of terrorist acts, including by provision of early warning to other States by exchange of information . . . [and] [a]fford one another the greatest measure of assistance in connection with criminal investigations or criminal proceedings relating to the financing or support of terrorist acts, including assistance in obtaining evidence in their possession necessary for the proceedings."[48]

The resolution also includes language barring state-sponsorship or harbouring of terrorists. States are to

> [r]efrain from providing any form of support, active or passive, to entities or persons involved in terrorist acts, including by suppressing recruitment of members of terrorist groups and eliminating the supply of weapons to terrorists; . . . [d]eny safe haven to those who finance, plan, support, or commit terrorist acts, or provide safe havens; . . . [p]revent those who finance, plan, facilitate or commit terrorist acts from using their respective territories for those purposes against other States or their citizens; [and p]revent the movement of terrorists or terrorist groups by effective border controls and controls on issuance of identity papers and travel documents, and through measures for preventing

---

47 *Security Council Resolution 1269*, SC Res. 1269, UN SCOR, 1999, S/RES/1269 at para. 4 [Resolution 1269].

48 Resolution 1373, above note 7 at para. 2.

counterfeiting, forgery or fraudulent use of identity papers and travel documents.[49]

In the specific area of nuclear terrorism, *Security Council Resolution 1540* also imposes important prevention and cooperation obligations. Under this instrument, for instance, states "shall refrain from providing any form of support to non-State actors that attempt to develop, acquire, manufacture, possess, transport, transfer or use nuclear, chemical or biological weapons and their means of delivery."[50]

Where a state consciously declines to suppress terrorist activity in a manner prescribed by these instruments, it is arguably complicit in attacks mounted by terrorist groups. Where it is incapable of suppressing these activities, that lack of capacity does injury to another state. In either instance, it may be that a sufficient connection exists between the state's actions or omissions and those of the terrorists who perform an armed attack to justify self-defence directed at terrorist assets themselves. The state's territorial integrity and its sovereignty interest are obviously impaired, even by an attack limited to terrorist assets. The degree of that impairment is, however, reduced by the terrorist-specific targeting, as compared to a use of military force directed against state institutions. To repeat, a higher level of attribution would be required before use of force in self-defence could be directed at state institutions themselves.

This bifurcated approach may not be attractive to many observers, not least because it does permit force against state territories on the basis of a much diminished attribution test. Nevertheless, it seems a more desirable approach than the Afghanistan situation, in which force was deployed against both state and terrorist without any apparent consideration of regular attribution rules. The *Ottawa Principles* might usefully have pronounced more clearly on this important issue.

ii) Terrorism, Proportionality, and Necessity

Even if the armed attack (with sufficient attribution) requirement for the use of force in self-defence is met, any armed response must still be proportional and necessary. The *Ottawa Principles* do not provide

---

49 *Ibid.*

50 *Security Council Resolution 1540*, SC Res. 1540, UN SCOR, 2004, S/RES/1540 at para. 1 [Resolution 1540].

unique insight on this issue, instead simply providing in principle 3.2.3 that "[t]he force used in self-defence must be necessary and proportionate in accordance with international law." There is a need, therefore, to cast greater light on these criteria.

a. Proportionality

Proportionality is usually taken to mean the use of force in self-defence that is no greater than is required to halt and repel the armed attack;[51] that is, proportional to the military objective of countering the threat. For some jurists, however, proportionality is assessed with reference to the armed attack defended against.[52] These are two very different measuring sticks. Gauged against the first standard, an armed response may become disproportionate if the consequences of the response, such as "collateral" civilian casualties, outstrip those of the initial armed attack. Assessed against the second standard, armed force is proportional if properly directed at forestalling the recurrence of attack. Proportional-

---

51   See discussion in Malcolm Shaw, *International Law*, 5th ed. (Cambridge: Cambridge University Press, 2003) at 1031, 88n; Duffy, above note 11 at 162:

> the proportionately test should be applied *vis-à-vis* the requirements of averting the threat, as opposed to in respect of the scale of that threat or of any prior armed attack. Arguments as to numbers of persons killed in the original attack outweighing numbers killed in subsequent counter-measures are of political relevance only.

52   For a discussion of the different methods of computing proportionality, applied in the specific case of terrorism, see Robert J. Beck & Anthony Clark Arend, "'Don't Tread On Us': International Law and Forcible State Responses to Terrorism" (1994) 12 Wis. Int'l L.J. 153 at 206. Notably, in several cases, the ICJ has apparently contrasted the harm caused by armed attack against the scale of the act of self-defence in assessing the existence of proportionality. In *Nicaragua*, above note 10 at para. 176, the ICJ described proportionality as "proportional to the armed attack," without further discussing this point. In the *Oil Platforms Case*, above note 22 at paras. 76–77, the Court concluded that the destruction by the United States of two Iranian oil platforms, "two Iranian frigates and a number of other naval vessels and aircraft was not proportionate to the mining, by an unidentified agency, of a single United States warship, which was severely damaged but not sunk, and without loss of life." See also *Case Concerning Armed Activities*, above note 13 at para. 147: noting, without deciding, "that the taking of airports and towns many hundreds of kilometres from Uganda's border would not seem proportionate to the series of transborder attacks it claimed had given rise to the right of self-defence."

ity persists even if the exercise of force for this purpose produces civilian causalities in excess of those injured in the initial armed attack.

These two disparate measuring sticks might have been usefully discussed in the *Ottawa Principles.* Measured against the first standard,
for instance, the armed response to 9/11 in Afghanistan (Operation Enduring Freedom) may become disproportionate if the consequences of
the response (in civilian casualties, for instance) outstrip those of the
terrorist attack.[53] Assessed against the second standard, armed force is
proportional if properly directed at dislodging the terrorists (and their
Taliban hosts, assuming that attribution rules are met), and thus forestalling the recurrence of the 9/11 attack. This is true, presumably, even
if the exercise of force produced civilian causalities in excess of those
injured in the initial armed attack.

If this second approach is the proper measure of proportionality in
the law of self-defence, then the legitimacy of these "collateral" consequences of resorting to force in self-defence fall to be measured simply by international humanitarian law, the *jus in bello* that applies when
armed conflicts are in progress.[54] Modest support for this view may be
extracted from the ICJ's reasoning in *Legality of the Threat or Use of Nuclear Weapons.* There, the Court did not preclude the above-noted first
view of proportionality. However, it did suggest that at the very least "a
use of force that is proportionate under the law of self-defence, must, in
order to be lawful, also meet the requirements of the law applicable in

---

53 9/11 produced roughly 3,000 casualties and substantial property damage. Estimates
    of civilian deaths in the initial conflict in Afghanistan are unofficial and suspect
    because of methodological difficulties, but in some studies estimates range from
    just over 1,000 (during the period 7 October 2001 to 1 January 2002) to 3,600 (7
    October 2001 to March 2003). See Carl Conetta, Project on Defense Alternatives,
    Briefing Report #11, *Operation Enduring Freedom: Why a Higher Rate of Civilian
    Bombing Casualties* (18 January 2002) and the database maintained by Professor
    Marc Herold online: http://pubpages.unh.edu/~mwherold/AfghanDailyCount.pdf.

54 For a discussion on this issue, see Judith Gardam, "Proportionality and Force in
    International Law" (1993) 87 A.J.I.L. 391. For instance, *Protocol Additional to the
    Geneva Conventions of 12 August 1949, and relating to the Protection of Victims of
    International Armed Conflicts (Protocol I),* 8 June 1977, 1125 U.N.T.S. 3, Article 51(5)(b)
    [Protocol I] provides, *inter alia,* that "[a]n attack which may be expected to cause
    incidental loss of civilian life, injury to civilians, damage to civilian objects, or a
    combination thereof, which would be excessive in relation to the concrete and
    direct military advantage anticipated."

armed conflict which comprise in particular the principles and rules of humanitarian law."[55]

b. Necessity

The "necessity" element of self-defence raises its own complexities. Force used in self-defence must be necessary to respond to (and presumably repel) the armed attack. In the *Nicaragua* case, there was no necessity because the use of force in alleged self-defence took place months after the putative armed attack had been repulsed.[56] In the *Oil Platforms Case* the ICJ viewed force as unnecessary where, on the facts, it was directed at targets considered targets of opportunity by the alleged defending state.[57]

Military responses to terrorism in particular have often precipitated debate among states and scholars as to whether they are truly necessary to repel the attack or, rather, simply retaliatory. International criticism describing military action as reprisals rather than self-defence was acute, for instance, after the 1986 U.S. bombing of Libya, and in reaction to at least some Israeli responses to terrorism.[58] Again, 9/11 constitutes an exception. After 9/11, Operation Enduring Freedom in Afghanistan was specifically justified by the United States as a response to an "ongoing threat" and "designed to prevent and deter further attacks on the United States."[59] Such justification was probably plausible, given the uncertainty of the period.

iii) Terrorism and Pre-emptive Self-Defence

A final, pressing issue in contemporary discussion of self-defence is whether the attack that prompts the act of self-defence must be im-

---

55 *Legality of the Threats or Use of Nuclear Weapons*, Advisory Opinion, [1996] I.C.J. Rep. 226 at para. 42.

56 *Nicaragua*, above note 10 at para. 237.

57 *Oil Platforms Case*, above note 22 at para. 76.

58 See discussion in William V. O'Brien, "Reprisals, Deterrence and Self-Defense in Counterterror Operations" (1990) 30 Va. J. Int'l L. 421.

59 Letter from Ambassador John Negroponte, Permanent Representative of the U.S.A. to the UN in New York, to the President of the Security Council, 7 October 2001, UN Doc. S/2001/946. See also the British statement, noting that the war in Afghanistan was designed to "avert the continuing threat of attacks." Letter from Stewart Eldon, Chargé d'Affaires, UK Mission to the UN in New York, to the President of the Security Council, 7 October 2001, UN Doc. S/2001/947.

mediate, or whether a more attenuated threat may justify an armed response. The issue of imminence was addressed most famously in *The Caroline* incident, a dispute between the United States and Great Britain involving an American ship. The British believed that *The Caroline* would be employed by American sympathizers to support the 1837 uprising in Upper Canada. The ship was destroyed by British forces, on the American side of the border. In a series of letters between the U.S. and U.K. governments, designed to resolve the resulting diplomatic dispute, the U.S. Secretary of State expressed the view, apparently shared by both sides, that self-defence was only warranted where the "necessity of that self-defence is instant, overwhelming, and leaving no choice of means, and no moment for deliberation."[60]

Article 51 of the UN *Charter* captures this sense of imminence. It specifies that the right to self-defence arises if "an armed attack occurs." Whether self-defence where the threat is less immediate is permitted in customary international law is a point of contention among international lawyers. It seems plausible (although far from universally accepted) that customary international law allows anticipatory self-defence: "where there is convincing evidence not merely of threats and potential danger but of *an attack being actually mounted*, then an armed attack may be said to have begun to occur, though it has not passed the frontier."[61] The *Ottawa Principles* capture a reasonably expansive understanding of the rule in principle 3.2.2: "Self-defence justifies the use of force against a state or within the territory of that state only in response to an act of terrorism that . . . has already occurred or is *evidently about to occur*" [emphasis added].

More contentious is whether anticipatory self-defence should be expanded to incorporate a concept of pre-emptive self-defence, sometimes referred to as the "Bush Doctrine." In the 2002 National Security Strategy of the United States, the Bush administration asserted the right to act in self-defence against nascent threats, and not just those that were imminent in the conventional or even anticipatory sense.[62]

---

60 Letter from Daniel Webster to Lord Ashburton (6 August 1842), online: www.yale.edu/lawweb/avalon/diplomacy/britain/br-1842d.htm.

61 C.H.M. Waldock, "The Regulation of the Use of Force by Individual States in International Law" (1952), 81 Hague Recueil des Cours 455 at 498 [emphasis added].

62 White House, U.S., *National Security Strategy of the United States of America* (September 2002) at 15, online: www.whitehouse.gov/nsc/nss.html. See also, reporting on President G.W. Bush's commencement address at West Point, Mike Allen &

Pre-emptive self-defence has not been readily welcomed by the international community. Not least among its shortcomings is its particular vulnerability to abuse. It is an easily-contorted justification for military force, capable of accommodating most acts of aggression. Unlike conventional self-defence, where the existence of an attack is readily and objectively ascertained, pre-emptive self-defence is built on intelligence and inferences of prospective enemy intentions, a notoriously difficult basis for decision-making. Ready acceptance of the doctrine would gravely undermine the historic restraints on use of force imposed by the UN *Charter*, with serious consequences for human rights and global stability. The UN Secretary-General's High-Level Panel addressed this issue persuasively in its 2004 report: "in a world full of perceived potential threats, the risk to the global order and the norm of non-intervention on which it continues to be based is simply too great for the legality of unilateral preventive action, as distinct from collectively endorsed action, to be accepted. Allowing one to so act is to allow all."[63]

The *Ottawa Principles* line up four-square behind this position, urging in principle 3.2.5 that "'[p]re-emptive self-defence'—the use of force in response to a feared security threat that is not evidently about to occur—is a violation of international law and is not a legitimate basis for use of military force."

D. *JUS IN BELLO* AND TERRORISM

The discussion to this point underscores the conceptual difficulties in fitting the proverbial round-peg of state-centric use of force law into the square-hole of militarized responses to acts of mass murder by non-state actors. The use of force in the Afghan theatre soon after 9/11 required an expansion of the concept of armed attack to include those by non-state actors. This expansion, in the Afghan case, ignored the problem of attribution and left unclear several uncertainties about proportionality. Nevertheless, the Afghan war had all the trappings of a state-state con-

---

Karen DeYoung, "Bush: US Will Strike Out First Against Enemies; In West Point Speech, President Lays out Broader US Policy" *Washington Post* (2 June 2002) A01.

63   General Assembly, High-level Panel on Threats, Challenges and Change, *A More Secure World: Our Shared Responsibility*, UN GAOR, 59th Sess., Agenda Item 55, UN Doc. A/59/565 (2004) 8.

flict, up to and including the occupation of the country and the removal of the enemy government. Had the international community reverted to a more traditional, law enforcement approach to anti-terrorism following the displacement of the Taliban, the "war on terror" would have undoubtedly bent international law, but in a way satisfactory to many observers.

The focus on armed force has persisted and in theatres far removed from either Afghanistan or Iraq. Press reports suggest, for instance, that the United States has a global targeted killing program, employing missiles from drone aircraft.[64] It would appear that some missile strikes have been made without the permission of the country in which the target was located.

News reports from 2006[65] suggest that approximately nineteen strikes have been made, with at least nine conducted outside Iraq. The actual locations of these attacks are closely guarded secrets. However, news reports suggest that missile strikes have occurred in Pakistan. In January 2006, for instance, a missile strike failed to kill Al-Qaeda second-in-command Ayman Zawahiri in Pakistan. It did, however, reportedly kill as many as eighteen civilians.[66] In 2005, Haitham Yemeni and Abu Hamza Rabia, both Al-Qaeda leaders, were killed in Pakistan. Several others, including possible civilians, were injured or killed in these attacks.[67] Earlier, in 2002, another Al-Qaeda leader, Qaed Sinan Harithi, and several associates were killed by a U.S. military drone aircraft in a missile strike in Yemen.

There was no credible claim that any of these missile strikes were precipitated by an imminent attack. They were, therefore, unlikely candidates for a self-defence justification. As one scholar observes, discussing the Yemeni case

> Can the mere fact that six men in the car were at a place vulnerable to attack and, eventually, planning future strikes against the U.S. justify their killing on the basis of anticipatory self-defence? Obviously not,

---

64 See, in particular, Josh Meyer, "CIA Expands Use of Drones in Terror War" *Los Angeles Times* (29 January 2006) A1.

65 *Ibid.*

66 Amnesty International, *Pakistan: US involvement in civilian deaths*, ASA 33/002/2006 (31 January 2006).

67 See Amnesty International, *Pakistan: Human rights ignored in the "war on terror,"* ASA 33/036/2006 (29 September 2006).

even if this was the only way to eliminate them effectively. The threat lacked specificity. The mere likelihood of future attacks does not even meet the broadest understanding of "imminence."[68]

Difficulty reconciling militarized anti-terrorism with conventional *jus ad bellum* rules is not, however, the only challenge to international law presented by this post-9/11 strategy. Perhaps even more troubling are the implications the war meme has for the *jus in bello*—the rules of law that should apply once a conflict is engaged.

Notably, a legitimate justification for use of force, measured by the *jus ad bellum*, does not authorize any and all forms of violence. The actual manner in which violence is used must comply with the *jus in bello*. The exact content of this *jus in bello* is usually assumed to be international humanitarian law (IHL). This fact is captured by the *Ottawa Principles* in principle 3.3.1: "In any situation of armed conflict, applicable customary and treaty-based international humanitarian law is to be observed by the combatants." However, not every use of violence by a state will trigger the application of IHL as a *lex specialis*.

1) International Humanitarian Law and Armed Conflict

IHL applies in circumstances of armed conflict, a term that is not precisely defined.[69] The existence of an armed conflict does not require a declared war.[70] Instead, armed conflict usually requires the use of military force reaching a certain threshold of intensity. The International Committee of the Red Cross sets this threshold very low: "Any difference arising between two States and leading to the intervention of armed forces is an armed conflict . . . even if one of the Parties denies the existence

---

68 Stahn, above note 31 at 875.

69 See Emanuel Gross, *The Struggle of Democracy against Terrorism* (Charlottesville: University of Virginia Press, 2006) at 53.

70 Christopher Greenwood, "Scope of the Application of Humanitarian Law" in Dieter Fleck, ed., *The Handbook of Law in Armed Conflicts* (Oxford: Oxford University Press, 1995) at 41 [*Handbook*]. The Geneva Conventions provide, in Common Article 2, that the conventions "shall apply to all cases of declared war *or of any other armed conflict* which may arise between two or more of the High Contracting Parties, *even if the state of war is not recognized by one of them*" [emphasis added]. A declared war may trigger the application of the Geneva Conventions, as will a situation of military occupation, even when not met by armed resistance: *Handbook* at 41.

of a state of war. It makes no difference how long the conflict lasts, or how much slaughter takes place."[71] In *Prosecutor v. Dusko Tadic*, the International Criminal Tribunal for the Former Yugoslavia concluded that

> an armed conflict exists whenever there is a resort to armed force between States or protracted armed violence between governmental authorities and organized armed groups or between such groups within a State. International humanitarian law applies from the initiation of such armed conflicts and extends beyond the cessation of hostilities until a general conclusion of peace is reached; or, in the case of internal conflicts, a peaceful settlement is achieved. Until that moment, international humanitarian law continues to apply in the whole territory of the warring States or, in the case of internal conflicts, the whole territory under the control of a party, whether or not actual combat takes place there.[72]

State practice, however, may suggest a more demanding threshold than mere "resort" to armed force. It is sometimes urged, for instance, that to constitute an armed conflict, the use of military force must involve more than isolated incidents; that is, more than occasional border skirmishes or naval exchanges.[73] On the other hand, even an isolated incident of great magnitude can cross the threshold of armed conflict. Further, a situation of armed conflict can exist even if only one side has used armed force.[74] As one jurist has noted, "if Iraq had used a special

---

71　International Committee of the Red Cross, "Commentary to Article 3, *Convention (I) for the Amelioration of the Condition of the Wounded and Sick in Armed Forces in the Field. Geneva, 12 August 1949*," online: www.icrc.org/ihl.nsf/COM/365-570005?OpenDocument.

72　*Prosecutor v. Dusko Tadic*, Decision of the UN International Tribunal for the Prosecution of Persons Responsible for Serious Violations of International Humanitarian Law Committed in the Territory of Former Yugoslavia since 1991, IT-94-1-AR72, reprinted in (1996) 35 I.L.M. 32 at para. 70 [*Tadic*].

73　Greenwood, above note 70 at 42; UK Ministry of Defence, *The Manual of the Law of Armed Conflict* (Oxford: Oxford University Press, 2004) at 29. See also discussion in Duffy, above note 11 at 219, n. 11 and the views canvassed in International Committee of the Red Cross, "International Humanitarian Law and Other Legal Regimes: Interplay in Situations of Violence," *XXVIIth Round Table on Current Problems of International Humanitarian Law* (2003) at 3, online: http://web.iihl.org/iihl/Album/Interplay_other_regimes_Nov_2003.pdf [Red Cross *Round Table*].

74　Silja Vöeky, "The Fight against Terrorism and the Rules of the Law of Warfare" in Walter *et al.*, eds., *Terrorism as a Challenge*, above note 31 at 903*ff.*

weapon and killed 3000 people in New York, one would not doubt that such an attack constituted an armed conflict, although it might have been isolated and sporadic."[75]

2) International Humanitarian Law as *Lex Specialis*

In a situation of armed conflict, IHL is without question the *lex specialis*. It now seems clear, however, that the mere existence of an armed conflict should not be viewed as automatically displacing other rules of international law, including human rights law.[76] International humanitarian law does not totally replace the more comprehensive rights guarantees of international human rights law. In its Advisory Opinion of 8 July 1996 on the *Legality of the Threat or Use of Nuclear Weapons*,[77] the International Court of Justice rejected arguments that the covenant was "directed to the protection of human rights in peacetime, and that all questions relating to unlawful loss of life in hostilities were governed by the law applicable in armed conflict." It held instead that "the protection of the *International Covenant on Civil and Political Rights* does not cease in times of war, except by operation of Article 4 of the Covenant whereby certain provisions may be derogated from in a time of national emergency." Under Article 4, key human rights are not derogable, even in the most extreme circumstances such as public emergencies that threaten the life of the nation.[78]

The ICJ amplified this position in *Legal Consequences of the Construction of a Wall in the Occupied Palestinian Territory*:

> the Court considers that the protection offered by human rights conventions does not cease in case of armed conflict, save through the effect of provisions for derogation of the kind to be found in Article 4 of the *International Covenant on Civil and Political Rights*. As regards the relationship between international humanitarian law and human rights law, there are thus three possible situations: some rights may be exclusively matters of international humanitarian law; others may be exclu-

---

75   *Ibid.* at 931.

76   Greenwood, above note 70 at 40.

77   Above note 55 at para. 24.

78   *International Covenant on Civil and Political Rights*, 19 December 1966, 999 U.N.T.S. 171, Can. T.S. 1976 No. 47, 6 I.L.M. 368 [*ICCPR*].

sively matters of human rights law; yet others may be matters of both these branches of international law.[79]

In both cases, the ICJ interpreted human rights and international humanitarian law harmoniously. It suggested that the *ICCPR*'s "right not arbitrarily to be deprived of one's life applies also in hostilities. The test of what is an arbitrary deprivation of life, however, then falls to be determined by the applicable *lex specialis*, namely, the law applicable in armed conflict which is designed to regulate the conduct of hostilities."[80] Under this reasoning, a violation of international humanitarian law may also constitute a violation of the *ICCPR*.

It is exactly this notion that the *Ottawa Principles* seek to convey in principle 3.3.2: "In a situation of armed conflict, international human rights obligations remain in force except where recognized international derogation provisions such as Article 4 of the *ICCPR* apply. International human rights and international humanitarian law are complimentary and mutually reinforcing, and should be interpreted in light of each other."

The principles might have further amplified this view by noting that these human rights obligations extend even outside of the territory of the state itself, to govern the conduct of its armed forces and agents. Article 2 of the *ICCPR* obliges state parties "to respect and to ensure to all individuals within its territory and subject to its jurisdiction" the human rights found in the treaty. Jurisdiction and territory are separate concepts in international law. For instance, states may exercise prescriptive jurisdiction in relation to their nationals irrespective of their location.[81]

Whether the *ICCPR* has extraterritorial reach has sparked animated discussion among states and commentators.[82] Logically, however, a state

---

79 Above note 24 at para. 106.

80 Above note 55 at para. 25, cited in *Israeli Wall Case*, *ibid.* at para. 105.

81 See *Restatement (Third) of the Foreign Relations Law of the United States* (St. Paul, MN: American Law Institute, 1987) § 402: Generally, "a state has jurisdiction to prescribe law with respect to . . . the activities, interests, status, or relations of its nationals outside as well as within its territory."

82 See, for example, Commission on Human Rights, *Report of the UN Special Rapporteur on the Situation of Detainees at Guantánamo Bay*, UN ESCOR, 62d Sess., UN Doc. E/CN.4/2006/120 (2006): concluding that the *ICCPR* has extraterritorial reach; discussion in Michael J. Dennis, "ICJ Advisory Opinion on Construction of a Wall in the Occupied Palestinian Territory: Application of Human Rights Treaties

cannot authorize its personnel to commit human rights abuses abroad that a state cannot inflict within its own territory. This view has prevailed in several international institutions. For instance, the UN Human Rights Committee has read Article 2 of the *ICCPR* as including a significant extraterritorial reach. In its recent *General Comment 31*, it noted that "a State party must respect and ensure the rights laid down in the Covenant to anyone within *the power or effective control* of that State Party, *even if not situated within the territory* of the State Party." [83] Rights are guaranteed "to those *within the power or effective control of the forces of a State Party acting outside its territory*, regardless of the circumstances in which such power or effective control was obtained, such as forces constituting a national contingent of a State Party assigned to an international peace-keeping or peace-enforcement operation."[84] The UN Human Rights Committee has applied this approach in its caselaw, for example, by allowing a complaint against Uruguay brought by an individual kidnapped in Argentina by the Uruguayan security forces.[85] In its review of state compliance reports, the committee has also raised *ICCPR* compliance concerns in relation to a state's armed forces stationed abroad.[86]

Extraterritorially in Times of Armed Conflict and Military Occupation" (2005) 99 A.J.I.L. 119: rejecting the notion that the International Covenant has extraterritorial reach and canvassing opinion on this matter.

83   UN Commission on Human Rights, *General Comment 31*, UN GAOR, 59th Sess., Supp. No. 40, UN Doc. A/59/40 (2004) Vol. 1 at 175, 177 [emphasis added]: noting that Article 2(1)'s reference to jurisdiction and territory "does not imply that the State party concerned cannot be held accountable for the violations of rights under the Covenant which its agents commit upon the territory of another State, whether with the acquiescence of the Government of that State or in opposition to it."

84   *Ibid.* [emphasis added].

85   *Lopez v. Uruguay*, U.N.H.R.C., Communication No. 52/1979, UN Doc. CCPR/C/13/D/52/1979 (1981), online: www.unhchr.ch/tbs/doc.nsf/o/e3c603a54b129ca0c1256ab2004d70b2?OpenDocument.

86   See, for example, UN Human Rights Committee, "Concluding Observations of the Human Rights Committee," UN CCPR, 72d Sess., UN Doc. CCPR/CO/72/NET (2001): relating to the "alleged involvement of members of the [Netherlands] State party's peacekeeping forces in the events surrounding the fall of Srebrenica, Bosnia, and Herzegovina, in July 1995." Online: www.unhchr.ch/tbs/doc.nsf/(Symbol)/CCPR.CO.72.NET.En?Opendocument.

Recently, the International Court of Justice referred to this committee jurisprudence in *Legal Consequences of the Construction of a Wall in the Occupied Palestinian Territory*. In that advisory opinion, it concluded that a state's covenant obligations had extraterritorial reach: "the Court considers that the International Covenant on Civil and Political Rights is applicable in respect of acts done by a State in the exercise of its jurisdiction outside its own territory."[87]

3) The Application of IHL to Extended Anti-terrorism

There is little doubt that IHL was the *lex specialis* for the 2001 conflict in Afghanistan. The scale of that war more than exceeded the intensity requirements triggering IHL. Most debate in relation to IHL in the Afghan theatre has centred on the specific application of several IHL concepts such as prisoner of war status and so-called "unlawful combatants." That discussion will not be repeated here. An area that has attracted less attention, however, concerns the legal environment in which the non-Afghan "war on terror" is conducted; that is, what is the applicable legal regime in theatres *other* than Afghanistan?

As noted, the "war on terror" is a metaphor, at least outside of Afghanistan (and post-invasion Iraq). It is not a declared conflict, with states arrayed on each side. None of the acts of terrorism post-9/11—most notably the bombings in Indonesia (Bali), Spain, and Britain—rise to the level of an "armed conflict" as this term is conventionally understood. Each is much more sensibly described as a crime, however horrific. There is no question, therefore, that state response to these acts might take the form of military force. For instance, a cruise missile attack against the apartment block in Madrid or London in which bomb-making materials are assembled by conspirators would be beyond the range of legitimate responses.

Nevertheless, military force has been deployed against terrorist targets outside of the Afghan and Iraq theatres. As noted above, the United States seemingly has a program of targeted killing, using drone aircraft, which is not confined by geographic boundaries. It seems implausible that the legitimacy of these acts is to be gauged against IHL standards. As already discussed, IHL constitutes the *lex specialis* only where it ap-

---

87   *Israeli Wall Case*, above note 24 at para. 111.

plies; that is, in situations of armed conflict. There was no armed conflict in Yemen or Pakistan at the time of the strikes, and it stretches all credulity to argue that the conflict in Afghanistan against, *inter alia*, Al-Qaeda created a geographically attenuated armed conflict existing everywhere Al-Qaeda might be found. If it did, then IHL, with its receptivity to the use of lethal force against combatants, would permit targeted missile strikes against housing developments across North America and Europe in which Al-Qaeda agents operate.

Nor could the missile strikes *themselves* constitute a use of military force triggering the IHL as *lex specialis*. Selective anti-terrorism strikes on terrorist targets within states that are not themselves targeted probably does not give rise to an armed conflict within the meaning of international humanitarian law. In deciding the application of IHL, the international criminal tribunals for the former Yugoslavia and Rwanda have suggested that acts of violence between states and non-state actors must be protracted for a situation of armed conflict to arise.[88]

Moreover, it is not clear that principles like Common Article 3 of the Geneva Conventions, which apply to truly non-international conflicts (that is, between states and non-state armed groups), extend also to actions against terrorists, acting clandestinely as part of a shadowy, geographically disparate network that do not act as dissident armed forces controlling territory.[89] Similar comments can be made about Additional Protocol II, dealing squarely with non-international armed conflicts.[90]

---

88 *Tadic*, above note 72 at para. 70; *Prosecutor v. Zejnil Delalic*, Judgment, IT-96-21 (16 November 1998) at para. 184 (ICTY, Trial Chamber): in internal conflicts, "in order to distinguish from cases of civil unrest or terrorist activities, the emphasis is on the protracted extent of the armed violence and the extent of organisation of the parties involved"; *Prosecutor v. Jean Paul Akayesu*, ICTR-96-4-T (2 September 1998) at para. 619 (ICTR, Trial Chamber) (citing *Tadic*).

89 International Committee of the Red Cross, Commentary to Article 3, above note 70, noting that Common Article 3 of the Geneva Conventions, is not intended to deal with banditry or unorganized and short-lived insurrections. Although clearly not meant as exhaustive, the criteria proposed by the Red Cross to distinguish the latter situation from a genuine non-international armed conflict tends to imagine insurgents formed as militaries and potentially controlling portions of state territory. See the debate on this issue in Red Cross *Round Table*, above note 73 at 5–8.

90 *Protocol Additional to the Geneva Conventions of 12 August 1949, and relating to the Protection of Victims of Non-International Armed Conflicts (Protocol II)*, 8 June 1977, 1125 U.N.T.S. 609, Article 1 [Protocol II]: applying to

The 2002 U.S. missile strike in Yemen and the more recent strikes in Pakistan against terrorist targets do not fit these criteria: they were incidental uses of armed force of insufficient intensity to truly constitute an armed conflict and were directed against a non-state actor who controlled no portion of the territory of the state and who, arguably, lacked the proto-military force qualities that IHL seems to anticipate. IHL was not, therefore, triggered to serve as the *lex specialis* applicable to the strikes.[91] In these circumstances, international human rights principles would apply in full form. One scholar has underscored this point:

> Where both states, the intervening state and the state exercising territorial jurisdiction over the terrorists, are bound by international human rights norms, there is no reason not to apply them to anti-terrorist raids. The obligation to respect the right to life is a peremptory norm of international law which may not even be suspended in times of a public emergency. Since limited strikes against terrorists on foreign territory in many cases will not meet the requirements of an — international or non-international — armed conflict, the wartime exceptions to the right to life are not applicable.[92]

4) Asymmetrical Law for Asymmetrical Warfare

This discussion begs the question of how missile strikes of the sort that occurred in Yemen and Pakistan are to be assessed. Human rights organizations[93] and the UN Special Rapporteur on extrajudicial execu-

---

> armed conflicts . . . which take place in the territory of a [state party] . . . between its armed forces and *dissident armed forces or other organized armed groups which, under responsible command, exercise such control over a part of its territory as to enable them to carry out sustained and concerted military operations* [emphasis added].

91   The analysis is different where targeted killings occur in a situation of armed conflict. The 2007 U.S. strike on Al-Qaeda targets during the armed conflict in Somalia likely fit the definition, as do (arguably) the Israeli targeted killings in the occupied territories. For a discussion of the IHL principles applicable to the latter, see *Public Committee against Torture in Israel v.. The Government of Israel* (2006), HCJ 769/02 (Israeli Supreme Court).

92   Rainer Grote, "Between Crime Prevention or Prosecution and the Laws of War" in Walter *et al.*, eds., *Terrorism as a Challenge*, above note 31 at 983.

93   See, for example, Amnesty International, *United States of America: An Extrajudicial Execution by the CIA?*, AMR 51/079/2005 (18 May 2005).

tions[94] have condemned these targeted attacks as illicit extrajudicial executions, inconsistent with human rights principles. There is support for this view. Article 6 of the *ICCPR* provides that "Every human being has the inherent right to life. This right shall be protected by law. No one shall be arbitrarily deprived of his life." This right is non-derogable, even in times of emergency that threaten the life of the nation.[95] For these reasons, the *Ottawa Principles* might have usefully underscored that death and injury caused by military force used outside of an armed conflict is always a human rights abuse.

Whether the principles could have addressed the related challenge of effective remedies is less clear. The international human rights system is notoriously bereft of effective remedies.[96] Moreover, while murder is a human rights violation, it is not an international crime *per se*. There is no treaty making murder an international crime, except when conducted on a scale sufficient to constitute a crime against humanity or genocide or in circumstances where it violates international humanitarian law, thereby amounting to a war crime.

On its face, the U.S. missile strikes might constitute terrorist bombings as prescribed by the 1997 *Bombing Convention*. Article 2(1) of that instrument requires state parties to criminalize

> unlawful and intentional delivery, placement, discharge or detonation of an explosive or other lethal device in, into or against a place of public use, a State or government facility, a public transportation system or an infrastructure facility:

---

94 Commission on Human Rights, *Civil and Political Rights including the Questions of Disappearances and Summary Executions: Extrajudicial, Summary or Arbitrary Executions, Report of the Special Rapporteur, Asma Jahangir, submitted pursuant to Commission on Human Rights resolution 2002/36*, UN ESCOR, 59th Sess., Item 11(6), UN Doc. E/CN.4/2003/3 (2003): noting that the "attack in Yemen constitutes a clear case of extrajudicial killing."

95 Above note 78 at Article 4.

96 For instance, the UN Human Rights Committee, established by the *ICCPR*, above note 78 at 52, and entitled to hear individual complaints in relation to states that have ratified that treaty's *Optional Protocol to the International Covenant on Civil and Political Rights*, GA Res. 2200A (XXI), UN GAOR, 21st Sess., Supp. No. 16, UN Doc. A/6316 (1966) 59, 999 U.N.T.S. 302, may be empowered to issue "views" in response to individual complaints. These views are, however, merely recommendations, and not at all analogous to binding court judgments.

(a) with the intent to cause death or serious bodily injury; or

(b) with the intent to cause extensive destruction of such a place, facility or system, where such destruction results in or is likely to result in major economic loss.[97]

Missile strikes against vehicles travelling on public roadways or against civilian housing blocks may fall within this definition.

However, the *Bombing Convention*, like several other anti-terrorism treaties, exempt (at least certain) state actors from their scope. Thus, in now standard language drawn from the *Bombing Convention*, the "activities of armed forces during an armed conflict, as those terms are understood under international humanitarian law, which are governed by that law, are not governed by this Convention."[98] This and several other conventions also single out state military forces for an even more emphatic, second exception: the convention does not apply to "military forces of a State in the exercise of their official duties, inasmuch as they are governed by other rules of international law."[99] "Military forces of a state" are defined in these treaties as "the armed forces of a State which are organized, trained and equipped under its internal law for the primary purpose of national defence or security and persons acting in support of those armed forces who are under their formal command, control and responsibility."[100]

A common critique is that because of these two exclusions, so-called "state terrorism" is unregulated by international law. To the extent this view suggests that states may use violence indiscriminately, it is an exaggerated claim, although it rightfully suggests that state violence is licit in international law to an extent non-state violence is not. The first exception—referring to armed forces and armed conflicts—is no *carte blanche* for state terrorism. It is instead a choice of law provision, confirming that international humanitarian law, rather than the terrorism conventions, govern armed forces in armed conflicts. IHL greatly restricts the nature and targets of armed forces violence in armed conflict situations. For instance, the Geneva Conventions and their protocols preclude armed forces in an armed conflict from targeting civilians and

97 *Bombing Convention*, above note 5.

98 *Ibid.*, Article 19.

99 *Ibid.*

100 *Ibid.*, Article 1.

emphatically outlaw acts of terror and terrorism.[101] Many of the acts of violence against civilians that comprise terrorism also constitute grave breaches of the Geneva Conventions,[102] attracting penal sanction.[103] There is no impunity, in other words, for attacks on civilians, even by armed forces in an armed conflict situation.

Of more concern for the Yemeni and Pakistani cases is the second exclusion for state military forces "inasmuch as they are governed by other rules of international law." This second exception is not confined to armed conflicts and is obviously intended to reach beyond the situations in which international humanitarian law applies. However, the actions of military forces operating outside of armed conflicts are only weakly "governed by other rules of international law." Making a point similar to that urged above, one scholar has noted:

> The other "rules of international law" that "govern" here would include a wide range of norms, from the prohibitions of genocide and crimes against humanity to the regional and international instruments of human rights law (as applicable), as well as the fundamental human rights norms protected under customary law. The results flowing from such norms vary widely . . . . [O]nly with torture does a clear conventional obli-

---

101 See, for example, *Geneva Convention (IV) Relative to the Protection of Civilian Persons in Times of War*, 12 August 1949, 75 U.N.T.S. 287 [*Geneva Convention IV*], Article 33: " all measures of intimidation or of terrorism are prohibited"; Protocol I, above note 54, Article 51: "acts or threats of violence the primary purpose of which is to spread terror among the civilian population are prohibited"; Protocol II, above note 90, Article 4: "the following acts . . . are and shall remain prohibited at any time and in any place whatsoever . . . (d) acts of terrorism." See also discussion at Becker, above note 6 at 104*ff.*

102 See, for example, *Geneva Convention IV, ibid.*, Article 147:

> Grave breaches to which the preceding Article relates shall be those involving any of the following acts, if committed against persons or property protected by the present Convention: wilful killing, torture or inhuman treatment, including biological experiments, wilfully causing great suffering or serious injury to body or health, unlawful deportation or transfer or unlawful confinement of a protected person, compelling a protected person to serve in the forces of a hostile Power, or wilfully depriving a protected person of the rights of fair and regular trial prescribed in the present Convention, taking of hostages and extensive destruction and appropriation of property, not justified by military necessity and carried out unlawfully and wantonly.

103 *Ibid.*, Article 148.

gation to extradite in the event of a failure to prosecute arise, while with genocide and crimes against humanity the view of the majority of commentators is that only a permissive universal jurisdiction exists at customary international law, without any "extradite or prosecute" obligation to serve as a bulwark against impunity . . . . As for human rights norms, their rules may "govern" a situation at a considerable level of generality, with potential enforcement often through only the sporadic and relatively weak supervision of international oversight bodies with their reporting requirements, special rapporteurs and sometimes visiting rights.[104]

Put another way, the exclusion of military forces from the *Bombing Convention* is more than simply a choice of law provision. It displaces scrutiny of violence perpetrated by the military to a body of international law potentially much less robust than the criminal law provisions in the anti-terrorism conventions.

The drafters of the *Ottawa Principles* chose not to engage the issue of state terrorism and the apparent asymmetry of equivalent acts of violence being a crime depending on who the perpetrators are. That may be the principles' most resounding shortcoming.

E. CONCLUSION

In an important critique of the George W. Bush administration's approach to the "war on terror," Mary Ellen O'Connell warns that the reference to war has not been employed as in past usages—such as the "war on poverty" or "war on drugs"—as metaphor. She accuses the Bush administration of using the expression literally, imagining a geographically unbounded conflict in which lethal military force may be deployed with impunity.[105]

The *Ottawa Principles* stand opposed to this militarization of anti-terrorism. But in many respects, their opposition is oblique. On matters such as the primacy of criminal law, and in underscoring that anti-terrorism does not change the fundamental rules on military force, the

---

104 Bruce Broomhall, "Terrorism on Trial: State Actors in an International Definition of Terrorism from a Human Rights Perspective" (2004) 36 Case W. Res. J. Int'l L. 421 at 435–36.

105 Mary Ellen O'Connell, "What Is War? When Is a War Not a War: The Myth of the Global War on Terror" (2005) 12 I.L.S.A. J. Int'l & Comp. L. 535.

principles make an important statement. However, in many instances, they restate international law without addressing its ambiguities. It is in those very ambiguities that the greatest danger to life, liberty, and security of the person lie. Thus, in the area of self-defence, the principles ignore uncertainty in the area of attribution of terrorist acts by non-state actors to states, and fail to grapple with whether attribution rules may vary depending on whether the target of self-defence is the state itself or merely the terrorists found on its territory, and thus leave the matter of proportionality ambiguous.

In relation to *jus in bello*, the principles underscore the importance of IHL without refining in detail its relationship to human rights in situations of armed conflict. They also fail to address the question of military force deployed outside situations of armed conflict and are silent on the question of military force as state terrorism.

Future iterations of the principles might usefully address each of these matters, especially if anti-terrorism strategies continue to disproportionately favour military response over criminal investigation and prosecution. The temptation for states with superior military power will be to employ the former over the latter, and to privilege rules of international law that support this strategy. However, militarized anti-terrorism amounts to fighting fire with fire. A *quid pro quo* of this sort may spark a series of regional conflagrations, with disastrous results for the protection of human rights.

Guarding Individual Rights in Cases Involving National Security

Lorne Waldman[1]

A. INTRODUCTION

In order to respond to perceived and actual threats to national security, states seek to implement protective measures. Although these measures may be viewed as the product of necessary vigilance, especially in the post-9/11 era, they may also have a severe impact on individual rights. Determining whether measures that are taken to protect national security are compatible with our democratic values is a difficult task. This problem arose well before the attacks on the twin towers. However, in the aftermath of 9/11, legislators felt compelled to expand the arsenal of powers available to the national security apparatus and, consequently, the issue of the impact of measures taken to protect national security on our democratic values has become even more pressing.

Among the powers that existed prior to, but were expanded after 9/11 was that of asserting confidentiality over information that was determined to put our national security or international relations in jeopardy if released. In Canada, the *Canada Evidence Act* was amended to allow the attorney general to overturn any determination by the Federal Court that information ought to be released after properly balancing the

1   The author wishes to acknowledge the contributions of Karin Baqri and Debbie Rachlis. Both provided invaluable assistance in the writing of this chapter.

need to protect the information with the public interest in disclosure.[2] Since 9/11 the assertion of confidentiality over sensitive evidence has become even more prevalent. Although this issue has arisen to a limited extent in the criminal context,[3] it is in the area of immigration law that government attempts to use secret information have been most common. While the Supreme Court has very recently declared one such attempt—that outlined by the security certificate provisions of the *Immigration and Refugee Protection Act (IRPA)*[4]—to be unconstitutional, it has not recommended a course of action for the legislature to adopt.[5]

However, the Supreme Court asserted that the extent to which procedural fairness is required is context-specific, and accepted that national security may often preclude full disclosure of information. In any event, it concluded that section 7 of the *Canadian Charter of Rights and Freedoms*[6] requires that "either the person must be given the necessary information, or a substantial substitute for that information must be found."[7] While certainly the next step, with respect to the impugned provisions, will involve the enactment of legislation by Parliament, the dilemma facing the legislature is determining the scope of procedural

---

2   *Canada Evidence Act*, R.S.C. 1985, c. C-5, s. 38.13.

3   See, for example, *Canada (Attorney General) v. Ribic*, [2002] F.C.J. No. 1835 (T.D.); *Ribic v. Canada (Attorney General)*, [2003] F.C.J. No. 1966 (F.C.), aff'd [2003] F.C.J. No. 1964 (C.A.); *Ribic v. Canada (Attorney General)*, [2003] F.C.J. No. 1965 (F.C.), aff'd [2003] F.C.J. No. 1964 (C.A.); *Canada (Attorney General) v. Ribic*, [2002] F.C.J. No. 1186 (T.D.); *Ribic v. Canada*, [2002] F.C.J. No. 384 (T.D.).

4   *Immigration and Refugee Protection Act*, S.C. 2001, c. 27 [*IRPA*]. The security certificate procedure is outlined in ss. 76–85 of the Act and allows for the detention and deportation of permanent residents, refugees, and foreign nationals on the grounds that they pose a threat to national security. Under the procedure, the person named in the security certificate issued by the minister of citizenship and immigration and the minister of public safety and emergency preparedness is not made aware of the precise allegations or evidence adduced against him. Further, neither he nor his counsel is given an opportunity to participate in the *in camera* hearings in which the minister's representatives present the Crown's case to a federal court judge. The security certificate regime is explained more fully in section C of this chapter.

5   *Charkaoui v. Canada (Citizenship and Immigration)*, 2007 SCC 9 [*Charkaoui v. Canada*].

6   *Canadian Charter of Rights and Freedoms*, ss. 8–12, Part I of the *Constitution Act, 1982*, being Schedule B to the *Canada Act 1982* (U.K.), 1982, c. 11 [*Charter*].

7   *Charkaoui v. Canada*, above note 5 at para. 61.

safeguards that must be afforded to non-citizens in the non-criminal context in the face of demands by national security agencies to protect their information and sources.

This paper traces both pre- and post-9/11 Canadian judicial approaches to evaluating the disclosure of secret evidence in cases where national security interests have arisen. More specifically, it will survey various approaches that have been pursued within the immigration context and assess their effectiveness in ensuring that the procedure designed to protect the security of information is consistent with our democratic values. This paper takes the position that the preservation of human rights must be the impetus behind, and an immutable constraint on, all anti-terrorism initiatives.[8] After all, protection of our "collective security must not be an assault on the individual's life, liberty and security of the person."[9] This position is consistent with that of the *Ottawa Principles on Anti-terrorism and Human Rights*, which state that administrative procedures that deprive a person of her liberty must ensure that the person has sufficient information to know and meet the case against her.[10]

The remainder of this paper is set out as follows: section B sets up the framework required to properly analyze security measures, taking into account constitutional and international human rights principles and highlighting Canadian courts' approaches to this analysis. Section C will discuss how security concerns have been addressed both prior to and after 9/11 under Canadian immigration legislation, with a particular focus on security certificates. After an evaluation of the deficiencies of security certificates, including those identified by the Supreme Court of Canada, section D canvasses alternative models of handling alleged national security cases, including the former Security Review Intelligence Committee (SIRC) model, the Arar Inquiry model, and the use of special advocates in the U.K. It ultimately proposes a "modified" Special Advocates model as an appropriate balance between security and human rights. Section E provides brief concluding remarks.

---

8 See the Introduction to the *Ottawa Principles on Anti-Terrorism and Human Rights*, found in Part One of this book [*Ottawa Principles*].

9 *Ibid.*

10 *Ibid.*, principle 5.1.3.

B. FRAMEWORK FOR ANALYSIS OF SECURITY MEASURES

> This is the fate of democracy, as not all means are acceptable to it, and not all methods employed by its enemies are open to it. Sometimes, a democracy must fight with one hand tied behind its back. Nonetheless, it has the upper hand. Preserving the rule of law and recognition of individual liberties constitute an important component of its understanding of security. At the end of the day, they strengthen its spirit and this strength allows it to overcome its difficulties."
>
> —Aharon Barak, President of the Israel Supreme Court

In the seven years since September 11, 2001, governments around the world have introduced new security and anti-terrorism measures. Some of these include: tightened border controls, broadened definitions of terrorist activity, legislation prohibiting financial contributions to terrorist organizations, and new restrictions to immigration and refugee claims.[12] Additionally, funding to national security agencies has been significantly increased and their intelligence gathering powers have been significantly expanded.

These newly implemented policies have been widely criticized for their impact on the fundamental human rights of those suspected of participating in terrorist activity or having links with terrorist organizations. The criticisms are part of a wider debate about the ethical and legal implications of the global "war on terror." At the core of the public debate is a need to ensure that efforts to protect national security interests do not undermine our democratic values.

This dilemma has often been depicted as a need to find the appropriate "balance" between protecting our national security and respecting civil liberties. However, such a balancing exercise is itself based on a false dichotomy. Aharon Barak, President of the Supreme Court of Israel,

---

11   *Public Committee against Torture in Israel v. The Government of Israel* (1999), H.C. 5100/94, 53(4) P.D. 817 at 845, cited in Aharon Barak, "The Supreme Court and the Problem of Terrorism" in *Judgments of the Israel Supreme Court: Fighting Terrorism within the Law* (2 January 2005) 9 at 15 [Barak].

12   For Canadian measures see, for example, the *IRPA*, above note 4. For U.S. measures, see, for example, *Uniting and Strengthening America by Providing Appropriate Tools Required to Intercept and Obstruct Terrorism (U.S.A. Patriot Act) Act of 2001*, Pub. L. No. 107-56, 115 Stat. 272.

has commented that rights and liberties are intrinsic to the definition of security in democratic societies.[13] Rather than viewing them as luxuries to be balanced against security, the more appropriate approach is to expand the conception of "national security" to include the protection of democratic values. That is, one must begin with the presumption that, in a free and democratic society, the legal system will be structured to operate in accordance with principles of fundamental justice. These principles, found in or informed in Canada by the *Canadian Charter of Rights and Freedoms* and various international human rights instruments, provide the procedural guarantees that characterize our legal system. Some of these include the right to be secure from unreasonable search or seizure; the right not to be arbitrarily detained or imprisoned; the right to counsel; the right to be presumed innocent until proven guilty in a fair and public hearing; the right not to be subjected to cruel and unusual treatment or punishment; and the right not to have incriminating evidence used against oneself in subsequent proceedings.[14]

Such procedural protections are especially important in times of crisis, when widespread fear and insecurity can result in pressure on the executive to depart from democratic principles and limit civil liberties. The United Nations' Economic and Social Council has noted that "[c]ounter-terrorism strategies pursued before and after 11 September have sometimes undermined efforts to enhance respect for shared human rights values,"[15] and reiterated the necessity of states to "adhere strictly to their international obligations to uphold human rights and

---

13   Barak, above note 11.

14   See *Charter*, above note 6. In *R. v. Malmo-Levine; R. v. Caine*, [2003] 3 S.C.R. 571, 2003 SCC 74 the Supreme Court of Canada held that balancing between individual and societal interests in considering the content of the principles of fundamental justice should not occur in s. 7, but, rather, should occur in s. 1. Where the balancing exercise occurs has critical implications. For example, if it is to occur in s. 7, the burden of proof rests with the claimant, whereas if it occurs in s. 1, the burden rests with the Crown. Furthermore, under a s. 1 analysis it is clear that the security certificate provisions should fail at the minimal impairment test, given that, as this chapter will demonstrate, there are many *less* rights-intrusive models to adopt that would adequately protect Canada's national security concerns. The Supreme Court affirmed this in *Charkaoui v. Canada*, above note 5.

15   Commission on Human Rights, *Human Rights: A Uniting Framework*, UN ESCOR, 58th Sess., Annex, Agenda Item 4, UN Doc. E/CN.4/2002/18 (2002) 4.

fundamental freedoms."[16] The Committee of Ministers of the Council of Europe also adopted *Guidelines on Human Rights and the Fight against Terrorism* to ensure that its member states remained attentive to their legal obligations.[17]

Free and democratic societies by definition require that government action, including measures taken to combat terrorist threats be lawful, precise, necessary, and proportional. The utmost objective should be to ensure that any proposed or adopted measures do not undermine the very rights and liberties that are the foundation upon which democratic societies are built.[18] Many experts have noted the difficulty of ascertaining either the potential or actual threat of a terrorist attack.[19] As a result, the necessity for responses curtailing fundamental freedoms is, to a large extent, speculative. However, even if we accept that there is a real legitimate threat to national security requiring protective measures, the impact of those measures must be thoughtfully considered. While the abrogation of some of the accepted principles of fairness may be justified in certain circumstances, this is not true of all of them. In each instance the context, the need for the measure, the expected effectiveness, and whether it impairs rights as minimally as possible must be examined.

There are two primary difficulties raised by the analytical exercise of evaluating what constitutes a "threat" to "national security." The first lies in the vague and highly politicized definition of "national security."

---

16   *Ibid.*

17   Council of Europe, Directorate General of Human Rights, *Guidelines on Human Rights and the Fight against Terrorism*, adopted by the Committee of Ministers on 11 July 2002 at the 804th meeting of the Ministers' Deputies (Council of Europe, 2002).

18   Alex Conte & Boaz Ganor, "Legal and Policy Issues in Establishing an International Framework for Human Rights Compliance When Countering Terrorism" (12 January 2005) online: www.ict.org.il/aarticles/ditems/c1901.php. Some commentators ask whether or not the effect of the proposed or adopted measure is proportional to the importance of its *objective* as a preliminary step in analyzing the appropriateness and potential effectiveness of a particular measure.

19   *Ibid.*, at 31–32. Establishing the existence of actual threats relies on intelligence, which is not always available or reliable, though certainly the absence of concrete intelligence does not necessarily connote an absence of threat. See also U.K. H.C., Constitutional Affairs Committee, *The Operation of the Special Immigration Appeals Commission (SIAC) and the Use of Special Advocates*, Seventh Report of Session 2004–5, HC 323-I, (2005) [*SIAC*].

As Craig Forcese points out, the phrase "national security" (or a similar expression) can be found in at least thirty-three federal statutes, yet the concept is defined in only nine.[20] Forcese adds that this ambiguity conveys significant discretion to the executive branch of government to define national security according to its own agenda.[21] Certainly the risk of politically motivated use of this discretion raises cause for alarm given the fundamental impact it has on the legal rights available to those suspected of terrorist activity. As we have seen in the post-9/11 era, national security concerns have been used as justification for draconian measures and have played a critical role in associating "foreignness" with danger.[22]

The second difficulty is that the courts have adopted a highly deferential approach to national security determinations made by the government. In *Henrie v. Canada*, Justice Addy stated:

> Public interest in the administration of justice requires complete openness of the judicial process. That principle must be jealously guarded and rigorously applied, especially where evidence which appears to be relevant to a judicial determination is at stake. That cardinal rule not only safeguards the rights of litigants generally but, more importantly, it is fundamental to the public interest in the preservation of our free and democratic society. There are, however, very limited and well-defined occasions where that principle of complete openness must play a secondary role and where, with regard to the admission of evidence, the public interest in not disclosing the evidence may outweigh the public interest in disclosure. This frequently occurs where national security is involved for the simple reason that the very existence of our free and democratic society as well as the continued protection of the rights of litigants ultimately depend on the security and continued existence of our nation and of its institutions and laws.[23]

In *Ruby v. Canada (Solicitor General)*, the Supreme Court reaffirmed the principle that the Government of Canada has a legitimate interest in protecting confidential information where its release would be detri-

---

20 Craig Forcese, "Through a Glass Darkly: The Role and Review of 'National Security' Concepts in Canadian Law" (2006) 43 Alta. L. Rev. 963 at 985.

21 *Ibid.*

22 The evocation of national security to justify practices such as "extraordinary rendition" or Guantanamo Bay are but two examples of this phenomenon.

23 *Henrie v. Canada (Security Intelligence Review Committee)*, [1988] F.C.J. No. 965 (T.D.).

mental to the national interest.[24] In *Suresh v. Canada (Minister of Citizenship and Immigration)*, the Court added that it would only review the executive's national security determinations where they were patently unreasonable.[25] As a result, given the deference that courts will give to assertions by the executive of "national security" privilege, it is crucial that, where the government raises national security concerns to maintain the secrecy of evidence, adequate safeguards are in place to ensure that the suspected individual is treated fairly.

In determining whether the public interest served by non-disclosure outweighs the interest in disclosure, the specific right affected by an assertion of confidentiality is an important consideration. For example, one could hardly imagine a situation in which the majority of the evidence was withheld from the accused in a criminal trial and where defence counsel was denied any opportunity to cross-examine witnesses. Such a procedure would run afoul of the basic principles of our legal system which protect an accused's right to know the case against them. However, while in *Ruby* the Court noted that, as a general rule, a fair hearing requires parties to know the opposing party's case, it accepted there, as it did recently in *Charkaoui*, that this principle tolerates certain exceptions.[26]

National security confidentiality claims are one such exception. In the non-criminal context especially, the extent to which the principles of fundamental justice will require disclosure has not been clearly defined, though the Supreme Court's recent *Charkaoui* decision makes it clear that the required analysis will be context-specific.[27] The Court held that when assessing whether or not a specific procedure is consistent with the principles of fundamental justice "the issue is whether the process is fundamentally unfair to the affected person."[28] Thus, although the context of national security can inform the analysis of whether a particular process is fundamentally unfair, it cannot be used to justify an otherwise unacceptable procedure.[29]

---

24 *Ruby v. Canada (Solicitor General)*, [2002] S.C.J. No. 73 at para. 43 [*Ruby*].

25 *Suresh v. Canada (Minister of Citizenship and Immigration)*, [2002] 1 S.C.R. 3 at para. 32 [*Suresh*].

26 *Ruby*, above note 24 at para. 40.

27 *Charkaoui v. Canada*, above note 5.

28 *Ibid.* at para. 22.

29 *Ibid.* at para. 23.

The Court held that the relevant principle of fundamental justice engaged in the special immigration procedures used in national security cases is that, before the state can detain someone for significant periods of time, it must accord him a fair judicial process.[30] The Court noted that the right to a fair judicial process encompasses the right to a hearing before an independent magistrate who has the power to make determinations of fact and law, the right to know the case put against oneself, and the right to answer that case.[31] The Court accepted that the *IRPA* procedures provided for a hearing before an independent magistrate. However, the Court concluded that because most, if not all, of the evidence that the magistrate considers is presented by the government and the magistrate does not have the power to independently investigate all of the relevant facts, the magistrate may not be exposed to all of the relevant evidence.[32]

In addition, the Supreme Court concluded that the procedure failed to ensure that the person was able to meet the case against him. The secrecy of the procedure prevents the accused from knowing the case against him and challenging the government's case. This limitation undermines the ability of the judge to render a decision based on all of the facts. The Court noted that there are other mechanisms that can provide greater protections to the individual while keeping critical information confidential and that section 7 of the *IRPA* requires that the concerned person either be given the necessary information or a substantial substitute for it must be found.[33] The following section provides a summary of the evolution of the procedures used in the immigration context where national security concerns have been raised so that this can be analyzed to determine whether or not they provide adequate procedural protections to meet the requirements of fairness and fundamental justice.

---

30 *Ibid.* at para. 28.
31 *Ibid.* at paras. 29–30.
32 *Ibid.* at paras. 48–53.
33 *Ibid.* at paras. 61 and 87.

C. ADDRESSING SECURITY CONCERNS IN THE IMMIGRATION CONTEXT

1) Security Intelligence Review Committee (SIRC) Proceedings under the Former *Immigration Act*

As early as *Canada (Minister of Employment and Immigration) v. Chiarelli*,[34] the Supreme Court signalled that permanent residents facing deportation should not expect the same degree of procedural fairness and substantive protections as persons involved in a criminal trial. In that case, Mr. Chiarelli was accused of being a member of an organized crime ring. In accordance with the former *Immigration Act*,[35] a security certificate was issued against him, the effect of which was to deny him an equitable review of his deportation order. While Mr. Chiarelli still had the right to a hearing where the allegations against him had to be proven, and a right to appeal any deportation order against him, the security certificate effectively deprived the Immigration Appeal Board (IAB) of the right to review the equitable circumstances surrounding his deportation.

Before the security certificate could be effective, Mr. Chiarelli was given a right to a hearing before the Security Intelligence Review Committee (SIRC). A SIRC is an administrative body created by Parliament with the enactment of the *Canadian Security Intelligence Service Act* to oversee CSIS. It also has other responsibilities including considering complaints by persons against CSIS. Under the previous legislation, SIRC considered some immigration cases involving permanent residents. In the *Chiarelli* case, while he was not given full access to all the evidence against him at that hearing, he was entitled to review summaries of the evidence adduced at the *in camera* hearings and to have counsel cross-examine witnesses and present evidence before the committee. In addition, independent counsel was present at the *in camera* hearings and also cross-examined the government witnesses. If SIRC was satisfied based on the evidence that the person concerned was connected with organized crime, the certificate would be upheld. If upheld, the right to an equitable review before the IAB would be extinguished.

---

34   [1992] 1 S.C.R. 711 [*Chiarelli*].
35   *Immigration Act*, R.S.C. 1985, c. I-2 [*Immigration Act*].

Further amendments to the *Immigration Act*, which took effect in 1989, expanded SIRC's role in cases involving permanent residents who were believed to be inadmissible on national security grounds.[36] While a more detailed explanation of the SIRC process is provided in the following section, in a nutshell, secret evidence was treated as follows: where the government had information about a permanent resident that it did not wish to disclose, it could request a hearing before SIRC to present some of it *in camera*. Independent counsel was available to cross-examine the witnesses and summaries of the cross-examination were made available to counsel for the concerned individual, subject to redactions made for national security concerns. Counsel for the accused could participate in all but the *in camera* sessions, could cross-examine government witnesses subject only to national security restrictions, and could present evidence. SIRC would then make a determination as to whether or not the allegations were well-founded. If the allegations were upheld, a deportation order would be issued. This procedure remained in effect in Canada for permanent residents until 2002 when the *Immigration and Refugee Protection Act* (*IRPA*) was implemented.[37] As discussed below, under *IRPA* security certificates can now be issued against permanent residents.

2) Security Certificates under the Former *Immigration Act*

Under the former *Immigration Act*, a separate procedure, involving the filing of a security certificate before a Federal Court judge, existed for "convention refugees" and all other persons who were not permanent residents.[38] Signed by the solicitor general and the minister of employment and immigration, the certificate was an indication that the two ministers had concluded that there were reasonable grounds to believe that the named individual was inadmissible to Canada on national security grounds. Upon issuance, the subject of the certificate was automatically detained and his case was referred to a Federal Court judge. The judge would, within one week of the issuance of the certificate, review the secret information and determine whether its release would be injurious to national security. If the judge determined that the information was relevant but could not be revealed without injuring national se-

---

36 *Ibid.*
37 *IRPA*, above note 4.
38 *Immigration Act*, above note 35, s. 40.1.

curity, she would provide only a summary of its contents. The detainee had the right to a hearing where he could respond to the allegations.

The major difficulties with this process were twofold. First, the summaries were usually so general that they did not provide the detainee with an adequate and meaningful opportunity to respond. Second, the secret evidence was not subject to any cross-examination or challenge except by the Federal Court judge, who was also the person required to make determinations as to its credibility. The exercise of this dual role is virtually impossible for many reasons. First, requiring the judge to test the information undermines her judicial independence. Second, the judge can hardly be expected to be an effective person to challenge the credibility of the government's evidence if she does not have any access to, or understanding of the position put forward by the person concerned.

Finally, in light of the conclusions of the Arar Commission of Inquiry in Canada, the reliability of evidence obtained and relied on by CSIS and other intelligence agencies that is used in administrative proceedings must be carefully scrutinized. The *Arar Report* found that Canadian intelligence agents did not appropriately assess evidence they obtained from foreign agencies, and erroneously concluded that Mr. Arar's statement given under torture was credible. This statement was subsequently relied on by the intelligence agencies in their characterization of Mr. Arar to his detriment. In light of this, it is clear that some form of effective challenge of the secret information provided by CSIS is essential to the viability of the security certificate procedure.[39]

3) Security Certificates under the *Immigration and Refugee Protection Act*

In 2002, the *Immigration and Refugee Protection Act* (*IRPA*)[40] was implemented, replacing the former *Immigration Act*.[41] *IRPA*'s security certifi-

---

39 Canada, Commission of Inquiry into the Actions of Canadian Officials in Relation to Maher Arar, *Report of the Events Relating to Maher Arar: Analysis and Recommendations* (Ottawa: Public Works and Government Services Canada, 2006) [*Arar Report*]. Justice O'Connor found that CSIS, which provides evidence and other information in the security certificate process, failed to do a proper reliability assessment of the information and statements obtained from Arar while under torture from the Syrian authorities.

40 *IRPA*, above note 4.

41 *Immigration Act*, above note 35.

cate provisions allow for the detention and deportation of permanent residents, refugees, and foreign nationals (including people admitted to Canada on student, work, or visitor's visas as well as non-status residents) on the grounds that they pose a threat to national security.[42] As noted, under the previous legislation security certificates were limited to convention refugees and non-status residents.

The security certificate process established under *IRPA* commences when the minister of citizenship and immigration and the minister of public safety and emergency preparedness review confidential information about an individual and conclude that he is inadmissible to Canada on security grounds. Section 34(1) provides that a permanent resident or foreign national is inadmissible for

a) engaging in an act of espionage or an act of subversion against a democratic government, institution or process as they are understood in Canada;

b) engaging in or instigating the subversion by force of any government;

c) engaging in terrorism;

d) being a danger to the security of Canada;

e) engaging in acts of violence that would or might endanger the lives or safety of persons in Canada; or

f) being a member of an organization that there are reasonable grounds to believe engages, has engaged or will engage in acts referred to in paragraph (a), (b), or (c).[43]

The ministers are then required to sign a certificate indicating their inadmissibility finding. They may also issue a warrant for detention of a permanent resident named in the certificate. Foreign nationals are subject to mandatory detention, without the requirement for a warrant. The matter is then referred to a Federal Court judge who has seven days to review the information or evidence upon which the certificate was issued, and determine its relevance to the detainee's inadmissibility. Where the judge believes that disclosure of this information or evidence would threaten national security, section 78(e) of the *IRPA* allows for all

---

42 See, for example, *IRPA*, above note 4, ss. 76–85.

43 *Ibid.*, s. 34.

or part of it to be heard in secret (that is, without the presence of the detainee or her counsel).[44]

The judge then prepares a summary of the evidence so that the detainee may be, according to the legislation, "reasonably informed of the circumstances giving rise"[45] to it, but must ensure that information that would be "injurious to national security or to the safety of any person if disclosed,"[46] remains confidential. Following receipt of the summary, the detainee can present evidence before the judge at a hearing.

Once the Federal Court judge decides there were reasonable grounds to issue a security certificate, it is considered to be conclusive proof of inadmissibility, and constitutes a deportation order—potentially even to countries where there is a risk of torture or even death.

There are several shortcomings of the security certificate process meriting grave cause for concern. First, the Federal Court has no power to decide whether or not the allegations upon which a security certificate is issued are indeed true; the judge can *only* decide whether there are reasonable grounds for its issuance. Furthermore, not only are the parameters of "reasonableness" not defined by the *IRPA*, but the determination itself can neither be appealed nor judicially reviewed.[47] In Canada, the courts have applied a very low threshold for finding that there are reasonable grounds and this further limits the person's ability to challenge the certificate.[48]

Second, the summary provided to the detainee is extremely general in nature; it does not contain the precise allegations against him nor is it accompanied by sufficient information to build an adequate defence.

Third, although the detainee can retain counsel, counsel's role is extremely minimal throughout the security certificate process. Counsel is only privy to the summary provided, and is not present when evidence is presented to the judge and, therefore, cannot test its credibility through cross-examination. Essentially the hearing is conducted in secret, and on the basis of secret evidence. At most, the detainee can only rely on the Federal Court judge to ensure his interests are protected during the

---

44 *Ibid.*, s. 78.

45 *Ibid.*, s. 78(h).

46 *Ibid.*

47 *Ibid.*, s. 79(3).

48 See *Chiau v. Canada (Minister of Citizenship and Immigration)*, [2000] F.C.J. No. 2043 (C.A.).

closed proceedings. Thus, not only must the judge act in her essential role as an impartial decision-maker, she must also assume these additional responsibilities, which may affect her ability to sufficiently test the government's case. This is wholly unsatisfactory.

For all of these reasons, the constitutionality of the security certificate process has been before the courts on more than one occasion. The Federal Court was first confronted with the question in *Ahani v. Canada*, where the plaintiff argued that the lack of disclosure and opportunity to challenge the evidence against him was a violation of the principles of fundamental justice.[49] However, the court concluded otherwise and held that the plaintiff's arguments were based on criminal law principles that were found to have no application in his case. Madame Justice McGillis found that a Federal Court judge was well-placed to effectively challenge *in camera* evidence on his own and ensure as full a disclosure as possible. She ruled that the security certificate procedure adequately balanced the state's interests in protecting confidential sources with the individual's right to defend himself against the allegations. The decision was upheld by the Federal Court of Appeal.[50]

In subsequent challenges the Federal Court came to similar conclusions.[51] However not all Federal Court justices are supportive of the procedure. In a public speech in 2002, Justice James Hugessen commented on the dual role Federal Court judges are to assume in secret proceedings:

> We do not like this process of having to sit alone hearing only one party and looking at the materials produced by only one party and having to try to figure out for ourselves what is wrong with the case that is being presented before us and having to try for ourselves to see how the witnesses that appear before us ought to be cross-examined . . . . We greatly miss, in short, our security blanket which is the adversary system

---

49 *Ahani v. Canada*, [1995] 3 F.C. 669 (T.D.).

50 *Ahani v. Canada*, [1996] F.C.J. No. 937 (C.A.).

51 See *Charkaoui (Re)*, [2003] F.C.J. No. 1816 (F.C.) and *Charkaoui (Re)*, [2006] F.C.J. No. 868 (C.A.). Also, in *Harkat (Re)*, [2004] F.C.J. No. 2101 (F.C.), Madam Justice Dawson rejected a request by counsel for the detainee to have a special advocate assist in the evaluation of evidence during the *in camera* hearing, stating that it was unnecessary.

that we were all brought up with and that . . . is for most of us, the real warranty that the outcome of what we do is going to be fair and just.

. . .

There is an analogy that is sometimes made by people who defend this system . . . . But the analogy is sometimes made to the much more traditional system of search warrants and the somewhat less traditional but pretty well established system of electronic surveillance warrants. It is not a very good analogy, I have to tell you, because persons who swear affidavits for search warrants or for electronic surveillance can be reasonably sure that there is a high probability that those affidavits are going to see the light of day someday. With these national security affidavits, if they are successful in persuading the judge, they never will see the light of day and that fact that something improper has been said to the Court may never be revealed.[52]

The Supreme Court of Canada was finally required to address the security certificate procedure in June 2006 when three detainees, Adil Charkaoui, Hassan Almrei, and Mohamed Harkat, challenged its constitutionality.[53] As is discussed in the following section, the Court concluded that the procedures in the *IRPA* do not conform to the principles of fundamental justice because they deny the person the opportunity to know and meet the case against her.

4) Supreme Court of Canada Ruling on Security Certificates

In *Charkaoui v. Canada*, the Supreme Court unanimously held that the current security certificate procedure outlined in the *IRPA* "unjustifiably violates section 7 of the *Charter* by allowing the issuance of a certificate of inadmissibility based on secret material without providing for

---

52 James K. Hugessen, "Watching the Watchers: Democratic Oversight" in D. Daubney, *et al.*, eds., *Terrorism, Law and Democracy: How is Canada Changing Following September 11?* (Montreal: Thémis, 2002) 381 at 384.

53 Two others, Mohammad Mahjoub and Mahmoud Jaballah, are also subject to security certificates and have been detained without charge since 2000 and 2001 respectively. However on 15 February 2007, Federal Court Justice Richard Mosley allowed Mr. Mahjoub to be removed from a federal immigration detention facility and instead be detained under house arrest.

an independent agent at the stage of judicial review to better protect the named person's interests."[54]

In its section 7 analysis, the Court held that the overarching principle of fundamental justice applicable to the security certificate regime is that "before the state can detain people for significant periods of time, it must accord them a fair judicial process."[55] The Court adds:

> This basic principle has a number of facets. It comprises the right to a *hearing*. It requires that the hearing be *before an independent and impartial magistrate*. It demands a *decision by the magistrate on the facts and the law*. And it entails the *right to know the case put against one*, and the *right to answer that case*. Precisely how these requirements are met will vary with the context. But for s. 7 to be satisfied, each of them must be met in substance.
>
> The *IRPA* process includes a hearing. The process consists of two phases, one executive and one judicial. There is no hearing at the executive phase that results in issuance of the certificate. However, this is followed by a review before a judge, where the named person is afforded a hearing. Thus, the first requirement that of a hearing, is met.
>
> Questions arise, however, on the other requirements, namely: that the judge be independent and impartial; that the judge make a judicial decision based on the facts and the law; and finally, that the named person be afforded an opportunity to meet the case put against him or her by being informed of that case and being allowed to question or counter it. I conclude that the *IRPA* scheme meets the first requirement of independence and impartiality, but fails to satisfy the second and third requirements, which are interrelated here.[56]

On the second requirement, that the judge make a judicial decision based on the facts and the law, the Court reiterated the exact concerns regarding the Federal Court judge's incompatible dual role, discussed in the preceding section:

---

54 *Charkaoui v. Canada*, above note 5 at para. 3. The Court also found that the impugned provisions also violated ss. 9 and 10(c) of the *Charter* as some of the time limits for continuing detention of foreign nationals are arbitrary.

55 *Ibid*. at para. 28.

56 *Ibid*. at paras. 29–31 [emphasis in original].

The designated judge under the *IRPA* does not possess the full and independent powers to gather evidence that exist in the inquisitorial process. At the same time, the named person is not given the disclosure and the right to participate in the proceedings that characterize the adversarial process. The result is a concern that the designated judge, despite his or her best efforts to get all the relevant evidence, may be obliged—perhaps unknowingly—to make the required decision based on only part of the relevant evidence.[57]

On the final requirement that the named person be afforded an opportunity to meet the case against him, the Court narrowed in on the relevant context:

> In the context of national security, non-disclosure, which may be extensive, coupled with the grave intrusions on liberty imposed on a detainee, makes it difficult, if not impossible, to find substitute procedures that will satisfy s. 7. Fundamental justice requires substantial compliance with the venerated principle that a person whose liberty is in jeopardy must be given an opportunity to know the case to meet, and an opportunity to meet the case. Yet the imperative of the protection of society may preclude this. Information may be obtained from other countries or from informers on condition that it not be disclosed. Or it may simply be so critical that it cannot be disclosed without risking public security. This is a reality of our modern world. If s. 7 is to be satisfied, either the person must be given the necessary information, or a substantial substitute for that information must be found. Neither is the case here.[58]

Two more recent judgments should also be instructive in reconsidering the participatory rights afforded to the named person in a security certificate. In *R. v. Khelawon*, the Supreme Court reiterated that the right to a fair trial is a principle of fundamental justice and stated:

> The right to make full answer and defence in turn is linked to another principle of fundamental justice, the right to a fair trial: *R. v. Rose*, [1998] 3 S.C.R. 262. The concern over trial fairness is one of the paramount reasons for rationalizing the traditional hearsay exceptions in accordance with the principled approach. As stated by Iacobucci J. in *Starr*,

---

57 *Ibid*. at para. 50.
58 *Ibid*. at para. 61.

at para. 200, in respect of Crown evidence: "It would compromise trial fairness, and raise the spectre of wrongful convictions, if the Crown is allowed to introduce unreliable hearsay against the accused, regardless of whether it happens to fall within an existing exception."

As indicated earlier, our adversary system is based on the assumption that sources of untrustworthiness or inaccuracy can best be brought to light under the test of cross-examination. It is mainly because of the inability to put hearsay evidence to that test, that it is presumptively inadmissible. However, the constitutional right guaranteed under s. 7 of the *Charter* is not the right to confront or cross-examine adverse witnesses in itself. The adversarial trial process, which includes cross-examination, is but the means to achieve the end. Trial fairness, as a principle of fundamental justice, is the end that must be achieved. Trial fairness embraces more than the rights of the accused. While it undoubtedly includes the right to make full answer and defence, the fairness of the trial must also be assessed in the light of broader societal concerns: see *R. v. Mills*, [1999] 3 S.C.R. 668, at paras. 69–76. In the context of an admissibility inquiry, society's interest in having the trial process arrive at the truth is one such concern.[59]

Furthermore in *Geza v. Canada (Minister of Citizenship and Immigration)*,[60] the Federal Court stated that decisions affecting refugees require a high degree of procedural fairness. This can be seen to temper the often-made claim that criminal law principles, such as the right to disclosure and to cross-examine evidence, do not apply in the immigration context. While it may well be that the full panoply of rights need not be extended to immigration hearings, there can be no doubt given the issues at stake that there must be a high level of procedural protection. Certainly, it is not whether a case falls within the ambit of "criminal law" or "immigration law" that is determinative of the applicable principles, but the implications of the decision. Where *Charter* rights are at stake, it cannot possibly be the case that fundamental safeguards are justifiably removed. Such an approach was affirmed by the Supreme Court's *Charkaoui* decision.[61]

In a free and democratic society there are less rights-invasive ways of protecting national security. After all, the preservation of human rights

---

59 *R. v. Khelawon*, 2006 SCC 57 at paras. 47–48.
60 2004 FC 1039.
61 *Charkaoui v. Canada*, above note 5.

and democratic liberties must be a central motivator to the fight against terrorism.

D. FINDING THE PROCEDURE THAT ENSURES ADEQUATE FAIRNESS: ALTERNATIVE MODELS

Accordingly, finding a preferred model of assessing security-sensitive evidence, one that includes sufficient participatory rights for the suspected individual, requires canvassing various alternatives.

At one end of the spectrum lies the current security certificate scheme, which fully privileges national security claims at the expense of procedural safeguards to the individual concerned. In this scheme, a person can be detained, in some cases for years, without any knowledge of the precise allegations or evidence against her. With no independent counsel available to challenge the assertions of confidentiality or the evidence presented in secret proceedings, the designated Federal Court judge is expected to take on this role for the detainee. While the current security certificate procedure guarantees that there will not be any leakage of confidential information, it provides virtually no participatory rights to the person concerned, and seems instinctively antithetical to democratic freedoms and principles.

At the other end of the spectrum, of course, would be a system in which the government could not at all rely on confidential information under any circumstances. Given the Supreme Court's decisions in *Ruby*,[62] and *Chiarelli*,[63] such a position is not one that is likely to find favour with our courts. What is required then is a careful consideration of alternative models between these poles. To date various arrangements have been employed or proposed in different contexts, including the SIRC model, the Arar Inquiry model (essentially a modified SIRC model), the Special Advocates model, used in the U.K., and the Modified Special Advocates model proposed for Canada, all of which will be discussed here.

Writing for the majority in *Charkaoui*, Chief Justice McLachlin also spent ample time canvassing these models as evidence of a litany of less intrusive models from which to choose. Ultimately, the chosen process or processes should ensure the individual's right to procedural fairness

---

62 *Ruby*, above note 24.
63 *Chiarelli*, above note 34.

and participation in proceedings while providing adequate protection of confidential security intelligence and other evidence. Where several models can achieve the desired result, the one that allows the fullest participation of the person, while ensuring protection of the confidential information, is to be preferred.

1) The SIRC Model

The SIRC model is set out under section 39(2) of the former *Immigration Act* and was applied in cases where the government sought to use secret evidence in the deportation of permanent residents.[64] Once a government report was received by SIRC, the chairperson would assign one or more members to investigate its accuracy. These members were provided with the information the government relied upon in making its findings. The suspected individual and the government would then be given the opportunity to make representations. The SIRC members decided what information could or could not be disclosed to the suspected individual. The government, as well as SIRC counsel, would make arguments with respect to disclosure. If certain material was deemed to be subject to national security confidentiality, it would be heard *in camera*, along with the testimony of any witnesses. The suspected individual would be provided with a summary of those hearings.

In the *ex parte* hearings, several counsel would be present: counsel to CSIS, counsel for any witnesses, counsel for any government departments with an interest in the case, and SIRC's own hired counsel, which could include inside and outside counsel. Inside counsel were directly employed by SIRC and had a close working relationship with CSIS and the security services. They would be charged with cross-examining witnesses brought before the committee and with representing, to the best of their ability, the appellant's interests. In more sensitive cases, where inside counsel were not fully capable of representing the appellant, or were reluctant to be involved in proceedings against CSIS, independent outside counsel were hired. Outside counsel were charged with challenging the confidentiality of the information contained in the closed evidence, as well as with cross-examining witnesses. They were also able to maintain contact with the person concerned throughout the process.

---

64 *Immigration Act*, above note 35, s. 39.

The SIRC procedures allowed for a fair procedure that maximized participation of the person concerned in the hearing, while allowing for the introduction of *in camera* evidence and the challenging of that evidence through independent counsel.

2) The Arar Inquiry Model

Maher Arar is a Canadian citizen who was detained by the United States while he was in transit. Instead of being allowed to return to Canada he was rendered by the United States to Syria. In Syria he was detained for more than one year and was subject to torture. Upon his return, the Canadian government called a public inquiry into his detention. During the course of the inquiry the government objected to the release of much of the evidence in public. As a result, the commissioner created a procedure for considering the secret evidence. The model used during the Arar Inquiry was essentially a modified version of the SIRC model described above. Commission counsel was appointed to review the government's evidence, interview potential witnesses, and call evidence at the hearings. They were also able to cross-examine the *in camera* evidence and meet with counsel for Mr. Arar and intervenors to receive suggestions for further cross-examination. In this manner, the concerned individual, Mr. Arar, was afforded some participatory rights with respect to secret evidence being adduced against him during the *in camera* proceedings. In his report, Justice Dennis O'Connor noted:

> When I reflect on the nature of the issues raised by the mandate for the Inquiry and the type of evidence I heard, I recognize that I could not have reported with confidence if the witnesses heard *in camera* had not been cross-examined . . . . Use of independent counsel thus makes a good deal of sense when all or a portion of proceedings are conducted *in camera*.[65]

Furthermore, additional independent counsel were appointed to act as *amici curiae* to test the government's national security claims. Their role was not to challenge the credibility of secret evidence, but merely to provide expert advice to the commissioner as to whether or not the government's claims for confidentiality were well-founded. Hence, as

---

65 *Arar Report*, above note 39 at 292–93.

opposed to the SIRC model, where one counsel had the dual roles of cross-examination and challenging assertions of confidentiality, in the Arar Inquiry model the commissioner chose to have different counsel fulfill each of the roles. This position makes eminent sense given that the specific type of expertise required for each of the two functions is different. As in the case of the SIRC model, the Arar procedures allowed for the fullest possible participation of Mr. Arar, while protecting confidential information.

3) The Special Advocates Model

In the Federal Court of Appeal decision of *Charkaoui,* the court specifically considered the special advocate procedures operating in the United Kingdom.[66] It concluded that implementing similar procedures in Canada would be a matter for the legislature and not the courts.

The appointment of some form of special advocate or *amicus curiae* for security certificate proceedings has received the support of most of the appellants and public interest groups that intervened in the Supreme Court hearings. However, the role to be played by the special advocates is the subject of some dispute. Both the administrative facility of creating a special advocates procedure and the fact that security-cleared special counsel would not compromise national security interests show the gross shortcomings and overbreadth of the current system. While acknowledging that the Special Advocates model is short of ideal, the Canadian Civil Liberties Association (CCLA) describes the implications of the failure to provide at least this level of protection to those named on security certificates:

> By denying access to special advocates, the Canadian system creates a greater risk that faulty and erroneous evidence will be used, and accepted, against impugned persons. To impose such a risk will always diminish procedural fairness. To do so unnecessarily must be fundamentally unjust.[67]

Special advocates have been used in the U.K. since 1997, following recommendations made by the European Court in *Chahal v. United*

---

66 *Charkaoui (Re),* [2004] F.C.J. No. 2060 (C.A.).
67 *Charkaoui v. Canada,* above note 5, (factum of the intervenor, Canadian Civil Liberties Association) at para. 38 [*Charkaoui Factum*].

Kingdom.[68] Since then the British government has created a Special Immigration Appeals Commission (SIAC) to hear cases involving security-sensitive evidence. Special advocates are appointed by the attorney general to act on behalf of the suspected security threat during the secret hearing process and can meet with them prior to reviewing the evidence to take direction.

While the Special Advocates model is certainly less draconian than *IRPA's* security certificate scheme, in that it affords at least some representation of the suspect's interests, critics in the U.K. have argued that it too is inappropriate where fundamental liberty interests are at stake.[69] Most of the criticism levelled against special advocates is the result of three major restrictions. Namely, that

1) once the special advocate has reviewed the secret evidence, (s)he is barred from having further contact with the suspected security threat and cannot take direction from them or their counsel;
2) the special advocate has no power to call witnesses; and
3) the special advocate does not have adequate resources to conduct a full defence.

The impact of each of these restrictions will be discussed more fully below.

a) Ability to be Instructed Only Prior to the Review of Secret Evidence

Once the special advocate has seen the closed material, she is barred in almost all circumstances from discussing the case with any other person. Thus, she has no means of ascertaining whether or not the suspected individual has any legitimate response to the secret evidence being adduced against him. Further, the special advocate is unable to discuss legal strategy with the suspected individual or his counsel and has no way of knowing whether or not they would choose to advance a specific line of argument.[70] Cross-examination of witnesses is also severely limited by the inability to seek informed instructions from the person concerned, as well as the inability to recognize exculpatory evidence.

---

68 *Chahal v. United Kingdom* (1996), 23 E.H.R.R. 413.

69 *SIAC*, above note 19.

70 See, for example, *ibid.* at 2 and 55–56.

Furthermore, many suspected individuals are skeptical of the impartiality and neutrality of special advocates themselves, given that they are appointed by the attorney general.[71] Many special advocates have revealed that appellants have often not used their services—likely a reflection that they are unilaterally appointed by the government (the opposing party).[72] This perceived lack of accountability towards the client remains another source of critics' consternation.

b) No Power to Call Witnesses

The relevance of sensitive secret evidence requires assessment. This assessment is made by members of British security services, who, for the purposes of a SIAC hearing, are treated as expert witnesses. However, the special advocate has no opportunity to call expert witnesses in reply.[73]

c) Inadequate Resources

Furthermore the lack of resources provided to special advocates itself represents another major restriction on their ability to adequately defend the appellant's interests.[74] They operate without substantive assistance, as they have no secretariat, and receive no expert help. They also lack access to interpreters, and adequate technical and administrative support. Severe research restrictions even prevent special advocates from conducting internet searches to verify what information provided in the hearing is already in the public domain.[75]

Moreover, the majority of special advocates are immigration lawyers with little or no expertise in the criminal law. Critics have thus suggested that criminal lawyers be added to the roster, especially given the limited contact special advocates can have with other people regarding the case in question.[76]

Several special advocates have resigned, claiming that the compounded restrictions have made a mockery of the process, though others have remained, simply because they have felt that the existence of special

---

71   See, for example, *ibid.* at 5, 19, and 45.
72   See, for example, *ibid.* at 55.
73   See, for example, *ibid.* at 10.
74   See, for example, *ibid.* at 19.
75   See, for example, *ibid.* at 6–7.
76   See, for example, *ibid.* at 7 and 20.

advocates, albeit hardly ideal, is more effective than what would exist in their absence.[77]

In April 2005, a U.K. parliamentary Constitutional Affairs Committee reviewed the procedure, considered some of the criticisms, and released a report containing three principal recommendations, two of which are especially instructive to a proposed model for Canada:

    a.　Steps are taken to make it easier for Special Advocates to communicate with appellants and their legal advisers after they have seen closed material, on a basis which does not compromise national security. This is for two reasons: first, to ensure that the Special Advocate is in a position to establish whether the charges or evidence can be challenged by evidence not available to the appellant; and second, so that the Special Advocate is able to form a coherent legal strategy with the appellant's legal team; and

    b.　Sufficient professional support is provided to the Special Advocates. We doubt that the proposals put forward by the Attorney General will be sufficient to meet the concerns expressed to us by the Special Advocates. The support provided should include security-cleared staff to assist in research and assessment of controlled material. These arrangements should be formalised into an "Office of the Special Advocate" to allow appropriate staffing and resources to be dedicated to ensuring suspects obtain fairer hearing.[78]

In a recent challenge to the control order scheme in the U.K., Justice Sullivan described the necessity for special advocates in reviewing secret evidence disclosed in closed hearings:[79]

77　See, for example, *ibid.* at 3–4.

78　*Ibid.* at 41.

79　The U.K. Home Office describes the control order regime operating in the U.K.:

    The *Prevention of Terrorism Act* allows for control orders to be made against any suspected terrorist, whether a UK national or a non-UK national, or whether the terrorist activity is international or domestic. The Home Secretary is required to report to Parliament as soon as reasonably possible after the end of the relevant three-month period on how control order powers have been exercised during that time.

    . . .

    Control orders enable the authorities to impose conditions upon individuals ranging from prohibitions on access to specific items or services (such as

That fairness requires the court to be able to take full account of the respondent's explanation at some stage in the decision-making process is obvious, as is the need to take account of, for example, potentially exculpatory information identified by the Special Advocate when reviewing the closed material and new closed material and/or submissions by the Special Advocate which might cast a different, and less unfavorable light, from the respondent's point of view, on the closed material that was available some months earlier.[80]

Justice Sullivan also noted the inherent limitations of the special advocate procedure in rectifying the shortcomings of the control order regime. He specifically considered the inability of the special advocate to communicate with the concerned person after viewing the closed evidence:

The role of the Special Advocate in control order proceedings presents a further and more fundamental difficulty. Section 7(1) enables the controlee to apply for revocation or modification if he considers that there has been a change of circumstances affecting the order. But the controlee will not know the full picture. In particular, he will not know whether anything in the Special Advocate's examination of the closed material might, either of itself or in conjunction with the material available to him, be described as a "change of circumstances." Once the Special Advocate has seen the closed materials he may not communicate with the respondent or his legal representatives unless the court so directs ... the Special Advocate does not have a roving commission to ascertain whether there might be new exculpatory material, or whether, for example, viewed in the light of the respondent's explanations which were not available to the Secretary of State, a different interpretation might have been given to the closed material.[81]

---

the Internet), and restrictions on association with named individuals, to the imposition of restrictions on movement or curfews. A control order does not mean "house arrest."

See online: www.homeoffice.gov.uk/security/terrorism-and-the-law/prevention-of-terrorism.

80 *Re MB*, [2006] EWHC Admin 1000 at para. 83.

81 *Ibid.* at para. 98.

4) The Modified Special Advocates Model

In light of the criticisms levelled against the U.K.'s Special Advocates model, some organizations have proposed modifications to it, taking into consideration recommendations made by the U.K. House of Commons Constitutional Committee's review. The Canadian Bar Association (CBA), also intervenors in the constitutional challenge to the security certificate regime, noted shortcomings of the U.K. model in its submissions. The CBA proposed a model where the special advocate would be able to meet with the concerned person both before and after the *in camera* hearing on the undertaking that she would not disclose any secret evidence.[82] Thus, while the special advocate would be prohibited from disclosing any confidential information to the appellant, the appellant would be able to at least participate in some meaningful way in the case against him by relaying information to the special advocate, who would in turn present it at the hearing. Such a procedure would correct some of the deficiencies identified so as to allow adequate participation of the person concerned in the hearing procedure. It appears that such a proposal has not fallen on deaf ears — in February 2007, the Special Senate Committee on the *Anti-terrorism Act* recommended a procedure in which a special advocate is able to communicate with the named person both *before* and *after* receiving the confidential information.[83]

5) Security-Cleared Counsel

Some of the intervenors before the Supreme Court in *Charkoui*, including the Canadian Council for Refugees, the African Canadian Legal Clinic, the International Civil Liberties Monitoring Group, and the National Anti-racism Council of Canada, endorsed a model in which counsel for the person named on the certificate would be present during the secret hearings on the condition that he would not disclose the closed material (that is, he would take an undertaking to this effect or be se-

---

82 *Charkaoui Factum*, above note 67 at para. 59.
83 Canada, Special Senate Committee on the *Anti-terrorism Act, Fundamental Justice in Extraordinary Times: Main Report of the Special Senate Committee on the Anti-Terrorism Act* (Ottawa: Senate Committees Directorate, 2007) at 35 (Chair: The Honourable David P. Smith, P.C.).

curity-cleared).[84] This is essentially the model that has been adopted in the Air India criminal trial. In such a procedure counsel for the person concerned would have full participatory rights in both the public and secret hearings, subject to an undertaking to not reveal any of the secret evidence to his client.

E. CONCLUSION

The various alternatives discussed above allow for different levels of participation by the person concerned in challenging the credibility of *in camera* evidence and present different levels of a threat of potential leakage of confidential information. However, wherever the line is drawn, it is clear that any proposed or adopted measures must meet two basic principles. First, that they uphold the right to a fair trial before an independent decision-maker by ensuring some meaningful, effective participation in all aspects of the proceedings (including those held *in camera*). Second, where it is determined that national security concerns preclude the direct participation of the concerned individual, it must be ensured that the counsel nominated to represent the interests of the person in the *in camera* proceedings can provide meaningful representation on her behalf, both in evaluating the scope of the Crown's assertion of confidentiality and in challenging the credibility of the Crown's case.

In terms of challenges to assertions of confidentiality, there would appear to be no need for any direct relationship between the person concerned and counsel. Counsel can effectively challenge assertions of national security confidentiality based on generally accepted principles and jurisprudence. However, when it comes to challenging the credibility of the government's evidence, it is clear that the representative nominated to do so on behalf of the person must have the ability to put forward, as fully as possible, the concerns of the named person.[85] Counsel can only do this if she is able to continue to communicate with the named person after she has reviewed the secret evidence. Therefore, at a minimum, counsel who plays this role must be able to interact with the

---

84 *Charkaoui v. Canada*, above note 5 (factum of the intervenors, Canadian Council for Refugees, the African Canadian Legal Clinic, the International Civil Liberties Monitoring Group, and National Anti-racism Council of Canada) at para. 48.

85 See *Charkaoui v. Canada*, above note 5 at para. 63.

concerned individual throughout the process (both before and after). As has been demonstrated in this paper, there are safeguards available to ensure that there is no leakage of confidential information (for example, requiring counsel to take an oath of secrecy and imposing stiff penalties if information is disclosed). In addition, counsel must have sufficient resources to be able to fulfill his function properly. These concerns would appear to eliminate the Special Advocates model implemented in the U.K. as an acceptable mechanism, and would militate in favour of either a SIRC or Arar Inquiry model or the Modified Special Advocates mechanism.

Certainly, if the government seriously wants to protect Canada's national security in a manner that preserves our democratic values, it must adopt a procedure that allows for the most fulsome participation of the named person while still protecting national security. The Supreme Court's ruling against the current security certificate regime is an important first step in ensuring a national security policy that reflects and protects our *Charter* values. It is now up to Parliament to rewrite the impugned *IRPA* provisions in a "*Charter*-proof" manner.

Consular and Diplomatic Protection in an Age of Terrorism: Filling the Gaps

Gar Pardy

A. INTRODUCTION AND BACKGROUND

The treatment of foreigners by governments has not received effective or conclusive attention by the international community. This lack of attention has been magnified enormously in recent years by the worldwide efforts to contain acts of international terrorism. Even existing relevant international legal instruments have been reinterpreted, ignored, and broken in the drive for illusory security. The Geneva Conventions,[1] the great bulwark providing the rules for war, did not adequately envisage

---

1   *Geneva Convention (I) for the Amelioration of the Condition of the Wounded and Sick in Armed Forces in the Field*, 12 August 1949, 75 U.N.T.S. 31; *Geneva Convention (II) for the Amelioration of the Condition of Wounded, Sick and Shipwrecked Members of Armed Forces at Sea*, 2 August 1949, 75 U.N.T.S. 85; *Geneva Convention (III) relative to the Treatment of Prisoners of War*, 12 August 1949, 75 U.N.T.S. 135; *Geneva Convention (IV) relative to the Protection of Civilian Persons in Time of War*, 12 August 1949, 75 U.N.T.S. 287; *Protocol Additional to the Geneva Conventions of 12 August 1949, and relating to the Protection of Victims of International Armed Conflicts (Protocol I)*, 8 June 1977, 1125 U.N.T.S. 3 (entered into force 7 December 1950); *Protocol Additional to the Geneva Conventions of 12 August 1949, and relating to the Protection of Victims of Non-International Armed Conflicts (Protocol II)*, 8 June 1977, 1125 U.N.T.S. 609 (entered into force 7 December 1978); *Protocol Additional to the Geneva Conventions of 12 August 1949, and relating to the Adoption of an Additional Distinctive Emblem*

the asymmetrical warfare of terrorism and the Geneva Conventions have been wilfully circumscribed. The provisions of the more recent *Convention against Torture and Other Cruel, Inhuman or Degrading Treatment or Punishment*[2] and its Optional Protocol,[3] while a rock of some standing, has been ignored by many governments in the belief that security concerns override its peremptory norms. And the anaemic *Vienna Convention on Consular Relations*[4] has demonstrated that this example of the lowest common denominator in treaty-making needs fundamental revision and/or replacement. In this climate, even the hortative prescriptions of the *Universal Declaration of Human Rights*[5] and the *International Covenant on Civil and Political Rights* and its Optional Protocol[6] have been of little direct value to persons snared in security webs. This paper makes proposals for a new multilateral treaty to provide additional protection for persons encountering difficulties in countries of second or non-citizenship.

An additional factor of considerable importance has emerged complicating the treatment of foreigners. This is the increasing incidence of dual citizenship or, as it is frequently misnamed in today's terminology, dual nationality. Improvements in transportation, especially the arrival of the jet engine, the spread of easy, inexpensive international communica-

---

(Protocol III), 8 December 2005 (entered into force 14 January 2007), online: www.icrc.org/ihl.nsf/FULL/615.

2   *Convention against Torture and Other Cruel, Inhuman or Degrading Treatment or Punishment*, 10 December 1984, 1465 U.N.T.S. 85 [*CAT*]; Signatories can be found online: www.ohchr.org/english/countries/ratification/9.htm.

3   *Optional Protocol to the Convention against Torture and Other Cruel, Inhuman or Degrading Treatment or Punishment*, GA Res. 57/199, UN GAOR, 57th Sess., UN Doc. A/RES/57/199 (2002) [*OPCAT*]. As of 19 April 2006, there were only eighteen parties (fifty signatories), two short of the required twenty for entry into force. Participants can be found online: www.ohchr.org/english/countries/ratification/9_b.htm.

4   *Vienna Convention on Consular Relations*, 24 April 1963, 596 U.N.T.S. 261, Can. T.S. 1974 No. 25, accession by Canada 17 August 1974) [*VCCR*].

5   *Universal Declaration of Human Rights*, GA Res. 217 (III), UN GAOR, 3d Sess., Supp. No. 13, UN Doc. A/810 (1948).

6   *International Convenant on Civil and Political Rights*, 19 December 1966, 999 U.N.T.S. 171, Can. T.S. 1976 No. 47, 6 I.L.M. 368 [*ICCPR*; *Optional Protocol to the International Covenant on Civil and Political Rights*, 23 March 1976, 999 U.N.T.S. 302.

tions, both personal and social, and the disappearance of the east-west divide in Europe and elsewhere has produced a complex new reality affecting the movement and migration of peoples. The vast migrations of the eighteenth and nineteenth centuries were permanent events in the lives of the people involved; there was little ability for such people to visit or maintain contact with family and friends in their previous countries of citizenship. Even up to and including the years after the First World War there was little expectation among migrants for a return to the old country or the maintenance of contacts across the oceans. The second half of the twentieth century saw the emergence of a new paradigm where migrants did not necessarily see the new country as being either permanent or, in the short term, establishing a new nationality.

The large migrations to Canada in the fourth quarter of the twentieth century illustrate many of the problems associated with dual citizenship. Particularly illustrative are the tens of thousands of Canadians who migrated from Lebanon. Initially the migrants were mainly from the Christian north, in the late-nineteenth and early-twentieth centuries. However, following the outbreak of the civil war in the mid-1970s, thousands more from all of the Lebanese confessionals fled to Canada. Once a semblance of normalcy was restored in the early 1990s, thousands decided to return. The events of the summer of 2006 surprised many Canadians when it was realized that there were in excess of 40,000[7] Canadians citizens in Lebanon needing consular protection and assistance. Similarly, there are estimates of over 200,000[8] Canadian citizens in Hong Kong, most also having Chinese citizenship; there are also large communities of Canadian citizens in Italy, Poland, the United Kingdom, the United States, Germany, Chile, and many other countries.

The reaction of many governments to the events of September 11, 2001 created an environment in which there was serious erosion of fundamental rights and freedoms. Nowhere was this more evident than in the treatment of foreigners suspected of being involved in terrorism or of being members or supporters of terrorist groups. Thousands have

---

7   Canada, Canada and the UN, *Press Review for July 22–24, 2006* (Ottawa: Government of Canada, 2006), online: http://geo.international.gc.ca/canada_un/ottawa/canada_un/unupdate-en.asp?id=7093&content_type=2.

8   Hong Kong Economic and Trade Office (Canada), *Facts and Statistics*, online: www.hketo.ca/invest/facts.html.

been detained in appalling conditions with serious allegations and, in many cases, confirmed acts of torture and abuse; preventative and secretive detentions have been used by normally democratic governments; international kidnappings and extra-legal deportations have occurred involving state agents; and police and security organizations have been conditioned through statements by democratic leaders of the almost "holy grail" nature of their work.[9] For many there was excessive *passion* for the mission and a willingness to ignore the rule of law.

Several years on from the seminal events of 2001 and the emerging ones from the wars in Afghanistan and Iraq, there is an increasing and deepening perspective on these worrisome developments. Importantly, there is widespread questioning of the value of these harsh, extra, or quasi-legal mechanisms in coping with worldwide ideological terrorist groups such as Al-Qaeda and its regional affiliates. There is a growing belief among security and intelligence professionals, and experts in academe and government, that many of the mechanisms were counterproductive and, in some instances, contribute to the threat.[10] Most importantly, courts, commissions, and legislatures are reasserting their authority in these areas and hopefully, over time, a more balanced and appropriate approach will emerge.[11]

At the level of individuals, several Canadians were the victims of the excesses of governments in the war on terrorism. Maher Arar was detained by the American authorities in September 2002 while transiting New York on his return to Canada and was subsequently deported to Syria, accused of being a member of Al-Qaeda. Arar also held Syrian cit-

---

9 Generally, see details on these events in the reports of Amnesty International, online: http://web.amnesty.org/library/engindex; Human Rights Watch, online: www.hrw.org/doc/?t=pubs; European Council, *Justice and Citizen's Rights,* European Commission, online: ec.europa.eu/news/justice/archives_en.htm; Council of Europe, *CPT Database,* European Committee for the Prevention of Torture and Inhuman or Degrading Treatment or Punishment, online: www.cpt.coe.int/en/database.htm; and numerous press articles.

10 See a summary of these ideas in James Fallows, "Declaring Victory" *The Atlantic* (September 2006) at 60. See also: U.S., Office of the Director of National Intelligence, *Declassified Key Judgments of the National Intelligence Estimate "Trends in Global Terrorism: Implications for the United States date April 2006"* (April 2006), online: www.dni.gov/press_releases/Declassified_NIE_Key_Judgments.pdf.

11 See *Hamdan v. Rumsfeld,* 126 S. Ct. 2749 (2006).

izenship. His experience was investigated by a Commission of Inquiry under Justice Dennis O'Connor and a report was issued in September 2006.[12] The report provides a comprehensive examination of the actions of Canadian officials that led to the wrongful identification of Arar as a terrorist and his detention and torture in Syria. Of significance to persons interested in consular matters, the report provides extensive details and analysis of the efforts to obtain access to Arar, his release, and the exercise of consular protection.[13]

Three other Canadians, Ahmad El-Maati, Abdullah Almalki, and Muayyed Nureddin, were also detained by the Syrians. El-Maati, a Canadian and Egyptian citizen, was subsequently transferred to Egypt and detained for several months. Abdullah Almalki and Muayyed Nurreddin held Canadian and Syrian citizenship. The three men were interviewed on behalf of the O'Connor Commission and it was reported that all three had been tortured while in Syrian custody.[14] Another Canadian, who was also a citizen of Iran, Zahra Kazemi, died in Tehran in July 2003 following torture and interrogation by Iranian officials.[15]

These cases, collectively, along with the report of Justice O'Connor, demonstrate the extreme difficulty in exercising consular protection in such circumstances and especially when the victims are in their country of second citizenship. Other countries have experienced similar difficulties and Justice O'Connor accords some attention to the issue of dual citizenship and its consequences in the war on terror.

---

12   Canada, Commission of Inquiry into the Actions of Canadian Officials in Relation to Maher Arar, *Report of the Events Relating to Maher Arar: Analysis and Recommendations* (Ottawa: Public Works and Government Services Canada, 2006).

13   The commission did not find fault with the word of consular officials in their efforts to assist Mr. Arar. The author provided testimony to the public and *in camera* sessions of the commission.

14   The Government of Canada, on 12 December 2006, appointed former Supreme Court Justice Frank Iacobucci as a commissioner under Part I of the *Inquiries Act*, R.S.C. 1985, C. I-11, "to conduct an internal inquiry into the actions of Canadian officials in relation to Abdullah Almalki, Ahmad Abou-Elmaati [*sic*] and Muayyed Nureddin": Canada, Internal Inquiry into the Actions of Canadian Officials in Relation to Abdullah Almalki, Ahmad Abou-Elmaati and Muayyed Nureddin, *Terms of Reference*, online: www.iacobucciinquiry.ca/en/terms-of-reference/index.htm. See online: www.iacobucciinquiry.ca for further details.

15   Various Iranian investigations and courts have not identified or punished those responsible for Ms. Kazemi's death.

B. CONSULAR AND DIPLOMATIC PROTECTION

The use of the terms *consular* and *diplomatic* in the context of the assistance and services provided by a country to its citizens while in another country, overlap in their meaning and intent. Consular is the more widely used term today although, historically, diplomatic protection appears to have had a longer run. Today, as John Currie writes, diplomatic protection takes the "form of the assertion by a state of an international claim on behalf of its national against another state."[16] Consular protection conceptually may be considered a subset of diplomatic protection or as an entirely separate and unique form of protection. In this paper, consular protection is treated as a unique form of protection and should not be confused with diplomatic protection.

To confuse matters even more, the term diplomatic protection is now often used to describe the police and security units providing protection to resident foreign diplomats and other foreign officials. For example, in the United Kingdom the Diplomatic Protection Group is part of the London Metropolitan Police. This paper is concerned with consular protection and will use that term throughout except when dealing with a recent International Law Commission initiative concerning the "bringing of a claim for diplomatic protection."[17] Some attention is given to this initiative since it provides an examination of a number of concepts (dual citizenship, obligation of states, differences with consular protection) valuable in the context of consular protection.

In his book, *The Professor and the Madman*, Simon Winchester provides an early example of consular protection in 1872 London, England.[18] The madman in this case was Dr. William Chester Minor, an American military officer living in London. The professor was Dr. James Murray, the man who gave us the *Oxford English Dictionary*. Dr. Minor was arrested for the murder of a British citizen and was in police custody.

> This put a wholly new complexion on the case. The American legation had now to be told. And so in the midmorning, despite it being a Sat-

---

16   John Currie, Craig Forcese, & Valerie Oosterveld, *Public International Law: Doctrine, Practice and Theory* (Ottawa: University of Ottawa, 2004) at 418.

17   "Report of the International Law Commission on the work of its fifty-sixth session" (UN Doc. A/59/10) in *Yearbook of the International Law Commission 2004*, vol. 2, part 2 (New York: United Nations, 2004) at para. 60 [*RILC*].

18   Simon Winchester, *The Professor and the Madman* (New York: Harper Collins, 1998).

urday, the Foreign Office formally notified the U.S. Minister in London that one of their army surgeons had been arrested and was being held on a charge of murder . . . .

Within days the American vice-consul was writing making sure that the hapless army officer was being well looked after. Might it be possible for "our poor friend," he prayed, to have some of his personal effects send down? . . . Is it in theory possible to visit? To cheer him up, could we send him a pound of his Dennis' coffee and some French plums? Mr Orange [the warden] was silent on the specific matter of plums, but told the consul that Doctor Minor could have whatever he liked so long as it didn't prejudice his safety or the asylum's disciplined running.[19]

C. THE INTERNATIONAL LAW COMMISSION (ILC)

For a number of years the ILC has been studying the issue of diplomatic protection. At its 48th session in 1996, it identified diplomatic protection "as one of three topics appropriate for codification and progressive development."[20] The General Assembly of the United Nations, in the same year, supported the initiative and requested that its scope be clarified and that the comments of member governments be taken into account. A special rapporteur was appointed and at the 3 August 2004 session of the ILC, draft articles on diplomatic protection were presented.

In part one, Article 1 dealing with *definition and scope*, the ILC emphasizes that the term diplomatic protection is to be used narrowly. Article 1 states:

Diplomatic protection consists of resort to diplomatic action or other means of peaceful settlement by a State adopting in its own right the cause of its national in respect of an injury to that national arising from an *internationally wrongful act of another State*.[21]

---

19 *Ibid.* at 13–14 and 121. At the request of his family, Dr. Minor was sent to an American asylum, an early example of the transfers that now take place under transfer of offender treaties.

20 "Report of the International Law Commission on the work of its forty-eighth session" (UN Doc. A/51/10) in *Yearbook of the International Law Commission 1996*, vol. 2, part 2 (New York: United Nations, 1996) at para. 248.

21 *RILC*, above note 17 at 59 [emphasis added].

The draft articles seem to be biased in the direction that the resort to diplomatic action would take place after an *injury* has taken place, and most likely there was an earlier termination point for the injury and certainly a need for earlier intervention by the state of citizenship of the person injured. The commentary associated with the ILC draft articles makes this point clear: "the present draft articles are confined to secondary rules only—that is, the rules that relate to the conditions that must be met for the bringing of a claim for diplomatic protection."[22] As such, it can be assumed that consular protection would be exercised first by the country of nationality of the injured person and in its failure the resort to diplomatic protection would take place. It is recognized that an internationally cognizable injury might be as simple as arbitrary detention of a national and may not involve physical or pecuniary injury.

The ILC report also makes a direct connection between its draft articles on diplomatic protection and another set of draft articles on state responsibility.[23] It notes that many of the principles contained in the state responsibility draft articles are relevant to diplomatic protection and goes on to further emphasize that its work has more to do with after-the-fact protection than with protection at the time an injury or wrongful act is occurring. The report states:

> This applies in particular to the provisions dealing with the legal conse-
> quences of an internationally wrongful act. A State responsible for injur-
> ing a foreign national is obliged to cease the wrongful conduct and to
> make full reparation for the injury, caused by the internationally wrong-
> ful act. This reparation may take the form of restitution, compensation
> or satisfaction, either singly or in combination.[24]

There is also an historical and contextual reason for using the term "consular protection" to describe the actions of a government to protect its nationals when in difficulty overseas. The *Hague Convention on Conflict of Nationality Laws*[25] was drafted in the aftermath of the 1919 Paris Peace Conference that confirmed numerous border changes in Europe

---

22   *Ibid.* at 23.

23   *Ibid.*

24   *Ibid.*

25   *Convention on Certain Questions Relating to the Conflict of Nationality Laws*, 12 April
     1930, 179 L.N.T.S. 89 [*CCNL*].

and elsewhere. These border changes were done with little regard for their effect on the people involved. As Richard Holbrooke wrote in the foreword to the Margaret MacMillan book, *Paris 1919*:[26]

> Some of the most intractable problems of the modern world have roots in decisions made right after the end of the Great War. Among them one could list the four Balkan wars between 1991 and 1999; the crisis over Iraq (whose present borders resulted from Franco-British rivalries and casual mapmaking); the continuing quest of the Kurds for self-determination; disputes between Greece and Turkey; and the endless struggle between Arabs and Jews over land that each thought had been promised them.
>
> As the peacemakers met in Paris, new nations emerged and great empires died. Excessively ambitious, the Big Four set out to do nothing less than fix the world, from Europe to the far Pacific. But facing domestic pressures, events they could not control, and conflicting claims they could not reconcile, the negotiators were, in the end, simply overwhelmed—and made deals and compromises that would echo down through history.[27]

Georges Clemenceau, the then President of France, "whose own behaviour contributed to the failure ... [is quoted as saying] yes, this treaty will bring us burdens, troubles, miseries, difficulties, and that will continue for long years."[28]

In the aftermath of the Paris Conference, there was appreciation that some of the conference decisions and the consequential border changes carried serious implications for the *nationality*[29] of the people affected and that there would be *conflicts* between the citizenship laws of states. The *CCNL* was an attempt to deal with these problems. Its preamble states:

> Being convinced that it is in the general interest of the international community to secure that all its members should recognize that every person should have a nationality and should have one nationality only;

---

26 Margaret MacMillan, *Paris 1919: Six Months That Changed the World* (New York: Random House, 2003).

27 *Ibid.* at ix.

28 *Ibid.*

29 The terms "citizenship" and "dual citizenship" are used as they are more accurate in today's environment.

Recognizing accordingly that the ideal towards which the efforts of humanity should be directed in this domain is the abolition of all cases both of statelessness and of double nationality;[30]

Canada, along with a number of other countries, was signatory to the *CCNL*. A number of countries remain signatories today, but not Canada. Article 4 of the *CCNL* states that "A state may not afford *diplomatic protection* to one of its nationals against a State whose nationality such person also possesses."[31] As mentioned earlier, many of the people affected by the human rights/anti-terrorism environment are nationals of more than one state. Consequently, to allow this language from more than seventy years ago to undermine consular protection today is unacceptable. The consular protection road is a difficult one as it is and to add to its bumps and ruts by retaining a principle that could be used to place persons beyond protection should be avoided.

Canada, along with a number of other countries, changed its policy in the early 1990s, reflecting the changing social, linguistic, and cultural makeup of the country. As well, earlier in 1977, when the Canadian *Citizenship Act*[32] was amended, the prohibition against dual citizenship was eliminated. These changes led Canada to denounce the *CCNL* on 15 May 1996[33] since its provisions were inconsistent with the emerging policy of ensuring that all Canadians were treated equally with respect to consular protection and services. The denouncement of the *CCNL* did not guarantee consular protection for Canadian nationals in their country of second nationality as any number of difficult cases has demonstrated. It does mean, however, that Canada will try and assist in whatever ways may be possible or permitted by the receiving state.

D. *VIENNA CONVENTION ON CONSULAR RELATIONS (VCCR)*

There is an extensive body of law, both national and international, on consular assistance and protection and there are numerous bilateral and

---

30   *CCNL*, above note 25, Preamble.
31   *Ibid.*, Article 4 [emphasis added].
32   R.S.C. 1985, c. C-29.
33   For the status of the *CCNL*, above note 25, see online: http://untreaty.un.org/ENG-LISH/bible/englishinternetbible/partII/Treaty-4.asp.

multilateral treaties on the matter. The most relevant is the multilateral *VCCR*,[34] which was negotiated and brought into service more than forty years ago. A companion treaty, the *Vienna Convention on Diplomatic Relations*,[35] was signed two years earlier, on 18 April 1961. Both conventions in the intervening years have been ratified by a large majority of the international community and both remain the foundation on which bilateral consular and diplomatic/political relations are exercised.

There is good reason for the *VCCR* to be called "Consular Relations" since it has little in its many provisions that could be labelled as protective measures a state could use in defending its citizens in other countries. The *VCCR* has seventy-nine Articles, only two of which can be defined as establishing protective standards. Article 36 requires that officials of the receiving state inform a detained person of the right to contact the consular authorities of her sending state.[36] Because of its importance, Article 36 is quoted in full:

Article 36
Communications and Contact with nationals of the sending State

1. With a view to facilitating the exercise of consular functions relating to nationals of the sending State:

(a) consular officers shall be free to communicate with nationals of the sending State and to have access to them. Nationals of the sending State shall have the same freedom with respect to communication with and access to consular officers of the sending State;

(b) if he so requests, the competent authorities of the receiving State shall, without delay, inform the consular post of the sending State if, within its consular district, a national of that State is arrested or committed to prison or to custody pending trial or is detained in any other manner. Any communication addressed to the consular post by the person arrested, in prison, custody or detention shall also be forwarded by the said authorities without delay. The said authorities shall inform the person concerned without delay of his rights under this sub-paragraph;

---

34 *VCCR*, above note 4.

35 *Vienna Convention on Diplomatic Relations*, 18 April 1961, 500 U.N.T.S. 95.

36 The terms "receiving state" and "sending state" follow the usage in the *VCCR*.

(c) consular officers shall have the right to visit a national of the sending State who is in prison, custody or detention, to converse and correspond with him and to arrange for his legal representation. They shall also have the right to visit any national of the sending State who is in prison, custody or detention in their district in pursuance of a judgement. Nevertheless, consular officers shall refrain from taking action on behalf of a national who is in prison, custody or detention if he expressly opposes such action.

2. The rights referred to in paragraph 1 of this Article shall be exercised in conformity with the laws and regulations of the receiving State, subject to the proviso, however, that the said laws and regulations must enable full effect to be given to the purposes for which the rights accorded under this Article are intended.

Article 36 establishes rights for the exercise of consular protection for persons who have been arrested or in detention. In respect to prisoners, Article 36 provides for "without delay" notification,[37] communications, access, delivery of written communications, visits, and legal representation between consular officers and their citizens. Of particular importance is that the rights conferred "shall be exercised in conformity with the laws and regulations of the receiving State [but that] the said laws and regulations must enable full effect to be given to the purposes for which the rights accorded under this Article are intended."[38] More often than not, the first part of this formula is what is applied, as the laws and regulations of the *receiving state* are well known to the authorities, but the *purposes* for these rights are much less known or acknowledged and are subject to the vicissitudes of local officials. The principles and rights in Article 36 are echoed and replicated in numerous other international instruments and resolutions where there is an issue, arrest, or detention.[39]

---

37 It should be noted that some countries through differences in privacy law standards are able to notify sending states of the detention of a national without the permission of the person involved. The United States is able to do this if there is a consular bilateral agreement in place, but Canada is unable to do so.

38 *VCCR*, above note 4 at 15.

39 Mark Warren, *Consular Rights of Foreign Nationals: International Norms*, January 2004, online: www3.sympatico.ca/aiwarren/norms.htm. The author is grateful to Mark Warren, Human Rights Research, Amnesty International, for the list.

Article 36 has also found support in several decisions by international courts. The Inter-American Court of Human Rights provided an advisory opinion to the United Mexican States on 1 October 1999. The court confirmed that Article 36 confers rights upon detained foreign nationals, including the right to information on consular assistance, and these rights carry associated obligations on the receiving state. In addition, the court was of the opinion that Article 36 concerns the protection of the rights of a national of the sending state and is part of the body of international human rights law. The expression "without delay" was seen to mean that a detained person has the right to be informed of the consular rights in Article 36(1)(b) at the time of arrest or at least before the detained person makes a first statement before the authorities. Finally, the court concluded that failure to observe a detained foreign national's right to information is prejudicial to due process of law.[40]

More recently the International Court of Justice (ICJ) in 2001 and 2004 reaffirmed Article 36 rights in both the *LaGrand*[41] and the *Avena*[42] cases. The United States was the defending state in both cases and the disputes centred on advising arrested persons of their right to contact their consulates. In the *LaGrand* case, decided on 27 June 2001, the Court ruled *inter alia*:

> by not informing [the arrested persons] without delay following their arrest of their rights under Article 36, paragraph 1(b) and paragraph (3), . . . the United States breached its obligations [to render assistance] to Federal Republic of Germany and to the *LaGrand* brothers.[43]

The same issues were in play in *Avena* and the Court, on 31 March 2004, ruled in much the same way as in *LaGrand*: the United States had breached its obligation under Article 36, paragraph (1)(b) and paragraphs 1(a) and (c) of the *VCCR*.

Significantly, there are numerous rights that are not covered in the *VCCR*. Article 36 does not provide for the following important rights that would significantly enhance consular protection: privacy for written

---

40 *Ibid.*

41 *LaGrand (Germany v. United States of America)*, [2001] I.C.J. Rep. 466 [*LaGrand*].

42 *Avena and Other Mexian Nationals (Mexico v. United States of America)*, [2004] I.C.J. Rep. 12 [*Avena*].

43 *LaGrand*, above note 41 at para. 128.

communications; confidential and private meetings with the detained persons; provision of personal articles and material; information from officials of the receiving state on the reasons for detention; provision of legal, forensic, and investigatory assistance; and access by family and friends.

The only other section of the *VCCR* that provides consular protection standards is Article 37. It requires a receiving state to provide a sending state with information concerning "Cases of Deaths, Guardianship or Trusteeship, Wrecks and Air Accidents." The seventy-seven other articles in the convention provide rules for the official conduct of consular relations between states, and, in and of themselves, do not establish standards of consular protection.

There are two Optional Protocols to the *VCCR*, both negotiated in Vienna on 24 April 1963, at the same time as the main *VCCR*. The first Optional Protocol deals with the acquisition of nationality by "members of the consular post and by members of their families."[44] It eliminates the possibility that such persons "shall not by the operation of the law of the receiving State, acquire the nationality of that State."[45] The second Optional Protocol provides for the compulsory settlement of disputes "arising out of the interpretation or application of the Convention to the compulsory jurisdiction of the International Court of Justice, unless some other form of settlement has been agreed upon by the parties within a reasonable period."[46]

More than 170 countries (including Canada) are parties to the *VCCR* and there are few if any of the remaining non-party countries that do not accept its provisions as the basis for the conduct of consular relations and consular protection. However, the acceptance of the Optional Protocols falls off sharply. Only thirty-nine countries are parties to the *Optional Protocol concerning Acquisition of Nationality* and just forty-five are parties to the *Optional Protocol concerning the Compulsory Settlement of Disputes*. Canada is not a party to either of the protocols.

The United States ratified the *Optional Protocol concerning the Compulsory Settlement of Disputes* on 24 November 1969, and was the first

---

44 *Optional Protocol to the Vienna Convention on Consular Relations concerning Acquisition of Nationality*, 24 April 1963, 596 U.N.T.S. 469, Preamble, para. 2.

45 *Ibid.*, Article II.

46 *Optional Protocol to the Vienna Convention on Consular Relations concerning the Compulsory Settlement of Disputes*, 24 April 1963, 596 U.N.T.S. 487, Preamble, para. 2.

"country to invoke the protocol before the ICJ, also known as the World Court, successfully suing Iran[47] for the taking of 52 U.S. hostages in Tehran in 1979."[48] The United States government wrote to the Secretary-General of the United Nations on 7 March 2005 and stated:

> This letter constitutes notification by the United States of America that it hereby withdraws from the aforesaid Protocol. As a consequence of this withdrawal, the United States will no longer recognize the jurisdiction of the International Court of Justice reflected in that Protocol.[49]

The withdrawal was a consequence of the ICJ decisions in the *LaGrand* and *Avena* cases. The spokesperson for the American state department was quoted at the time as saying: "The International Court of Justice has interpreted the Vienna Consular Convention in ways that we had not anticipated that involved state criminal prosecutions and the death penalty, effectively asking the court to supervise our domestic criminal system."[50]

E. BILATERAL CONSULAR AGREEMENTS

There are literally hundreds of bilateral consular agreements. For the most part these, more or less, replicate the provisions of the *VCCR*. Article 73 of the *VCCR* provides explicit permission for such agreements. "Nothing in the present Convention shall preclude States from concluding international agreements confirming or supplementing or extending or amplifying the provisions thereof."[51] Many of these bilateral agreements predate the *VCCR* although, more recently, there have been initiatives by a number of countries to use bilateral agreements to extend consular protection into areas not covered by the *VCCR*.

Canada, in recent years, signed three such agreements. There is a bilateral agreement with the People's Republic of China that covers several consular issues and considerably broadens the consular protection rights of the sending state for detained persons. There are also bilateral

---

47 *United States Diplomatic and Consular Staff in Tehran (United States of America v. Iran)*, [1980] I.C.J. Rep. 3.

48 Charles Lane, "U.S. Quits Pact Used in Capital Cases" *Washington Post* (10 March 2005) A01.

49 *Ibid.*

50 *Ibid.*

51 *VCCR*, above note 4, Article 73.

agreements with Egypt and Lebanon providing for mutual assistance and support in cases of parental child abduction.

The agreement with China was negotiated prior to the return of Hong Kong to Chinese sovereignty in 1997 and sought to establish the right to provide consular assistance to dual citizens in certain circumstances. The negotiations provided an opportunity to improve some of the provisions in the *VCCR* with respect to arrested or detained persons. Specifically, the bilateral agreement provides improved language on notification by the receiving state of persons arrested, detained, or deprived of freedom; specific standards with respect to the languages that can be used in communicating with such persons; the right to visit such persons within two days of the date of notification by the receiving state and that visits can take place at intervals of no longer than one month; the obligation of the receiving state to provide information on the charges against a national of the sending state; the right of a consular officer of the sending state to attend the trial or other legal proceedings; the obligation of the receiving state to make available adequate interpretation services; and the rights granted in the treaty will not be restricted by the application of other laws of the receiving state.[52]

In addition to these improvements the treaty created a precedent in providing protection for dual citizens who are in their country of second citizenship. The treaty states that signatories will use the passport for entry to determine citizenship for consular protection purposes. As such a Canadian citizen who is also a citizen of China, and who enters China using a Canadian passport, will be considered by the Chinese authorities as being solely a citizen of Canada. The relevant provision states:

> A national of the sending State entering the receiving State with valid travel documents of the sending State will, during the period for which his status has been accorded on a limited basis by visa or lawful visa-free entry, be considered a national of the sending State by the appropriate authorities of the receiving State with a view to ensuring consular access and protection by the sending State.[53]

---

52 *Consular Agreement between the Government of Canada and the Government of the People's Republic of China*, 28 November 1997, Article 8, online: www.voyage.gc.ca/main/legal/can_china-en.asp.

53 *Ibid.*, Article 12(3).

Australia and the United States signed similar agreements with China. These are the only treaties breaking new ground in the extension of consular protection to dual citizens. As discussed later, this precedent could provide a model for this contentious matter.[54]

The bilateral agreements with Egypt and Lebanon were designed to improve cooperation with these countries on "Consular Elements of Family Matters" in the case of Egypt[55] and on "Consular Matters of a Humanitarian Nature" in the case of Lebanon.[56] These treaties became necessary as it was unlikely either Egypt or Lebanon would sign the multilateral *Convention on the Civil Aspects of International Child Abduction*.[57] The *Hague Convention* reflects a concept of family and social law that differs considerably from that found in many Islamic countries, but, as the treaties reflect, there is a concern to provide a mechanism to resolve cases of parental child abductions. Both treaties are similar in that they recognize the need to resolve such cases and to do so a joint consultative commission has been established. As stated in the Lebanese treaty,

The Commission shall be competent to:

a) consider problems related to individual consular cases involving persons possessing the nationality of either Party with a view to

---

54 The personal experience of the author, up to 2003, was that the new treaty worked well. However, in recent months there is some questioning of the treaty as a result of the Huseyin Celil case. In that case, a Canadian citizen who was born in the Uyghur region of China was detained in Uzbekistan in 2006, subsequently extradited to China, and sentenced to a lengthy prison term for terrorism-related offences. China has refused all requests from the Canadian government for consular access. Specific details are not available but if Mr. Celil was returned to China using Chinese travel documents, then the bilateral consular agreement would not apply.

55 *Agreement between the Government of Canada and the Government of the Arab Republic of Egypt Regarding Cooperation on Consular Elements of Family Matters*, 10 November 1997, online: www.voyage.gc.ca/main/legal/can-egypt_family-en.asp.

56 *Agreement between the Government of Canada and the Government of the Lebanese Republic Regarding Cooperation on Consular Matters of a Humanitarian Nature*, 13 April 2000, online: www.treaty-accord.gc.ca/ViewTreaty.asp?Language=0&Treaty_ID=103477.

57 *Convention on the Civil Aspects of International Child Abduction*, 25 October 1980, 1343 U.N.T.S. 89 [*Hague Convention*].

facilitating their resolution, in accordance with the laws of each Party.

These cases shall include matters pertaining to personal status such as child custody, and those which require measures pertaining to the protection of a child's right, and of basic human rights in general.[58]

F. OTHER MULTILATERAL INSTRUMENTS

There are few enforcement mechanisms in the historical human rights instruments with respect to the treatment of foreigners or consular protective standards generally. The *Universal Declaration of Human Rights*, the *International Covenant on Civil and Political Rights* and its Optional Protocol, and a variety of other instruments, while part of customary international law and thus binding on all states, largely rely on evolutionary self-improvement as the main mechanism for change. While the standards are quite clear, they do not provide any direct, practicable, enforcement mechanisms and as such these instruments offer little direct or timely assistance for individuals whose fingernails are being shortened or whose feet are being beaten.

One exception is the *Convention against Torture and Other Cruel, Inhuman or Degrading Treatment or Punishment*[59] (*CAT*) and its Optional Protocol (*OPCAT*).[60] The *CAT* provides comprehensive language establishing standards of state behaviour related to some of the more abusive elements involved in the war on terror. However, these standards have more to do with establishing a requirement not to engage in or be a party to such activities than establishing mechanisms through which a state can protect the interests of its citizens in other countries. It was recognized early on that the *CAT* lacked appropriate enforcement mechanisms and efforts were undertaken to provide contemporaneous

---

58 Above note 56, Article 4. The personal experience of the author was that these were valuable initiatives on a very sensitive subject. They have been useful in providing a framework to obtain solutions to several cases and the Joint Consultative commissions for each country have met at least once. It is still early days in determining whether or not such bilateral treaties can continue to assist in parental child abduction cases.

59 *CAT*, above note 2.

60 *OPCAT*, above note 3.

protective and enforcement mechanisms in order to achieve the *CAT's* laudatory goals.

Eighteen years and eight days after the *CAT* was opened for signature, an Optional Protocol was adopted at the 57th session of the General Assembly and it provides a practicable and timely set of enforcement mechanisms that give reality to the goals of the main convention. The *OPCAT* requires the establishment of a Subcommittee of the Committee against Torture and would " establish a system of regular visits undertaken by independent international and national bodies to places where people are deprived of their liberty, in order to prevent torture and other cruel, inhuman or degrading treatment or punishment."[61] Unfortunately, the enthusiasm for the original *CAT* (less than three years from adoption to entry into force) is not yet evident for the Optional Protocol, as it does not yet have the requisite support for entry into force.

G. THE FUTURE

As the preceding paragraphs demonstrate, there is an absence of appropriate international legal enforcement mechanisms to assist states in providing consular protection. This absence is made all the more serious and urgent by the willingness of many states to place national security above human rights and international obligations. In these circumstances, there is a need for an additional international instrument that would fill the existing gaps and deal with the consular protection issues that are not covered by the *VCCR*. There is a reluctance to make such a proposal at this time since the international agenda is crowded and the comity of nations appears more distant than ever. Nevertheless, the need is urgent and there is an increasing understanding that national security does not exist in a vacuum, void of human rights and adherence to international obligations.

It is suggested that, prior to the war on terrorism, the existing international rules and standards for consular protection were already weak and insufficient to deal with the significant global changes affecting the movement of peoples. These changes have become more manifest since the events of September 11, 2001. Fundamentally and conceptually, there is a gap between the rules and standards needed by a sending state to

---

61 *Ibid.*, Article 1.

provide consular protection to its citizens and what a receiving state may be prepared to grant. That dynamic was evident in the original negotiations for the *VCCR* and it is not overly pessimistic to suggest that not much has changed in the intervening years. The need for reciprocity has also ensured that standards in this area are kept at the lowest level possible.

There have been occasional attempts over the years to improve and broaden these rules and standards but there has not been significant progress. What there is today is what there was in 1963, and what there was in 1963 was what there was for the previous several centuries. The possibility of a diplomatic review conference for the *VCCR* has been mooted from time to time, but the idea foundered due to the fear that the review could lead to the loss or diminution of existing rules and standards, meagre as they are.[62]

The war on terrorism and its attendant attack on human rights, along with the emergence of dual citizenship as an issue for many countries, provide an opportunity to revisit the idea of a review conference for the *VCCR*. Equally, it may be more appropriate to leave the *VCCR* as it is and, instead, attempt to negotiate a new convention or optional protocol to the *VCCR* that would deal exclusively with consular protection issues. Such a new convention would compliment the *VCCR* and, in doing so, provide the specificity that many believe is necessary if countries are to protect the interests of their citizens in other countries.

A new treaty, tentatively called, *Convention on Consular and Diplomatic Protection*[63] ideally would be a companion treaty or an optional protocol to the *VCCR*.[64] The new treaty would have the following objectives:

- Establish elaborate standards of conduct for receiving and sending states for the protection of nationals of the sending state

---

62 The author discussed the proposal with consular and legal experts from other countries on several occasions but was unable to evince enthusiasm at the time for a diplomatic review conference for the *VCCR*, above note 4.

63 The author has retained the words "diplomatic protection" despite earlier reservations since "consular" may not be inclusive enough to contain the range of protective actions proposed. However, the term would need to be carefully defined to avoid the limitations mentioned earlier.

64 Draft articles of the new *Convention on Consular and Diplomatic Protection* have been prepared and are available from the author at garp@rogers.com.

- Establish rules for determining "predominant citizenship" when a person has more than one citizenship
- Establish rules on access to nationals of the sending state imprisoned or detained by the receiving state
- Establish rules for the movement of detained persons between states, other than through extradition
- Provide a mechanism for the settlement of disputes

The new treaty could also reflect the recent work of the ILC in dealing with diplomatic protection. The ILC developed draft articles providing procedures for state intervention for redress on behalf of its nationals as a result of "injury"[65] arising from action by the receiving state determined to be an "internationally wrongful act."[66] Conceptually, there would be coherence in having both consular and diplomatic protection standards associated in the same treaty. The new treaty could also provide a bridge to the Geneva Conventions of 1949 and its two protocols of 1977[67] for civilian combatants. This would address, among others, issues associated with access to civilian combatants as determined under the Geneva accords.

The new treaty should provide the sending state with pre-eminent status on consular protection. It should create obligations for the sending and receiving states to ensure consular protection is available to all persons. In addition, it should confirm that the VCCR creates individual rights[68] and imposes obligations on the receiving state. Often in treaty negotiations low expectations provide the basis for low achievements. The draft treaty on *Consular and Diplomatic Protection* should aim high both in its expectations and its objectives.

There are two significant issues associated with the ability of states to exercise consular and diplomatic protection on behalf of its nationals that need to be addressed in the new treaty. These issues have become

---

65 "Draft Articles on Diplomatic Protection with Commentaries 2006" (UN Doc. A/61/10) in *Yearbook of the International Law Commission 2006*, vol. 2, part 2 (New York: United Nations, 2006) at para. 50(1) [*ILC Draft Articles*].

66 *Ibid.*

67 Above note 1. These can be found at Society for Professional Journalists, *Geneva Conventions: A Reference Guide*, online: http://spj.org/gc-texts.asp?.

68 *Khadr v. Canada (Minister of Foreign Affairs)*, 2004 FC 1145 at paras. 26–27: "[T]he International Court of Justice's decision in *LaGrand* . . . states that the VCCR does create individual rights to the services requested" [*Khadr*].

more manifest and acute following the intensification of the war on terrorism after September 11, 2001. The first is associated with persons with
more than one citizenship, or in common language — dual citizens. This
has been an ongoing issue, probably since the emergence of the modern
state, and one with which the international community has had difficulty in establishing standards and rules for resolving disputes.

The *ILC Draft Articles*[69] attempt to provide language, but do not go
far enough in resolving the many practical issues that arise. The concept of "dominant or effective nationality"[70] has emerged and is used in
the *ILC Draft Articles*. The ILC commentary points out that there is considerable precedent for this, but suggests in paragraph 5 that there will
always be a need to balance the strengths of competing nationalities; a
more appropriate term would be "predominant" when "applied to nationality [rather] than either 'effective' or 'dominant.'"[71]

The *ILC Draft Articles* state that it makes no attempt to "describe
the factors to be taken into account in deciding which nationality is
predominant,"[72] but does provide an illustrative list of factors that might
be taken into account when there is a need to resolve disputes. The list
of factors includes

> habitual residence, the amount of time spent in each country of nation-
> ality, date of naturalization . . . place, curricula and language of educa-
> tion; employment and financial interests; place of family life; family ties
> in each country; participation in social and public life; use of language;
> taxation, bank account, social security insurance; visits to the other
> State of nationality; possession and use of passport of the other State;
> and military service.[73]

It could be useful to add to this list the passport used most recently to
enter the state that has given rise to the dispute.

The second significant issue that would need attention in the new
treaty is that of consular access. The *VCCR* establishes a weak access
standard based on national treatment. That is, the right of access is

---

69 *ILC Draft Articles*, above note 65.
70 "Nationality" has been retained in order to be faithful to the *ILC Draft Articles, ibid.*
71 *Ibid.* at 46.
72 *Ibid.*
73 *Ibid.*

exercised in "conformity with the laws and regulations of the receiving State."[74] Experience has shown that a stronger standard is required. The OPCAT[75] gives exclusive attention to this issue and its approach needs to be extended to other areas in order to provide the level of protection that detained and imprisoned persons require. The Optional Protocol provides for regular inspections or the threat of inspection of prison and detention facilities by "independent international and national bodies"[76] and would provide a positive force for improvements for such places and what goes on within them. The possibility of a state being able to request such an inspection with respect to one of its citizens would add significantly to its consular protective capacity. The new *Convention on Consular and Diplomatic Protection* should provide the sending state with the right to request such an inspection along with the means to establish the frequency and environment (privacy, confidentiality of communications, services) around which access is exercised.

H. ASSOCIATED ISSUES

A significant issue associated with consular protection is whether or not states are or should be obligated to provide consular protection and assistance to its citizens. The issue has taken on added urgency in the war on terrorism. In the action of some states there is the view that persons alleged to be involved in terrorism should be treated differently than others and the treatment should be bereft of the normal protections and guarantees. The recent action by the United States Congress, to provide the administration with new authority following the decision of the Supreme Court striking down the earlier system for trying detainees, illustrates the issue. The new law includes provisions that would limit the use of *habeas corpus* for terrorism suspects, allow prosecutors, in some circumstances, to use hearsay evidence or evidence collected through coercive interrogation, limit the right to a speedy trial, and impose on defendants military defence attorneys. Equally significant, the new law limits access to federal civilian courts. Other governments have also placed serious restrictions on long-established legal rights, all in

---

74   *VCCR*, above note 4 at 15.
75   Above note 3.
76   *Ibid.*, Article 1.

the name of national security. These include the United Kingdom, which has established new rules for the fast tracking of extradition in terrorism cases, and Canada, where limitations are placed on evidence that is made available to terrorism suspects.

There is wide variation in the practices of states in the exercise of consular protection. At one end of the spectrum are states that extend little or no protection and/or services to their citizens while they are in a foreign country. At the other end, are states, including Canada, which provide a wide range of consular protection and services to their citizens overseas. The latter states have an extensive network of points of service through embassies, high commissions, consulates general, consulates, and non-diplomatic offices where officials assist citizens. These overseas offices are backed by dedicated units at headquarters, usually in the Foreign Ministry, that coordinate policy and direct the actions of the overseas officials.

There is little, however, in international law to provide a guide on the obligation of states to provide consular protection to their citizens. In 1924 the Permanent Court of International Justice held that "a State is entitled to protect its subjects, when injured by acts contrary to international law committed by another State, from whom they have been unable to obtain satisfaction through the ordinary channels."[77]

It is, however, necessary to separate "obligation" from "practice." The Court went on to say that in extending such protection, a state was merely preserving its own rights, namely, "its right to ensure in the person of its subjects, respect for the rules of international law."[78] The *VCCR* does not oblige states to extend consular protection, rather the convention provides a set of rules under which such protection can be extended if a state is required to do so by its own laws, regulations, or policies. In the *VCCR*, a sending state has the right of access to its detained citizens, but Article 36 does not impose an obligation to seek that access. In a 1970 case, the ICJ ruled that the "State must be viewed as the sole judge to decide whether its protection will be granted, to what extent it is granted, and when it will cease. It retains in this respect a discretion-

---

77 *Mavrommatis Palestine Concessions (Greece v. Britain)* (1924), P.C.I.J. (Ser. B) No. 3 at 12.

78 *Ibid.*

ary power the exercise of which may be determined by considerations of a political or other nature, unrelated to the particular case."[79]

In 2000, the ILC rapporteur coordinating the draft articles on diplomatic protection suggested that the discretionary standard be altered in certain circumstances. It was proposed that there be a duty to extend diplomatic protection in instances where the injury results from a grave violation of international law, specifically, those violating *jus cogens* — or peremptory norms. A peremptory norm is defined in the *Vienna Convention on the Law of Treaties*[80] as one "accepted and recognized by the international community of States as a whole as a norm from which no derogation is permitted and which can be modified only by a subsequent norm or general international law having the same character."[81] The rapporteur went on to state that there would be an obligation on states "to provide in their municipal law for the enforcement of this right [for diplomatic protection] before a competent domestic court or other independent national authority."[82] However, when it released its draft articles on diplomatic protection in 2004, the full ILC decided to retain the classic position on the matter. The draft article on the matter stated: "A State has the right to exercise diplomatic protection on behalf of a national. It is under no duty or obligation to do so. The internal law of a State may oblige a State to extend diplomatic protection to a national, but international law imposes no such obligation."[83]

Among states the situation is mixed, with no distinct trend yet in evidence. The German Constitutional Court, for example, has written that the German state has "a constitutional duty to provide protection for German nationals and their interests in relation to foreign States."[84] In the United States obligations are included in statutes[85] that require

---

79 *Barcelona Traction, Light and Power Company, Limited (Belgium v. Spain)*, [1970] I.C.J. Rep. 3 at 44.

80 *Vienna Convention on the Law of Treaties*, 23 May 1969, 1155 U.N.T.S. 331.

81 *Ibid.*, Article 53.

82 International Law Commission, *First report on diplomatic protection by Mr. John R. Dugard*, Special Rapporteur, UN ILCOR, 2000, UN Doc. A/CN.4/506, at para. 74.

83 *ILC Draft Articles*, above note 65 at 29.

84 *Rudolf Hess Case*, BVerfGE 55, 349, 2 BvR 419/80, [1992] 90 I.L.R. 387 at 395 (Ger. Const. Ct.).

85 See U.S., Department of State, *Foreign Affairs Manual, Vol. 7 — Consular Affairs*, 1 November 2007, online: http://foia.state.gov/masterdocs/07FAM/07fam0020.pdf.

the executive arm of government to provide such protection and services. In the United Kingdom a 2002 decision by the Court of Appeal for England and Wales found that "a legitimate expectation to some form of consular service had been created as a result of previous actions and statements by the British government."[86] It is not evident that the government of the United Kingdom completely accepts that view. In another decision on 11 October 2006, the British Court of Appeal refused to extend consular or diplomatic protection to long-term residents of the United Kingdom who were imprisoned in Guantanamo Bay. Lord Justice Laws stated, in giving the decision, that "This suffering is the consequence of the actions of a foreign sovereign state for which the United Kingdom bears no responsibility under the *European Convention on Human Rights* or the *Human Rights Act*."[87] A recent decision by the South African Constitutional Court came to a similar conclusion, but from a different direction. In *Kaunda and Van Zyt*,[88] the Court ruled that it will scrutinize refusals to extend diplomatic protection against a standard of rationality, bad faith, arbitrariness, or some other equivalent concept, as such transgressions would be contrary to the *South African Bill of Rights*.

In Canada there is also uncertainty. Historically, the government has asserted it is under no legal obligation to provide consular protection or services to its nationals. Uncertainty was created following a recent decision by the Federal Court of Canada in *Khadr*.[89] The case has not reached the merits stage, but in a decision released on 18 August 2004, Justice K. von Finckenstein rejected a government effort to have the matter dismissed. In doing so, he made a number of relevant comments on the obligation of the government to provide consular services. Justice von Finckenstein stated "indeed, Canadians abroad would be surprised, if not shocked, to learn that the provision of consular services in an individual case is left to the complete and unreviewable discretion of

86 *R (on the application of Abbasi and another) v. Secretary of State for Foreign and Commonwealth Affairs and another*, [2002] EWCA Civ 1598, [2002] E.W.J. No. 4947 [*Abbasi*].

87 "Guantanamo Men's Return Bid Fails" *BBC News* (12 October 2006), online: http://news.bbc.co.uk/2/hi/uk_news/6043594.stm.

88 *Kaunda and Van Zyl v. Government of RSA* (2005), 11 B.C.L.R. 1106 (S. Afr. Const. Ct.).

89 *Khadr*, above note 68.

the Minister."[90] He draws a parallel with the case in the United Kingdom of *Abbasi v. Secretary of State for Foreign and Commonwealth Affairs*,[91] and goes on to state that he was of the view that a "persuasive case can be made that a legitimate expectation to consular services has been created through the DFAITA [Department of Foreign Affairs and International Trade Act], the Guide [A Guide for Canadians Imprisoned Abroad] and on the basis of the jurisprudence cited."[92] Justice von Finckenstein also cites favourably the ICJ decision in the *LaGrand* case in that the "*VCCR* does create individual rights to the services requested by the Applicants."[93]

These cases and decisions suggest that the traditional approach to these issues is now fluid and it is likely that the courts might add some certainty to the situation in the near future. In doing so, it is to be expected that the standard for consular and diplomatic protection will be the same for all persons in all situations and there should not be a special set of rules for persons alleged to have been involved in terrorism and for whom there are human rights concerns, or not for that matter. It would be wrong and contrary to the principles of the democratic state to suggest that there should be two classes of citizenship, one for persons against whom there are allegations of involvement in terrorism and another for those where there are no such allegations. Richard Wilson has argued, quoting Alexis de Tocqueville, that rights must remain "a fundamental part of democratic politics since they define the boundary between individual license and government tyranny."[94]

I. CONCLUSION

International migrations, including labour mobility, and travel will become an even more pronounced feature of life in the years to come. Political turmoil, social, cultural, and economic inequality, and even climate change will drive millions of people to seek a better life beyond the horizon. The existing international mechanisms and standards of behaviour

---

90 *Ibid.* at para. 23.
91 *Abbasi*, above note 86.
92 *Khadr*, above note 89 at para. 25.
93 *Ibid.* at para. 27.
94 Richard A. Wilson, ed., *Human Rights in the "War on Terror"* (Cambridge: Cambridge University Press, 2005).

for governments, particularly enforcement mechanisms, even today, are unequal to ensuring that a person beyond her country of citizenship will be treated equitably and justly. The experience in the aftermath of September 11, 2001 and the consequential war on terrorism demonstrated the willingness of normally enlightened states to draw the shades and tolerate an erosion of carefully crafted norms governing the relationship of the individual to the state. If the individual is a foreigner then this toleration is more pronounced. This will become more accentuated as the problems of the global village become part of our village. At a time when humanity, through travel, has the opportunity to lower the historical barriers of speciality, sectarianism, and self-aggrandizement, the lack of widely acceptable international standards and norms will make such a transition more dangerous and add to our inhumanity.

The international rules dealing with migration and travel need a fundamental reordering. Generally, in the past there has been little specialization for those of us who migrate and travel. It has been assumed general standards and norms would be sufficient to deal with this special subset of humanity. The nation state continues to create the centripetal force around which all such standards and norms are calibrated. Like the weather, travel is a global phenomenon and needs to be unshackled from the particularities of the nation state. The transoceanic migrations of earlier centuries are poor illustrations of our future needs. Concepts of citizenship, single and multiple, migratory rights, rights of aliens, entry and departure standards, and the responsibility and obligation of governments for citizens beyond their borders need to be addressed and standards and norms, especially enforcement mechanisms, need to be elaborated. To do so would give the future new meaning and security to millions.

Principled Secrets in an Age of Terror: International Obligations and the Canadian Experience with the Principle of Presumed Access

David M. Paciocco

A. INTRODUCTION

It is hackneyed to describe "information as power" only because that observation is true enough to bear so much repetition. It is true in life generally and it is true in matters of government. If governors have unlimited control over information, they have power to abuse public trust, to err, and to be left unaccountable to those who are governed. Still, as important as access to information is, there will be times when governments have to refuse to release information on national security grounds. It is common to say it is all a matter of balance. Yet standing alone that observation is empty. It takes on meaning only if principles are identified for determining how that balancing is to be done. This paper is about the fortunes of the key principle in attaining an appropriate balance between access to information and its suppression—what I will call the "principle of presumed access." The principle of presumed access is the simple but critical notion that, even in matters of national security, governments are obliged to demonstrate that the suppression they seek is truly necessary.

The case in favour of placing the burden on states to prove necessity before suppressing information is an imposing one, built on the firm foundation of experience and history. It rests on the public ownership of government information, on the role that access plays in securing responsible government, and on the consequences that occur when access to information is denied. It is also built around a long legacy of nations abusing national security suppression. Even so, the case for imposing the burden on the state depends on a realistic conception of what demonstrated necessity entails. This requires an appreciation that national security only exists if serious threats do not become consequences; its stock in trade, therefore, is risk management. When we speak of "necessity" in the national security context we are in the business of prediction rather than certainty. "Necessity" cannot require foregone conclusions. It can be built on real and reasoned risks that outweigh the benefits of access or disclosure. Bearing this in mind, an examination of the considerations that normally affect the assignment of burdens of proof gives firm support to the wisdom of putting the burden on those who would suppress information rather than on those who seek it.

I am going to make the case in favour of this principle of presumed access that I have described, even though readers can be forgiven for thinking that it is a trite and obvious principle. I need to make that case because, notwithstanding that the principle is a central tenet of the influential *Johannesburg Principles on National Security, Freedom of Expression and Access to Information*,[1] its stature in international law is not as secure as it deserves to be. In fact, even in my own country, Canada, while the principle has received impressive protection in the courts, it is not assured. While it has been adopted in our *Access to Information Act*,[2] the prevailing view of those few courts that have addressed the issue is that the principle of presumed access is not constitutionally required. As a result, Canadian practice respecting the control of government

---

1   Commission on Human Rights, *Johannesburg Principles on National Security, Freedom of Expression and Access to Information*, UN ESCOR, 52d Sess., Item 8, Annex, UN Doc. E/CN.4/1996/39 (1996) 28 [*Johannesburg Principles*]. These principles, adopted by international experts at a conference in Johannesburg, South Africa, have been endorsed by the UN Special Rapporteur on freedom of expression and opinion, relied upon by the UN Commission on Human Rights, and cited by the House of Lords in *Secretary of State for the Home Department v. Rehman*, [2003] 1 A.C. 153 at 181, Slynn L.J.: Craig Forcese, "Clouding Accountability: Canada's Government Secrecy and National Security Law 'Complex'" (2005) 36 Ottawa L. Rev. 49 at 65–66.

2   R.S.C. 1985, c. A-1.

information is uneven, a condition I will describe below. While there have been many important victories, the principled foundation needed to fully respect access to information has yet to be set.

The situation in Canada is unfortunate not only because it jeopardizes the proper balance between access to information and national security in my own country, but also because of the example Canada's practices provide internationally. Canada has the potential to be a fitting role model for access practices. It is a stable democracy committed to the rule of law that has made constitutional commitments to liberty and democracy in an instrument, our *Canadian Charter of Rights and Freedoms*,[3] which allows for the responsible protection of competing public interests. Moreover, while we in Canada have not been scarred directly by post-9/11 acts of terrorism, our closest allies have been and we have been threatened directly. More importantly, we have endured more distant terrorist acts, both during the FLQ crisis[4] and most significantly with the Air India bombings.[5] These experiences have made national security a higher priority here than it is in many other states[6] without, at the same time, tincturing our judgment with the close emotion that

3   Part I of the *Constitution Act, 1982*, being Schedule B to the *Canada Act 1982* (U.K.), 1982, c. 11 [*Charter*].

4   Known in Canada as the "October Crisis," the Front de Libération du Québec (FLQ), a domestic organization seeking independence for the Province of Quebec, kidnapped a British diplomat, James Richard Cross, and a minister in the Quebec provincial government, Pierre Laporte in 1970. Mr. Laporte was murdered. The FLQ was linked to a number of bombings.

5   In June of 1985 bombs were loaded onto two Air India flights in Vancouver by Sikh extremists. CP Air 003 landed safely at Japan's Narita Airport but a bomb in a suitcase set for transfer to an Air India flight exploded shortly afterwards, killing two baggage handlers and injuring four more. Air India Flight 182 was downed by the other bomb on June 23, killing all three hundred and twenty-nine persons on board. A judicial inquiry, being conducted by retired Supreme Court of Canada Justice John Major, relating to the investigation and ultimate acquittal of two of the primary suspects, is underway in Canada.

6   It has been observed, for example, that Latin American and Caribbean countries have been less active in limiting access to information based on security concerns post-9/11 than the United States, Canada, and many European countries: Kati Suominen, "Access to Information in Latin America and the Caribbean: An Overview" in *Access to Information in the Americas* (Washington: Inter-American Dialogue, 2002) 18 at 19–20, online: http://thedialogue.org/PublicationFiles/Access%20Report.pdf.

immediate, direct victimization can cause. In essence, our national security concerns are real, but in a way that should be unburdened by an intense and inevitably distorting sense of crisis.[7] Both in the interests of our domestic government and our international example then, it is critical that we get the balance right here, for if it cannot be achieved in Canada, it has little hope elsewhere.

The place to begin, however, is not with the Canadian experience but rather with international law. Unfortunately, the contours of international law are almost invariably debatable. This is because of the absence of both a central government and a firm system of precedent and judicial hierarchy. The case that the principle of presumed access is protected by international law standards is nonetheless compelling. In the end, it is so compelling that the principle of presumed access should be secure in any responsible nation. The principle is supported by treaty law in most nations, and should even find comfort in the fickle and often unpredictable embrace of customary international law. The case in favour is simply too imposing to ignore. For this reason it should receive constitutional recognition here in Canada. The international community, beginning with Canada, has to give the principle of presumed access better regard or we will not achieve an appropriate balance between access and security. We will continue with an imbalance that paradoxically makes all of us less secure by making our governments less responsible.

B. THE CASE FOR THE PRINCIPLE OF PRESUMED ACCESS TO INFORMATION IN INTERNATIONAL LAW

1) The Treaty-based and Customary Law of Freedom of Expression

If the principle of presumed access to information is protected as a matter of international law, it is as part of a "freedom of expression."

---

7   For studies of access to information in nations, such as Israel and South Korea, facing persistent international threats see Ruth Gavison, "National Security, Freedom of Expression and Access to Information: The Israeli Situation" at 333, and Kyo Ho Youm, "Freedom of Expression and National Security in South Korea" at 413, both in Sandra Coliver *et al.*, eds., *Secrecy and Liberty: National Security, Freedom of Expression and Access to Information* (The Hague: Martinus Nijhoff, 1999).

Without question, "freedom of expression" is a binding international law obligation on those states that have agreed to multilateral treaties that guarantee that freedom. In 1966, the *International Covenant on Civil and Political Rights*, which has now been ratified, joined in, or acceded to by 156 nations, provided for "freedom of expression" in its Article 19.[8] Freedom of expression has also been affirmed in other regional multilateral treaties, including in Article 13 of the *American Declaration of the Rights and Duties of Man* that was proclaimed in 1948 by the Organization of American States.[9] Two years later freedom of expression was agreed to in the *Convention for the Protection of Human Rights and Fundamental Freedoms*,[10] and in 1978, the *American Convention on Human Rights*,[11] adopted by the Organization of American States, came into force. In 1981, the *African Charter on Human and People's Rights*, adopted by the Organization of African Unity, affirmed freedoms of expression, albeit in less stirring terms.[12] It is clear that an overwhelming majority of nations have made legal commitments to freedom of expression by treaty.

As impressive as this record is, treaties bind only the parties to them. By contrast, as a general rule, customary rules of international law bind all states. This is because custom is broadly analogous to the common law. It rests on the precedent of the actual practice of states internationally, and is supported by *opinio juris*—that is, international agreement that those practices are adhered to because they are legally binding. When customary legal principles are considered to be fundamental enough according to a general consensus of the international commun-

---

8   *International Covenant on Civil and Political Rights*, 19 December 1966, 999 U.N.T.S. 171, Can. T.S. 1976 No. 47, 6 I.L.M. 368, last updated 26 January 2006 [*ICCPR*]. See online: www.ohchr.org/english/countries/ratification/4.htm.

9   The *American Declaration of the Rights and Duties of Man*, 1948, O.A.S., adopted by the Ninth International Conference of American States in Bogata, Columbia on 2 May 1948 [*American Declaration*].

10   4 November 1950, 213 U.N.T.S. 221, Eur. T.S. No. 5 [*ECHR*].

11   22 November 1969, 1144 U.N.T.S. 123, O.A.S.T.S. No. 36 [*American Convention*].

12   *African Charter on Human and People's Rights*, 27 June 1981, OAU Doc. CAB/LEG/67/3 rev. 5, 21 I.L.M. 58 (1982) (entered into force 21 October 1986) [*African Charter*]. By 1986, the *African Charter* had been ratified by fifty-one countries: Jean-Bernard Marie, "International Instruments Relating to Human Rights" (1997) 18 H.R.L.J. 79 at 84. The right to receive information is stated in unqualified terms in Article 9(1), but Article 9(2) only assures the right to express and disseminate opinions "within the law."

ity, they are considered to be peremptory or *jus cogens*—matters that cannot be varied by treaty or opted out of.[13] What, then, does the customary international law say about freedom of expression?

Without question, freedom of expression has received the kind of widespread endorsement internationally that can support a finding that it is a customary legal right. That support is to be found not only in the multilateral treaties described, but in UN General Assembly resolutions. Indeed, in 1946, during its first session, the United Nations General Assembly adopted Resolution 59(1) in which it described "freedom of information" as "a fundamental human right," the "touchstone of all freedoms." Then in 1948 the UN General Assembly, in Article 19 of the *Universal Declaration of Human Rights*, expressed, under the rubric of "freedom of expression," the right "to seek, receive and impart information and ideas through the media and regardless of frontiers."[14]

In spite of the widespread recognition of both freedom of expression and its importance, there are those who doubt that customary international law buttresses the treaty obligations that protect freedom of expression. Professor Schacter, for example, argues that freedom of expression, including in its paradigmatic form of a qualified entitlement to communicate information free from restraint, is not protected by customary international law.[15] Schacter was not persuaded that customary international law can be identified by evidence of what states say, even in solemn international instruments, where what they say diverges from actual state practice.[16] In short, he wondered how international law can be said to require freedom of expression when that freedom is violated internationally more than it is respected.

---

13   See Article 53 of the *Vienna Convention on the Law of Treaties*, 23 May 1969, 1155 U.N.T.S. 331 [*Vienna Convention*].

14   ARTICLE 19, Global Campaign for Free Expression, "International Standards and Comparative Best Practice" in *Access to Information in the Americas*, above note 6 at 34, online: www.thedialogue.org/page.cfm?pageID=32&pubID=359&s=Internati onal%20Standards%20and%20Comparative%20Best. See also *Universal Declaration of Human Rights*, GA Res. 217(III), UN GAOR, 3d Sess., Supp. No. 13, UN Dec. A/810 (1948) [*Universal Declaration*].

15   Oscar Schacter, "International Law in Theory and Practice" (1982) 178 Recueil des Cours 334 at 335–36.

16   *Ibid*. See also Prosper Weil, "Towards Relative Normativity in International Law?" (1983) 77 A.J.I.L. 413, and his criticisms.

The reality that caused Schacter to deny that freedom of expression is customary law has not disappeared; even today, a quarter century after he wrote about it, international state practice is pocked if not marred by the widespread abuse of information by states, including through the punishment of simple expression. "[While] the majority of African governments have ratified international treaties in which they pledge to uphold freedom of expression,"[17] "unwillingness to honour commitments to international human rights treaties have characterized the majority of African states in their thirty-five or more years of independence."[18] "Latin American military elites have used national security to suppress rights far beyond the limitations allowed under international law."[19] And despite customary international law and "despite the existence of constitutional provisions guaranteeing freedom of speech, the press and publication, like other communist parties, the Chinese Communist Party (CPP) has ... characterized the suppression of its critics as a necessary aspect of the 'class struggle' carried out to protect the socialist revolution."[20] This problem is easiest to identify in authoritarian regimes but the reality is that, internationally, freedom of expression practices tend to be dramatically less vibrant than international legal instruments proclaim, casting at least some doubt on what is "customary" for nations.

At the other extreme there are those who believe that anything housed in the *Universal Declaration of Human Rights* is customary international law, without more, in spite of widespread violations. Since the *Universal Declaration* includes freedom of information, it is considered by them to be a customary international law right.[21] Then there are those

17   Claude E. Welch, Jr., "The African Charter and Freedom of Expression in Africa" in Coliver *et al.*, eds., above note 7, 145 at 151.

18   *Ibid.* at 145.

19   Vivianna Krsticevic *et al.*, "The Inter-American System of Human Rights Protection: Freedom of Expression, 'National Security Doctrines' and the Transition to Elected Governments" in Coliver *et al.*, eds., above note 7 at 161.

20   Sophia Woodman & Yu Ping, "'Killing the Chicken to Frighten the Monkeys': The Use of State Security in the Control of Freedom of Expression in China" in Coliver *et al.*, eds., *ibid.* at 223.

21   Louis Sohn, "The New International Law: Protection of the Rights of Individuals Rather than States" (1982) 32 Am. U. L. Rev. 1 at 17. In 1995, the Honourable Christine Stewart, speaking as a representative of the Government of Canada, said "Canada regards the principles of the Universal Declaration of Human Rights as

commentators who use more traditional international law techniques to make the case that freedom of expression is indeed protected by customary international law,[22] a position I have no doubt courts in my country would accept.

The case for customary protection of freedom of expression benefits from the fact that in the interests of improving the lot of humanity, when it comes to human rights, what states say tends to be given more currency than what they do.[23] Torture provides a good illustration. In spite of its widespread practice, the prohibition on torture is accepted in international law as a matter of customary obligation.[24] With respect to the basic human right of freedom of expression, an imposing majority of states have said that it is binding on them. They have done so passively, by endorsing United Nations General Assembly declarations assuring freedom of expression, and they have done so actively, by joining treaties in which they agree to respect freedom of expression. International law has been creative in treating widespread endorsement of multilateral covenants by states as generalized expressions of international consensus representative not only of the views of those who have chosen to sign on to treaties, but also those who have refused.[25] Using international law's familiar tools then, the non-binding UN declarations and the multilateral treaties support the case for customary protection.

---

entrenched in customary law binding on all governments": Hon. Christine Stewart, "Statement 95/I Notes for an Address by the Honourable Christine Stewart, Secretary of State (Latin America and Africa)" (Presented to the 10th Annual Consultation between Non-Governmental Organizations and the Department of Foreign Affairs and International Trade, Ottawa, Ontario, 17 January 1995) cited in Forcese, above note 1 at 56, n. 33, along with *Alvarez-Machain v. United States*, 331 F.3d 604 at 618 (9th Cir. 2003).

22 See Forcese, *ibid.*, and ARTICLE 19, above note 14.

23 See, for example, the recognition by Meron that international law-making conferences are often less interested in codifying actual behaviour than promulgating more protective rules of conduct: Theodor Meron, *Human Rights and Humanitarian Norms as Customary Law* (Oxford: Clarendon Press, 1989) at 44. While in my view technically problematic, it does reflect an understandable aversion to the conservative tendency of looking at past practice when moving the law forward.

24 *Prosecutor v. Furundzija*, Case No. IT-95-17/1-A (21 July 2000) (ICTY, Appeals Chamber).

25 See Meron, above note 23 at 81, who expresses caution about this tendency, calling for an irreproachable rather than an aspirational legal method.

Then there are the authorities, those international experts and interpretive bodies that serve informally, in the absence of international government and a precedent-imposing court structure, as reporters on the state of international law. An assembly of experts who identified the *Johannesburg Principles* had no doubt that freedom of expression is a legally binding norm. Although arguably less an assembly of experts than an interest group, the Inter American Press Association adopted the *Declaration of Chapultepec* that, not surprisingly, contains a powerful endorsement of freedom of expression. What gives this declaration credibility is that "the heads of state of governments of 22 countries in the Americas ... have signed the Declaration."[26] And there are other expert organizations and conferences that have affirmed freedom of expression.[27] All indications from the authorities are that freedom of expression is protected by customary international law.

2) The Right of Access to Information As a Component of Freedom of Expression

The more difficult question is: Exactly what is protected? This is a problem endemic in the generality that international law normally trades in. While there seems little controversy that international law protects the qualified right to communicate information that is known,[28] what is less clear is whether the right to access government information is secured by international law.

To be sure, there remain problems in making a magisterial declaration that international legal rights to freedom of expression include the

---

26 ARTICLE 19, above note 14 at 38, citing the "Report of the Office of the Special Rapporteur for Freedom of Expression, Chapter III" in the *Annual Report of the Inter-American Commission on Human Rights 1998, vol. III*.

27 See Appendix D to Coliver *et al.*, eds., above note 7, including the Organization on Security and Cooperation in Europe; the Document of the Copenhagen Meeting of the Conference on the Human Dimension; and the Document of the Moscow Meeting of the Conference on the Human Dimension.

28 See the discussions and cases collected in Elizabeth Evatt, "The International Covenant on Civil and Political Rights: Freedom of Expression and State Security" in Coliver *et al.*, eds., *ibid.* at 83; and Paul Mahoney & Laurence Early, "Freedom of Expression and National Security: Judicial Policy Approaches under the European Convention on Human Rights and Other Council of Europe Instruments" in *ibid.* at 109.

right of citizens to obtain access to information held by their states. There are two sources for this insecurity. First, "traditionally, the right has been understood to be limited to the right to receive and impart information free from government interference, and not to establish a general right to receive information from the government or others."[29] Second, within nations, even constitutional provisions on freedom of speech tend not to be interpreted as requiring positive rights of access to official information.[30] This pessimistic appraisal, made by Lawrence Lustgarten, is consistent with the jurisprudence in Canada where to date the *Charter*'s "freedom of expression" provision has failed to require access to government information.[31] Lustgarten's observation also finds further support in the American experience. While many scholars believe that the First Amendment protects the right to know government information, there has been little caselaw identifying an enforceable right of this kind other than a largely undefined common law right to inspect and copy public records.[32] This trend, against finding a right of access inherent in constitutional rights documents within nations, is

---

29 Sandra Coliver, "Commentary on the Johannesburg Principles on National Security, Freedom of Expression and Access to Information" in Coliver *et al.*, eds., *ibid.*, 11 at 55, citing *Open Door & Dublin Well Woman v. Ireland* (1992), 246-A. E.C.H.R. (Ser. A) 71 & 72; *Leander v. Sweden* (1987), 116 E.C.H.R. (Ser. A) 74; OAS, Inter-American Commission on Human Rights, *Annual Report of the Inter-American Commission on Human Rights 1980–81*, OAS Doc. OEA/Ser.L/V/II.54, doc. 9, rev. 1 (1981) at 121.

30 Laurence Lustgarten, "Freedom of Expression, Dissent and National Security in the United Kingdom" in Coliver *et al.*, eds., *ibid.*, 457 at 464.

31 *Criminal Lawyers' Assn. v. Ontario (Ministry of Public Safety and Security)* (2004), 184 O.A.C. 223, [2004] O.J. No. 1214 at para. 42 (Div. Ct.), rev'd without resolving the constitutional status of "access to information" (2007), 280 D.L.R. (4th) 193, 220 C.C.C. (3d) 343, 2007 ONCA 392 [*Criminal Lawyers' Assn.*]; *Ontario (Attorney General) v. Fineberg* (1994), 19 O.R. (3d) 197 at 204, [1994] O.J. No. 1419 (Div. Ct.) [*Fineberg*]; *Yeager v. Canada (Correctional Service)*, [2003] 3 F.C. 107 at para. 65, 2003 FCA 30 [*Yeager*]. See the discussion of these decisions in section 8(c), below in this chapter.

32 See Paul Hoffman & Kate Martin, "Safeguarding Liberty: National Security, Freedom of Expression and Access to Information: United States of America" in Coliver *et al.*, eds., above note 7, 477 at 487, citing Thomas Emerson, "Legal Foundation of the Right to Know Why" (1976) Wash. U.L.Q. 1; Mary Cheh, "Judicial Supervision of Executive Secrecy: Rethinking Freedom of Expression for Government Employees and the Public Right to Access to Government Information" (1984) 69 Cornell L. Rev. 690 at 719–34. For the common law right, see *Nixon v. Warner Communica-*

arguably relevant to the contours of any international right of freedom of expression because, if granting access to information is a legal obligation states have as a matter of international human rights law, then the law within states should reflect that, and rights of access to information should be recognized, particularly at the constitutional level.[33]

In spite of these concerns, the more recent trend among international law commentators has been to include access to information within the framework of those international treaties that protect freedom of expression. Although, in 1983 the UN Human Rights Committee wanted clear evidence of state practice before describing the contours of freedom of expression,[34] ten years later the UN Commission on Human Rights created the office, UN Special Rapporteur on freedom of opinion and expression, assigning it the task of clarifying the content of the right.[35] By 1995 freedom of expression was defined by the special rapporteur to include access to information, albeit in ambiguous terms.[36] By

---

tions, 435 U.S. 589 (1978), and *Schwartz v. Dept. of Justice*, 435 F. Supp. 1203 (D.C. Cir. 1977), aff'd 595 F.2d 888 (D.C. Cir. 1979).

33 In *Criminal Lawyers' Assn* (Ont. C.A.), above note 31, Justice Jurianz, dissenting on other grounds, noted that international law does not require states to give constitutional stature to international obligations, so long as those obligations are respected. That is true technically, but if a right or freedom relating to the treatment of citizens within a state is foundational enough to become an international law obligation owed by the state, it arguably warrants the kind of commitment that only a constitutional instrument can assure. This, of course, is why, in Canada, international law obligations are used to interpret the provisions of the *Canadian Charter of Rights and Freedoms*.

34 *Report of the Human Rights Committee*, UN GAOR, 38th Sess.,, Supp. No. 40, UN Doc A/38/40 (1983) 109.

35 Commission on Human Rights, *Right to Rreedom of Opinion and Expression*, C.H.R. Res. 1993/45, UN ESCOR, 49th Sess., UN Doc. E/CN.4/RES/1993/45 (1993).

36 Commission on Human Rights, *Promotion and Protection of the Right to Freedom of Opinion and Expression, Report of the Special Rapporteur, Mr. Abid Hussain, Pursuant to Commission on Human Rights Resolution 1993/45*, UN ESCOR, 51st Sess., UN Doc. E/CN.4/1995/32 (1995) at paras. 34 & 35. The ambiguity stems from the distinction drawn by the rapporteur in the general comments found in para. 19 between "freedom of access to the state" and "freedom from the state," and the statement that "in principle, the State has no obligation to guarantee [freedom from the state] with positive measures." In the Canadian *Charter* case of *Criminal Lawyers' Assn.*, above note 31, the Ontario Divisional Court had interpreted this to mean that the rights of access to information discussed in paras. 34 & 35 were

1999 there was no ambiguity at all. The special rapporteur, in response to a request for clarification,[37] said the "right to seek and receive information . . . imposes a positive obligation on States to ensure access to information, particularly with regard to information held by Government in all types of storage and retrieval systems."[38] The inclusion of access to information as a corollary of freedom of expression has now been elaborated upon in successive reports that have been received with approval by the Commission on Human Rights.[39] Significantly, UN special rapporteurs have not been alone among experts in reaching that conclusion. The Special Rapporteur for the Inter-American Commission on Human Rights agrees that a positive obligation exists on states to provide access to government information,[40] and that the *Johannesburg Principles* treat access to government information as an international legal right.

There is also an increasing trend among nations to accept legal obligations to give access to information to their citizens. There are now close to seventy nations,[41] and possibly as many as 100,[42] who have adopted access to information laws. This international trend within domestic systems arguably provides a mirror, in which international law can see its work being reflected. Along with the broad acceptance by the authorities, this is an increasingly powerful indication that inter-

---

"freedoms from the state," meaning that they did not entail positive obligations on the state to furnish information. The passages are confusing and it is clear that the rapporteur felt aspects of the law were "subject to debate," but he did decry attempts of governments to withhold information from the people.

37   Commission on Human Rights, *Right to Freedom of Opinion and Expression*, C.H.R. Res. 1998/42, ESCOR Supp. No. 3, UN Doc. E/CN.4/1998/42 (1998) 147 at para. 9(d).

38   Commission on Human Rights, *Report of the Special Rapporteur on the Protection and Promotion of the Right to Freedom of Opinion and Expression, Mr. Abid Hussain*, UN ESCOR, 1999, 55th Sess., UN Doc. E/CN.4/1999/64 at para. 12.

39   See ARTICLE 19, above note 14 at 36, and see Commission on Human Rights, *Report of the Special Rapporteur, Ambeyi Ligabo, The Right to Freedom of Opinion and Expression*, UN ESCOR, 61st Sess., UN Doc. E/CN.4/2005/64 39.

40   ARTICLE 19, *ibid.*, 34 at 38.

41   See David Banisar, "Freedom of Information and Access to Government Record Laws around the World" (2006), online: www.accessdemocracy.org/library/2044_ww_freeinfo_010504_ara.pdf.

42   Privacy International, Freedom of Information, "Map of Freedom of Information Laws Around the World," online: www.privacyinternational.org/foi/foi-laws.jpg. The huge discrepancy in number may be explained because of the specific content various statutes have. What exactly is it that makes them freedom of information laws?

national law's freedom of expression, whether housed in treaty or custom, embraces not only the ability to communicate what is known, but also the right to access from governments what is not known. It is not surprising that Professor Coliver spoke several years ago of recent developments suggesting a positive duty on governments to provide access to information.[43]

There are good reasons for this maturation in the understanding of what freedom of expression entails. At its most technical level, the case that international treaties secure rights to access to information arises from the "ordinary meaning to be given to the terms of the treaty in their context and in light of their object and purpose."[44] Certainly, the UN Special Rapportuer Ligabo considered that a right of access to information was "easily deduced" from the expression "to seek [and] receive information" that is found in Article 19 of the *International Covenant on Civil and Political Rights*, and, based on that, he went on to describe standards that states should observe in giving access.[45] This is a particularly compelling interpretation given the usual practice in interpreting human rights instruments. The *Universal Declaration* and the relevant covenants it spawned are to be given large and liberal interpretation: "in interpreting legal norms, [the principle of freedom of expression] must be interpreted broadly and the permissible restrictions restrictively."[46] Confirming protection for information that is known but granting none for access to state information is a narrow rather than broad interpretation of international instruments, especially given that those instruments speak overtly of a right to "receive" information.

A natural reading of the text that imposes on states an obligation to enable individuals to "seek [and] receive information" from them is also more consonant with the basic mission of international human rights law than the competing interpretation that has been offered for that phrase. As indicated, the "traditional" view would secure only a right be-

---

43 Coliver, above note 29, citing *Gaskin v. United Kingdom* (1989), 160 E.C.H.R. (Ser. A) at para. 49.

44 See *Vienna Convention*, above note 13, Article 31.

45 *Report of the Special Rapporteur, Ambeyi Ligabo*, above note 39 at 39.

46 Subcommission on the Prevention of Discrimination and the Protection of Minorities, *Report of the Special Rapporteurs, Danilo Turk & Louis Joinet, The Right to Freedom of Opinion and Expression: Final Report*, UN ESCOR, 44th Sess., UN Doc. E/CN.4/Sub.2/1992/9 (1992) at paras. 20 and 25.

tween individuals to seek and receive information from each other. Yet international human rights instruments only rarely attempt to regulate the relationships between individuals themselves.[47] Their ordinary function is to describe obligations that states have to those they govern.[48] It would be a curiosity if these solemn instruments were to be interpreted to regulate access to information between individuals by imposing negative obligations on states to keep them from interfering with the receipt of information between those they govern, yet not binding the states themselves in terms of how they deal with government information.

Although many international lawyers are chary of placing too much emphasis on purposive interpretation of treaties,[49] it is significant in my view that a natural interpretation of the right to "seek [and] receive information" that includes rights of access to information from states is uniquely consistent with the "object and purpose" of freedom of expression, a point I will develop shortly. Object and purpose in the looser sense of "function" or "role" enhance, as well, the case that access to information is a corollary of freedom of expression in customary international law. This is so because, even though customary law is identified by observing state practice and gleaning *opinio juris*, the identification of customary human rights obligations is a highly normative exercise and normative reasoning simply demands that freedom of expression carry with it a right of access to information. This can be seen by examining, in turn, the undeniable public ownership of government information, the role that access to information plays relative to freedom of expression, and the consequences that occur when information is permitted to be suppressed.

a) The Undeniable Public Ownership of Government Information

Some would prefer to avoid ownership rhetoric because focusing on property notions arguably demeans the stature of access to information

---

47   The sole exception is individual responsibility in international criminal law.

48   Because they describe individual rights, those instruments do not perform the paradigm role of international law of conferring rights on states in the interests of their citizens, which are tenable against other states.

49   See Ian Brownlie, *Principles of Public International Law*, 6th ed. (Oxford: Oxford University Press, 2003) at 602–7 and Anthony Aust, *Modern Treaty Law and Practice* (Cambridge: Cambridge University Press, 2000) at 184–93.

as a human right. Nonetheless, public ownership of information is one of the most compelling arguments favouring a right of access.[50] The case for public ownership is implicit in everything from rule of law notions that consider governors to be the guardians and ministers who serve the community;[51] to liberal social contract traditions in which the state exists with the consent of its citizens;[52] to the democratic sentiment popularized in President Abraham Lincoln's Gettysburg Address with its promise of "government of the people, by the people, for the people."[53] Community ownership of public information is also implicit in those natural law notions that support the concept of sovereignty—ideas that ascribe "rights" to states not as an end in themselves but as a convenient way to express and protect the underlying entitlements of a state's citizens.[54] Simply put, if government and the sovereign power of states are meant for the people then the information governments acquire and use is for the people; some of it private to the individuals to whom it pertains,[55] but most of it for the public at large.

I am certain there is no need to venture further into what could easily become a deeply philosophical discussion about political theory, for there is apt to be little opposition to the central point. Whether we speak using the Westernized preoccupation with ownership, which in its extreme form claims access rights based on taxpayer status, or with the more gentile language of public trust and benefit, it is difficult to deny that government information is held for the public, a feature that strengthens claims for access to information.

It is not surprising then to see the UN Special Rapporteur for freedom of expression for the Inter-American Commission of Human Rights

---

50 See Roberto Saba, "The Right to Access to Government Information" in *Access to Information in the Americas*, above note 6, 24 at 25.

51 Ernest Baker, *The Politics of Aristotle* (Oxford: Clarendon Press, 1962), Book III, Chapter XV, 1286 at 140–44.

52 See Brian Z. Tamahana, *On the Rule of Law: History, Politics, Theory* (Cambridge: Cambridge University Press, 2004) at 32–36.

53 Abraham Lincoln, The Gettysburg Address, 19 November 1863, Bliss Copy, online: www.thelincolnmuseum.org/new/research/gettysburg.html.

54 Charles De Visscher, *Theory and Reality in Public International Law*, trans. by P.E. Corbett (Princeton: Princeton University Press, 1968) at 9 and 16.

55 See, for example, the *Privacy Act*, R.S.C. 1985, c. P-21: a Canadian statute that understandably limits access by the public to private information held by government.

comment in 1997 that "[i]t is to the individual who delegated the administration of public affairs to his or her representatives that belongs the right to information that the State uses and produces with taxpayer money."[56] Nor was it a surprise to see the UN Special Rapporteur on freedom of opinion and expression reporting to the UN Commission on Human Rights that he had "concern," in 2000, about "the tendency of Governments and the institutions of Governments, to withhold from the people information that is rightly theirs."[57]

In Canada public ownership or benefit was an important consideration in securing access to information in the criminal disclosure context. The decision in *R. v. Stinchcombe* was a ground-breaking one in which the Supreme Court of Canada held that prosecutors are obliged to disclose to accused persons any relevant information found during a police investigation. Among the primary justifications for the holding was Justice Sopinka's observation that

> the fruits of the investigation which are in the possession of counsel
> for the Crown are not the property of the Crown for use in securing
> a conviction but the property of the public to be used to ensure that
> justice is done.[58]

b) The Roles Access Performs
While ownership or beneficial entitlement helps drive the case for a right of access to information, it is not the typical rationale offered. The primary rationale, at least in the pure access to information cases where efforts are being made to secure information from a state, is the impera-

---

56   Above note 26.

57   Commission on Human Rights, *Report of the Special Rapporteur on the Promotion and Protection of the Right to Freedom of Opinion and Expression*, UN ESCOR, 56th Sess., UN Doc. E/CN.4/2000/63 (2000) at para. 43, cited in ARTICLE 19, above note 14 at 36.

58   *R. v. Stinchcombe*, [1991] 3 S.C.R. 326 at 333. In *Criminal Lawyers' Assn.*, above note 31 at para. 116, the Ontario Divisional Court, in dealing with an access to information request, said that this passage from *Stinchcombe* was inapplicable because *Stinchcombe* involved an accused seeking disclosure of information to defend himself. It is true that the use to which the information is to be put differs between straight access and criminal disclosure cases, and that in criminal disclosure cases the need for the information to defend a criminal charge makes the call for access particularly urgent, but if the information is public information, it is public in both contexts. Where, then, is the distinction?

tives of democracy. The leading Canadian case is *Dagg v. Canada (Minister of Finance)*, where Justice La Forest said:

> the overarching purpose of information legislation ... is to facilitate democracy. It does so in two related ways. It helps to ensure first, that citizens have the information required to participate meaningfully in the democratic process, and secondly, that politicians and bureaucrats remain accountable to the citizenry.[59]

It would be an easy matter to salt this discussion with powerful quotes from courts, philosophers, and politicians, extolling the relationship between access to information and democracy—everything from James Madison's admonition that without popular information "knowledge will forever govern ignorance," to then opposition leader Joe Clark's echoing warning when pushing for a Canadian access to information law that "there is excessive power concentrated in the hands of those who hide public information,"[60] to the stirring if not ironic words of former U.S. Secretary of Defense Donald Rumsfeld, extolling the democratic imperatives of access to information, including his declaration that "ultimately truth prevails."[61] There are few areas in the law where the sentiment is powerful enough to inspire the kind of lofty rhetoric one finds in access to information materials.[62] Suffice it to say that the case for simple access to information is built on the reality that corruption, misjudgment, and incompetence thrive on secrecy, while access to information permits governments to be held to account and helps to prevent mistakes. Access to information is all about responsible government.

I have used the term "responsible government" instead of "democracy" advisedly. I have done so because hitching the right of access to evidence to democracy in an article that treats the coverage of international law can invite distracting arguments about whether the right to

---

59   [1997] 2 S.C.R. 403 at para. 61.

60   Andrew Osler, "Journalism and the FOI Laws: A Faded Promise" (March 1999) 17 Government Information in Canada, online: www.usask.ca/library/gic/17/osler. html, quoted in Alasdair Roberts, *Blacked Out: Government Secrecy in the Information Age* (Cambridge: Cambridge University Press, 2006) at 87.

61   Roberts, *ibid.* at 51, quoting from a 22 April 2004 luncheon address to the American Society of Newspaper Editors in Washington, D.C.

62   See, for example, the collection of made-in-Canada quotes catalogued in Forcese, above note 1.

democracy is itself protected by international law;[63] after all, if it is not, and access to information is simply the handmaiden of democracy, then access to information is not protected by international law either. More importantly, even though access to information statutes had their origin in the United States with the passage of the *Freedom of Information Act*[64] in 1966 and then gained their initial foothold in clearly democratic states during the next twenty years, there has been something of an access to information trend since 1989 in which statutes are being passed in states that few would describe as democratic. Some of those states are either "weakly democratic or authoritarian."[65] As indicated, there may now be more than 100 states that have passed similar legislation.[66]

When it manifests itself in weakly democratic or authoritarian states, this wave of access laws can be explained cynically as an example of credibility-contagion in which repressive regimes pass laws for the sake of international consumption, knowing that those laws can be observed in the breach. Still, even in China there is an apparent recognition that the transparency gained through access to information can help stem corruption[67] and foster confidence in the government, thereby discouraging dissent and civil unrest.[68] In other words, even in weak democracies or authoritarian states it is possible to recognize that access statutes are passed in the interest of promoting responsible government.

---

63   Although I do not purport to have researched the question specifically, I do note that Thomas M. Franck, in *Fairness and International Law and Institutions* (Oxford: Clarendon Press, 1995) at 139, expressed the view that democratic entitlement was not yet a customary norm. He argued that, based on its rapid recognition and rapid evolution, it is becoming one. He encouraged older democracies to use universal voluntary standards of compliance to help that transformation. To the contrary see "General Comments" on Article 1 of the political covenant, where the Human Rights Committee declared democracy's cousin, self-determination, as a right of international law: UN GAOR, 39th Sess., Supp No. 40, UN Doc. A/39/40 (1984) 142. *Quaere* whether the undemocratic features of the UN structure compromise the claim that democracy is a matter of customary law.

64   *Freedom of Information Act of July 4, 1966*, Pub. L. No. 89-487, 80 Stat. 250 (5 U.S.C. § 552).

65   Roberts, above note 60 at 20.

66   Privacy International, above note 42.

67   Roberts, above note 60 at 110.

68   *Ibid.* at 8.

The thing to notice about this rationale, whether it is styled as the facilitation of democracy or the promotion of responsible government, is that it is identical to one of the central or base rationales offered for freedom of expression generally.[69] There are three major theories supporting freedom of expression:[70] (1) the pursuit of the truth that emerges from competition in the marketplace of ideas;[71] (2) the facilitation of the liberty of individuals to grow as responsible moral agents through the development of their intellect, interests, tastes, and personality;[72] and the most relevant consideration, namely, (3) furnishing necessary support for democracy[73] or responsible government. Indeed, this last rationale, supported most famously by the American philosopher Alexander Meikeljohn,[74] is perhaps the most secure rationale for freedom of expression because it represents the lowest common denominator among commentators and legal systems. Meikeljohn's work has been criticized, for example, not because he erred in identifying this rationale, but because of his belief that this is the only foundation for freedom of expression.[75]

---

69 See generally, Paul Rishworth *et al.*, *The New Zealand Bill of Rights* (New York: Oxford University Press, 2003) "The Theoretical Basis of the Right [to Freedom of Expression]" at 309–11.

70 All three have been identified: by Lawrence Tribe in *American Constitutional Law*, 2d ed., (Mineola, NY: Foundation Press, 1988) at 786–87, as being used: by the United States Supreme Court in explaining the American constitutional right of freedom of expression in the United States; by the Supreme Court of Canada in the foundational freedom of expression case, *Irwin Toy v. Quebec (Attorney General)*, [1989] 1 S.C.R. 927 at 976; and by the United Nations Human Rights Committee in *Ballantyne, Davidson and McIntyre v. Canada* (1994), 1 I.H.R.R. 145 at 156.

71 John Stuart Mill, "On Liberty" in *Three Essays* (1859; repr., New York: Oxford University Press, 1975) at 24; and see the classic dissent of Holmes J. in *Abrams v. United States*, 250 U.S. 616 at 630 (1919).

72 Ronald Dworkin, "Why Must Speech Be Free" in *Freedom's Law* (Cambridge, MA: Harvard University Press, 1996) at 195, and see *Whitney v. California*, 274 U.S. 357 at 375 (1927), Brandeis J.

73 See *New York Times v. Sullivan*, 376 U.S. 254 (1964).

74 Alexander Meikeljohn, *Free Speech and its Relation to Self-Government* (1948; repr., Union, NJ: Lawbook Exchange, 2000); Alexander Meikeljohn, "The First Amendment is an Absolute" (1961) Sup. Ct. Rev. 245, and Alexander Meikeljohn, *Political Freedom: The Constitutional Powers of the People* (New York: Oxford University Press, 1965).

75 See T.I. Emerson, *The System of Freedom of Expression* (New York: Random House, 1970); Robert Post, "Meikeljohn's Mistake: Individual Autonomy and the Reform

The European Court and Commission tend to see freedom of expression less as a means for individual self-fulfillment than as "a vital tool of democratic society."[76] Meanwhile, the High Court of Australia has held that freedom of political communication is inherent in the concept of representative democracy and is thereby constitutionally protected in that country,[77] even though other forms of expression are not. The point of this detour into the rationales for freedom of expression writ large is that, if international law's freedom of expression exists in material part to facilitate responsible government, then the interpretation of the term "receive" in international law provisions protecting freedom of expression should derive its meaning from that same objective. So understood, the promise of freedom to receive information, found in declarations and covenants, has to be recognized as including the kind of receipt needed to support democracy or responsible government, namely, the receipt of, or access to, government information. Only an interpretation of freedom of expression in international law that is severed from its *raison d'etre* can hold otherwise, a reality that should surely influence international law.

c) The Consequences When Access Is Denied

While it is possible to make the case for the principle of presumed access by simply describing, as I have done, the role of access to information, that case becomes more compelling when a quick tour is taken of what can happen when access to information is abridged or information is manipulated by states. Slobodan Milosevic, for example, manipulated the mass media to inflame nationalistic fervour through the selective and distorted presentation of information, while following a practice of distributing government information "in accordance with the program of the Government and the plan of the Ministry of Information."[78] Apartheid was maintained in South Africa for as long as it was

---

of Public Disclosure" (1993) 64 U. Col. L. Rev. 1109; and see William Brennan, "The Supreme Court and the Meikeljohn Interpretation of the First Amendment" (1965) 79 Harv. L. Rev. 1.

76 Mahoney & Early, above note 28, 109 at 111–12.

77 *Australian Capital Television Pty Ltd. v. Commonwealth (No. 2)* (1922), 177 C.L.R. 106 (H.C.A.); *Nationwide News Pty Ltd. v. Wills* (1992), 177 C.L.R. 1.

78 Branislav Milinkovic, "The Federal Republic of Yugoslavia: Suppression of Dissent to Protect 'The National Interest'" in Coliver *et al.*, eds., above note 7, 508 at 508 and 515.

through a number of limits on freedom of expression, including the "se-lection of news by state-controlled media."[79] Moreover, while the rest of the world watched as the South African Defense Force invaded Angola, South Africans were "among the last to know."[80] Brazilians were left in the dark about the extermination of members of an insurgent force by their government in the 1970s and Argentines were unable to secure information about a concentration and extermination centre operated during the "dirty war."[81] It is not only in military, authoritarian, or endem-ically rights-abusing states where the restriction on access to informa-tion works to stifle informed dissent and protect against accountability. Perhaps the most famous case of all involved the leakage of the sup-pressed Pentagon papers by Daniel Elsberg, which revealed that the United States government "lied to the U.S. Congress and the American people about its bombing of Cambodia."[82] Americans have learned too late of radiation experiments on "unwitting American citizens," of sup-port by the CIA and FBI of Nazi war criminals in the aftermath of World War II, and of the U.S. Government's role in the Pinochet coup of 1973.[83] More recently, the American and the international public were and still are being left in ignorance about the use of extraordinary rendition in the war against terror, and it was only through unauthorized leaks that torture of detainees by American soldiers and contractors in Abu Ghraib was revealed. It was sixty years before the British learned that their own government operated a torture program after World War II, not against Nazis but against communist sympathizers; a minister in the govern-ment of the day wrote in a memo at the time of the lengths taken to hide "the fact that we are alleged to have treated internees in a manner reminiscent of the German concentration camps."[84] Perhaps most dra-matically, the initial widespread support within the United States for the invasion of Iraq was generated using flawed and selective intelligence

---

79   Gilbert Marcus, "Freedom of Expression and National Security: The South African Experience" in Coliver *et al.*, eds., *ibid.* at 389.

80   *Ibid.*, 389 at 395.

81   Krsticevic *et al.*, above note 19 at 184.

82   Coliver, above note 29 at 66.

83   Roberts, above note 60 at 32.

84   Ian Cobain, "Revealed: Victims of UK's Cold War Torture Camp" *The Guardian* (3 April 2006).

claiming non-existent Al-Qaeda links and weapons of mass destruction, while complete information was being suppressed.

Having laid out this sad list I want to make three points about it. The first is that nobody can reasonably believe that the Serbian atrocities, the Apartheid, the Cambodian bombings, or even the invasion of Iraq would necessarily have been prevented by access to information. Still, these and the other events described took place behind a shield of secrecy that doubtlessly lowered inhibitions and suppressed the kind of public knowledge and debate that might have averted or at least lessened the scale of errors and atrocities. Speaking of Iraq, Alasdair Roberts argues that secrecy "prevented a more complete view of the available evidence." Complete information could have changed political choices, or at least revealed the inadequacy of post-occupation planning[85] that so many are now paying for. Access to information does not have to be a foolproof panacea to be worthy of jealous protection.

The second point I want to make is that I have selected these illustrations because the information that was suppressed in each case reveals what are arguably, and in most cases were certainly, violations of international law. Should there be any doubt about whether access to government information is included in international laws' own treaty-based or customary notion of freedom of expression, we would do well to note, bearing these and similar illustrations in mind, that "freedom of information" was described in the original UN General Assembly Resolution 59(1) as the "touchstone of all freedoms." This was done with good reason. "Informed public opinion is one of the most effective means of preventing violations of [other] international norms."[86] And even when violations cannot be prevented by access to information, at the very least accountability can be achieved.[87]

The final point I want to make is that in each of the illustrations I have selected suppression of the information was done in the name of national security. I chose national security examples in order to illustrate how the purpose underlying freedom of expression not only applies in the national security context, but to show how it can take on particu-

---

85 Roberts, above note 60 at 44–45.
86 Coliver, above note 29 at 72.
87 Roberts, above note 60 at 33, describing how belated access was given to victims of state security agencies in Argentina to help them call their tormentors to account.

lar urgency when nations are threatened and individuals are being processed through legal hearings bent on protecting national interests. As
a number of these cases show, it is in the face of terror or perceived
threat that nations lose their character and their commitment to democratic principle. They abridge civil liberties, compromise their fair trial
standards, suspect classes of people rather than people themselves, and
even send citizens off to war. These are profound outcomes, the wisdom
or folly of which can only be identified in the sanitizing light of publicity
and with the kind of informed debate that only publicity can enable.

Of course, no responsible commentator can claim an absolute right
to access. There are times when "openness must be tempered by practical exigencies, lest the very values it supports come under threat."[88]
And that threat is real. People have been incinerated in their offices,
blown up in trains and buses, torn apart by car and body bombs, suf-
focated in subways, kidnapped, taken hostage, and obliterated in plane
crashes. This has happened across the globe. There are, in many states
and for many reasons, people who are committed to causing harm and
to destabilizing, if not destroying, governments and states and harming
their citizens. Given that information is power, it is obvious that there
will be cases where the failure to suppress information can empower
those who would destroy the state or do obscene harm to its public.
The commitment to access to information loses its currency, then, when
it risks becoming self-destructive. Without attempting to be exhaustive, suppression of information can be necessary to protect the security
of investigations from premature disclosure of critical information that
could frustrate the detection of terrorists or insurgents. It can be needed to mask the identity of informants, to reserve information so that
international relations and effective diplomacy can be maintained,[89] and
it can be required to ensure the physical safety of troops and civilians.[90]
It is undoubtedly true that even *some* information pertaining to the list
of infamous secret abuses and gaffes I have provided above warranted

---

88   Stanley A. Cohen, *Privacy, Crime and Terror: Legal Rights and Security in a Time of
     Peril* (Markham, ON: LexisNexis Canada, 2005) at 290.

89   *Ibid.* at 290–91.

90   Subcommission on the Prevention of Discrimination and the Protection of Minor-
     ities, *Report of the Special Rapporteurs, D. Turk & L. Joinet, Update of the Prelimin-
     ary Report Prepared for the UN Subcommission on Prevention of Discrimination and
     Protection of Minorities*, UN ESCOR, 43d Sess., UN Doc. E/CN.4/Sub.2/1991/9 (1991).

suppression in the interests of national security. The question, as it is often said, is one of balance.

3) Balancing Competing Interests: The Principle of Presumed Access and the Burden of Proof

Whenever the law balances competing interests it assigns burdens of proof. These burdens serve two key functions: first, they give the responsibility to one side to initiate the proof and arguments needed to make its case, while the other side is called upon to respond; and second, burdens allocate the risk of loss—if, at the end of the case, the evidence and merits are too equivocal to inspire a clear decision one way or the other, then the party bearing the burden loses. The principle of presumed access imposes the burden of proof on the state to justify suppression. Provided standards of proof are assigned that recognize that national security is about avoiding events and therefore involves evaluating risks rather than proving certain, impending consequences (a point I will return to below), then imposing the burden on the state to justify suppression commends itself both as a matter of international law and as a matter of reason.

Dealing first with the contribution of international law, there is little doubt that if access to information is an international law right, then it is supported, even in the face of national security claims, by the principle of presumed access. I say this with confidence for two reasons. First, the relevant international instruments make freedom of expression the norm and national security suppression the exception. They do so by describing freedom of expression as a right in overt terms, and by presenting it initially as an absolute.[91] Only then, after it is extolled in this way, do those instruments make that right subject to public order or national security exceptions which apply only when designated criteria are met.[92]

91   *Universal Declaration*, above note 14, Article 19; *ICCPR*, above note 8, Article 19(2); the *American Convention*, above note 11, Article 13; the *American Declaration*, above note 9, Article 4; *ECHR*, above note 10, Article 10(1). The sole exception is the *African Charter*, above note 12. Curiously, it confers an absolute right to receive information, but it imposes the proviso on the right to express opinions that this be done within the law.

92   *Universal Declaration*, *ibid.*, Article 29(2), subject to limitations for securing the rights and freedoms of others and public order and general welfare in a democratic society; *ICCPR*, above note 8, Article 19(3), including necessary restrictions

Disclosure would be the rule and suppression the exception, even on national security grounds. Not surprisingly, both the *Siracusa*[93] and *Johannesburg*[94] *Principles* respect this by largely dedicating themselves to constraining the meaning of national security, lest it erode the rights protected in Article 19 of the *Universal Declaration*.

Second, it is an indisputable proposition of international law that the burden of limiting fundamental rights like freedom of expression falls to the state, just as it does under domestic constitutional instruments like the *Canadian Charter of Rights and Freedoms*. Under the *International Covenant on Civil and Political Rights*, "the presumption is always in favour of freedom of expression . . . [and] the proponent of a restriction bears the burden of proof."[95] The same holds true in the case of the application of related instruments, like the *American Convention on Human Rights*[96] and the *European Convention on Human Rights*.[97] The *Johannesburg Principles* make express what is implicit in these international instruments. Principle 11 of the *Johannesburg Principles* provides that

> Everyone has the right to obtain information from public authorities, including information relating to national security. No restriction on this right may be imposed on the ground of national security unless the government can demonstrate that the restriction is prescribed by law

---

on national security, provided by law; *American Convention*, above note 11, Article 13(2), including necessary restrictions on national security, provided by law; and the *ECHR*, above note 10, Article 10(2), including necessary restrictions on national security, provided by law as well as the preservation of information received in confidence. Curiously, Article 4 of the *American Declaration*, above note 9, is not subject to expressed limits.

93 Commission on Human Rights, *The Siracusa Principles on the Limitation and Derogation Provisions in the International Covenant on Civil and Political Rights*, UN ESCOR, 41st Sess., Annex, UN Doc. E/CN.4/1985/4 (1985) 1 [*Siracusa Principles*].

94 *Johannesburg Principles*, above note 1.

95 *Report of the Special Rapporteurs, Danilo Turk & Louis Joinet*, above note 46 at paras. 20 and 25. The *Siracusa Principles* confirm that "[t]he burden of justifying a limitation upon a right guaranteed under the Covenant lies with the State." *The Siracusa Principles*, above note 93, principle 12, reprinted in (1985) 7 Hum. Rts. Q. 3.

96 *Velasquez Rodriguez Case* (1988), OEA/Ser. C, No. 4 (Inter-Am. C.H.R.), cited in Krsticevic *et al.*, above note 19 at 177, n. 65.

97 See *Sunday Times v. United Kingdom*, (1979), 30 E.C.H.R. (Ser. A) paras. 49 and 63–66.

and is necessary in a democratic society to protect a legitimate national
security interest.

This, then, is the principle of presumed access: if access to government
information is a corollary right to freedom of expression, it can be subject to the needs of national security, but only if the state justifies suppression.

Leaving aside the technical support international law furnishes to
the principle of presumed access, imposing the burden on the state
when it is seeking to suppress information is a wise choice. This can be
seen by examining the kinds of things that ordinarily influence the assignment of burdens of proof, by considering the balance of risks, and by
exploring the operation of that burden.

a) Factors Affecting the Assignment of Burdens

The first and most common factor in assigning burdens of proof is that
ordinarily the party making a claim has to justify it. This can be observed in civil cases, where the claimant has to prove its case. In a technical sense it may seem in the access to information context that the
members of the public who are seeking the release of the information
are making the claim. What has to be remembered, however, is that the
information belongs to the applicants as members of the public. In a real
sense it is in fact the state that is making the relevant claim, namely, the
right to withhold that information. This is why international law holds
that if the state wants to bring itself into the national security exception
to suppress information it should have to establish its case.

Another factor in assigning burdens of proof is that if a claimed proposition of fact is largely self-evident, the burden will generally be placed
on the party disputing that fact. The theory is that unlikely factual scen-
arios may be rare enough that overall accuracy is better achieved by
erring in favour of the highly probable. This is how many legal presump-
tions work. Sadly, national security and related grounds for suppression
simply cannot be given this kind of presumptive credit. There is a demonstrated tendency internationally for states and state agents to abuse
claims of national security, either wittingly or not. The decision to suppress information is often taken for political purposes, to avoid accountability, for litigation advantage, or because of inadequate commitment
to the virtues of open government.

This comes as no surprise in the case of repressive regimes.[98] In fact, over-classification is an endemic problem in all states. "Experience . . . has shown that . . . access exemptions tend to be widely interpreted by governments" of all stripes.[99] In the United States "there is . . . 'massive over-classification.'"[100] It was estimated by the U.S. Under Secretary of the Defense for Counterintelligence and Security in 2004 that as many as half of all classified documents have been misclassified.[101] Proof of over-classification lies in the fact that "much information originally classified on national security grounds is released under the Freedom of Information Act."[102] In Britain, Clive Ponting was prosecuted in the interests of national security for "leaking" classified information that did nothing to put the United Kingdom at risk, but rather exposed official lies about the sinking of *The General Belgrano* during the brief Falklands war; only jury nullification prevented his conviction when Ponting was prosecuted.[103] Here in Canada, the Hon. Justice O'Connor, conducting an inquiry into the role that Canadian officials may have played in the extraordinary rendition to Syria of Canadian Maher Arar, who was subsequently tortured there, issued an interim report critical of unmeritorious national security claims being made by the Canadian government.[104] In the challenge to search warrants issued in the "leak" investigation of journalist Juliet O'Neill, successive court applications resulted in the disclosure of the bulk of information the government initially sought to suppress based on national security and related grounds.[105] In another case, the Attorney General of Canada used national security grounds to fight an

---

98 See Ceclia Medina & Felipe Gonzalvez, "Chile: National Security, Freedom of Expression and the Legacy of Military Dictatorship" in Coliver *et al.*, eds., above note 7 at 208; Sophia Woodman & Yu Ping, above note 20 at 233.

99 Lustgarten, above note 30 at 464.

100 Hoffman & Martin, above note 32 at 486.

101 Roberts, above note 60 at 142, citing "Hearing of the National Security, Emerging Threats and International Relations," Subcommittee of the House Government Reform Committee (24 August 2004).

102 Hoffman & Martin, above note 32 at 488.

103 See Lustgarten, above note 30 at 465.

104 The Hon. Justice Dennis O'Connor, Commission of Inquiry into the Actions of Canadian Officials in Relation to Maher Arar, "Ruling on National Security" (20 December 2004).

105 *Canada (Attorney General) v. O'Neill*, [2004] O.J. No. 4649, 192 C.C.C. (3d) 255 (S.C.J.).

application by the *Ottawa Citizen* newspaper to force the disclosure of names that had been redacted in six national security search warrants. The objection lacked integrity because the attorney general's office knew that all of the relevant redactions simply repeated the names of two people, each of whom the *Ottawa Citizen* was already aware of and who were co-operating with the newspaper to the knowledge of the government.[106]

Not only do politics, opportunism, and often befuddling judgment influence national security characterizations for information sought to be suppressed, but the choice about what otherwise classified information to release is often undertaken for political expedience. The most notorious current example is the allegation that higher-ups in the Bush administration authorized the leak of classified information about Valerie Plame's CIA identity in order to discredit her husband, a political opponent of the president's.[107] John D. Rockefeller IV, Vice-Chair of the United States Senate Select Committee on Intelligence felt impelled to write to the director of national intelligence, John D. Negroponte, on 17 February 2006 because "'leaks' and damaging revelations of intelligence sources and methods are generated primarily by the Executive Branch officials pushing a particular policy." Rockefeller noted how selective leaks were undertaken to support the case for war in Iraq and to undo political damage caused by the revelation that the president had approved a National Security Agency (NSA) warrantless surveillance program.[108] Elsewhere Rockefeller expressed his disquiet at the classified material shared with journalist Bob Woodward by the executive, which was done according to a former senior administration official because "the White House . . . considered it good public relations."[109] The most recent example of the politically inspired release of purportedly classified information was the decision by the White House to disclose large portions of a top-secret

---

106 *Ottawa Citizen Group Inc. v. Canada (Attorney General)*, [2005] O.J. No. 2209 (C.A.). Costs were awarded against the Attorney General of Canada for causing pointless litigation. See *Ottawa Citizen Group Inc. v. Canada (Attorney General)*, [2005] O.J. No. 4487 (C.A.).

107 Pete Yost, "Papers: Cheney Aide Says Bush OK'd Leak" *Associated Press* (6 April 2006).

108 Letter of 17 February 2006 [copy on file with the author].

109 Murray Waas, "Did the White House 'Authorize' Leaks to Woodward" *The Huffington Post* (24 Feburary 2006), online: www.huffingtonpost.com/murray-waas/did-the-white-house-auth_b_16263.html.

national intelligence estimate on "Prospects for Iraq's Stability: Some Security Progress but Political Reconciliation Elusive, Update to NIE, Prospects for Iraq's Stability: A Challenging Road Ahead." That information was not released by the White House because the security picture changed. It was released in an attempt to counter the political fallout that occurred after portions of that document, suggesting that the war on terror was actually increasing the risks of terrorism, were leaked to *The New York Times*.[110]

Politics is not only pursued through selective leaks. Damage control declassification also occurs. It occurred with respect to information about what the FBI knew of the impending 9/11 attacks, and about presidential knowledge of Osama bin Laden's intent to strike the U.S.[111] It is evident that government perspectives on the intensity of national security risks often wax and wane with the political implications of release. This kind of practice is in keeping with other, broad political practices in response to access requests. The Irish justice minister, for example, has acknowledged pre-releasing information to friendly journalists to neutralize access requests by the opposition,[112] and, in Canada, federal government departments have been known to create documents to spin information after receiving access demands.[113]

The point, of course, is that it would be unwise to give presumptive credit to claims of national security given that they are often not meritorious and disclosure practices are often tinctured by political judgment and self-interest. There can be no presumption that information claimed to be too sensitive to release is in fact too sensitive to release. Prudence alone requires that national security claims be vetted closely, making the assignment of the burden on the state appropriate.

By far, however, the most significant factor favouring international law's choice to impose the burden on states is the relative balance of informational power. Only the party in possession of the information has the tools to make a cogent case, and this is the party often called upon in law to prove relevant facts. Citizens or even the typical access appli-

---

110 The declassified portions of the document can be seen online: www.odni.gov/press_releases/20070823_release.pdf (August 2007).
111 Roberts, above note 60 at 74 & 75.
112 *Ibid.* at 85.
113 *Ibid.* at 93.

cants (journalists, advocacy groups, and opposition politicians[114]) cannot be expected to generate arguments about the relevance of information or challenge the relative integrity of national security claims when the information they require to make those arguments is denied them. It would invite error to assign the burden to the party least in the know. Quite simply, "responsibility for establishing the need for restrictions to the freedom of expression falls to the State; it is in a better position to assess threats to national security than the applicant whose rights or freedoms have been restricted."[115]

In sum, key factors normally influencing the assignment of burdens support the wisdom of imposing that burden on states in access to information contexts.

b) Considering the Balancing of Risks

The strongest counter-argument against putting the burden on the state is that burdens assign the risk of loss when a tribunal cannot make up its mind and that, in national security matters, it is best to err on the side of suppression, given the horrific costs to public safety when national security is compromised through the imprudent release of information. This "err on the side of caution" sentiment, if not the argument itself, has been influential internationally. This concern no doubt supports the marked tendency among domestic tribunals to defer to the claims made by states that information has to be suppressed for national security reasons.[116] In Canada, albeit in a case that did not deal with burdens of proof, the Supreme Court of Canada has arguably supported the case for erring on the side of suppression by accepting that it was appropriate for the Government of Canada to refrain, under the *Privacy Act*,[117] from offering judicial summaries of the innocuous parts of national security files to those who want to challenge suppression because requiring judicial summaries "would increase the risk of inadvertent disclosure of the information or its source."[118]

---

114   *Ibid.* at 116–17.
115   Krsticevic *et al.*, above note 19 at 177.
116   See Joan Fitzpatrick, "Introduction" in Coliver *et al.*, eds., above note 7 at xiii: summarizing a theme that reappeared time and again in the anthology of access articles contributed by international authors.
117   Above note 55.
118   *Ruby v. Canada (Solicitor General)*, [2002] 4 S.C.R. 3 at para. 37 [*Ruby*].

In spite of this implicit judicial support for erring in favour of suppression, it is both undesirable and unnecessary to do so when assigning burdens of proof. First, it is easy to exaggerate the benefits of suppression. It has been observed that when classified information has been leaked, the calamitous consequences almost never materialize.[119] Roberts speaks of unprecedented levels of disclosure in the Bush administration;[120] those leaks have in fact done more to embarrass the government than to undermine national security, an obvious corollary of over-classification. Even when the *Chicago Tribune* revealed, during World War II, by obvious implication that the Japanese codes had been broken—an indiscretion that folklore claims caused President Roosevelt to consider occupying the press office with marines—no harm was done. The Japanese, it seems, were not *Chicago Tribune* readers, for they never caught on.[121] And it is not just a case of an exaggerated fear of the implications of release. There are even times when open debate using apparently dangerous information can in fact enhance national security, such as by exposing gaps in security systems to attract public pressure to do things better.[122] After NBC leaked information that federal investigators managed to carry the material needed to make bombs through twenty-one airport security systems without detection, the U.S. Transport Security Agency responded to the public outcry by committing to improve airport security.[123] Armed forces often leak otherwise classified combat

---

119 Hoffman & Martin, above note 32 at 486.

120 Roberts, above note 60 at 73.

121 Susan Buckley, "Reporting on the War on Terror: The *Espionage Act* and Other Scary Statutes" (March 2002) Media Law Resource Center Bulletin 2002:2.

122 Roberts, above note 60 at 40.

123 See Lisa Myers, Rich Gardella, & the NBC Investigative Unit, "Airline Screeners Fail Government Bomb Tests: 21 Airports Nationwide Don't Detect Bomb-making Materials" (17 March 2006), online: www.msnbc.msn.com/id/11863165; and Peter Williams, "TSA Responds to Airlines Failing Bomb Tests: Probe Fails to Consider Full Array of Security Measures" (17 March 2006), online: www.msnbc.msn.com/id/11878391. When the Canadian Senate Committee on National Security and Defence was criticized for exposing security risks, according to the World War II adage "loose lips sink ships," it replied: "Our basic premise: You can be sure that ships really will sink if they have a lot of holes in them. And those holes aren't likely to get patched unless the public applies pressure to get the job done. They certainly aren't patched yet": Canada, Standing Senate Committee on National Security and Defence, *Fifth Report: The Myth of Security at Canada's Airports* (21

capability information to embarrass governments into increasing funding. In many cases, even when the case for suppression is sound, the desire to suppress can be futile. This is why public domain information tends not to warrant suppression. In an internet and technological age, when masses of information can be searched and transmitted in nanoseconds,[124] when spy satellites and remote listening devices make personal infiltration unnecessary, and when the world of nations is diverse enough to have citizens and therefore civil servants with complex loyalties, attempts to achieve security by suppressing information can be pointless. None of this is to say that secrecy is never called for, or that it is such a futile ambition that we should just open a help desk for terrorists. The point is simply that it would be wrong to adjust the entire balance between access and suppression based on an exaggerated sense of the benefits suppression can provide. That balance has to be undertaken with a realistic sense of the imperatives of secrecy.

Just as it is easy to overestimate the benefits of suppression, it is an easy matter to underestimate its costs. As described above, achieving the balance is not simply a contest between the relative risks of error; there is a consistent pattern internationally of the intentional abuse of national security classifications, and these practices have been used consciously by governments to mask horrendous human rights abuses and to insulate controversial policy from challenge. Imposing a *de jure* or even a *de facto* burden on the applicant would do too much to facilitate information abuse.

Nor can the broader implications of assigning the burden of proof be ignored when relative risks are being evaluated. I appreciate that it is a value judgment, but international law would do better to prize imperfect but reasonable security within open governments, than secure governments that are unreasonably closed. As Stanley Cohen has noted, "Human security may be the precondition to liberty, but that should not be valued above liberty for, when it is weighed, it is capable of destroying liberty."[125] It cannot be forgotten that the decision of where to assign the burden is a profoundly important statement of principle about how

---

January 2003) at 11, online: www.parl.gc.ca/37/2/parlbus/commbus/senate/com-e/defe-e/rep-e/rep05jan03-e.htm#Symbolism%20and%20Reality.

124　Roberts, above note 60 at 38–39.

125　Cohen, above note 88 at 546–47.

the balance should be conducted; as a matter of democratic values, that burden has to be assigned to the state.

Ultimately, what needs to be realized is that the mere imposition of the burden on the state, even given that the main role performed by burdens of proof is in assigning the risk of loss in cases of uncertainty, does not have to entail material public risk. To think that it necessarily must is to confuse burdens of proof and standards of proof. The argument in favour of erring on the side of national security in decision-making is predicated on calamitous consequences, on the fear of threats as profound as nuclear sabotage, dirty bombs, the slaughter of innocents, or the very overthrow of responsible governments by insurgents all occurring because well-intending tribunals or access administrators make mistakes and release what proves to be devastating information over the objection of governments. When tribunals and administrators evaluate the case for suppression according to international law, however, the degree and nature of the demonstrated risk is a critical variable. Where risks are high, or consequences extreme, the case for suppression will almost certainly be powerful enough to achieve suppression, even with the burden on the state. Assigning the burden of proof to the state allows for responsible outcomes, while at the same time endorsing key or base values.

c) The Operation of the Burden

Jurisprudence dealing with the *International Covenant on Civil and Political Rights*, mimicked for other conventions,[126] identifies three key issues that are to be considered when states seek to limit rights. Applied to the question of when information can be suppressed in the interests of national security, those standards ask (1) whether the restrictions are provided by law; (2) whether there is an established need for the restrictive measures to protect national security; and (3) whether the restrictions are kept to the minimum necessary to protect national security.[127] This is an approach that is broadly familiar to Canadian lawyers as it generally mirrors the requirements of section 1 of our *Charter*.

---

126 Mahoney & Early, above note 28 at 113: describing practices of the European Court of Human Rights; and Krsticevic *et al.*, above note 19 at 173: describing the practice of the Inter-American Court.

127 Evatt, above note 28 at 86.

The first requirement, that the restriction be provided by law, is needed to respect the rule of law.[128] It is an inquiry that is intended to prevent arbitrary or selective treatment by requiring infringements to be based on pre-existing rules so that those whose rights are abridged are treated equally by the state. The law must not only exist, but it must also be "adequately accessible" and be "formulated with precision" to enable individuals to (a) understand their obligations and (b) foresee whether particular action is unlawful.[129] Moreover, it must be a law that is binding on public authorities. For this reason administrative practices are not enough.[130] Finally, if the government claims that there is a law that limits a right, it must show that the law clearly applies in the circumstances of the case.[131]

The requirement of "necessity" has a number of components to it. First, there must be a "democratic necessity" for abridging the international law right.[132] In other words, the restriction must be undertaken for purposes consistent with legitimate needs of democratic society, and not for improper objectives.[133] When the claim is based on national security, this means that suppression cannot be undertaken to protect a government from embarrassment or to conceal wrongdoing or to suppress information about the functioning of public institutions[134] nor can it be done to gain a litigation advantage. It must be a legitimate national security threat.

Moreover, the risk that justifies the suppression of information must be real and compelling.[135] This means that

---

128 Mahoney & Early, above note 28 at 113; see *Malone v. U.K.* (1984), 7 E.H.R.R. 14 at para. 67 [*Malone*].

129 In international law, if a law can be applied in a given case consistently with the requirements of international law, its application can still be valid even though it may be vague in its reach. See Evatt, above note 28 at 87. This is not a fitting approach where the issue is the validity of the law itself, as it is where statutes are challenged, for example, under the *Canadian Charter of Rights and Freedoms*.

130 Coliver, above note 29 at 24; Mahoney & Early, above note 28 at 114; *Malone*, above note 128 at para. 67; Krsticevic *et al.*, above note 19 at 173.

131 Coliver, *ibid.* at 24.

132 Evatt, above note 28 at 88.

133 Krsticevic *et al.*, above note 19 at 174.

134 *Johannesburg Principles*, above note 1, principle 2(b).

135 Coliver, above note 29 at 30.

A state must make a three part showing. The State must establish that: (1) there exists a threat to the nation as a whole; (2) the expression at issue has caused or contributed to that threat; and (3) the restrictive measures are necessary to prevent the threat and [are] proportional to it.[136]

In cases where the controversy is whether to release information, the reference to "threat" in the foregoing passage is critical.[137] It affirms that to suppress information, the state does not have to prove that national security *would* be harmed if the information is made known or communicated. Necessity can be based on the risk of harm alone. This is appropriate because national security is about risk management; it is about preventing tragic consequences, not addressing them after they occur. Still, the risk cannot be fanciful. A real threat has to be "established." As the Supreme Court of Canada put it in a non-disclosure context, "there must be a real and serious possibility of . . . harming Canadian security."[138]

In some contexts adjudicators have permitted states a "margin of appreciation" so that international law can accommodate different standards of tolerance between nations. When it comes to a right as fundamental as freedom of expression, however, it would be wrong to do so for three simple reasons. First, whether there is a "real and substantial" risk is a question of objective fact, not of standards, so there can be no room for variable levels of tolerance. Second, it is inherent in the notion of a burden of proof that margins of appreciation work against the party carrying the burden, in this context the state. Third, and of most importance, freedom of expression is too fundamental to be treated as a relative thing. Accordingly, as Judge Martens said of freedom of expression in a European case

---

136 Evatt, above note 28 at 88.

137 In cases where the issue is not disclosure but, rather, whether to punish those who have disclosed information, an unmaterialized risk of harm that existed at the time of disclosure may not be enough. There is "a developing trend to refrain from punishing or even prosecuting the media unless disclosure actually harmed a legitimate national security interest and the harm resulting from disclosure outweighed the public interest in knowing the information": Coliver, above note 29 at 63. See, for example, Germany: Ulrich Karpen, "Freedom of Expression and National Security: The Experience in Germany" in Coliver *et al.*, above note 7, 289 at 297.

138 *Suresh v. Canada (Minister of Citizenship and Immigration)*, [2002] 1 S.C.R. 3 at 51.

[T]here is no room for leaving to the national courts a margin of appreciation as to the assessment of relevant standards, but [rather a tribunal] will affect a full review of such assessments.[139]

Finally, to meet the necessity test, "the restrictive measures [must be] necessary to prevent the threat and [must be] proportional to it."[140] In other words, even though a threat may exist, the apprehended damage may be too minimal to make suppression necessary, or too remote to warrant it. By contrast, even though a risk is relatively unlikely to eventuate, if it would produce horrendous consequences, suppression is appropriate. In effect, although it is not put this way in the authority, the necessity test has inherent in it the need to consider whether the public interest is better served by disclosure or suppression. If the public interest is better served by disclosure, then suppression is hardly "necessary."

In addition to necessity, international law requires that the restriction on freedom of expression must be the minimum infringement necessary. This has two components to it. First, although in some contexts a "reasonable proportionality standard" is applied, where freedom of expression is implicated it appears that a strict proportionality test has to be respected.[141] Consistent with that standard, the Inter-American Court applies a "least restrictive means" test that obliges a state to narrowly tailor its conduct to meet the needs it is pursuing.[142] In the suppression context it would seem to follow that, where redaction or editing can remove the risk, it should be undertaken in preference to denying information absolutely. Second, although it is not likely to be a factor in controlling access to information, consistent with general principles of treaty interpretation,[143] a restriction on a right cannot be broad enough to defeat the right; as it has been put by the UN Special Rapporteur on freedom of expression, "restrictions can ... be considered acceptable only if they do not jeopardize the principle itself."[144] For example,

---

139   *Schwabe v. Austria* (1992), E.C.H.R. No. 242-B (Ser. A).

140   Evatt, above note 28 at 88.

141   Coliver, above note 29 at 30.

142   *Ibid.*; *Compulsory Membership in an Association Prescribed by Law for the Practice of Journalism*, Advisory Opinion OC-5/85, (13 November 1985) Inter-Am Ct. H.R. (Ser. A No. 5) at para. 46.

143   Krsticevic *et al.*, above note 19 at 168.

144   *Report of the Special Rapporteurs, Danilo Turk & Louis Joinet*, above note 46 at 20.

national security restrictions cannot be used to suppress speech that challenges a particular political philosophy since to permit this would be to enable the exception to destroy the right.[145]

It is evident that the principle of presumed access is not a feeble one. It is supported by international law standards developed by tribunals and proposed by commentators that are rigorous by design, intended to reduce the risk that the important prerogative of protecting national security will be abused by states who suppress public information. At the same time, however, this state burden not only permits, but accepts suppression that is supported by law and based on, and proportional to, realistic risk assessments. The operation of the burden, therefore, supports imposing it on states because there is nothing in placing this burden on states that should jeopardize the ability of states to protect their citizens.

4) Summarizing the Case for a Customary Principle of Presumed Access

In sum, international treaty law and probably even customary international law include the principle of presumed access. While courts internationally have yet to give it firm embrace, they should do so given the widespread international consensus that access to information is a *sine quo non* to the kind of responsible government that the international law right of freedom of expression is meant to assure, and given international practices relating to the assignment of burdens of proof. Ultimately, whether customary international law does include the principle of presumed access should not matter to responsible nations, which are the only ones likely to respond in a meaningful way to international human rights standards in any event. This is because, like constitutional instruments, international law purports to do no more than set out minima for behaviour. For responsible nations, the vital case for the principle of presumed access should rest on the fact that access to information is essential to responsible government and can be rejected only corruptly, perversely, or without full reflection in times of panic.

---

145 Krsticevic *et al.*, above note 19 at 168.

5) The Canadian Experience

To evaluate the depth of Canada's commitment to the principle of presumed access, the three different contexts in which the principle of presumed access should operate need to be identified. Those three contexts correlate to the three ways in which government information can be accessed publicly. Government information can be (1) "disclosed" through legal proceedings, (2) "released," either officially or by leak, or (3) "secured" through formal "access to information" regimes. Governments can control the extent to which information is disclosed publicly during litigation by closing courts; the release of information by prosecuting or imposing administrative sanctions on those who distribute information that governments do not want released; and the degree to which access can be secured on request by defining their own obligation to share information with the public.

Unfortunately, the way that Canadian law responds to national security concerns in these three areas has been inconsistent, a point that has been made by Craig Forcese in his article, "Clouding Accountability: Canada's Government Secrecy and National Security Law 'Complex.'"[146] The reason why this has happened is that Canadian access laws have never been integrated. They have, like the access laws of most nations, developed piecemeal, at times in response to real or perceived crises rather than with a view to basic underlying principles and without the kind of general reflection that permits the law to develop in a coherent way.

6) The Law on Disclosure of Information

There are two distinct ways in which government information can be gained during legal proceedings. The first is through disclosure made by governments to the opposing party when governments are litigating. This kind of disclosure is not intended to advance the interests of responsible government; its functions are to ensure the fairness and efficiency of litigation in civil cases and to enable the government's opposing litigant to know the case it has to meet, a crucial consideration in those contexts where liberty or physical safety is at stake, including but not limited to the criminal context. Since disclosure of this kind is

---

146 Above note 1.

not relevant to the principle of presumed access linked to freedom of expression, I will not discuss it further.[147]

The second form of disclosure of government information that occurs during litigation in which the government is implicated is the "open court principle." That principle serves two functions. It ensures that justice is done and seen to be done between the parties, and it helps ensure responsible government. As La Forest J. explained in *Canadian Broadcasting Corp. v. New Brunswick (Attorney General)*,

> It is in this forum [namely courts] that the rights of the powerful state are tested against those of the individual. As noted by Cory J. in *Edmonton Journal*, courts represent the forum for the resolution of disputes between citizens and the state, and so must be open to public scrutiny and to public criticism of their operations.[148]

The open court principle is therefore a context-specific corollary of the more general principle of presumed access. This principle provides access both to the proceedings and to the information relied on during those proceedings,[149] and it applies at all stages. It can furnish access to

---

147 It is worth mentioning in passing that, in criminal cases, the claim by a criminal accused to have presumed access to information sought to be suppressed on national security grounds has been undermined in part by s. 38 of the *Canada Evidence Act*, R.S.C. 1985, c. C-5. Where the Crown makes a national security-based privilege claim, the onus is said to be on the state to establish that disclosure would be injurious to national security, however, Canadian courts lighten that burden by beginning from a posture of deference to executive claims of national security and by imposing the burden on the accused to show that competing disclosure-based interests outweigh any demonstrated national security considerations: *Ribic v. Canada (Attorney General)*, 2003 FCA 246 at paras. 17–21; *Khawaja v. Canada (Attorney General)*, 2007 FC 490 at paras. 61–67, 90, and 92 [*Khawaja*]. This is troubling from a full answer and defence perspective where the state should carry the full burden. More germane to the current discussion is that this line of authority, if it ultimately proves to withstand *Charter* scrutiny in the Supreme Court of Canada, does not augur well for the principle of presumed access that is linked to freedom of speech; if a principle of presumed access can be gutted this way when the liberty of a subject is at stake, the principle of presumed access in the freedom of expression context is not apt to be given the full force it deserves.

148 *Canadian Broadcasting Corp. v. New Brunswick (Attorney General)*, [1996] 3 S.C.R. 480 at para. 20.

149 *Sierra Club of Canada v. Canada (Minister of Finance)*, [2002] 2 S.C.R. 522 at 526 [*Sierra Club*].

the evidence used to secure search warrants,[150] to appeal documents,[151] and it applies in criminal cases,[152] civil litigation,[153] and in administrative reviews.[154] It even applies, albeit in a highly qualified fashion, in immigration cases.[155] Canadian law is vigilant in protecting the open court principle because it is, without controversy, secured by the freedom of expression and freedom of the press found in section 2(b) of the *Charter*. Courts apply the aggressive *Mentuck* test,[156] which employs the kind of rigorous necessity test and proportionality standards described above in the international law context.

How, then, has Canadian law done in balancing the imperatives of access to information against the demands of national security in the open court context? There is no doubt that there has been a reduced commitment to the open court principle on the part of government since 9/11,[157] although Canadian courts have been rolling back state efforts at using national security claims to close courtroom doors. The Supreme Court of Canada gave strong endorsement to the open court principle, even in the national security context, by holding in *Re Vancouver Sun*[158] that interrogations of terrorism witnesses during investigative hearings before courts will presumptively be held in open court, and the Court held in *Ruby* that arguments about national security under the *Privacy Act* are also presumptively to be made in open court.[159] In

---

150 *Toronto Star Newspapers Ltd. v. Ontario*, [2005] S.C.J. No. 41 [*Toronto Star Newspapers*].

151 *Vickery v. Nova Scotia Supreme Court (Prothonotary)*, [1991] 1 S.C.R. 671.

152 *R. v. Mentuck*, [2001] 3 S.C.R. 442 [*Mentuck*].

153 *Sierra Club*, above note 149.

154 *Ruby*, above note 118.

155 *Majoub v. Canada (Minister of Citizenship and Immigration)*, [2004] F.C.J. No. 1335 (F.C.).

156 *Mentuck*, above note 152.

157 David M. Paciocco, "When Open Courts Meet Closed Government" (2005) 29 Sup. Ct. Law Rev. (2d) 385.

158 [2004] 2 S.C.R. 332.

159 *Ruby*, above note 118. In the aftermath of *Ruby*, the Government of Canada was left with no choice but to amend s. 37 of the *Canada Evidence Act*, above note 147, to reverse its legislated attempt to oblige courts to hold closed hearings whenever the Crown argues for the non-disclosure of evidence in a specified public interest that is other than international relations, national defence, or national security; now judges are *empowered* to close their courts at such hearings after balancing competing interests but they can choose to keep courtroom doors open; S.C. 2004, c. 12, s. 18.

Toronto Star Newspapers Ltd. v. Canada[160] the Federal Court of Canada "read down" several provisions in section 38 of the *Canada Evidence Act*, which provides for hearings to suppress information in the interests of international relations, national defence, and national security, because of the "open court" principle. The court held that a number of that statute's mandatory suppression provisions were unconstitutionally "overbroad." As a result, unless there is a risk that national security information or foreign confidences would be disclosed during hearings, those hearings and the documents generated are to be "presumptively open to the public."[161]

Still, the principle of presumed access is not yet universally respected in the open court context. Most significantly, at least taken in isolation, the *Toronto Star Newspapers Ltd., 2007* decision came up short. This is because the court held that the open court presumption does not apply to *ex parte* hearings, which are to be automatically closed.[162] Since, on its face, section [38.11(2) of the statute obliges courts to give the attorney general the absolute right to make *ex parte* submissions, even without any demonstrated need, this would effectively leave the attorney general with the choice of whether to close courtroom doors, which would of course be incompatible with the operation of the principle of presumed access. Subsequently in *Khawaja*, however, the same court upheld the "right of the government to make *ex parte* submissions in national security matters," but qualified that right as being "subject to the control of the reviewing court and the applicable principles of fundamental justice."[163] If this qualification means, as it should, that to enjoy the "right" to make *ex parte* submissions the attorney general must first persuade the court that excluding other parties is necessary to protect international relations, national defence, or national security, then the principle of presumed access will be respected indirectly; in demonstrating the need to exclude other parties, the attorney general would necessarily be discharging its burden of rebutting the principle of presumed public access.

---

160 [2007] F.C.J. No. 165 (F.C.) [*Toronto Star Newspapers Ltd., 2007*].
161 *Ibid.* at para. 86.
162 *Ibid.* at para. 87.
163 2007 FC 463 at para. 45.

While there remains some issue as to whether the section 38 procedure fully respects the principle of presumed access, section 83.05(6)(a)
of the *Criminal Code* clearly does not. It purports to *oblige* judges to hold
closed judicial review hearings into challenges as to whether an "entity,"
which can include an individual, should be listed as a terrorist group. In
the face of Canadian authority, the constitutional validity of this section
is also doubtful.

It can be seen, then, that while the principle of presumed access
finds significant support in the open court context, it is only because
of the constitutional support that the open court principle finds in the
Charter's freedom of expression provision. This is the only reason why
the principle of presumed access is holding its own in the context of
national security disclosure. Sadly, it has not been respected because
the open court principle enjoys widespread, institutionalized support
within the Government of Canada, a disturbing reality that reinforces
the importance of constitutional rights and freedoms.

7) Controlling the Release of Government Information

As described, government information can be accessed publicly when it
is either released officially or leaked. Until recently, the release of government information was controlled by leakage provisions of the *Security of Information Act*.[164] These sections purported to make it a criminal
offence for anyone to communicate, receive, or retain "official secret" information. The provisions were, in fact, vestiges of the infamous, heavily
criticized, British *Official Secrets Act 1989*, an enactment since overhauled
in the United Kingdom,[165] revised elsewhere,[166] and which continues to
be held up in the United States as a model to be avoided.[167]

---

164 R.S.C. 1985, c. O-5, as amended.
165 *Official Secrets Act 1989* (U.K.), 1989, c. 6.
166 South Africa replaced the *Official Secrets Act* in 1982 with the *Protection of Information Act 1982*, No. 84 of 1982. It continues to operate with some modification in
Australia, and has been modified in India: K.S. Venkateswaran, "India: National Security, Freedom of Expression and Emergency Powers" in Coliver *et al.*, above note
7, 321 at 329. It is reported that in India a definition of secret information including
a prejudice component has been adopted.
167 See Harold Berger & Benno C. Schmidt, Jr., "Curtiss-Wright Comes Home: Executive Power and National Security Survey" (1986) 21 Harv. C.R.-C.L. L. Rev. 349 at
401–6.

The original British *Official Secrets Act, 1889*,[168] which was replicated in Canada,[169] was passed in response to the failed prosecution of a disgruntled clerk who in 1878 divulged to a newspaper a secret Anglo-Russian Treaty, after other national defence information was released in two other incidents.[170] Although the bill was presented to the public as a national security initiative, the opportunity was taken in it to criminalize breaches of trust by government officials including the release of any information by government officials contrary to the public interest, whether dealing with national security or not.[171] In 1911 the British made their Act much more strict by making it an offence for anyone, government official or not, to leak *or receive* official or secret official information, whether or not that leak or receipt damaged the public interest.[172] This statute, which applied throughout the dominions overseas including Canada,[173] was passed within one day by a government beset with a constitutional crisis (a violent railway strike that required the intervention of the army, and the Agidir crisis in which a German U-Boat entered the Agidir harbour in Morocco, threatening British interests).[174] Again, the bill was sold to the public as a national security initiative even though it applied to the leakage of any information, harmful or not, whether on national security grounds or otherwise.[175] The law was

---

168 *Official Secrets Act, 1889* (U.K.), 52 & 53 Vict., c. 52.

169 *Criminal Code*, S.C. 1892, c. 29, ss. 76–78.

170 M.L. Friedland, *National Security: The Legal Dimensions: A Study prepared for the Commission of Inquiriy Concerning Certain Activities of the Royal Canadian Mounted Police* (Hull, QC: Canadian Government Publishing Centre, 1980) at 81; U.K., Departmental Committee on Section 2 of the *Official Secrets Act, 1911*, "Report of the Committee Presented to Parliament by the Secretary of State of the Home Department by Command of Her Majesty," Cmnd. III, Appendix III at 121, Chairman Lord Franks ["Report on Section 2 of the *Official Secrets Act, 1911*"].

171 Friedland, *ibid.* at 32, citing the House of Commons (England) Debates. See Ann Rogers, *Secrecy and Power in the British State: A History of the Official Secrets Act* (London: Pluto Press, 1997) 15–18.

172 *Official Secrets Act, 1911* (U.K.), 1 & 2 Geo. 5, c. 28.

173 *Ibid.*, s. 10(1).

174 "Report on Section 2 of the *Official Secrets Act, 1911*," above note 170, vol. 1 at 24.

175 See the account of Major General J.E.B. Seeley, Under Secretary of War, in D.G.T. Williams, "Official Secrecy and the Courts" in *Reshaping the Criminal Law: Essays in Honour of Glanville Williams*, P.R. Glazebrook, ed., (London: Stevens & Sons, 1978) 154 at 159–62; and the account of Christopher Andrew, *Secret Service: The Making of the British Intelligence Community* (London: Heinemann, 1985) at 63–64.

then tightened even further in the aftermath of World War I, shortly after Bloody Sunday (1920) during the Irish War of Independence at a time when the streets of London were blockaded.[176] It was on the eve of World War II when Canada rapidly passed the current Canadian *Official Secrets Act*.[177] That Act was largely a compilation of the British laws that had already been in force here. Again, it was presented to the Canadian public exclusively as a national security bill.[178] Then, in the aftermath of 9/11, the government integrated this statute's leakage and receipt provisions bolus and untouched into its new *Security of Information Act*.[179] It also created additional forms of liability, including for "persons permanently bound to secrecy," but as Forcese points out, these new, narrower, and more restrained forms of liability are moot because you cannot commit those offences without also offending the broader leakage provisions transplanted without material change from the *Official Secrets Act*.[180] With the exception of minor grammatical amendments,[181] then, the law that purported to apply in Canada for controlling the release of government information was the antiquated progeny of crisis, real or perceived.

Not surprisingly given its anxious genesis, the law controlling the receipt of government information in Canada was not fashioned with the priority of honouring the principle of presumed access in mind. There can be no effective presumption of openness if the cast of information that can be suppressed by prosecution is ill-defined, yet the *Security of Information Act* leakage provisions failed to define exactly what information is protected by its leakage provisions. Indeed, in England, the view was taken that the equivalent British statute extended to *all* government information,[182] making it possible, contrary to the principle of presumed

---

176 *Official Secrets Act, 1920* (U.K.), 10 & 11 Geo. 5, c. 75; Friedland, above note 170 at 33.

177 *Official Secrets Act*, R.S.C. 1939, c. 49.

178 *House of Commons Debates Re: Official Secrets Act 1939* (30 May 1939) at 4718–25; *Senate Debates Re: Official Secrets Bill* (31 May 1939) at 552–55.

179 Government of Canada, Press Release (18 December 2001) [the day Bill C-36 received Royal Assent], cited in Canadian Security Intelligence Service, *Security of Information Act* (2 April 2002) at 1 of 2 and 3 of 5, online: www.csis-scrs.gc.ca/en/ newsroom/backgrounders/backgrounder12.asp.

180 Forcese, above note 1 at 85–86.

181 *Canadian Forces Act, 1951*, S.C. 1951 (2d Sess.), c. 7, s. 28.

182 "Report on Section 2 of the *Official Secrets Act, 1911*," above note 170, vol. 1 at 14.

access, to prosecute the leakage or receipt of any government information without limit. The competing and probably prevailing view in Canada was that the Canadian statute protects only "secret official" or "official" information,[183] but, even then, there was no definition furnished of what "secret official" or "official" information was. Unfortunately, the administrative procedures for classifying the secrecy of government information that are currently in place in Canada[184] are not created under any statutory authority and were not integrated into the *Security of Information Act*.[185] Nor was there anything in the statute to identify information as "secret official" or "official" information. Instead information is "classified" administratively if it relates to a "national interest" that may qualify for exemption under the *Access to Information Act*[186] or the *Pri-*

183 See Donald C. Rowat, *Administrative Secrecy in Developed Countries* (New York: Columbia University Press, 1979) at 286; *R. v. Toronto Sun Publishing Limited* (1979), 24 O.R. (2d) 621 (Prov. Ct. (Crim. Div.)); *R. v. Rose* (1946), 88 C.C.C. 114 at 130 (Que. K.B. (Appeal Side)), "The Report of the Commission of Inquiry into Complaints Made by George Spencer" at 57, cited in Friedland, above note 170 at 42–43, but challenging the opinion of the author, *ibid.* at 41–43.

184 Those policies are contained in Canada, Treasury Board of Canada Secretariat, *Government Security Policy* (1 February 2002): see policies on "Security Organization and Administration," online: www.tbs-sct.gc.ca/pubs_pol/gospubs/TBM_ 12A/21RECON_e.asp; and "Security Policy—Manager's Handbook," online: www. tbs-sct.gc.ca/pubs_pol/gospubs/TB_J2/SPMH_e.asp.

185 The exception is the 17 March 2003 "Government Security Policy—Operational Standard for the Security of Information Act," which implements the "special operational information" provisions of the *Security of Information Act*, above note 164, but does not otherwise classify information or deal with leakage or receipt of information under s. 4.

186 Above note 2. Information is classified when it is "related to the national interest [and] may qualify for exemption of exclusion under the *Access to Information Act* or *Privacy Act*, and the compromise of which would reasonably be expected to cause injury to the national interest." National interest is broadly defined and "concerns the defence and maintenance of the social, political and economic stability of Canada." When information is classified in the national interest it is given a classification level of "top secret," "secret," or "confidential," depending on the detrimental effect that might reasonably be expected to occur from its compromise. Shared classified information, including information secured on promises of confidentiality from another nation, is classified as extremely sensitive, particularly sensitive, and low-sensitive. It can be seen that these categories do not integrate symmetrically with the *Security of Information Act* concepts of "secret official" or "official" information.

vacy Act.[187] Meanwhile, the *Security of Information Act* was not linked in any way to either of these statutes. It was therefore technically possible to prosecute individuals for leaking or receiving information that they would be entitled to access under the *Access to Information Act* simply because they had not made formal application for access.

Even though the leakage and receipt provisions of the *Security of Information Act* and its predecessor statutes had repeatedly been sold to the Canadian public as having been passed in the interests of national security, they applied to information having nothing to do with national security, and the statute made no attempt to define national security.[188] Nor was there a requirement in law that the leak or receipt of information be harmful or injurious, making it possible to prosecute the release of innocuous information.[189]

It is evident that the Canadian regime for controlling the release of government information was not based on a presumed right of access; it was a law that purported to permit the suppression of access at the whim of governors. It therefore failed to respect the principle of presumed access and it did so without the definition required by law, unnecessarily, and in a non-minimally impairing fashion.

Fortunately, the leakage provisions of the *Security of Information Act* did not survive *Charter* challenge. In *O'Neill and the Ottawa Citizen Group Inc. v. Canada (Attorney General)*,[190] an Ontario Superior Court Judge found them to be contrary to freedom of expression since each of the communication, receipt, and retention provisions were too broad and too vague to constitute a justified limit on the freedom to communicate and receive information.[191] The Government of Canada decided against

---

187 Above note 55.

188 The statute does define "special operational information," which "basically means military and intelligence-related information that the government seeks to 'safeguard,' an undefined expression." Forcese, above note 1 at 70. The term "special operational information" does not apply, however, to the leakage and receipt offences in s. 4.

189 There is a "public interest defence," but it applies solely to ss. 13–14 offences involving those "permanently bound to secrecy," and is not an available defence under s. 4 (the general leakage and receipt section).

190 [2006] O.J. No. 4189 (S.C.J.).

191 The provisions were also void for vagueness, and unconstitutionally overbroad, contrary to s. 7 of the *Charter*.

appealing the decision and currently recognizes that its *Security of Information Act* leakage provisions are of no force or effect. The Government of Canada has done nothing to replace these sections, in spite of a wholesale amendment to its anti-terrorism legislation; it has either been unable to identify a constitutionally sound method of creating a general leakage provision, or it has decided for political reasons not to try. Once again, it is only because of *Charter* litigation that the principle of access is currently being respected in the receipt context.

8) The Law on Securing Access to Information

Ironically, the federal law of Canada[192] dealing with securing access to information by request is much more respectful of the principle of presumed access, irrespective of *Charter* challenges. It is probably because the Canadian *Access to Information Act* was passed in a period of stability in Canada when the greatest issues had to do with "frustration over the declining power of Parliament, deteriorating economic performance, constitutional instability, fiscal indiscipline and abuses of power by the national police force."[193] It was adopted as part of the crest of initiatives by democratic, stable nations following the American lead.[194] To its credit, the *Access to Information Act* specifically incorporates the principle of presumed access in its primary provision, section 4. That section confers a right on Canadian citizens and permanent residents to access information controlled by the government, and it treats national security suppression as the exception. Where a denial of access is challenged, the burden is on the government to bring itself within that exception.[195] Moreover, the national security exceptions are generally respectful of the principle of presumed access. They are well defined and discretionary, meaning that access administrators and reviewing bodies can balance competing considerations in a way that conforms to international

---

192 As a result of Canadian federalism, each provincial government has its own access to information legislation for provincial government information. Since national security matters tend to arise at the federal level, I will not be referring to the provincial access regimes in this discussion.

193 Roberts, above note 60 at 86.

194 *Ibid.* at 14–15 and 93.

195 *Access to Information Act*, above note 2, s. 48.

law standards.[196] Moreover, those standards all describe what could, in the circumstances of particular cases, be credible bases for denying access. They reference things like military tactics, strategies, and capabilities; intelligence gathering; investigations into unlawful threats to the security of Canada, and the like. If the principle of presumed access is not honoured then, it is because of the application of the law and not its design. There are, however, three problems that impact on access to government information: section 38.13 of the *Canada Evidence Act*,[197] the statutory protection of "third-party agreements," and the equivocal state of Canadian constitutional law.

a) The Impact on Access of Section 38.13

As a result of the flurry of national security initiatives passed after 9/11 as part of Canada's *Anti-terrorism Act*,[198] the *Access to Information Act* was made subject to certificates issued under section 38.13 of the *Canada Evidence Act*.[199] This provision empowers the Attorney General of Canada to issue a section 38.13 certificate that will override the orders of courts and other tribunals declaring a right of access. The attorney general can do this "for the purpose of protecting information obtained in confidence from, or in relation to a foreign entity, or for the purpose of protecting national defence or national security." None of these terms are defined.

This certificate process is inherently inconsistent with the principle of presumed access given that (1) access can be denied on grounds that are undefined, (2) the decision to suppress the relevant information does not require any balancing of competing interests to be undertaken, and

---

196 Some might quibble with this by arguing that the rules fail to respect the necessity principle by empowering decision-makers to deny access where there is a "reasonable expectation" of harm rather than a sustainable determination that harm will occur, but this would be an unmeritorious objection. The statute is about risks. By definition, whether risks will evolve into harm can only be known with the benefit of hindsight. Moreover, the law as interpreted requires a reasonable exception of probable harm: *Rubin v. Canada (Ministry of Transport)*, [1998] 2 F.C. 430 (C.A.).

197 Above note 147.

198 S.C. 2001, c. 41 (commonly referred to as Bill C-36). The specific provision is now incorporated in the *Access to Information Act*, above note 2, as s. 69.1.

199 Above note 147.

(3) there is no real review possible once a certificate has been issued. The sole appeal possible is pointless. It is to a single judge of the Federal Court of Appeal, whose only power is to determine whether the information does "relate to" the undefined purposes for which the attorney general can suppress information. Section 38.13 is manifestly inconsistent with the principle of presumed access.

b) Third-Party Agreements: Internationally Shared Information

The second problem with Canadian law relating to the securing of information from the federal government is the treatment in the *Access to Information Act* of information that has been obtained in confidence from the government of a foreign state or institution. Section 13 of the *Access to Information Act* requires that access to such material be denied unless the foreign state or institution consents to its disclosure or makes the information public.[200] Section 13 is an illustration of the "third-party rule," which gives the state of origin control over the release of shared information by the recipient state, whether that information is classified or not, and regardless of its contents.[201] No showing of national security interest relating to the content of the information is even required. All that is needed to suppress information under section 13 is proof that the information was obtained after a promise of confidence was made to a foreign state or institution. Since there are many standing information-sharing treaties promising confidence, this showing is easily made. For example, in the *International Convention for the Suppression of the Financing of Terrorism*,[202] internationally shared information is presumed to be confidential unless there is an agreement to the contrary.

The third-party rule appears to have originated with the North Atlantic Treaty Organization (NATO). In the early 1950s after information that had been shared between NATO states revealing NATO military plans was leaked, NATO pressured its members to develop tighter con-

---

200 It is not just the *Access to Information Act*. Section 38.13 certificates under the *Canada Evidence Act* can be used to suppress information on similar grounds, an authority the minister of justice claimed necessary in the wake of 9/11 in order to share sensitive information with allies: House of Commons, Standing Committee on Justice and Human Rights, Evidence of the Minister of Justice, Anne McLellan in Meeting 29, Bill C-36 Combat Terrorism (18 October 2001) at 1610.
201 Roberts, above note 60 at 129.
202 10 January 2000, 39 I.L.M. 270, 2002 Can. T.S. 9.

trols over information protection, with harsher penalties. Several existing NATO members obliged[203] and others passed new secrecy laws as a
condition of membership.[204] The third-party rule was born. Third-party
agreements have now become the norm in international relations. The
United States, for example, claims that it will not share information with
a nation that does not agree to a bilateral Security of Information Agreement that entrenches the third-party rule, and such provisions are commonly found. In the Canadian-Australian agreement, for example, "each
government promised to 'take all steps legally available' to block disclosure of shared information under its national laws—a direct reversal of
the presumption of openness."[205] The European Union members agreed
to similar terms.[206]

It is evident that the third-party rule is contrary to the principle
of presumed access. It contravenes that principle by taking the focus
away from whether the information itself should be suppressed in its
own right and by asking instead *how* that information was obtained.
It therefore permits the Government of Canada to suppress harmless
information by simply extending blanket promises of confidentiality to
foreign states, and it permits those foreign states to set the standards
for access here in Canada by giving them the right to decide upon the
release of information even where Canadian officials have acted upon
it. This is instinctively disconcerting. As Roberts puts it, "Why should a
citizen's capacity to hold his *own* government accountable hinge on the
transparency rules adopted by *another* government?"[207] There is surely
something to this disquiet. Once a promise of confidence has been extended, section 13 permits, indeed requires, Canadian government officials to suppress information even if there is a heavy public interest in
its release unless the foreign government consents to its release. If the
United States requested in confidence that the Canadian government
allow it to use Canadian airspace and landing facilities to accommodate
the transportation of terrorism suspects and "enemy combatants," for
example, Canadian officials would have to suppress this information re-

---

203 Roberts, above note 60 at 128.
204 *Ibid.* at 130.
205 *Ibid.* at 133–34.
206 *Ibid.* at 134–35.
207 *Ibid.* at 148.

gardless of any heightened national interest there may be in disclosure, and regardless of whether this information would be proof of Canada's knowing participation in violations of international law, unless the United States consented to its release. Indeed, given that foreign countries are not likely to give standing to Canadians to seek access in their courts, the suppression of shared information in Canada prevents any hearing into the need for suppression of the information itself. This is part of the broader problem identified by Coliver when she commented that "too many governments consider that, because good relations with foreign governments form part of their national security, they are entitled to keep secret a broad spectrum of foreign relations information."[208]

Given that the principle of presumed access is not respected by the third-party rule, if that principle is indeed a matter of treaty obligation or a tenet of customary international law or of Canadian constitutional law, the question that emerges in this country is whether the rule is a justified limitation. The first problem is with its necessity. The rule is overbroad with respect to the information secured. Since the rule is based on the source rather than on the content of the information, the necessity claim has to be based not on the quality of the information itself but rather on the general need to make and honour promises of confidentiality. In *Ruby*[209] the Supreme Court of Canada dealt with this issue only indirectly because the question the Court faced was whether access hearings under the federal *Privacy Act* into internationally shared information could be held *in camera* and *ex parte*. The Court held that *in camera, ex parte* hearings were justifiable because of the risk that international confidences would otherwise be inadvertently breached. In coming to that conclusion the Court referred uncritically to evidence that, without absolute assurances of confidentiality, Canada would be unable to secure information from foreign countries, a necessity, particularly in an age of terror.[210] Although the Court did not address a direct challenge to the legitimacy of the absolute suppression of internationally shared information, its acceptance of the need for the blanket closure of disclosure hearings involving internationally shared confiden-

---

208 Coliver, above note 29 at 22.
209 Above note 118 at paras. 41–51.
210 See Cohen, above note 88, c. 8.

tial information gives some qualified support to the case for blanket suppression of the information itself.[211]

Still, the matter of necessity is not yet resolved and there is time for full consideration. It is worth noting that, subject to the notable exception of "informer's privilege,"[212] class claims based on a generalized fear that information-sharing would cease unless blanket protection is given have fallen out of fashion in Canadian law.[213] Case-by-case, contextual evaluation is by far to be preferred. Moreover, the claim that foreign governments would cease to share all information because of fear that Canadian courts might disclose some of that information deserves critical examination. In the end, the class protection argument holds that if Canadian courts release information that they have determined to be harmless or harmless enough to release in the public interest, then foreign states will take their marbles home and try to combat terrorism without Canada's help. It is an argument predicated either on distrust about the judgment of Canadian courts, or on a claimed right to suppress even harmless information.

Then there is the fact that automatic suppression of internationally shared confidential information does not seem necessary in other contexts. In the release context, the now defunct *Security of Information Act* leakage provisions did not indicate whether "secret official" or "official" information included all internationally shared material.[214] Certainly

---

211 That support is only "qualified" because until the hearing is held, there is a risk of the disclosure of truly sensitive information, hence the case for closed hearings; once the information is vetted and it is seen that it is innocuous, however, the need for perceived secrecy might disappear.

212 "Police informant privilege" protects the identity of those who give information in confidence to the police in criminal cases. In *Named Person v. Vancouver Sun*, 2007 SCC 43, given the risks that would be posed to police informants should their identities become known and the chilling effect that the risk of identification could have on police informants, the Supreme Court of Canada rejected an invitation to weaken this privilege by giving the judge discretion to make the kind of case-by-case assessment that tends to be practised for other areas of privilege in Canada.

213 See *Carey v. Ontario*, [1986] 2 S.C.R. 637, and *R. v. Gruenke*, [1991] 3 S.C.R. 263.

214 "The Government of Canada does, however, require its departments to treat information received from other governments or international organizations in accordance with . . . agreements or understandings between the parties concerned," although the failure to integrate this policy with the scope of the *Security of Infor-*

Canada was not careful in crafting leakage and receipt provisions that would give clear and absolute protection to such information. In the disclosure context, it is clear that there is no absolute suppression. Section 38 of the *Canada Evidence Act* protects "potentially injurious information," which includes "information of a type that, if it were disclosed to the public could injure international relations." The regime permits courts to release such information if a judge concludes that disclosure would not in fact be injurious, or if the public interest in disclosure outweighs in importance the avoidance of the injury. Although the attorney general could use a section 38.13 certificate to prevent the release of internationally shared confidential information to countermand a judge's disclosure order, this is a discretionary power of the attorney general. The provision therefore contemplates the possible release of internationally shared confidential information without the consent of foreign states. If absolute suppression is necessary in the access context, why is it not necessary here? Then there are Mutual Legal Assistance Treaties (MLATs), which contemplate that information might be shared internationally without absolute protection:

> If investigators anticipate that they may be required to disclose information as part of a criminal prosecution, they must warn the agency providing the information. The agency then has the option of refusing to cooperate if doing so would prejudice the country's "sovereignty, security, public order or other essential interests."[215]

Finally, while there is provision for Canadian courts to shut their doors where public access to internationally shared confidential information might otherwise occur, there is no absolute rule requiring courts to do so; it is a discretionary authority, meaning that the possibility of public access to such information is contemplated.[216] Each of the legal contexts where disclosure of internationally shared confidential information is contemplated weakens the claim that blanket suppression is necessary.

---

mation Act makes the policy unenforceable through the *Security of Information Act*: Treasury Board of Canada Secretariat, "Security Organization and Administration," above note 184 at para. 8.5 (currently being revised).

215 Roberts, above note 60 at 139.
216 *Criminal Code*, R.S.C. 1985, c. C-46, s. 486(1).

Still, there are legal standards and then there is *realpolitiks*. Would Canadian courts, or courts in other nations, put their nations to the risk of losing access to national security information by calling the bluff of an information boycott, or by exploiting an unintended inconsistency in domestic legislation? It is not likely. What international law can do, however, is ask whether legislation and government action supporting third-party agreements are minimally impairing. Canadian law has moved towards achieving this by recognizing that, where the third-party rule is invoked to deny access, the government is under an obligation to make reasonable efforts to seek the consent of the third-party state.[217] In the criminal disclosure context, where information is sought by the accused, the government cannot rely on this rule if Canada was aware of the information before receiving it from the third-party state, or if the information has already been publicized. Those same principles would seem to apply in the access context as well.[218]

Although the judicial creation of these obligations and limits on the government is commendable, it does not go far enough to support the minimal impairment requirement that international law would require. First, if according to Canadian law the *content* of information will not justify suppression, the Government of Canada should not only be asking whether the third-party state will release it, the government should be making the case for its release on behalf of the access applicant. Second, the Canadian regime is not minimally impairing at the front end — there are no standards imposed for limiting when Canada should extend promises of confidentiality. Indeed, in the MLAT-context those promises are furnished by field officers,[219] and assurances are often given in blanket terms by treaties before the nature of the protected information is even identified. It cannot be forgotten that Canada, or any other country that extends third-party rule protection, is making a choice to do so and should bear some responsibility to ensure that it extends protection only to information that deserves protection. Finally, it is not minimally impairing to do as Canada does and enter into international treaties per-

---

217 *Cemerlic v. Canada (Solicitor General)*, [2003] F.C.J. No. 191 (F.C.), and *Ruby v. Canada (Solicitor General)*, [2000] 3 F.C. 589 (C.A.), rev'd in part by S.C.C., above note 118, although this may not require a case-by-case request if there are adequate general protocols in place that respect the spirit of access and the letter of the law.

218 *Khawaja*, above note 147 at paras. 146–54.

219 Cohen, above note 88 at 382–83.

mitting the foreign state of origin to decide whether Canada can give access to information, without extracting agreements that Canadians will be given standing to seek access in the courts of the state of origin.[220] In the end, there is no place to go to have suppression reviewed based on the content of the information. The outcome of all of this is that even innocuous information of tremendous public importance can be suppressed, not because that information needs secrecy but because a foreign government or entity insists on suppression for information that international law would not allow to be suppressed even in the state of origin. If blanket suppression ultimately proves to be accepted as necessary by Canadian courts, understandably diffident about working in the international relations area, Canadian law still fails to respect the principle of presumed access because it has not done enough to ensure that the principle is minimally impaired. The question of whether a Canadian court might do anything about that is closely linked to the third problem with Canadian access law. Namely, the regrettable tendency of Canadian courts not to recognize constitutional rights of access.

c) The Canadian Constitutional Right to Access
The third problem with Canadian access law I alluded to is that it is unclear whether the rights of disclosure contained in the *Access to Information Act* are supported by constitutional protection grounded in the *Canadian Charter of Rights and Freedoms*.[221] Those few decisions and judgments that are directly on point deny the existence of a constitutional right of access to information,[222] but the matter is far from settled. Without embracing the question directly, the Federal Court referred to the Canadian *Access to Information Act* as quasi-constitutional,[223] and there are non-binding comments made in other decisions that can be

---

220 Alasdair Roberts does not think this would be an effective remedy, but in my view it is better than the alternative: above note 60 at 148.

221 Forcese, above note 1 at 60.

222 Those cases are *Fineberg*, above note 31; *Yeager*, above note 31; and the Ontario Court of Appeal decision in *Criminal Lawyers' Assn.*, above note 31. In the last decision, Justice Jurianz was the only one to directly address the question of whether the *Charter* guarantees access to information. In his dissenting judgment, he held that it did not.

223 *Canada (Attorney General) v. Canada (Information Commissioner)*, [2002] 3 F.C. 630 at para. 20 (T.D.).

taken to support a full *Charter* right.[224] It is also possible to find general observations about freedom of expression protecting "listeners and readers" that can be used to ground rights of access.[225] There is also the apt analogy to the constitutionalized "open court" cases. Courts opposed to the constitutionalization of an access to information right have attempted to distinguish the "open court" authorities by observing that the open court principle is intended to ensure that courts arrive at fair conclusions,[226] and that this is not a consideration in other access to information contexts. This, however, is not a point of distinction given that, as explained above, the open court authorities, like other access to information initiatives, are also intended to protect the integrity of government and the laws in use by exposing them to the sanitizing light of day. It is important that when the Supreme Court of Canada spoke robustly about the open court principle in its most recent case, *Toronto Star Newspapers*,[227] it cited a broad supporting principle that applies to government information generally. Speaking of freedom of communication and freedom of expression, Justice Fish said "these fundamental and closely related freedoms both depend for their vitality on public access

---

224 See, for example, *Re Rideout*, [1987] N.J. No. 407 (S.C.) in the context of the open court principle, and *International Fund for Animal Welfare Inc. v. Canada*, [1987] 1 F.C. 244 at para. 36 (T.D.).

225 See Forcese, above note 1 at 61, citing *Ruby*, above note 118 at para. 52. In my view, this is not a compelling indicator of a constitutional right — that concession might extend only so far as passive listeners and readers; not to those who try to secure access to government information.

226 In *Criminal Lawyers' Assn.*, above note 31 (Ont. C.A.), Justice Jurianz agreed that the "open court" analogy was not instructive in the access to information context (at para. 140), but based his conclusion primarily on the fact that the open court principle applies only to judicial and quasi-judicial activity, and not to non-adjudicative bodies or to other parts of the criminal justice system. With respect, the fact that it developed in the adjudicative context does not change the indisputable fact that one of the primary functions of the open court principle is to provide access to information. Its failure to apply other than in courts is not a function of a conscious decision to promote secrecy everywhere but in courts; its failure to apply in other contexts is simply a function of the fact that courts are its relevant sphere of operation. The case being made in favour of a constitutional principle of access to information is that, just as openness has been recognized as essential in judicial institutions, it is needed in other governmental contexts for the same reason — to protect the integrity of public institutions and decision-making.

227 See above note 150.

to information of public interest."[228] He was speaking in the open court context but, in referring to the public interest, he was clearly speaking with generality about the interplay among access, public debate, and accountability in a way that gives firm support to a constitutional right of access to information.

This current suspense over whether the *Charter* protects access to information may not continue for long. There is now an application before the Supreme Court of Canada for leave to appeal the Ontario Court of Appeal decision in the *Criminal Lawyers' Assn.*[229] case. If permission to appeal is granted, Canada's highest court is apt to resolve the question of whether the constitutional right of access to information exists.

In truth, the majority decision that is being appealed in the *Criminal Lawyers' Assn.* case is a peculiar one. The majority of the court said that it was not resolving the question of whether the *Charter* includes a right of access to information,[230] but it then turned around and used the *Charter* to protect access to information. It did so by employing creative but arguably questionable reasoning. The majority held that, since Ontario's *Freedom of Information and Protection of Privacy Act*[231] confers a *prima facie* statutory right of access to information, decisions by state agents to deny access, having the purpose or effect of impairing freedom of expression, will violate section 2(b) of the *Charter*. In order to prevent *Charter* violations of this kind, the court reasoned that the *Freedom of Information and Protection of Privacy Act* was constitutionally defective unless it gave access officials the power to override, in the public interest, the statutory discretion of government officials to deny access requests. In effect, the majority used the *Charter* to protect access to information while purporting to avoid deciding whether access to information is even constitutionally protected, and it did so by employing the controversial if not suspect means of recognizing a constitutional right to enjoy a mere statutory right.[232]

---

228 *Ibid.* at para. 2.

229 *Criminal Lawyers' Assn.*, above note 31, leave to appeal to S.C.C. granted, [2007] S.C.C.A. No. 382.

230 *Ibid.* at para. 25 (Ont. C.A.).

231 R.S.O. 1990, c. F.31.

232 This is suspect for two reasons. First, it is illogical. It is implicit in the majority's decision not to resolve the question of whether the *Charter* includes a right of access to information that it may not do so. How can the claim that the *Charter*

With respect, the majority in *Criminal Lawyers' Assn.* should have done directly what it did indirectly; it should simply have recognized overtly that a functional or purposive interpretation of freedom of expression leads to no other conclusion but that access to information is constitutionally protected because it is a *sine quo non* to the core value of section 2(b), namely furnishing necessary support for democracy or responsible government. While it is true that Canada had an enviable democracy and responsible government before it had access to information legislation, it also had enviable democracy and responsible government before it had the *Charter*. It had these things because, in the main, governors acted honourably, yet that governors have acted honourably in the past is no reason to consider constitutional rights to be dispensable. The virtue of the *Charter* is that it transforms the indulgences of the honourable into the legal entitlements of the people. No democracy can survive without reasonable access to public information, and no formal legal blueprint for democracy is complete without guaranteeing reasonable access. Simply put, without reasonable access to government information, citizens are left dependent on the choices of governors and civil servants about what they should know about the conduct of government. This is not a recipe for supporting democracy or responsible government. It is at best a refuge for incompetence, and at worst a prescription for the abuse of power and, as so many international examples illustrate, for the violation of human rights.

For the most part, Canadian courts that have rejected this constitutional right have done so under the influence of distracting considerations. The first decision to do so, in *Fineberg*,[233] rested primarily on the fact that prior to the passage of the *Access to Information Act* there was no tradition in Canada of governments conferring rights of access to in-

---

may not protect access to information be true if the *Charter* can be used to protect access to information as it was in this case? Second, subject to constitutional override or meeting a reasonable limitations test, a *Charter* right is a mandatory obligation imposed on governments. Since the *Charter* right that was used by the court is available only because there is a statutory right of access, the government can effectively undercut that *Charter* right by repealing or amending that statutory right. The majority in *Criminal Lawyers' Assn.* has effectively created a *Charter* obligation that is contingent on the government choosing to be bound, which is no obligation at all.

233 Above note 31.

formation. This kind of historical argument is not only a retrograde way of pouring content into a constitutional instrument, it prizes longevity over function and purpose. Of more importance than longevity is the fact that for a quarter of a century access to information systems have become a primary means of ensuring government accountability in Canada.

The now overruled Divisional Court decision in *Criminal Lawyers' Assn. v Ontario (Ministry of Public Safety and Security)*[234] did not rely as heavily on longevity or tradition. It supported its rejection of a constitutional right by invoking international authorities that have stopped short of declaring a positive right of access to information.[235] Making the point that there are international decisions opposing the applicants' position was fair enough given that the applicants had invoked international standards to support their claim. Still, there are two key problems with relying as heavily as this court did on international authorities. First, this technique is prone to selective reasoning, and the body of authority selected is not the body that should have been used. There are other international decisions supporting a right of access to information[236] and as I have attempted to demonstrate, the preferable reading of international law is that access to information is indeed protected, both in the *International Covenant on Civil and Political Rights* that Canada is a signatory to and as a matter of customary international law. And while it is indeed true that our international commitment can be discharged without grounding it in a domestic constitution, as argued above[237] it is equally true that the most effective way to fulfill any state commitment is to treat the obligation as constitutionally based. Second, and most importantly, the ultimate measure of constitutional stature in Canada is a functional and purposive interpretation of the *Charter* itself. International experiences can illustrate purpose, and international commitments can colour interpretation, but the opinion of some bodies that

---

234 Above note 31.

235 See, for example, *Houchins v. KQED, Inc.*, 438 U.S. 1 (1978); *Guerra v. Italy* (1998), 26 E.H.R.R. 357; and the ambiguous document, *Report of the Special Rapporteur, Mr. Abid Hussain*, above note 36.

236 Such as *Netherlands v. Council*, C-58/94, [1996] E.C.R. I-2169; *S.P. Gupta v. President of India and Ors*, [1982] A.I.R. (S.C.) 143; and Commission on Human Rights, *The Right to Freedom of Opinion and Expression*, ESC Res. 1999/36, UN ESCOR, 1999, Supp. No. 3, UN Doc. E/CN.4/1999/167-E/1999/23. See also the foregoing discussion.

237 See above note 33.

international law does not require access to information should not be allowed to deflate Canadian values and standards.

One of the more discreditable reasons advanced by courts for rejecting a *Charter* right of access to information holds that there cannot be a general constitutional right of access to information because any regime that provides a right of access invariably recognizes access exceptions to account for competing interests.[238] This is closely related to the argument, also made, that there are competing interests at stake such as privacy concerns that may have their own constitutional dimension and that oppose rights of access.[239] This is all true, but exceptions or the need for exceptions do not disprove a rule. No constitutional right is absolute. The *Charter* specifically allows for exceptions where they are reasonable and justified. The fact that exceptions have to be allowed for provides no basis for rejecting constitutional rights.

Equally discreditable was the court's attempt in *Fineberg* to demonstrate that access to information laws are unnecessary. The court apparently accepted the essential purpose that access to information serves, but found it to be sufficient that other methods, apart from a *Charter*-based right, help to preserve the important democratic mission that access to information supports. The court referred, for example, to the parliamentary system with opposition parties posing questions, and the option of resort to the Ombudsman of Ontario, and to statutory regimes including the *Access to Information Act* itself.[240] With respect, none of this is a reason for rejecting a constitutional right of access to information. While opposition questioning is a constitutional convention, it is no substitute for access to information; indeed, opposition parties are among the heaviest users of access to information regimes,[241] since they need government information to engage in meaningful debate. As for the non-constitutionalized modes listed, these are creatures of statute that can easily be repealed.[242] With respect, the fact that governments

---

238 *Criminal Lawyers' Assn.*, above note 31 at paras. 79 and 82 (Ont. Div. Ct.).

239 *Fineberg*, above note 31 at 204.

240 *Ibid.*

241 Roberts, above note 60 at 116–17.

242 Indeed, before the appointment of the current Ombudsman of Ontario, André Marin, the abolition of the office was being considered: Ombudsman of Ontario, André Marin, *Annual Report 2005–2006* (tabled before the Legislative Assembly of Ontario 22 June 2006) at 10.

have taken voluntary measures to help fulfill the purpose underlying a *Charter* provision cannot qualify the content of the *Charter* right itself. Simply put, the content of a constitutional rule does not vary with the extent to which non-constitutional rules or practices address the interests at stake. Indeed, the fact that the *Fineberg* court took solace in the existence of alternative means of achieving access-based accountability is indirect recognition of the essential purposive link between access and democracy.

The most formidable objections to recognizing a constitutional right of access to information are found in the dissenting decision of Justice Jurianz in the Ontario Court of Appeal decision in the *Criminal Lawyers' Assn.* case. He addressed the purposive interpretation argument I have just offered head on, and rejected it for two reasons. First, he urged that the purpose of the provision has to be understood in light of its juridical nature, and section 2(b) of the *Charter* confers a "freedom" of expression, as opposed to a positive "right." That being so, he concluded that the purpose of section 2(b) is to ensure that government does not interfere with or constrain expression, a purpose that does not easily carry with it any right to "positive government action." It therefore follows, he concluded, that the purpose of section 2(b) cannot encompass rights of access to information. To hold that it does is to overshoot the mark.[243] Second, he called into aid the legislative history of the *Charter*, most notably that when the *Charter* was in the committee stage the Special Joint Committee of the Senate and House of Commons, in a formal vote, expressly decided not to include a proposed access to information clause.[244]

To be sure, these arguments pose difficult legal obstacles to constitutionalization, but they are not insurmountable. As Justice Jurianz recognizes, the juridical divide between constitutional "rights" and "freedoms" is not sure enough to apply rigidly.[245] For example, we speak in Canada of a right to silence when, in substance, it has hitherto been little more than the choice or freedom of whether to speak. Given the absence of tight meaning, it is not surprising that the *ICCPR* elides the two concepts, speaking of "the right to freedom of expression." This makes heavy reliance on the choice of the *Charter*'s drafters to use "free-

---

243 *Criminal Lawyers' Assn.*, above note 31 at paras. 108–12 (Ont. C.A.).
244 *Ibid.* at paras. 113–19.
245 *Ibid.* at para. 110.

dom" language rather than "rights" terminology, an inherently unstable platform for decision.

More importantly, there are two reasons why the constitutional stature of access to information should not turn on the fortuity with which the constitutional guarantee for expression was articulated. First, what is at stake here is information belonging to the public; finding constitutional assurances of reasonable access is not so much a question of creating a right as it is a means of assuring access to what the public already has a right in. If we are to speak in terms of rights, the question should be whether government officials have the right to restrict the freedom of access that the public should have to its own information. Second, and of greatest importance, unless the freedom of expression includes a right of access to information, political speech can effectively be undermined or defeated. If a right to access to information is not constitutionally secured, *ex hypothesi* the government has the constitutional competence to keep all government information secret. It is important to realize that we are not speaking of a claimed right to logistical support, such as government-funded megaphones,[246] nor are we speaking about access to a particular mode of expression, such as a vote in a referendum.[247] What is at stake if the "freedom" does not include the "right" is acceptance of the vulnerability of the constitutional freedom of political speech to government fiat. That state of affairs should not be tolerated simply because the framers chose the word "freedom" to express a concept that could equally have been styled to be a right.

As for the legislative history argument, there is no question that the conscious decision of the Special Joint Committee of the Senate and House of Commons to reject a proposed access to information provision gives pause for concern, even though "originalism" has been entirely rejected in the Canadian constitutional tradition. There are, however, compelling reasons why the legislative history argument should not prevail. First, there is the omnipresent objection to trying to glean the actual state of mind of legislators when searching for "legislative intent."

---

246 In *Haig v. Canada*, [1993] 2 S.C.R. 995 at 1035, the Court used this illustration to explain that ordinarily s. 2(b) of the *Charter* operates as a negative obligation rather than a positive right to government assistance [*Haig*].

247 This was the issue in *Haig, ibid.*, where the unsuccessful applicant argued that denial of his participation in the referendum compromised his freedom of expression.

Whose "intent" should we be looking at: the committee's or all members of Parliament and the nine legislatures who passed the *Charter* into law? Indeed, even the decision to include or not include a provision can be ambiguous—was it rejected because it was opposed, or because it was considered inherent in the "freedom of expression," or was it considered a matter for courts to resolve using their interpretative power? In making this point I understand that it is unconvincing to argue that there were probably parliamentarians and legislators who actually believed that freedom of expression would carry a right of access to information, and who therefore concluded that no express access provision would be needed. The likely truth is that most would never have thought the matter through, which is precisely why, as a legal construct, "legislative intention" is best conceived of by examining the basic and evident underlying concepts of those rights that are expressed, rather than the conceptions of legislators. Relying on legislative history in preference to purpose to jettison a constitutional right of access to information is to conclude that the evident underlying concepts animating freedom of expression, including the promotion of responsible government and democracy, are not to be fulfilled because on a particular day in 1981 a committee chose not to include an express right that would have helped secure the clearly recognized purpose of a constitutional provision that was enshrined. With respect, this is not a method of analysis that is conducive to securing fundamental rights and freedoms.

In any event, if legislative history is to be consulted, it must be consulted in context. When the committee deliberations were underway there was no tradition of access to information in Canada; the federal *Access to Information Act* was not even passed into law until the following year, in 1982. As this paper seeks to illustrate, there has been a significant maturation in the concept of effective democracy since the passage of the *Charter*, linked to openness, transparency, and access to information. To freeze the reach of section 2(b) in the inferred intention of a rump of elected and appointed officials in 1981, is a poor way to structure an effective constitutional regime.[248] What should matter is purpose and function, and we in Canada, like so many of our internation-

---

248 This argument was not put before Justice Jurianz; he observed that no arguments had been made to suggest that circumstances had changed since the *Charter*: *Criminal Lawyers' Assn.*, above note 31 at para. 119 (Ont. C.A.).

al neighbours, have come to realize that the purpose of encouraging expression as a way to ensure responsible and democratic government is dependent on access to information.

The last word has not been spoken about the constitutional stature of the principle of presumed access. When it is spoken, if a purposive and functional interpretation is used, the principle of presumed access will be embraced in Canada. It must be. As the Canadian experience in the disclosure context shows, even a state such as Canada will act on an exaggerated need for secrecy; had it not been for the settled and vital constitutional status of the open court principle in the context where it operates, those excesses would have gone unchecked. The constitutional open court principle should be joined by its democratic partner, the constitutional right of access to information, operating through the principle of presumed access.

C. CONCLUSION

The elusive balance between access to information and national security depends on the operation of the principle of presumed access. This principle has the twin virtues of giving profound expression to a necessary commitment to responsible and accountable government while still accommodating suppression of information where suppression is truly needed in the interests of national security. The principle of presumed access almost certainly finds protection not only in treaty law but in customary international law as well. Only the inherent uncertainty of international law itself, and the inexplicable but soft trend among some courts and commentators to treat the recognized international right to receive information as a direction to states to permit a free market exchange of known information, leaves room for uncertainty.

At the end of the day, whether or not treaty-based or customary international law protect the principle of presumed access should not matter to responsible governments. They should not only accept it but also nurture it because the case for the principle of presumed access is decisive. The fact that government information is public information should sustain a presumptive right of access, but more so should the critical role that access plays in securing responsible government. It is when information is suppressed that governments become most corrupt and rights and liberty fall into deepest peril, and it is when information is suppressed that violations of international human rights law are most apt to occur. Access to information can only be protected meaningfully by putting the burden of suppression on states in accordance with the principle of presumed access. There have simply been too many cases internationally and over time where governments have secreted their sins, omissions, and errors behind falsified claims of national security for the law to assume national security claims have integrity. Moreover, only states can truly enlighten tribunals about the need for national security given that they are the ones in possession of the information needed to do so. Finally, this burden can be safely imposed on states without risking calamity, since the burden can be discharged by states in cases where suppression really is needed by providing real and reasonable proof of what could happen without having to go farther and establish what will happen; the degree of damage at risk and the chances that it will happen should enable tribunals to make intelligent and reasoned assessments about suppression. It is simply unrealistic to think that placing the burden on states will undermine the safety of nations.

Unfortunately the Government of Canada, doubtlessly a responsible nation, has not been as scrupulous about respecting the principle of presumed access as it should be. This is not because of corrupt conspiracy or any *mala fide* desire to hide dishonesty or incompetence. It is because Canadian parliaments have developed the law of access largely in an atmosphere of crisis and without an integrated, principled approach. The principle of presumed access is given vigorous expression in the disclosure context of litigation only because of the intercession of courts, wielding *Charter* rights related to, but distinct from, that principle. Moreover, the principle of presumed access was dismally represented under the leakage and receipt provisions of the *Security of Information Act*. This overbroad and ill-defined statutory regime, erected on a platform of panic and misrepresented national security imperatives, failed on every count to respect the principle of presumed access. It permitted the use of oppressive criminal prosecutions in the interests of suppressing the innocuous. Fortunately, again aided by the *Charter*, it has been a court that has shaped the law to give high regard to the principle.

By contrast, the Canadian record where those who are governed seek to secure access to information from their government is mixed. By and large the *Access to Information Act* respects the principle of presumed access, but there are problems. Making access subject to section 38.13 certificates is disconcerting because section 38.13 of the *Canada Evidence Act* gives unbridled and unreviewable power to a politician to have the last word on access issues. It is a "trust me" provision, pure and simple, and it defeats accountability. The *Access to Information Act* also suffers from an overly muscled ban on internationally shared confidential information. The case for the necessity for absolute suppression of internationally shared confidential information is questionable, and Canada has not done enough to minimize the risk of its abuse.

The biggest problem for Canadians is that the right of access to information is left more vulnerable than it should be because of the reticence of Canadian courts to recognize a constitutional right of presumed access residing in the right of freedom of expression. Canada will provide the principle of presumed access its full respect, and the international community its sage example, only when Canadian courts recognize a constitutional principle of presumed access. The case for doing so is decisive. It is how to achieve the promised balance. Without a deep commitment, in law and Canadian legal and political culture, to the principle of presumed access, we will have responsible government in the national security context only by chance, and we will never have a truly accountable government.

Casting a Light into the Shadows: Why Security Intelligence Requires Democratic Control, Oversight, and Review

Andrea Wright[1]

A. INTRODUCTION

Activity that threatens a state's security is usually carried out surreptitiously. To counter and monitor this activity, states must often operate covertly as well. States use special powers to plant listening devices, monitor telephone calls, decipher codes, dispatch spies, seize computers, intercept e-mail, exchange data, and question people. While vital to a state's security, these exceptional, secretive activities can pose risks to a liberal democratic society built on the rule of law, on fundamental principles of openness and accountability, and on individual rights and freedoms. If the sanctity of these institutions and precepts is to

---

1   Prior to writing, Andrea Wright was Legal Counsel to the Commission of Inquiry into the Actions of Canadian Officials in Relation to Maher Arar, advising the Honourable Justice Dennis O'Connor on his policy review mandate to recommend an independent, arm's-length review mechanism for the national security activities of Canada's national police force. Justice O'Connor submitted his report to the Canadian government in December 2006: Canada, Commission of Inquiry into the Actions of Canadian Officials in Relation to Maher Arar, *A New Review Mechanism for the RCMP's National Security Activities* (Ottawa: Minister of Public Works and Government Services, 2006) [*Arar Policy Review Report*]. The views expressed in this chapter are the author's own and should not be taken to represent those of Justice O'Connor or the commission.

be preserved, while at once protecting national security, states should establish a robust regime for democratic control, oversight, and review[2] of security intelligence activities. It is only through the auspices of such safeguards and scrutiny that a populace can effectively demand that security intelligence activities proceed according to its pre-set standards: of legality and propriety, of success in achieving security goals, and of transparency and accountability. It is only through such a regime that a populace can cast light into the shadows of security intelligence activities and thereby make them legitimate.

The *Ottawa Principles on Anti-terrorism and Human Rights* set out a number of basic tenets of such a regime. This chapter elaborates on those principles, by discussing their rationales, their modes of practical application, and their inherent challenges. It also touches upon some emerging challenges for democratic control, oversight, and review (DCOR) of security intelligence, in an era of expanding security intelligence activity.

B. THE REASONS FOR A REGIME OF DEMOCRATIC CONTROL, OVERSIGHT, AND REVIEW

1) The Nature of Security Intelligence Activities

Security intelligence activities,[3] while vital to the protection of the state,

---

2   There are no universally agreed upon definitions of these concepts. This chapter uses "democratic control" to denote measures that a state's legislative branch—the democratic representatives of the people—enacts or otherwise applies to exercise control over the conduct of security intelligence activities. "Oversight" is the ongoing supervision and direction of security intelligence activities by the executive branch of government, which is ultimately accountable for their conduct. "Review" is *post-facto* scrutiny of the activities, independent of any authority to direct them. This chapter elaborates on these concepts by setting out rationales for their conceptual separation, the distinct objectives of each, and the vehicles through which they may be exercised.

3   As with the concepts of oversight and review, there are no universally agreed upon definitions of "security intelligence activities." In this chapter, the term is used broadly, to denote the full range of "actions taken by any state or private actor, typically covertly, in order to gather and collate information that may be relevant to the protection of national security, as the state may define it." See Andrea Wright, "Security Intelligence—Everybody's Doing It: New Challenges for Democratic Control and Oversight" (Paper presented to the European Consortium for Political Research General Conference, Pisa, Italy, 7 September 2007) [Wright, "Security

its institutions, and its people,[4] are activities that can paradoxically risk treading on a liberal democratic state's foundations—its rule of law, its guaranteed rights and freedoms, and its principles of openness and accountability.

Security intelligence typically involves activity such as the monitoring of telephone calls and e-mail, decoding of signals intelligence, surveillance, seizure of possessions and data, infiltration of target groups, questioning of targets, and acquisition of financial, medical, criminal, physical, professional, family, and travel information. These activities can risk infringement of many individuals' rights and freedoms, both domestically and abroad. They risk adversely affecting rights such as privacy, mobility, equality, and the principle of innocence until proven guilty, in addition to protections against unreasonable detention, arrest, inhuman and degrading treatment and torture, and fundamental freedoms such as association, expression, and religious and political beliefs.[5]

Intelligence"]. This definition therefore includes activity that is undertaken by private actors on behalf of state agents, and activity that may or may not exceed statutory bounds. In designing a DCOR regime, the scope of activity for scrutiny should be as wide as the scope of activity that poses risks. Indeed, it is the activity on the margins of propriety, proportionality, and legitimacy that often requires particular attention by a DCOR regime.

4   For a discussion of the role of security intelligence activities to a state's security, see Marina Caparini, "Challenges of Control and Oversight of Intelligence Services in a Liberal Democracy" (Paper presented at the Workshop on Democratic and Parliamentary Oversight of Intelligence Services, Geneva, 3–5 October 2002), online: www.dcaf.ch/pcaf/ev_geneva_021002_prog_caparini.pdf at 2 [Caparini, "Challenges"]; and Greg Hannah, Kevin O'Brien, and Andrew Rathwell, "Intelligence and Security Legislation for Security Sector Reform" (Paper prepared for the United Kingdom's Security Sector Development Advisory Team, June 2005), online: www.rand.org/pubs/technical_reports/TR288/index.html at 1*ff.*

5   The specific risks of intrusion on individual rights and freedoms will vary from country to country, depending on the rights instruments in place and the permitted or undertaken security intelligence activities, but a number of rights intrusions are also proscribed by international instruments. Findings of adverse impact of security intelligence activities on domestic and, in some cases, international rights and freedoms have been made in numerous countries, including, most recently, in Canada: Commission of Inquiry into the Actions of Canadian Officials in Relation to Maher Arar, *Report of the Events Relating to Maher Arar: Analysis and Recommendations* (Ottawa: Minister of Public Works and Government Services, 2006) [*Arar Report*]; in Sweden: Parliamentary Ombudsmen, *A Review of the Enforcement by the Security Po-*

When security intelligence actors[6] utilize special powers, act surreptitiously, or act at the direction of political masters, they also risk

---

lice of a Government Decision to Expel Two Egyptian Citizens, online: www.jo.se/Page.
aspx?MenuId=106&MainMenuId=106&Language=en&ObjectClass=DynamX_SFS_
Decision&Id=1662 [*Melin Report*]; in the United States: U.S., Office of the Inspector
General of the Department of Justice, *The September 11 Detainees: A Review of the
Treatment of Aliens Held on Immigration Charges in Connection with the Investigation
of the September 11 Attacks*, online: www.usdoj.gov/oig/reports/FBI/index.htm [*The
September 11 Detainees*]; and, in recent decades, in Norway: Commission headed by
Justice Ketil Lund, *Report of Surveillance by Norwegian Security Intelligence Agencies
from 1945–Present* (Dok. Nr. 15, 1995–96) [*Lund Report*], discussed in Fredrik Sejer-
sted, "Intelligence and Accountability in a State without Enemies" in Hans Born,
Loch K. Johnson, & Ian Leigh, eds., *Who's Watching the Spies? Establishing Intelligence
Service Accountability* (Washington, DC: Potomac Books, 2005) [*Who's Watching the
Spies?*] 119 at 123 [Sejersted, "Intelligence and Accountability"]; in Belgium: Chambre
des Représentants de Belgique, *Enquête parlementaire sur la manière dont la lutte
contre le banditisme et le terrorisme est organisée—Rapport fait en commun au nom de
la commission d'enquête* (59/8-1988, 59/9-1988, 59/10-1988) [*Belgium Report*]; in the
United States: Senate, Select Committee to Study Governmental Operations with
Respect to Intelligence Activities, *Final Report, 94th Congress* (S. Rep. No. 94-755)
[*Church Report*]; in Australia: Royal Commission on Intelligence and Security, *Fourth
Report* (Canberra: Australian Government Printing Service, 1977) and Royal Com-
mission on Intelligence and Security, *General Report* (Canberra: Australian Govern-
ment Printing Service, 1984) [*Hope Reports*]; and in Canada, Commission of Inquiry
Concerning Certain Activities of the Royal Canadian Mounted Police, Second Re-
port, *Freedom and Security under the Law* (Ottawa: Ministry of Supply and Services
Canada, 1981) [*McDonald Report*]. The Council of Europe has also stated that it

> is concerned about certain practices that have been adopted, particularly in
> the fight against terrorism, such as the indefinite imprisonment of foreign
> nationals on no precise charge and without access to an independent tribunal,
> degrading treatment during interrogations, the interception of private com-
> munications without subsequently informing those concerned, extradition to
> countries likely to apply the death penalty or the use of torture, and deten-
> tion and assaults on the grounds of political or religious activism, which are
> contrary to the European Convention on Human Rights (ETS No. 5) and the
> protocols thereto, the European Convention for the Prevention of Torture and
> Inhuman or Degrading Treatment or Punishment (ETS No. 126) and the Frame-
> work Decision of the Council of the European Union.

Council of Europe, P.A., 23rd Sess., *Democratic oversight of the security sector in
member states*, Text Adopted, Rec. 1713 (2005), No. 7 [*Recommendation 1713*].

6   This chapter frequently uses the phrase "security intelligence *actor*," because
security intelligence activities are increasingly carried out by more than just

straying into the targeting of legitimate activities in a liberal democratic state, such as peaceful political dissent,[7] or selectively interpreting intelligence to serve political ends.[8] Moreover, they risk disproportionate or improper use of their special powers and access[9] and improprieties, when acting in cooperation with other states.[10] These possibilities, together with the potential for intrusions on individual rights and freedoms, all endanger a state's rule of law, since they risk placing state actors and/or the executive branch in a position of unchecked power over a population and its democratically elected representatives.

Further, security intelligence actors can falter in their genuine efforts to carry out their work. They have a highly demanding job in which the stakes are often not just life and death, but mass societal harm. In the acute pressure and challenges of their role, security intelligence actors can fail to identify critical threats and relevant individuals. They can fail to adequately assign resources, hire requisite skill sets, or collect sufficient information. They can also fail to correctly analyze inexact information, fail to take necessary operational and/or preventative action, or fail to act as briskly or adroitly as hindsight might prove necessary.[11]

Finally, security intelligence activities, by virtue of their covertness and preventative nature, proceed with less transparency and mandated

---

conventional, dedicated intelligence agencies. See sections B and C, below in this chapter, and Wright, "Security Intelligence," above note 3.

7   See, for example, *Lund Report*, above note 5, *McDonald Report*, above note 5, *Church Report*, above note 5.

8   For a discussion of the potential for "politicization of intelligence," see H.H. Ransom, "The Politicization of Intelligence," in S.J. Cimbala, ed., *Intelligence and Intelligence Policy in a Democratic Society* (Dobbs Ferry, NY: Transnational, 1987) 25–46; Hans Born & Ian Leigh, *Making Intelligence Accountable: Legal Standards and Best Practices for Oversight of Intelligence Agencies* (Oslo: Publishing House of the Parliament of Norway, 2005) at 68 [*Making Intelligence Accountable*]; Peter Gill, "The Politicization of Intelligence: Lessons from Iraq" in *Who's Watching the Spies?*, above note 5 at 12.

9   See, for example, *The September 11 Detainees*, above note 5; *McDonald Report*, above note 5; *Lund Report*, above note 5; and *Church Report*, above note 5.

10 See, for example, *Melin Report*, above note 5.

11 For example, writing "with the benefit and handicap of hindsight," the 9/11 Commission identified a number of specific "operational failures" of the U.S. government's security intelligence apparatus prior to 9/11. See U.S., National Commission on Terrorist Attacks upon the United States, *9/11 Commission Report Executive Summary* (Washington, DC: National Commission on Terrorist Attacks upon the United States, 2004) at 8 [*9/11 Commission Report*].

scrutiny than other intrusive state action. That is, in contrast to activities such as conventional policing, in which the aim of bringing criminals to justice can only be achieved if the information-collecting methods pass rigorous and bright-light evidentiary tests applied by courts, security intelligence activities often aim to disrupt or prevent the threat from ever being realized. Without any *post-facto* evaluation of the methods used, a society has little way of knowing if they were legal, proportionate, and as effective as possible. Further, ordinary democratic state actors operate with a fair degree of transparency for a number of reasons that do not typically apply in the security intelligence setting. For example, the interface between ordinary state agencies and individuals is, in principle, direct and open. Individuals submit tax returns and are advised of decisions made; they receive medical treatment from state hospitals; they seek permits to drive; and they file unemployment insurance claims. In general, individuals in a liberal democratic society know when a state agency has a file concerning them and make a decision based upon it. This knowledge, together with ordinary systems of complaints and legal challenges, affords scrutiny and testing of state action against collectively-decided standards and rules. In contrast, when a security intelligence actor has a file on an individual, that individual seldom knows it, or has little recourse in the absence of a regime of controls and scrutiny. Further, ordinary state actors do not typically work with data that are restricted from disclosure on the grounds of national security. Information generated or possessed by ordinary state actors can therefore be discussed and challenged in open forums, and it can form part of uncensored public reports, as is typically required of state actors in liberal democratic societies. Historically, intelligence agencies have either had no reporting requirements (indeed the existence of the agencies themselves was often denied),[12] or they have published reports that are redacted of any sensitive information.

It is this lack of ordinary democratic scrutiny, combined with the inherent risks of security intelligence activities, that necessitates a regime of democratic control, oversight, and review. If a populace is to allow such activities to proceed in its name, and if it is to have confidence that the activities are genuinely succeeding in protecting it without contravening or impairing the state's rule of law and societal standards

---

12   See below note 25.

of conduct, a system of safeguards and scrutiny should be put in place. Without such a regime, security intelligence activities have no legitimacy in a liberal democratic state.

2) Objectives of a Regime for Democratic Control, Oversight, and Review

The foundational objective of a democratic control, oversight, and review regime, therefore, is to legitimize a state's security intelligence activities. This is achieved by giving the populace confidence that the activities are complying with collectively-agreed limits on the rights intrusions that may occur and the special powers being exercised. It is also achieved by ensuring that the means employed by the security intelligence apparatus are actually achieving their ends; that the actions of the security intelligence actors are subject to as much scrutiny as possible without jeopardizing national security; and that government is accountable for security intelligence activities. In other words, a regime of democratic control, oversight, and review should seek to assure[13] the populace[14] of the

---

13   While even the most competent regime of safeguards will not prevent every possible error or misdeed, nor guarantee effectiveness and transparency, its *objective* should nonetheless be to assure a state's populace that the agency in question is functioning as it should. In other words, the regime should be sufficiently designed and empowered to genuinely *seek* to ensure the propriety, effectiveness, transparency, and accountability of security intelligence activities. The corollary of this premise is that, when the regime falters, either due to lack of powers or resources or cooperation or other circumstances, the responsible individuals should identify this fact and seek to change or rebalance the system. To do otherwise would be to do a disservice to the legitimacy platform that the system is intended to forge. In fact, it would risk lending a specious legitimacy to security intelligence activities, a result that would arguably be more harmful than a lack of DCOR regime in the first place.

14   Assurances should be given to the wider *populace* of a state, rather than to its citizenry, because it is the broad society of persons within a state that should confer legitimacy upon a security intelligence apparatus, particularly given that all persons enjoy certain fundamental rights and freedoms, and given that security intelligence activities can target both citizens and non-citizens. While non-citizens living in a state may have a lesser capacity to hold government accountable for its security intelligence activities, their confidence in the system is nonetheless important.

Further, while it is the legitimacy of a liberal democratic state's populace that is required in order to avoid compromising the foundations it is seeking to protect, there is potential harm that a security intelligence system can do to the rights of foreign citizens located outside state borders. These individuals are due at least the

- *propriety* of the state's security intelligence activities;
- *effectiveness*[15] of the activities;
- maximal *transparency* of the activities; and
- government *accountability* for the activities.

These objectives are discussed in more detail below.

a) Propriety

A DCOR regime should seek to ensure the propriety of the state's security intelligence activities. This means that it should require that security intelligence activities comply with strict and certain rules. It should also scrutinize adherence to these rules.

These rules should prohibit certain intrusions on rights and liberties, and should define, in advance, the circumstances in which certain kinds and degrees of rights intrusions and investigative methods will be acceptable.[16] The regime should then provide for monitoring of compliance

---

rights and protections recognized in international law (see the *Ottawa Principles on Anti-terrorism and Human Rights* in Part One of this book), and a DCOR regime should seek to ensure that its state's security intelligence apparatus adheres to at least these minimum protections. However, it remains the populace to whom assurances are due, because it is they who can hold the government accountable and force change.

15   Some scholars also refer to the objective of "efficacy." See, for example, Caparini, "Challenges," above note 4 at 8, referring to an intelligence service's "capacity to successfully fulfill its mandate." The Oxford Dictionary defines "effective" as "having a definite or desired effect" and "efficacious" as "producing or sure to produce the desired effect": *Concise Oxford Dictionary of Current English*, 9th ed. (Oxford: Clarendon Press, 1995). If there is any nuance of distinction between these terms, it is not relevant in its application in a DCOR regime, since it is desirable that those charged with supervising the effectiveness, or the efficaciousness, of security intelligence activities, give this objective its broadest definition. This chapter therefore uses "effectiveness" and "efficacy" synonymously.

16   A 1981 Canadian inquiry concluded that the fundamental principles that should inform the formulation of propriety controls are that

- the rule of law must be observed;
- the investigative means used must be proportionate to the gravity of the threat posed and the probability of its occurrence;
- the need to use various investigative techniques must be weighed against possible damage to civil liberties or to valuable social institutions;
- the more intrusive the technique, the higher the authority that should be required to approve its use;

with these legal limits. In addition to measures aimed at legality, a DCOR regime should develop and monitor further standards of conduct and policies that both support and supplement the legal constraints.

Scrutiny for propriety also involves the examination of operational decision-making, and evaluation of the processes that a security intelligence actor has developed to secure compliance by its staff and the criteria it develops to guide discretionary decision-making. Propriety reviews should also look behind representations or conclusions that security intelligence actors provide to support their decisions to use intrusive action, and should scrutinize the underlying collection and conclusion processes. Finally, propriety controls should also involve reporting of non-compliance, evaluation of reasons for non-compliance, and recommendations for change.

Systems for effective supervision of the propriety of security intelligence activities can vary according to the societal, legal, and constitutional context. These are discussed in detail below,[17] but at minimum, they should include the following:

- statutory and internal controls;
- an independent body charged with assuring compliance with these controls; and
- requirements for judicial scrutiny and approval of the use of proposed intrusive activities.

b) Effectiveness

A critical objective of democratic control, oversight, and review is the assurance of the effectiveness of security intelligence activities. The populace—whose security is at stake, whose tax dollars are being spent, and whose civil liberties and societal norms are in jeopardy—should have confidence that the system is functioning optimally to protect it. Supervision of the effectiveness of security intelligence activities therefore involves evaluations of strategic decision-making and operational competence, including intelligence-gathering and -collating methods, analysis outcomes, and target selection; budget and resource allotment;

- except in emergency circumstances, the least intrusive techniques of information collection must be used before more intrusive techniques.

McDonald Report, above note 5 at 513–14.

17   See section C, below in this chapter.

recruitment, training, and management processes; and policy formulation and execution.[18]

The institutions within a DCOR regime that should be charged with supervision of the efficacy of security intelligence activities are discussed in detail below.[19] They include a representative of the executive branch, since one or more ministers should be responsible and accountable for the actions of the security intelligence services, and a committee of the legislative branch, which is the democratically elected representative of the populace and a rightful supervisor. It is arguable whether independent review bodies, which should be primarily charged with reviews for propriety, should also be charged with reviews for effectiveness, since the latter mandate risks compromising the former.[20] This issue is discussed below, and is one of the challenges that a multifaceted regime of safeguards and scrutiny can address.

c) Transparency

Security intelligence activities are normally carried out covertly. They are not subject to the courtroom scrutiny of conventional evidence-gathering activities by police. They are seldom subject to complaint-based scrutiny in a tribunal or otherwise, typically because intelligence targets are not aware they are being watched. Further, they are not subject to routine democratic scrutiny by parliamentary committees and independent officers of the legislative branch because the activities and information are generally secret. They are also seldom subject to media and public scrutiny and access to information about them is ordinarily denied under freedom of information instruments. The inherently secretive nature of security intelligence activities, combined with exemptions from ordinary rules on disclosure, necessitate a focus by the oversight regime on transparency. Security intelligence activities should at least be fully transparent to designated bodies, individuals, and/or committees of the utmost trustworthiness, or else oversight and review mandates will be meaningless.[21] Reviews of propriety and effectiveness can

---

18 See, for example, Australia, Inspector-General of Intelligence and Security, *Bali Inquiry Report* (Canberra: Commonwealth of Australia, 2003); *9/11 Commission Report*, above note 11.

19 See section C, below in this chapter.

20 See sections C(2) & (3), below in this chapter.

21 See section C(3)(b)(iv), below in this chapter.

only truly take place if the activities are transparent to those charged with review.

Security intelligence activities should also be sufficiently transparent to the populace. While most security intelligence will require high levels of secrecy in order to be effective, these activities only remain legitimate as long as the populace gives them their continual, informed endorsement. It is not enough that oversight bodies give opaque assurances of propriety and effectiveness. These assurances should be informative, to the greatest extent possible without jeopardizing national security, providing information on the activities that are being undertaken, the policies that are being applied, the strategic priorities that are being pursued, the resources being expended, and the errors and deficiencies that are being identified and corrected. As discussed below, this transparency role is typically played by an independent review body that makes public reports of its findings and recommendations to the legislative and/or executive branch. However, the executive branch and state and civil society institutions also have a role to play in publicly scrutinizing security intelligence activities, and in maximizing public disclosure of information, without jeopardizing national security.

d) Accountability

A DCOR regime should also hold individuals accountable for the conduct of security intelligence activities. That is, if deficiencies or abuses are identified, there must be a mechanism for the populace to force change. The people, through their elected representatives, should be able to cause policy, strategic, or operational change, or other remedial action such as dismissals of individuals involved. Ultimately, they should be able to force ministers to resign and governments to fall. In a liberal democratic state in which the government (the executive branch) is responsible to the people through their elected representatives (the legislative branch), it is ministers, then, that must bear primary responsibility for a state's security intelligence activities. This political accountability should be underpinned by a hierarchy of individuals to whom operational responsibility is assigned—from directors of agencies to front-line supervisors.

A DCOR regime should therefore include a robust component of supervision by ministers, who can be held to account by the legislative branch and the public. But legislatures and the people can only hold ministers accountable if they have adequate information to identify the need for change or correction. They require evaluations of propriety and efficacy on which to base their ongoing approbation or calls for improvement. The objective of accountability therefore follows from, and relies on, the achievement of other objectives of a regime of control and oversight: transparency of activities, and the evaluations of propriety and effectiveness that transparency facilitates. It is the integrally linked pursuit of these four goals — accountability, transparency, propriety, and effectiveness — that permits public confidence in the security intelligence activities of its government, despite the risks these activities present to some of the society's most fundamental principles.

C. THE COMPONENTS OF A REGIME OF DEMOCRATIC CONTROL, OVERSIGHT, AND REVIEW

Achieving legitimacy then, requires a multifaceted approach. A number of mechanisms are required to shine a light on security intelligence activities and to facilitate the pursuit of the four underlying objectives of accountability, transparency, propriety, and effectiveness. Most of the components are essential, such as statutory control and ministerial accountability. But some facets are variable or optional, depending on the constitutional, legal, and societal context, the nature and structure of the security intelligence activities that the state undertakes, and the design of the rest of the DCOR system. While in limited circumstances some avenues of monitoring and control may overlap, the objective is the creation of separate but complementary accountability instruments, which, taken together, will prevent gaps in scrutiny and achieve all four objectives. As the Parliamentary Assembly of the Council of Europe has recommended

> Democratic supervision makes use of a series of specific tools intended to ensure the political accountability and transparency of the security sector. These instruments include constitutional principles, legal rules and institutional and logistical provisions, as well as more general activities aimed at fostering good relations between the various parts of the security sector on the one hand, and the political powers (the executive, legislative and judiciary) and representatives of civil society (NGOs, the media, political parties, etc.) on the other.[22]

---

22 Council of Europe, *Recommendation 1713*, above note 5.

This section discusses both the essential components of a control, oversight, and review regime, and the variable features that states may incorporate. It provides examples from existing systems, and notes a number of factual or structural difficulties that must often be surmounted. This section also discusses a number of emerging challenges for a DCOR regime that are posed by the changing nature of security intelligence activities.

1) Clear Statutory and Internal Controls

a) Statutory Controls

An indispensable element of ensuring popular legitimacy of security intelligence activities, particularly the exceptional and rights-intrusive powers, is the placement of such activities on a footing that the public has expressly endorsed. Security intelligence activities should be provided for and limited by legislation, which a democratically elected assembly has formulated as its expression of the role that it wishes the security intelligence actors to play, the powers that it wishes to grant, and the limits that it wishes to place on the exercise of those powers. Such democratic control of security intelligence activities, particularly any interferences with rights and liberties, also preserves the rule of law, for "(w)ithout such a framework there is no basis for distinguishing between actions taken on behalf of the state and those of law-breakers."[23] Further, in Europe, a legislative basis for security intelligence services is effectively required by, at least, the right to privacy, enshrined at Article 8 of the *European Convention on Human Rights*.[24]

Security intelligence activities have historically been an inscrutable prerogative of the executive branch of government, seldom discussed or even acknowledged,[25] let alone mandated by parliaments. However, a

---

23 Born and Leigh, *Making Intelligence Accountable*, above note 8 at 17.

24 *Harman and Hewitt v. U.K.* (1992), 14 E.H.R.R. 657. An executive branch instrument in the United Kingdom (the Maxwell-Fyfe Directive of 1952) was found to be an insufficient basis for the Article 8 requirement that privacy intrusions occur "in accordance with the law." Further, the instrument failed to provide the "requisite degree of certainty" and failed to set out the "scope and the manner of the exercise of discretion by the authorities in the carrying out of secret surveillance activities" (at para. 40). See also *Convention for the Protection of Human Rights and Fundamental Freedoms*, 4 November 1950, 213 U.N.T.S. 221, Eur. T.S. No. 5, Article 8.

25 For example, the Canadian government did not acknowledge the existence of its long-standing signals and foreign intelligence agency, now known as the Communi-

number of states have enacted legislation that expressly creates or continues the existence of security intelligence agencies, and variously sets
out their mandates, their powers, and certain limits on these powers.[26]
Statutes can vary in content and in the degree of control they impose
over security intelligence activities, but at minimum they should set out
the following: the type of threat(s) that the agency is mandated to protect against (e.g., domestic threats, foreign threats), including geograph-

---

cations Security Establishment, until 1983 during proceedings of a Special Committee of the Senate. *Arar Policy Review Report*, above note 1 at 143.

26   For example, all of Australia's dedicated security intelligence agencies are provided
for and/or controlled to some extent by statute (see the *Australian Security Intelligence Organisation Act 1979*, No. 113 of 1979 (Cth.) [the *ASIO Act*], and the *Office
of National Assessments Act 1977*, No. 107 of 1977 (Cth.)) with the exception of one,
which a recent inquiry has recommended "be formalized in legislation": Australia,
Inquiry into Australian Intelligence Agencies, *Report of the Inquiry into Australian
Intelligence Agencies* (Canberra: Commonwealth of Australia, 2004) at 180 [*Flood Report*]. In Belgium, the two dedicated security intelligence agencies were placed on
a statutory footing by the *Loi organique des services de renseignement et de sécurité*,
dated 30 November 1998, file no. 1998-11-30/32. Canada's two dedicated security intelligence agencies are also controlled by statute, though one agency was
formally established by statute in 1984 (*Canadian Security Intelligence Service Act*,
R.S.C. 1985, c. C-23 [*CSIS Act*]), and the other was "continued" by statute in 2001
(*National Defence Act*, R.S.C. 1985, c. N-5, ss. 273.61*ff.*), following numerous calls
for a statutory basis. For a discussion, see Canada, Commission of Inquiry into the
Actions of Canadian Officials in Relation to Maher Arar, "Accountability of Security
Intelligence in Canada: Background Paper," online: www.ararcommission.ca/eng/15.
htm at 35*ff.* In Norway, the three dedicated security intelligence services have
various statutory footings (*Act of 20 March 1998 No. 10 relating to Protective Security Services, Act of 20 March 1998 No. 11 relating to the Norwegian Intelligence Service*, and *Act of 4 August 1995 No. 53 relating to the Police*). In the United Kingdom,
the three dedicated security intelligence agencies—MI-5, MI-6, and the Government Communications Headquarters—have all been given a statutory basis (*Intelligence Services Act 1994* (U.K.), 1994, c. 13, *Security Service Act 1989* (U.K.), 1989, c.
5). Other countries with statutes that establish, continue, and mandate security
intelligence agencies include Argentina (*National Intelligence Law No. 25520 of
2001* [*National Intelligence Law*]); the Netherlands (*Act of 7 February 2002, No. 148,
providing for rules relating to the intelligence and security services and amendment of
several acts*); New Zealand (the *Security Intelligence Service Act 1969* (N.Z.), 1969/24;
and the *Government Communications Security Bureau Act 2003* (N.Z.), 2003/9); and
South Africa (*National Strategic Intelligence Act, 1994*, No. 39 of 1994 (South Africa),
and the *Intelligence Services Act, 1994*, No. 38 of 1994 (South Africa)).

ic responsibilities and limits;[27] a comprehensive[28] list of the intrusive methods that may be employed and the restrictions on these, such as threshold conditions for their use;[29] the lines of accountability running from the directors of security intelligence agencies to the executive branch;[30] safeguards against ministerial abuse;[31] and the mechanism(s) for independent and other scrutiny of the agency.[32] Depending on the scope of the statute, other legislation may also play a critical role in

---

27 For example, the Australian Security Intelligence Service may only collect intelligence that relates to security threats posed by "capabilities, intentions or activities of people or organizations outside Australia": *Intelligence Services Act 2001*, No. 152 of 2001 (Cth.), s. 11; and the Communications Security Establishment in Canada may only intercept communications that are *directed* at "foreign entities located outside Canada": *National Defence Act*, above note 26, ss. 273.64 and 273.65.

28 A Canadian inquiry has written:

> [N]o technique of intelligence collection should be employed which entails the violation of criminal law, other statutory law or civil law . . . . If for national security purposes it is considered essential that the security intelligence agency use an investigative technique which involves the violation of law, then those responsible or enacting laws . . . must be persuaded to change the law so that the use of that technique by the security intelligence agency is made lawful.

   McDonald Report, above note 5 at 513.

29 Conditions may include impossibility of less intrusive means, necessity, urgency, and proportionality of the risk and the means. See, for example, the criteria laid out in Canada's *CSIS Act*, above note 26, ss. 12, 19, 21, and 33; the U.K.'s *Regulation of Investigatory Powers Act 2000* (U.K.), 2000, c. 23, ss. 5, 28, 29, and 32 [*RIPA*]; Australia's *ASIO Act 1979*, above note 26, ss. 25*ff*.

30 For example, s. 6 of Canada's *CSIS Act*, above note 26, states that the director of CSIS is "under the direction of the Minister"; that the minister may issue written directions and must file these with the independent review body; and that the director must consult the deputy minister on "general operational policies" and any matter that a written direction may determine. The statute also sets out requirements for ministerial consent or requests in order for the service to enter into certain arrangements or carry on certain activities (ss. 13, 16, and 17).

31 These can include prohibitions on certain kinds of activities such as Argentina's prohibition on the "[e]xert[ion of] influence over the institutional, political, military, police, social, and economic situation of the country, its foreign policies, and the existence of legally formed political parties, or influence of public opinion, individuals, the media, or any kind of associations whatsoever" (*National Intelligence Law*, above note 26, Article 4). Other measures to achieve independence are discussed under section C(3)(b)(i), below in this chapter.

32 See section C(3), below in this chapter.

providing further safeguards, particularly related to the investigative methods employed by the agencies,[33] and the general human rights and privacy norms that apply.[34]

Clear statutory controls on a security intelligence agency's mandate and its powers will also assist the other components of a DCOR regime — the executive branch, independent review bodies, parliamentary committees, other statutory officers — in doing their jobs, since these latter groups will have concrete standards and benchmarks against which to evaluate activities.

b) Emerging Challenge — Statutory Control of New Security Intelligence Actors

The legislative instruments discussed above generally mandate and limit only dedicated intelligence agencies; that is, those agencies charged solely with the collection and analysis of intelligence relevant to national security. Most of these statutes do not place similar limits on the security intelligence activities increasingly carried out by other state and private-sector actors.[35]

State actors that play an increasingly front-line role in security intelligence include law enforcement agencies charged with counter-terrorism mandates, and border authorities.[36] But other departments and agencies also play a role when they collect information from the public that takes on a national security character because it is of interest to dedicated security intelligence agencies and investigating officers.[37] These bodies may have constraints on their powers deriving from constituting and other rights and data-protection statutes, as well as caselaw sources,

---

33 *RIPA*, above note 29.

34 See section C(6), below in this chapter.

35 This issue is discussed in Wright, "Security Intelligence," above note 3.

36 See, for example, the discussion in the *Arar Policy Review Report*, above note 1, of the role of the Royal Canadian Mounted Police and the Canada Border Services Agency (at 83–121 and 151–69) and of police agencies and border authorities in other countries (at 309–424). See also Otwin Marenin, "Democratic Oversight and Border Management" in Marina Caparini & Otwin Marenin, eds., *Borders and Security Governance: Managing Borders in a Globalised World*, publication and pagination pending; online: www.dcaf.ch/publications/bm_borders_securitygov.cfm [*Borders*].

37 See, for example, the discussion of the Canadian national security landscape, as well as that of a number of other countries in *Arar Policy Review Report*, above note 1 at 127–242 and 309–424. See also Wright, "Security Intelligence," above note 3.

but they seldom have statutes that expressly address their roles as security intelligence collectors in any way comparable to the statutes that govern dedicated security intelligence agencies.[38]

Security intelligence is also increasingly acquired by private-sector actors, either because a given security intelligence activity is contracted out or because a private company happens to hold information that is of value to a security intelligence actor.[39] In many cases, such activities and/or information collection and transfer, will be subject to far fewer safeguards than if they had been carried out by a state actor.[40]

Security intelligence activity is also increasingly integrated. Dedicated security intelligence agencies increasingly work out of the same offices and on joint task forces with other domestic and foreign officials, including police forces, border authorities, and other government departments. They also transfer data between agencies and countries, and work together to analyze data and facilitate investigative and intelligence collection activity.[41] These various agencies have disparate

---

38 An exception is *RIPA* in the United Kingdom, above note 29, which places controls on certain interceptions and surveillance activity, regardless of which state agency carries out the activity. The fact that "national security activities" have become an increasingly formalized part of the mandate of Canada's national police force also recently led to recommendations, *inter alia*, for specific statutory controls. See *Arar Report*, above note 5 at 311*ff.*; and *Arar Policy Review Report*, above note 1 at 499*ff.*

39 For a discussion, see, for example, Alan Bryden & Marina Caparini, eds., *Private Actors and Security Governance* (Geneva: Centre for the Democratic Control of the Armed Forces, 2006), online: www.dcaf.ch/publications/kms/details. cfm?lng=en&id=25736; Virginie Guiraudon, "Enlisting Third Parties in Border Control: A Comparative Study of Its Causes and Consequences" in *Borders*, above note 36; and Fred Schreier & Marina Caparini, *Privatising Security: Law, Practice and Governance of Private Military and Security Companies* (Geneva: Centre for the Democratic Control of the Armed Forces, 2005), online: www.dcaf.ch/publications/ kms/details.cfm?lng=en&id=18346 ["Privatising Security"].

40 See, for example, Bryden & Caparini, *Private Actors and Security Governance, ibid.*; and Schreier & Caparini, *Privatising Security, ibid.*

41 See, for example, Gijs de Vries, "The European Union and the Fight against Terrorism" (Paper presented at a Centre for European Reform seminar, Brussels, 19 January 2006), online: www.consilium.europa.eu/uedocs/cmsUpload/ 060119CenterEuropeanReform.pdf ["EU Fight against Terrorism"]; *Melin Report*, above note 5; Canada, Commission of Inquiry into the Actions of Canadian Officials in Relation to Maher Arar, *Report of the Events Relating to Maher Arar: Factual*

statutory controls, and their joint and integrated activity can mean that some officials may be involved in activity that is tightly controlled for some, but not for others.[42]

These changes in security intelligence activity present challenges for a DCOR regime. Enactment of identical statutory controls would, in most cases, be conceptually and operationally clumsy, since other agencies and private actors typically operate in different legal contexts and sectors, and are often marginally or seldom involved in security intelligence activities, particularly the most exceptional and rights-intrusive ones. Identical regulation of these other state and non-state actors could therefore be unduly burdensome and over-inclusive. Conversely, ill-considered replication of statutory controls could be under-inclusive, insomuch as it might fail to address the particularized risks that a sector of activity carries with it. Security intelligence activities carried out by police, for example, carry special risks, in part because they are combined with mandated coercive powers, such as forcible entry, detention, and arrest.[43]

Ideally then, tailored statutory controls should be placed on the activities of any agency or private actor that is involved in security intelligence

---

Background, volume 1 (Ottawa: Minister of Public Works and Government Services, 2006) 30–114; Arar Policy Review Report, above note 1 at 136ff., 163ff., and 309ff.

42 For a discussion, see, for example, Claire Pitham & John McMillan, "Who's Got the Map? The Changing Landscape of National Law Enforcement, Homeland Security and the Role of Administrative Accountability Bodies" in Chris Finn, ed., Shaping Administrative Law for the Next Generation: Fresh Perspectives: Papers Presented at the 2004 National Administrative Law Forum (Hobart, Tasmania: Australian Institute of Administrative Law, 2004); Australia, Commonwealth Ombudsman, "Annual Report 2003–04" (Canberra: Commonwealth of Australia, 2005) at 55 [Commonwealth Ombudsman Report 2003–04]; Australia, Commonwealth Ombudsman, "Annual Report 2004–05" (Canberra: Commonwealth of Australia, 2006) at "Law Enforcement" section of Chapter 4, online: www.comb.gov.au/publications_information/Annual_Reports/ar2004-05/chapter_4/chapter_4h.html; Arar Policy Review Report, above note 1 at 580–97; and Wright, "Security Intelligence," above note 3.

43 Other reasons include the decentralized nature of front-line policing, and the inherent differences in respective mandates of law enforcement and security intelligence agencies. For examples and a discussion of the particular risks created by the conduct of security intelligence activities by police forces, see Sejersted's discussion of the Lund Report, "Intelligence and Accountability," above note 5 at 123; McDonald Report, above note 5 at 95ff. and 418ff.; Arar Policy Review Report, above note 1 at 428ff.

activities. These controls should take account of the specific role that the agency or actor plays in the field of security intelligence, the general and exceptional nature of the activities carried out, and the degree of risk to individual rights and the rule of law. It may be, for example, that robust but generalized data-protection and human rights instruments, combined with some form of independent monitoring and other account-ability instruments, will provide sufficient safeguards. On the other hand, where activity poses particular, significant, and/or novel risks, such as the combined intelligence, enforcement, immigration/customs, and counter-terrorism role increasingly played by border authorities, it may be that an original set of rules and supervisory mechanisms will be required.[44] For example, states should expressly provide for communication and collab-oration among monitoring bodies in order to prevent questionable activ-ities from slipping between the cracks of a DCOR regime.[45]

c) Internal Controls

The first level of responsibility for the efficacy and propriety of security in-telligence activities should be the internal hierarchy and structures of the respective agencies. Directors and other managers within the organiza-tions should ensure that procedures and policies are put in place to ensure

---

44 For a discussion, see, for example, Marenin, "Democratic Oversight and Border Management," above note 36.

45 Several states have made provision for collaboration in various forms. In Belgium, ss. 52*ff.* of the *Loi organique du contrôle des services de police et de renseignements,* 18 July 1991, file no. 1991-07-18/53 [*Loi organique du contrôle*], require the respect-ive bodies for review of intelligence agencies and police agencies to exchange information, hold joint meetings, and collaborate on investigations where desir-able. In Australia, the Commonwealth Ombudsman (who has review jurisdiction over numerous bodies including the Australian Crime Commission but not any of the country's security intelligence agencies) has statutory authority to enter into arrangements with other monitoring bodies: *Ombudsman Act 1976,* No. 181 of 1976 (Cth.), s. 8. For a discussion of examples of such mechanisms and those in other countries, see *Arar Policy Review Report,* above note 1 at 313–16 and 317–424, and Canada, Commission of Inquiry into the Actions of Canadian Officials in Relation to Maher Arar, "International Models of Review of National Security Activities: A Supplementary Background Paper to the Commission's Background Paper on Inter-national Models" [*Arar Supplementary Background Paper on International Models*], online: www.ararcommission.ca/eng/15.htm. A recent Canadian inquiry has also recommended "statutory gateways," integrated review, and a coordinating commit-tee: see *Arar Policy Review Report,* above note 1 at 582–600.

compliance with applicable laws and rules. Indeed, as certain commentators have written, "[t]he most reliable information about illegal action by a security or intelligence agency is likely to come from within the agency itself."[46] Directors and their subordinate managers should therefore ensure that they provide proper training in relevant law and policy and the risks of non-compliance. They should develop and apply rigorous procedures for the selection of targets and the use of intrusive methods,[47] as well as formulate criteria to guide discretionary decision-making. Duties (and corresponding whistle-blower protections) should be created to report breaches of legal or procedural requirements along with disciplinary procedures and competent self-review and internal investigations. Where incidences of impropriety or inefficiency are found, appropriate steps should be taken, including corrective measures, ameliorative procedures, and reporting to the executive branch and/or the independent review body.

Rigorous internal procedures and review mechanisms will contribute to public confidence, and will also facilitate the job of other components of the DCOR regime (particularly the independent review body), since they will offer additional gauges for evaluation of activities, and concrete, traceable procedures to which improvements, where necessary, can be made.

2) Accountability of the Executive Branch

It is a basic maxim of liberal democratic systems that governments are held accountable for their actions, ultimately through the tool of free elections.

---

46   Born & Leigh, *Making Intelligence Accountable*, above note 8 at 46.

47   For example, the Canadian Security Intelligence Service has developed a Target Approval Review Committee (TARC), which is chaired by the director of the service. Its authorization must be requested in writing in order for the service to target an individual and commence the use of intrusive methods against him or her. The request is evaluated on the basis of statutory and other requirements including reasonable grounds to believe there is a threat, necessity, and proportionality. Approval must be specifically granted for investigative methods with increasing degrees of intrusiveness, and for an application for a judicial warrant. For descriptions of the TARC process, see Canada, Security Intelligence Review Committee, *Annual Report 1999–2000* (Ottawa: Public Works and Government Services Canada, 2000) at 13; and Canada, Commission of Inquiry into the Actions of Canadian Officials in Relation to Maher Arar, "Testimony of William John Hooper at the Public Hearing" (22 June 2004), online: www.ararcommission.ca/eng/11e.htm at 458*ff.*

They are also held accountable through the ordinary mechanisms of scrutiny of liberal democratic systems—public reports, complaints processes, media investigation, etc. This accountability causes elected officials to supervise government activity and control the actions of departments and agencies, lest errors or abuses happen and their elected party pay the price. Since it is unworkable for the entire legislative branch to carry out plenary supervision, in many systems it is ministers who are assigned responsibility for various portfolios and who are held accountable by the legislative branch on behalf of the people. Such executive supervision and control is necessary in the security intelligence arena in particular, since the secrecy and sensitivity of much of the activity precludes the possibility of diffuse legislative scrutiny. And since there is a risk of abuse where ministers are given responsibility for agencies with exceptional powers, ministers' specific supervisory and controlling roles should be fixed by statute,[48] and their directions should be given in writing.

This executive branch role should take several forms, including ongoing ministerial direction of strategic goals, occasional involvement in particular investigative and strategic decisions,[49] and priority- and standards-setting. This supervision and control should be exercised over all security intelligence actors, not just dedicated intelligence agencies, particularly in an expanding security intelligence landscape.[50]

---

48 The recent inquiry into the Australian Intelligence Agencies recommended that "ministerial accountabilities" be extended in statute to include a further security intelligence agency, the Defence Imagery and Geospatial Organisation: *Flood Report*, above note 26 at 180. See also Born & Leigh, *Making Intelligence Accountable*, above note 8 at 55–56.

49 Ian Leigh has discussed examples of U.K. ministerial involvement in certain kinds of day-to-day operational and investigative decisions: "Accountability of Security and Intelligence in the United Kingdom" in *Who's Watching the Spies?*, above note 5, 79 at 84–85. For a counter-argument about the appropriate level of ministerial involvement in operational decision-making, due to the risk of abuse and dilution of effective ability to supervise, see Born & Leigh, *Making Intelligence Accountable*, *ibid.* at 55–56.

50 This raises several challenges for a DCOR regime. First, since security intelligence activities now straddle numerous ministerial portfolios, states must decide how to exercise adequately centralized supervision (for example, by transferring the security intelligence aspects of all portfolios into one, or by assigning a coordination function to a close-knit committee of ministers), without losing coherent supervision of the integrally linked remainders of the mandates. Second, there are

Ministerial accountability should also include the authority to demand any information from the security intelligence agencies that the minister may need in order to be satisfied of the effectiveness and propriety of the activities. The activities are being carried out on behalf of the government in the name of state security, and there should be no "no-go zones" for responsible ministers or else the security intelligence agencies become a regime unto themselves. Indeed a DCOR system could mandate a designated body or individual to be the minister's "eyes and ears,"[51] and to supervise the activities on her behalf, in particular because the many competing demands of executive branch government may often prevent a minister from carrying out a sufficient degree of supervision.

It is worth noting that the establishment of an executive branch supervisor does not, however, vitiate the need for an independent re-

---

special considerations in devising a system for ministerial direction of police agencies that are involved in security intelligence activities, for there is tension between a requirement for active ministerial responsibility and the rule of law requirement that police must be free from improper governmental interference in their investigative decisions, lest they become the agents of the government rather than enforcers of the law. Where police forces engage in security intelligence activity, the line between ministerial non-interference and ministerial responsibility will therefore be very difficult to draw. Nonetheless, ministerial oversight of security intelligence activities is as much an imperative for police agencies as it is for dedicated security intelligence agencies, particularly where the activities are not subject to the judicial scrutiny to which ordinary policing work is subject, and particularly where the exceptional powers of security intelligence work are combined with the coercive powers of law enforcement. States must therefore ensure that the responsible minister for police agencies is answerable for their activities, and is actively involved in the direction and supervision of their security intelligence activities. Two Canadian inquiries have recently explored this issue. See Canada, Commission of Inquiry into the Actions of Canadian Officials in Relation to Maher Arar, "Police Independence from Governmental/Executive Direction: Background Paper," online: www.ararcommission.ca/eng/15.htm; and recommended that the minister continue to issue directives to the police force (*Arar Report*, above note 5 at 329), but that the principle of police independence be respected (*Arar Policy Review Report*, above note 1 at 473–4). See also Canada, Ipperwash Inquiry, *Report of the Ipperwash Inquiry*, vol. 2, online: http://www.ipperwashinquiry.ca/report/vol_2/index.html at 301*ff* and Kent Roach, "Four Models of Police-Government Relationships," online: www.ipperwashinquiry.ca/policy_part/meetings/pdf/Roach.pdf. See also *McDonald Report*, above note 5 at 1005*ff*.

51 Canada, Inspector General of the Canadian Security Intelligence Service, *Certificate for 2005*, online: www.psepc-sppcc.gc.ca at para. 2.

view body. The latter should ordinarily perform a different function, as discussed below.

3) Review by an Independent Body

a) Rationale

While supervision by the executive branch or its agents serves as essential, it is not sufficient on its own to assure the populace of the propriety and efficacy of the state's security intelligence activities. Indeed there is much risk in the command and control relationship of the executive branch to the security intelligence agencies, which should be checked, and there is a philosophical divide between oversight by the government of its own activities, particularly ones so hidden from public view, and scrutiny of these activities to ensure that they conform to established norms. Further, there should be an avenue of recourse for individuals who have allegedly been the subject of rights intrusions. There should be an independent forum for the consideration of complaints by individuals, one which is not housed within or answerable to the supervisors of the impugned system. For these reasons, there should be a robust independent review mechanism to carry out ongoing examinations of security intelligence activities on behalf of the people.

Since the basic representative of the people is the legislative branch, it is often debated whether the creation of a dedicated committee of that branch is sufficient to review security intelligence activities on behalf of the people. Parliamentary,[52] congressional,[53] and other legislative

---

52 It should be noted that some commentators, states, and agencies use the adjective "parliamentary" when referring to the body that carries out the review of security intelligence activities on behalf of the legislative branch, even if the body is not comprised of members of the elected assembly. This is sometimes because the legislative branch may have played a role in selecting the members of the body, and/or simply because the body is carrying out its mandate on behalf of the parliament (i.e., the elected legislators and representatives of the public). For example, the review body in Norway (Utvalget for kontroll med etterretnings-, over-våknings-og sikkerhetstjeneste), whose members are elected by the Norwegian parliament but cannot themselves be parliamentarians, often translates its name as the Norwegian Parliamentary Intelligence Oversight Committee (see Born & Leigh, *Making Intelligence Accountable*, above note 8 at 133).

53 In the United States, for example, one commentator has noted that committees of the people's representatives—Congress—have played a "consistent and serious"

committees typically examine government activities in detail, through reporting requirements, information demands, and hearings, and members of the executive branch are called to account in plenary sessions. However, as government activity has become more complex and voluminous, parliaments have created offices and agencies to carry out certain areas of scrutiny on their behalf, such as data protection and human rights commissions and elections officers. The creation of a similarly dedicated office would seem equally imperative if a state is to assure sufficient review of its security intelligence activities. As discussed at the beginning of this chapter, these activities are carried out largely in secret, and they carry risks of rights intrusions and abuse by the executive branch. Rigorous examination is therefore required, which is too onerous a task for members of legislative assemblies, who have numerous other priorities.

Further, elected individuals owe allegiances to their parties, to their parties' agendas, and to individuals and interests that helped elect them. Their skill sets, and their levels of experience in public life and law, vary. There is therefore a risk that day-to-day scrutiny of security intelligence activities, if carried out by elected individuals, could lack the requisite rigour, and could be tainted by partisan or inappropriate motives.[54] This caution does not, however, mean that a parliamentary role is inappropriate. Indeed I discuss the merits of a parliamentary committee in section C(4) below.

Skeptics of independent review bodies often cite a concern about the security of sensitive information because it is being handed to people outside of the conventional "ring of secrecy" of security intelligence agencies and their political masters. It is argued that any increase in the number of individuals in possession of classified information increases the probability that mistakes or leaks may happen. It is also argued that

---

role in the review (and oversight) of American security intelligence activities. See Loch Johnson, "Governing in the Absence of Angels" in *Who's Watching the Spies?*, above note 5, 57 at 58.

54 Speaking about Norway's review body, which is comprised of individuals who are appointed by the legislature but not members of it, Fredrik Sejersted has suggested that it is appropriate to have a committee of appointed members to represent the legislative branch, because the "oversight they conduct is of a legalistic and professional rather than political nature": "Intelligence and Accountability," above note 5 at 121.

foreign states will be wary of sharing vital national security information with a state that widens its ring of secrecy to too many people. However, practice has shown that appointment of sufficiently qualified individuals for the positions, combined with other safeguards such as oaths or statutory enjoinders, will ensure that the information is protected and handled responsibly, and that foreign allies feel confidence in the system.[55] Further, it is now well accepted in many states that the "slight" risk of compromising national security operations is "justified by the greater risk to . . . democracy that lies in the absence of any effective independent check on the government's conduct of security operations."[56]

b) Components

i) Independence
To be effective, a body that examines security intelligence activities on behalf of the populace should be independent of the agencies within its purview and independent of government. The review body should be at "arm's length" from the executive branch and the security intelligence activities in order to ensure objectivity, critical analysis, and a perception of same.

Independence ordinarily requires a combination of measures. These include an appointment mechanism that prevents any perception that

---

55 One study analyzed the safeguards in place and the number of leaks by review bodies in eight countries, and found that the majority of the bodies had had either no leaks or very few. See Hans Born & Loch K. Johnson, "Balancing of Operational Efficiency and Democratic Legitimacy" in Born, Johnson, & Leigh, *Who's Watching the Spies?*, above note 5, 225 at 236. The Canadian Security Intelligence Service also recently stated that

> concerns that comprehensive [review body] access to Service files would cause nervous international partners and liaisons to restrict intelligence exchanges have not, in the long run, come to pass. Related worries about [review body] ability to afford proper security to Service information and protect its human sources and sensitive collection methodologies have not been justified — "leakage" of classified information has not been a factor.

Canadian Security Intelligence Service, "Control, Accountability and Review: The CSIS Experience" (Submission to the O'Connor Commission of Inquiry, 21 February 2005), online: www.csis-scrs.gc.ca/en/newsroom/speeches/speech21022005. asp?print_view=1.

56 *McDonald Report*, above note 5 at 881–82.

the appointee owes allegiances to the government or the security intelligence agency. This usually means ensuring a measure of transparency or input into the appointment. In some countries, this is accomplished through elections by parliamentarians, including requirements that the political spectrum be represented.[57] Other countries have executive branch appointments that are conditional upon consultation with opposition leaders.[58] Other measures could include the appointment of persons who in the aggregate have a range of experience,[59] or who are near the end of their careers.[60]

The process should also include security of tenure for appointees. Their jobs should not be at risk when they criticize the actions of security intelligence agencies and, impliedly or expressly, the government. The term of appointment should be fixed by statute, as should any mechanism and grounds for removal.

The review body should also have its tasks clearly set out in statute. In some cases this may include limiting the body's mandate to a review for propriety, and not effectiveness.[61] The body should also be equipped with adequate budgetary resources to carry out its mandate, without having to rely on examination of a token or limited sample of operational activity. There should be mechanisms in place to ensure that the execu-

---

57   The governing statute for Norway's independent review body requires that the members shall be elected by the legislature, the Storting: *Act of 3 February 1995 No. 7 relating to the Monitoring of Intelligence, Surveillance and Security Services*, s. 1 [*Intelligence Monitoring Act*]; and "care is . . . taken to ensure that they reflect the main political interests represented in Parliament": Sejersted, "Intelligence and Accountability," above note 5 at 127. Belgium's *Loi organique du contrôle*, above note 45, ss. 4 and 28 also provide for election of independent review body members.

58   For example, in Australia, the Inspector-General of Intelligence and Security is appointed by the Prime Minister after consultation with the Leader of the Opposition in the House of Representatives (*Inspector-General of Intelligence and Security Act 1986*, No. 101 of 1986 (Cth), s. 6 [*IGIS Act*]); and in Canada, members of the Security Intelligence Review Committee are appointed by the Prime Minister after consultation with leaders of all parties with twelve or more members in the House of Commons (*CSIS Act*, above note 26, s. 34).

59   See section C(3)(b)(ii), below in this chapter.

60   In Canada, a former Information Commissioner has recommended "an end-of-career appointment" for that office, to prevent the appointee from "looking for future favours": Hugh Winsor, "Ottawa Accused of Trying to Tame Watchdog" *The Globe and Mail* (13 September 2006).

61   See discussion in section C(3)(b)(iii), below in this chapter.

tive branch does not control the budget of the review body such as to affect its decisions about areas of inquiry or criticism.

ii) Composition

To be effective, there are a number of qualities and competencies that a review body should have at its disposal, either in its statutory appointees, or in its staff.

The character and professional experience of the statutory appointees should be such that they will be unafraid to criticize senior government and security intelligence officials in what are often high-stakes circumstances. They should be able to exercise this power responsibly, and should have a strong sense of the public interest and civic duty, and of the challenges and competing public policy objectives that such appointments can hold. They should have the capability and determination to carry out the substantial task of rigorously scrutinizing activity that is secretive and complex. They should have the integrity and discipline to protect national security information and they should instill confidence in both domestic and foreign agencies that the information is safe. They should have the ability to ensure productive interaction with the security intelligence agencies, yet the restraint and awareness to avoid "capture" of their vital external review mandate.[62] They should have the stature to inspire public confidence.[63]

There are other competencies that states should consider in determining the make-up of an effective review body. For example, there are certain essential skills, knowledge, and experience sets that may not need be found in the statutory appointees, but which should at least be found among staff members. These include knowledge and experience in the law and/or the judiciary, public accountability and public

---

62 For a discussion of the risk of "capture" or "co-optation" of review bodies by the security intelligence agency and its mandate, see, for example, Loch Johnson, "Governing in the Absence of Angels," above note 53 at 72; and James G. March & Johan P. Olsen, *Democratic Governance* (New York: The Free Press, 1995) at 164, discussed in Sejersted, "Intelligence and Accountability," above note 5 at 132–33. See also section C(3)(b)(iii), below in this chapter.

63 See, for example, the recommendation made by the Commission of Inquiry into the Actions of Canadian Officials in Relation to Maher Arar: *Arar Policy Review Report*, above note 1 at 552.

policy, civil liberties protections and security intelligence, and law enforcement.[64]

a.   Emerging Challenge: Diversity of Perspectives

To return to first principles, the fundamental objective of a DCOR regime for security intelligence activities is to confer popular legitimacy on the activities, despite the risks of rights intrusions that they present to the state's cornerstone principles. The populace, whose conferred legitimacy is required, necessarily includes all constituent members of a society, in particular those individuals whose professional and personal experiences have contributed to the vibrancy and growth of human rights protection, minority rights advocacy, and cross-cultural understanding in the state. It also includes those individuals and communities that may be targeted without due cause or propriety, and whose rights, freedoms, relationships, and state allegiance may be adversely impacted by illegal, improper, ineffective and/or unaccountable surveillance, detention, or other intrusive activity. If democratic review of security intelligence activities is to confer legitimacy on behalf of all members of a society, an independent review body should represent a spectrum of perspectives (that is, persons who have demonstrated expertise or experience in minority rights issues or advocacy, and matters of cross-cultural understanding). Essentialism and tokenism should of course be avoided in formulating appointment and staffing requirements, but a diversity of perspectives and expertise is vital in matters of popular legitimacy and rights intrusions, particularly in liberal democratic states that

---

64   In Belgium, the heads of the review bodies for security intelligence activities and for police activities must be judges, and the committee members must have at least seven years of high-level experience in areas of criminal law, criminology, public law, or management, acquired in a police, intelligence, or a similar setting: *Loi organique du contrôle*, above note 45, ss. 4 and 28*ff*. In addition, certain staff competencies are required by statute, including linguistic requirements, law degrees, and experience in posts associated with policing or intelligence: *Loi organique du contrôle*, *ibid.*, ss. 5, 17, 31, and 41. In the United Kingdom, the individuals appointed to examine certain aspects of certain investigative activities, such as communications interceptions and surveillance, must hold or have held high judicial office: *RIPA*, above note 29, ss. 57, 59, and 63; and *Police Act 1997* (U.K.), 1997, c. 50, s. 91. In Canada, the person charged with review of the signals and foreign intelligence agency's activities must be a retired judge: *National Defence Act*, above note 26, s. 273.63.

are increasingly focused on domestic terror threats and the avoidance of racial profiling and minority-community alienation.[65]

iii) Mandate

a. Propriety versus Effectiveness

The review body should have a clear purpose. Its mandate should be set out in statute, and should be specific enough to provide clear guidance to the review body and the agencies within its purview of the areas that will be scrutinized, yet broad enough to allow for discretionary decision-making on the part of the review body to investigate matters and areas of operational activity as it sees fit.[66]

The review body should seek to ensure the propriety of the security intelligence activities in question. Review for propriety, as discussed in section B(2)(a) above, essentially involves the scrutiny of security intelligence activities to ensure compliance with strict and certain rules

---

65 In Canada, a Cross-Cultural Roundtable on Security was established in February 2005 to bring together individuals with

> awareness of security matters as they relate to the community and relevant community dynamics . . . knowledge and experience in engaging diverse and pluralistic communities . . . [the] ability to facilitate the exchange of information with communities . . . [and the] commitment to building community capacity and safer communities.

The Committee is mandated to

> [provide] insights on how national security measures may impact Canada's diverse communities . . . [promote] the protection of civil order, mutual respect and common understanding . . . [and facilitate] a broad exchange of information between the government and communities on the impact of national security issues consistent with Canadian rights and responsibilities.

See online: www.psepc.gc.ca/prg/ns/ccrs/ccrstor-en.asp#2. See also the Diversity & Citizen Focus Directorate of the U.K.'s Metropolitan Police, online: www.met. police.uk/dcf/index.htm.

66 The review body in Norway, for example, is granted the discretion to inquire into matters as it sees fit, "particularly matters that have been subjected to public criticism": *Intelligence Monitoring Act*, above note 57 at s. 3. On the other hand, a lack of discretionary scope appears to have precluded the Security Intelligence Review Committee in Canada from reviewing new statutory activities with which the intelligence service has been mandated: Canada, Security Intelligence Review Committee, *Annual Report 2004–05* (Ottawa: Public Works and Government Services Canada, 2005) at 4.

found in applicable law, policy, and procedure. These include rules that prohibit certain intrusions on rights and liberties, and that define the circumstances in which certain kinds and degrees of rights intrusions and investigative methods may be used.

While some bodies have dual mandates to review the propriety and the effectiveness of security intelligence activities,[67] some view that the latter carries too great a risk of tainting the body's indispensable role of assuring propriety.[68] There is a risk that such a mandate could immerse the body at times in results-based examinations of matters such as the choices of investigative methods and selection of targets, and even budgetary considerations. Such scrutiny would consume valuable resources and skills, and would effectively involve the body in strategic decision-making. This could in turn divert the body from its priority mandate of reviewing activity for propriety, and taint its objectivity. For example, highly intrusive means might be sanctioned where lesser means might have been adequate, or circles of targets for surveillance might become wider than necessary. The review body could lose its critical perspective and find itself captured or co-opted by the community of security intelligence and its goals, leaving the external territory of review behind.[69] Further, assurances of the efficacy of security intelligence activities can be adequately provided by other instruments, namely the ongoing oversight of the executive branch, and the scrutiny of a committee of the legislative branch.[70]

---

67 For example, Belgium's review body for its intelligence agencies is mandated by its statute to monitor the "protection of the rights conferred upon the individual by the Constitution and by law as well as the coordination and efficiency of . . . intelligence and security services": *Loi organique du contrôle*, above note 45, s. 1.

68 In his article "Intelligence and Accountability," above note 5 at 132–33, Sejersted notes the importance of a distinction between review and ongoing direction of security intelligence agencies. He notes Norway's prohibition on "consultations" by its review body with the security intelligence agencies under review. Section 2 of the *Intelligence Monitoring Act*, above note 57, states that "[t]he Committee may not instruct the monitored bodies or be used by these for consultations."

69 Above note 62.

70 In one commentator's view, discussing the mandate of the Norwegian review body for the activities of three security intelligence agencies, "[t]he Committee has neither the competence nor the qualifications to evaluate the intelligence and analysis supplied by the secret agencies, nor to question their effectiveness and

This said, review bodies should be empowered to pass information on to other bodies within the oversight and review regime that are charged with review for effectiveness, such as the executive branch oversight body or the dedicated parliamentary committee. Patterns of impropriety can often be indicative of bigger problems of efficacy and leadership in an agency, and a review body should therefore have an avenue to report its findings to the appropriate body for further scrutiny.

b. Emerging Challenge: The Need for Particularized Mandates

Statutes setting out the mandates of independent review bodies tend to contain few details about the standards against which security intelligence conduct should be examined. Rather, they tend to set out conditions for the use of certain kinds of powers, and rules about authorizations that are required. They then mandate the agencies to review for compliance with these statutory controls.[71] Some may additionally, or instead, set out a mandate to monitor "general performance;"[72] or the "protection of rights"[73] or "human rights;"[74] or "to ascertain and prevent any exercise of injustice against any person . . . undue damage to civil life . . . (and violations of) statute law, administrative or military directives and non-statutory law."[75] Review for compliance with internal controls and ministerial directives also tend to be either express or easily implied.

However, these statutes do not often mandate review bodies to review the activity of security intelligence agencies against the requirements of domestic and international human rights instruments, data protection instruments, and international law generally. This book, for example, contains discussion of a substantial set of well-established international law and principles that should constrain counter-terrorism operations, few of which are expressly incorporated into the mandates of external review bodies.

---

efficiency. Such evaluations are left to executive oversight procedures." (Sejersted, "Intelligence and Accountability," above note 5 at 125.)

71 See, for example, *CSIS Act*, above note 26, ss. 12, 13, 17, 21, and 38; the *RIPA*, above note 29, ss. 57 and 59.

72 *CSIS Act, ibid.*, s. 38.

73 *Loi organique du contrôle*, above note 45, s. 1.

74 *IGIS Act*, above note 58, s. 4.

75 *Intelligence Monitoring Act*, above note 57, s. 2.

In an era in which security intelligence activities are increasingly being impugned for failures to comply with fundamental human rights instruments,[76] states should establish external review mandates that include express requirements for monitoring of compliance with applicable international law standards.[77]

Review bodies should also be mandated to review agencies against rules of conduct that have been developed with the particular risks of that agency's activity in mind. For example, a recent Canadian inquiry made twenty-one detailed recommendations for particularized rules that should govern the national security activities of Canada's national police force (and other Canadian agencies); and stated that the recommendations, if adopted, would provide standards against which the police force's activities would be measured by the independent review body that it also recommended.[78] These recommendations included rules for information sharing, investigative interaction with countries with questionable human rights records, the prohibition of racial, religious, or ethnic profiling, and the conduct of border activity.[79]

Establishing mandates that are tailored to address areas of contemporary concern will also go a long way to ensuring the legitimacy of security intelligence activities among the diverse spectrum of perspectives found in contemporary western societies. Indeed review bodies,

---

76 See *Recommendation 1713*, above note 5 at no. 8.

77 Two officials in the United States, albeit internal to government departments, have recently been tasked with particularized mandates that go some way to addressing areas of substantial contemporary concern: reviewing and reporting on "information and . . . complaints alleging abuses of civil rights and civil liberties by employees and officials" of authorities that included the Federal Bureau of Intelligence and the Department of Homeland Security: *Uniting and Strengthening America by Providing Appropriate Tools Required to Intercept and Obstruct Terrorism (U.S.A. Patriot Act) Act of 2001*, Pub. L. No. 107-56, 115 Stat. 272, s. 1001; *Homeland Security Act of 2002*, Pub. L. 107-296, 116 Stat. 2135, s. 705. The mandates are conferred upon the Inspectors General of the Departments of Justice and Homeland Security respectively. These mandates, the fact of which must be publicized in numerous languages by the officials, have led to systemic investigations such as the inquiry by the U.S. Inspector General for the Department of Justice into alleged rights abuses in the detentions and immigration charges that followed September 11, 2001: see *The September 11 Detainees*, above note 5.

78 *Arar Report*, above note 5 at 311*ff*; and *Arar Report*, above note 1 at 503*ff*.

79 *Arar Report*, *ibid*.

oversight bodies, and politicians can elaborate on such mandates by formulating policies and training that will help instill confidence in affected communities.[80]

c.   Emerging Challenge: Mandate to Review the Activities of Which Agencies?

As discussed in section C(3) above, the field of security intelligence actors is expanding. In many states, police forces, border agencies, foreign affairs departments, transport authorities, tax agencies, private sector companies, and integrated cross-border teams all play a role in maintaining national security. Yet the security intelligence roles of these agencies vary immensely. In some cases, the agencies are front-line collectors of information that directly interface with the public and have significant powers (e.g., law enforcement agencies charged with counter-terrorism policing), and in other cases the agencies and departments are largely repositories of personal information that may be of importance to front-line agencies (e.g., employment, health, tax authorities).

The integration and data sharing of these agencies poses an emerging challenge for states that wish to ensure that they leave no "accountability gaps"[81] in their DCOR regimes. They should address how to ensure that appropriate controls and review mandates are established for each agency, given the risks its activities pose. They should also address how to prevent migration of rights-intrusive activity from the agencies with robust review bodies watching over them to other agencies, including foreign ones, which do not have the same degree of statutory and review controls. Many states are grappling with this issue and have either put certain measures in place[82] or have received recommendations.[83]

---

80 For example, Canadian security intelligence agencies have recently implemented policies that attempt outreach and dialogue with affected communities, such as changes in lexicon and regular meetings and engagement with community leaders. See Omar El Akkad, "CSIS, RCMP Briefed Muslim Leaders before Going Public with News of Arrests" *The Globe and Mail* (9 September 2006); Colin Freeze, "Muslims, RCMP Start Talking" *The Globe and Mail* (12 August 2006). See also the Diversity and Citizen Focus Directorate of the U.K.'s Metropolitan Police, above note 55.

81 *Commonwealth Ombudsman Report 2003–04*, above note 42 at 55.

82 See the discussion of statutory information exchange and cooperation powers discussed, above note 45.

83 A recent Canadian inquiry recommended "statutory gateways" and other institutional cooperation among review bodies, as well as an Integrated National Security

iv) Functions and Powers

There are certain minimum functions and powers that an arm's-length review body must be granted in order for it to effectively scrutinize security intelligence activities, and for it to provide public assurances that the activities are being carried out in compliance with applicable law, policies, and prescribed norms.

The review body's functions should include the authority to conduct regular and ongoing inspections of any aspect of operational activity;[84] initiate investigations into any matter or category of activity;[85] investigate complaints about the conduct of the individuals within its purview; inquire into matters referred to it by the legislative branch; and accept or refuse requests from the executive branch to inquire into a matter.[86] The review body should make findings and recommendations and it should report these to the legislative branch in special reports, where appropriate, and otherwise in annual reports.[87]

Review Coordinating Committee to address any disputes about how and by whom integrated security intelligence activity should be reviewed: *Arar Policy Review Report*, above note 1 at 582–600. See also above notes 42 and 45.

84   A complete inspection power in existing statutes is as vague as "[t]he Committee shall regularly monitor": *Intelligence Monitoring Act*, above note 57, s. 3 or "shall review": *CSIS Act*, above note 26, s. 38.

85   An inquiry in Australia recently recommended that the authority of the Inspector-General of Intelligence and Security, to initiate investigations into the activities of only some of the agencies within its purview, be extended to all the agencies within its jurisdiction: *Flood Report*, above note 26 at 180.

86   While it is logical that the democratic legislative assembly should be able to task its delegate — the review body — with matters for inquiry, it is also appropriate to prevent the review body from becoming beholden to a governmental request for an inquiry into a matter. This said, the request could be valid and indeed a matter of executive branch knowledge only. The system should allow for the review body to accept such requests if it sees fit.

87   Westminster countries tend to provide for reporting to the executive branch, with copies of the report subsequently laid before parliament. This reporting line derives from the principle of ministerial accountability. However, in a DCOR system in which the executive branch is provided with its own supervisory representative, the legislature's delegate (the independent review body) should report to it. There should be no undermining of the principle of ministerial accountability because the legislature is the recipient of the reports. Indeed, Westminster systems include numerous "independent officers of parliament" who

To carry out these functions effectively, the review body should have the authority to compel information, including all levels of sensitive information, in the possession or control of the agencies within its purview, and compel the agencies' personnel. Given the increasing integration of security intelligence activity, it should also have the power to compel information that may not be in the possession or control of the agencies strictly under its purview, in order to ensure that information vital to its investigation does not slip through the cracks.

The body should produce public reports and should have clear guidelines as to how to report sensitive information. The statute should set out who makes the decision as to what information may be released. In many cases it is the executive branch that retains the final decision, sometimes with a requirement to provide a public explanation,[88] and sometimes with the prior involvement of the judicial branch through a dispute resolution mechanism between the government and the review body.[89] The review body should otherwise aim, within its statutory limits, for maximal transparency without jeopardizing national security.

a. Emerging Challenge: Recourse and Redress for Complainants

Complaints processing and adjudication is a vital tool of accountability and legitimacy. It provides the public, including victims of improper conduct, with opportunities for transparency and redress, and it provides oversight and review bodies with windows into operational activity that they might not otherwise have.

In order to be effective as a legitimacy tool, the complaints process should provide effective access, fair procedures, and concrete redress. Access can ordinarily be improved by legal challenges funds and by

---

report to the legislative branch, without disrupting the foundations of ministerial accountability.

88 For example, while the United States executive branch has a veto over disclosures by the Inspectors General of the Department of Justice (including the Federal Bureau of Intelligence), the Central Intelligence Agency, and the Department of Homeland Security, the obligation for the executive to publish reasons for its refusal has generally curtailed the use of the veto in the view of one Inspector General: *Arar Supplementary Background Paper on International Models*, above note 45 at 29.

89 See, for example, *Canada Evidence Act*, R.S.C. 1985, c. C-5, ss. 38*ff*.

allowing complaints to be made by third parties, such as community groups and rights advocates. But redress is an element that complaints systems in the security intelligence context largely have yet to provide.[90] A common view appears to be that a review body should not get mired in the imposition of disciplinary measures and monetary compensation, lest this function impact its focus and objectivity and sour the relationship with the agencies within its purview. There is also an argument that a review body should leave the imposition of policy and operational change to responsible ministers. However, these arguments would seem to have no application if a dedicated tribunal for adjudication of such complaints is established as an adjunct or separate body.[91]

A further challenge is how to provide a fair complaints process when relevant information cannot be shown to the complainant because of its national security character. Emerging solutions adopted by states appear to include the use of designated individuals to scrutinize information on behalf of complainants or in lieu of complainant scrutiny.[92]

4) Review by a Body of the Legislative Branch of Government

Security intelligence activities have historically been the preserve of the executive branch of government. Their inherent secrecy, particularly where they are not the subject of a legislative statute, has meant that the activities have seldom been openly debated in legislatures or scrutinized in detail in ordinary committee processes. Their vital im-

---

90 An exception is the power of the Investigatory Powers Tribunal in the United Kingdom to award compensation or such other order as it thinks fit. See *RIPA*, above note 29, s. 67.

91 For example, the Investigatory Powers Tribunal in the United Kingdom is established as a separate body from a number of commissioners charged with review of certain security intelligence activities. See *RIPA*, *ibid.*, s. 65*ff*.

92 The role of special advocates in the U.K., as well as lawyers in secret proceedings in Canada, is explored by Lorne Waldman in Part Two, chapter 6 of this book. See also *Charkaoui v. Canada (Citizenship and Immigration)*, 2007 SCC 9 at paras. 70–79, in which the Supreme Court of Canada outlined a number of statutory and other processes employed in Canada; and *Arar Policy Review Report*, above note 1 at 549, in which security-cleared counsel is recommended in certain circumstances for complaints proceedings involving national security activities of the national police force.

portance to the nation's security has also led to the widely held view that they should not be the subject of ordinary partisan politics.

But, as argued above, security intelligence activities are done in the name of protecting the populace and its institutions and values. The activities, which pose risks to fundamental rights and to the rule of law, must have popular legitimacy and the people, through their representatives, must therefore play a role in their conduct and in their examination. Placing security intelligence agencies on a statutory footing goes a long way to facilitating the involvement of the legislative branch in matters of national security, but security intelligence work should still be the subject of direct parliamentary scrutiny.[93] There should be a committee of the legislative branch with access to sensitive information and agency personnel, thereby allowing it to conduct an informed review of the government's strategies and operations to protect national security.

To avoid the risk of criticism levelled for politically partisan reasons rather than in the interest of national security accountability, and to minimize the risk of wrongful disclosure of sensitive information, such bodies should be bipartisan and small. They should have less frequent turnover in their membership than is typical for parliamentary bodies, given the specialized knowledge required to review security intelligence activities; and they should be comprised of individuals with the experience and qualifications to inspire public, parliamentary, and security and intelligence sector confidence. The committee's reports should be submitted to the legislative branch.

The committee should also be aware of its role in a larger regime of control, oversight, and review. It should not seek to duplicate the detailed work of the independent review body—it should complement it, by using the review body's findings and recommendations to question security intelligence officials and by focusing on areas that the review

---

93 For a discussion of the arguments in favour of scrutiny by a committee of the legislative branch, see *McDonald Report*, above note 5 at 896*ff*; Born & Leigh, *Making Intelligence Accountable*, above note 8 at 77*ff*; and Canada, "A National Security Committee of Parliamentarians: A Consultation Paper to Help Inform the Creation of a Committee of Parliamentarians to Review National Security" (Ottawa: Public Safety and Emergency Preparedness Canada, 2004) at 8, online: ww2.psepc-sppcc. gc.ca/publications/national_security/pdf/nat_sec_cmte_e.pdf.

body does not, or is not mandated to, review, such as the effectiveness of the activities in protecting state security.

5) Judicial Control

Courts play a fundamental role in liberal democratic countries in scrutinizing government activity to ensure the supremacy of the rule of law, and in ensuring protection of individual rights and freedoms. In most liberal democratic countries, courts are routinely required by legislative instruments to authorize, by warrant, the state's more intrusive activity, such as searches of homes and workplaces, seizures of personal possessions and data, and arrests.

This institutional role as an objective check on government activity is all the more vital in the case of covert security intelligence activity that not only uses exceptional powers, but also occurs largely outside ordinary avenues of scrutiny. In the security intelligence context, judges should be conferred with the role of determining whether to authorize the most intrusive activities of the security intelligence agencies, including surreptitious entries and communications interceptions.[94] Their role as gatekeeper to such activity should not be diminished by virtue of the existence of internal controls, independent review, or ministerial oversight; but it may be that more or less judicial control is required for other intrusive activity, such as ordinary target surveillance, depending on the robustness of the other elements of the DCOR regime in providing assurances of propriety.

Depending on the complaints mechanisms that are established, states may also allow recourse to the courts to facilitate redress for illegal activity on the part of security intelligence actors.[95]

---

94 See, for example, the "Judicial Control" provisions of the *CSIS Act*, above note 26, s. 21*ff*, which enumerate the matters and thresholds that CSIS must demonstrate in order to receive a warrant for certain intrusive activities, such as urgency, and which detail the procedure prior to and following issuance of a warrant.

95 The Parliamentary Assembly of the Council of Europe has stated, "[t]he judiciary, in turn, plays a crucial role because it can punish any misuse of exceptional measures in which there may be a risk of human rights violations": *Recommendation 1713*, above note 5 at no. 6.

6) Supplementary Controls: Other Instruments

Statutory, constitutional, and international instruments that enshrine human rights, privacy protections, and freedom of information rights, together with authorities charged with monitoring compliance with these instruments, play an invaluable accountability and transparency role in the security intelligence sphere. So too do numerous other instruments such as financial audit schemes, whistle-blower protections, and public-inquiries statutes.

These safeguards not only supplement an agency's particularized statutory controls with more general, but still fundamental codes of conduct (norms against which conduct can be judged by the review body, ministers, and a parliamentary committee), but they also close critical gaps in proprietary controls and review, which may increasingly exist in an era of multifarious security intelligence activity by the state. For example, where personal data are in the possession of a public authority or a private-sector company that is not ordinarily involved in the security intelligence trade and is therefore not governed by the controls applicable to the dedicated security intelligence agencies, it is only international and national data protection instruments that govern the use and transfer of this information.

Whistle-blower protections are a different breed of supplementary instrument, but a valuable one in shining a light on the secret activities of security intelligence agencies. As with any public or private entity, it is often the individuals on the inside that are in the best position to identify errors and misconduct. In a system of covert activity on which both security and the rule of law are riding, it is important that these individuals have avenues to report their observations, without jeopardizing national security and without fear of reprisal. States should therefore codify protections for whistle-blowers with security intelligence agencies, and provide mechanisms for them to report their suspicions without jeopardizing the security of any classified information.

Finally, states should have instruments in place that allow for the establishment of public inquiries into matters that come to light from time to time. This kind of extraordinary transparency and accountability mechanism has been used a number of times by liberal democratic states in recent decades, and in many cases has led to fundamental reforms to the security intelligence apparatus and/or its control, oversight, and review.[96]

7) Free and Independent Civil Society Institutions, Including the Media and Advocacy Groups

States should nourish a societal environment in which non-governmental organizations, community, advocacy, and pressure groups, and the media can be free and independent critics of government activity. They must be free to investigate, free to report, free to criticize, free to provide alternative perspectives, free to inform policy, free to lobby, free to advocate. Their contributions should be valued for the often courageous, probing, enlightening, and persuasive roles that they may play. Indeed the case could likely be made that, without media and pressure groups, misconduct and allegations would go mostly unnoticed by the public and unanswered by the government, even in systems with review and oversight bodies that can produce damning reports.[97] States must therefore lay foundations that allow societal institutions, such as the media and non-governmental organizations, to flourish, for they play an essential role in holding states and their security intelligence apparatus to account for their activities.

D. CONCLUSION

This chapter has elaborated on the basic tenets of control, oversight, and review of security intelligence activity, as set out in the *Ottawa Principles on Anti-terrorism and Human Rights*. It has discussed not only the fundamental challenges of designing a comprehensive and competent regime for democratic control, oversight, and review of security intelligence activities, but also a number of new challenges that are being

---

96 See, for example, *Hope Reports*, above note 5; *Belgium Report*, above note 5; *McDonald Report*, above note 5; *Lund Report*, above note 5; *Church Report*, above note 5; *9/11 Commission Report*, above note 11.

97 One scholar has argued that "[t]he press serves as a sort of 'unofficial opposition' or fall-back accountability mechanism: when internal control does not check questionable behaviour, and external control does not identify and challenge it, the potential exists in a free society for insider whistle blowing (leaks) or an investigative journalist's report to draw attention to it." Caparini, "Challenges," above note 4 at 11.

posed by the changing landscape of security intelligence. The irony of prescriptive standards for such emerging challenges is that the majority of states in the world still do not have basic DCOR regimes for their conventional, dedicated intelligence agencies. Indeed even the most sophisticated DCOR systems are not much more than a decade or two old, and are still being refined or developing fundamental components and features. States therefore have different degrees of challenges ahead. While DCOR oversight discourse is evolving in some states to tackle issues of supra-national safeguards and scrutiny, other states still have much work to do to establish even a basic regime for democratic control, oversight, and review of security intelligence activities.

PART THREE

Beyond the *Ottawa Principles*: Issues for Future Iterations

Beyond the *Ottawa Principles*: Social and Institutional Strategies and Counter-Terrorism

Victor V. Ramraj

A. INTRODUCTION

Human rights, it is often said, are not only compatible with a counter-terrorism strategy, they are also an essential part of an effective one.[1] But however much we might try to reconcile national security impera-tives with human rights principles, the complex relationship between the two, and our efforts to make sense of it, have exposed deep cleav-ages between realists and idealists. Idealists would stand firmly behind fundamental principles, clinging to lofty human rights aspirations even in the face of a crisis; realists are prepared to bend those principles, so as not to have them cast aside altogether, in the quest to be more effect-ive in constraining state power if they make "realistic" demands. Any at-tempt to articulate a set of principles governing counter-terrorism laws must come to terms with the chasm between realism and idealism. The *Ottawa Principles*[2] are no exception.

---

1   See, for example, Lord Phillips of Worth Matravers, Lord Chief Justice of England and Wales, "Terrorism and Human Rights" (Singapore Academy of Law Annual Lec-ture 2006, 29 August 2006) at para. 90 (forthcoming publication in the *Singapore Academy of Law Journal*; copy on file with author).
2   The *Ottawa Principles on Anti-Terrorism and Human Rights*, found at Part One of this book [*Ottawa Principles*].

The principles set out in this volume are a sophisticated attempt to come to terms with this basic tension. They hold states to aspirant standards of conduct while acknowledging, for instance, through an overarching principle of proportionality, that departures from these standards are inevitable, and that states of emergency must be provided for in advance. Yet, in many respects, the tension between realism and idealism persists. Should human rights espouse only unadulterated principles or should they take into account the reality that, when faced with a crisis, states tend to use whatever tools they have at their disposal, testing the outer bounds of legality? The problem in trying to resolve this question is that it assumes that human rights law is the main mechanism for restraining state power in times of crisis.

This chapter unsettles this assumption by reconsidering the role of human rights principles in constraining state power in the first place. Specifically, it attempts to situate the role of human rights principles in a broader counter-terrorism context, examining the role that other strategies—from social and political to institutional and good governance strategies—might play in restraining state power and reducing the incidence of terrorism. The basic argument in this chapter is that, although human rights principles take an important role in both of these respects, we would be well-advised to be conscious of the limits of human rights and the limits of the law in a comprehensive counter-terrorism and state-restraining agenda.

B. TERRORISM, IDEALISM, AND PRAGMATISM

The story of contemporary counter-terrorism is in many ways a story about the demise of idealism and human rights. We have seen how quickly legal norms have been cast aside. At the very least, states have thought little of pushing the boundaries of legality—creating legal "black holes"[3] in Guantanamo Bay, turning a blind eye to violations of the absolute prohibition against torture,[4] and purporting to derogate

---

3   Johan Steyn, "Guantanamo Bay: The Legal Black Hole" (2004) 53 I.C.L.Q. 1.

4   See Karen J. Greenberg & Joshua L. Dratel, eds., *The Torture Papers: The Road to Abu Ghraib* (Cambridge: Cambridge University Press, 2005).

from human rights norms[5] or negotiating diplomatic assurances to circumvent the prohibition on *refoulement*.[6] The post-9/11 political rhetoric itself reflects the notion that a departure from ordinary rules is necessary, with then British Prime Minister Tony Blair declaring famously that "the rules of the game have changed."[7]

For two legal theorists, Oren Gross and David Dyzenhaus, none of this comes as a surprise; they posit that it is naïve to think that states, in a time of crisis, can simply continue to apply ordinary laws, adopting a "business-as-usual"[8] approach to law. Gross rejects this business-as-usual approach by arguing that it is "either naïve or hypocritical in the sense that it disregards the reality of governmental exercise of extraordinary measures and powers in responding to emergencies."[9] Instead, he proposes an "extra-legal measures" model, which holds that "there may be circumstances where the appropriate method of tackling grave dangers and threats may entail going outside the constitutional order, at times even violating otherwise accepted constitutional principles, rules and norms."[10] This model "calls upon public officials having to deal with catastrophic cases to consider the possibility of acting outside the legal order while openly acknowledging their actions and the extra-legal

---

5   The United Kingdom purported to derogate from Article 5 of the *Convention for the Protection of Human Rights and Fundamental Freedoms*, 4 November 1950, 213 U.N.T.S. 221, Eur. T.S. No. 5 [*ECHR*], to enable it to detain indefinitely, foreign terrorist suspects whom it could not deport as a consequence of *Chahal v. United Kingdom* (1996), 23 E.H.R.R. 413; it was prevented from doing so by the House of Lords in *A v. Secretary of State for the Home Department*, [2004] UKHL 56.

6   See generally Human Rights Watch, *Still at Risk: Diplomatic Assurances No Safeguard against Torture* (2005), online: www.hrw.org/reports/2005/eca0405/eca0405. pdf.

7   Press Conference (5 August 2005). In announcing a new set of counter-terrorism initiatives, the prime minister declared: "What I'm trying to do here is . . . to send a clear signal out that the rules of the game have changed." Online: www.number-10.gov.uk/output/Page8041.asp.

8   Oren Gross, "Chaos and Rules: Should Responses to Violent Crises Always be Constitutional?" (2003) 112 Yale L.J. 1011, 1023–24.

9   *Ibid.*

10 Oren Gross, "Stability and Flexibility: A Dicey Business" in Victor Ramraj, Michael Hor, & Kent Roach, eds., *Global Anti-terrorism Law and Policy* (Cambridge, Cambridge University Press, 2005) 90 at 92.

nature of such actions."[11] It is then for the public, perhaps through the political process, to decide whether to ratify the official misconduct.

Dyzenhaus rejects Gross's extra-legal measures model for granting too much unchecked power to the executive.[12] But despite his disagreement with Gross, Dyzenhaus nevertheless accepts that a rigid adherence to ordinary legal principles in times of crisis is unrealistic. For Dyzenhaus, however, modern administrative law is sophisticated enough to allow the executive to protect security intelligence and confidential sources, while at the same time preserving the rule of law. This can be done through the use of specialized administrative tribunals, such as the Special Immigration Appeals Commission (SIAC) in the United Kingdom, which has the institutional expertise to assess claims of national security, the procedural power of holding closed sessions, and, at the same time, the ability to implement rule of law norms under the broad supervision of the ordinary courts. Imaginative experiment in institutional design is needed to enable institutions to respond effectively in times of crisis. What is notable about this approach is its attempt to accommodate the presumably changed security landscape of an emergency while preserving norms of legality.

As distinct as these theories are—with one espousing extra-legal, political checks on abuses of power and the other insisting on strict compliance with the principle of legality—what these two theoretical approaches to emergencies demonstrate is a willingness to depart from ordinary norms in times of crisis. This is perhaps the definitive characteristic of the contemporary response to international terrorism; the assumption that ordinary rules no longer apply. Pragmatism has become the standard against which all policies, and even human rights norms, must be measured. Indeed, the defence of human rights standards has taken on a distinctly instrumental tone; in these pragmatic times, the strongest argument for human rights is thus the argument that they play an integral role in counter-terrorism strategy.[13] The best defence of human rights is thus to emphasize their strong counter-terrorism credentials.

---

11   *Ibid.*

12   *Ibid.*; and David Dyzenhaus, "The State of Emergency in Legal Theory" in Ramraj *et al.*, eds., *Global Anti-terrorism Law and Policy*, above note 10, 65–89.

13   Above note 1.

C. THE *OTTAWA PRINCIPLES*

Given the strength and currency of these instrumental arguments and the correlative decline of idealism, any effort to articulate human rights principles to govern counter-terrorism measures must steer a course between ideal, aspirant standards that stand symbolically apart from the pragmatic ethos of our time, and pragmatic standards that recognize the reality of state counter-terrorism measures and sacrifice the purity of our principles in order to contain the state's response. How, then, do the *Ottawa Principles* navigate the course? Examination of the *Ottawa Principles* shows both a commitment to some core, non-negotiable principles and a pragmatic attempt to limit the harm done by counter-terrorism measures actually adopted by states. Consider these examples.

At their most idealistic, the *Ottawa Principles* are uncompromising in their rejection of torture and cruel, inhuman, or degrading treatment or punishment.[14] The prohibition against torture is expressed as a peremptory norm of international law (*jus cogens*) in respect of which no derogation is possible: "No circumstances whatsoever, including a state of war, a threat of war, a threat to national security, an emergency threatening the life of the nation, internal political instability or any other public emergency, may be invoked by a state as a justification for torture or cruel, inhuman or degrading treatment or punishment."[15] The sub-principles in part 4 place unqualified obligations on states to prevent torture and ill-treatment, whether internally or at the hands of another state to which a person is transferred. Thus, the principle of *non-refoulement* is affirmed and the use of diplomatic assurance against torture is declared to be "legally insufficient to overcome the transferring state's obligation to refrain from transferring an individual to a known risk."[16] Absent from these principles is any hint of the need to balance human rights and national security considerations.[17] Similarly, the use of statements obtained by torture in judicial, administrative, or other proceedings or

---

14 *Ottawa Principles*, above note 2, principle 4.1.1.

15 *Ibid.*, principle 4.1.2.

16 *Ibid,*. principle 4.2.7.

17 In contrast, see *Suresh v. Canada (Minister of Citizenship and Immigration)*, [2002] 1 S.C.R. 3, where the Supreme Court of Canada refused to prohibit absolutely the deportation of terrorist suspects who face a risk of torture in the destination country, allowing the government to weigh the risk of torture against national security concerns.

for other national security purposes is expressly prohibited.[18] The *Ottawa Principles* also provide for remedies and reparations for victims of torture or other forms of ill-treatment.[19] It should be noted here that the mere provision of such remedies and reparations is not in itself a dilution of ideal standards any more than a penalty for murder is a concession to pragmatism. In both instances, the prohibition is expressed in absolute terms; the fact that there are consequences for a breach does not compromise the absolute nature of the prohibition. A similarly uncompromising approach can be found elsewhere in the *Ottawa Principles*, including, for instance, in the non-discrimination principle,[20] the prohibition against enforced disappearances,[21] and the subjugation of the UN Security Council to human rights of a *jus cogens* character.[22]

Yet equally evident in the aforementioned document are principles that (1) recognize that states will depart from human rights in times of crisis and (2) are designed to contain these departures within reasonable limits. Consider, for instance, the principle of proportionality that governs departures from ordinary criminal law and procedure. This paragraph provides that "[a]ny departures from ordinary principles of criminal law or derogable international human rights standards must be strictly necessary to prevent the identified harm and be rationally connected to the achievement of this goal; they should infringe the rights of those subject to the law as little as possible; and their effectiveness should be weighed against the degree of rights infringement that they permit."[23] In contrast with the absolute prohibition on torture and ill-treatment, and in the spirit of many modern human rights instruments—from the *ECHR*[24] to the *Canadian Charter of Rights and Freedoms*[25] to the *South African Bill of Rights*[26]—this principle acknowledges textually that many rights are not absolute, while attempting to limit departures from those rights to what

---

18   *Ottawa Principles*, above note 2, principle 4.3.

19   *Ibid.*, principle 4.4.

20   *Ibid.*, principle 1.

21   *Ibid.*, principle 5.2.

22   *Ibid.*, principle 10.

23   *Ibid.*, principle 2.3.1.

24   Above note 5.

25   Part I of the *Constitution Act, 1982*, being Schedule B to the *Canada Act 1982* (U.K.), 1982, c. 11.

26   *Constitution of the Republic of South Africa 1996*, No. 108 of 1996, c.2.

is "strictly necessary" and carefully tailored to prevent harm. Principle 2.4 added to this substantive principle several procedural mechanisms that serve as a brake on the use of officially declared emergency powers.[27]

This attempt to subordinate the use of emergency powers to legal norms might seem perfectly consistent with human rights. After all, the principles governing states of emergency are manifestly inspired by the best practices in national constitutional law[28] and expressly incorporate the best practices of international human rights law.[29] So it is easy to forget that the express provision for states of emergency in human rights documents is itself contentious.[30] The tension here can again be seen as a tension between idealists and pragmatists—between those who see human rights as holding fast even in times of emergency and those who acknowledge that states will assume emergency powers one way or another, and seek to subject the use of such powers to the discipline of the rule of law.

The mere articulation of a principle of proportionality might not be sufficient in itself to suggest a pragmatic strand in the *Ottawa Principles*. But other principles are difficult to explain in any other way. Consider, for instance, the exception in principle 2.1.8. to the general rule in principle 2.1.7 that the state "must disclose all relevant evidence in its possession to a person accused of committing a terrorist act so as to ensure that the defendant can prepare a full and effective defence, and to ensure that the defendant has a fair trial."[31] The exception allows the state to withhold evidence to protect national security provided that it discloses the evidence to security-cleared defence counsel who have given undertakings of non-disclosure and to a security-cleared, independent advocate who can "review the evidence and challenge it." This exception is also subject to the overriding requirement that the non-disclosure is "a proportionate limit on the accused's right to disclosure that is

---

27 *Ottawa Principles*, above note 2, principle 2.4.

28 *Constitution of the Republic of South Africa 1996*, above note 26, s. 37.

29 *International Covenant on Civil and Political Rights*, 19 December 1966, 999 U.N.T.S. 171, Can. T.S. 1976 No. 47, 6 I.L.M. 368, Article 4. See also *ECHR*, above note 5, Article 15.

30 See, for example, Bruce Ackerman, "The Emergency Constitution" (2004) 113 Yale L.J. 1029; Laurence H. Tribe & Patrick O. Gudridge, "The Anti-emergency Constitution" (2004) 113 Yale L.J. 1801.

31 *Ottawa Principles*, above note 2, principle 2.1.7.

necessary to protect legitimate national security interests of the state" and that the refusal "is consistent with a fair trial."[32]

What this principle demonstrates is an attempt in the *Ottawa Principles* to acknowledge, in effect, that "the rules of the game have changed"[33] by allowing the state, consistent with David Dyzenhaus's recommended approach, to re-craft its institutions in a manner that recognizes national security imperatives while preserving human rights principles to the greatest extent possible. It is here that the pragmatic strand of the *Ottawa Principles* becomes clear. The goal is not to articulate absolute human rights standards to govern all cases without exception as is the case with the prohibition against torture. Rather, the goal is to accommodate the legitimate national security interests of the state within a broad human rights framework, while leaving the core of human rights principles intact.

So the tension between idealistic and pragmatic approaches to emergencies leaves the basic problem unresolved. Should human rights principles espouse only unalterable standards or should they take into account the reality that states will use whatever tools they have at their disposal, testing the bounds of legality, when faced with a crisis? One problem, identified by Gross, is that both the business-as-usual and the accommodative approaches to emergencies are problematic: the former in its naïvité, the latter in its dilution of ordinary law through seepage.[34] A second problem in trying to resolve the tension between idealism and pragmatism is the underlying assumption that human rights constitute the main instrument for restraining state power in times of crisis. This is the assumption that I want to examine.

D. BEYOND HUMAN RIGHTS: SOCIAL AND INSTITUTIONAL STRATEGIES

Like those who advocate a legislative response to terrorism, those who view human rights as the main way of restraining state power assume that law is the best answer to contemporary problems. Both look to the legal system to provide the necessary instruments to address the situation; just as the state rolls out preventive detention and enhanced pow-

---

32   *Ibid.*, principle 2.1.8 at para. c.

33   Above note 7.

34   Above note 8.

ers of investigation and surveillance, human rights advocates roll out the writ of *habeas corpus* and the full panoply of international human rights conventions. Yet, in some ways, this automatic tendency to rely on the law to solve our problems can distract us from other strategies—social, political, economic, and cultural strategies (all of which I group under the term "social strategies")—and institutional strategies for resolving the underlying problem. In this section, I explore these social and institutional strategies for dealing with terrorism and counter-terrorism, strategies that rely less on law as the main answer to contemporary problems.

David Kennedy, in a skeptical essay on the international human rights movement, has argued that "human rights crowds out other ways of understanding harm and recompense."[35] We need not fully embrace this kind of generalized skepticism to see the force of the suggestion that human rights discourse "crowds out" other ways of addressing problems in the counter-terrorism context. Indeed, it may be that the most effective strategies are those that focus on the social and political issues—including social strategies to address questions of minority alienation and social cohesion, and political strategies that address exclusion from politics broadly construed. The latter might include not only exclusion from the formal political process, but also exclusion from the realm of political influence, where questions of foreign policy, to take an obvious contemporary example, seem unresponsive to minority concerns.[36] This is not to say that human rights do not play a role in restraining state power; indeed, respect for human rights may well be a crucial step in overcoming social and political exclusion. But it is here that the problem rests, for the courts can just as easily inspire cyni-

---

35   David Kennedy, "The International Human Rights Movement: Part of the Problem" (2001) 3 Eur. H.R.L. Rev. 245 at 251.

36   See Riazat Butt, "Warning on 'Criminalising Muslims'" *The Guardian* (5 December 2005) 8: reporting that the secretary general of the Muslim Council of Britain, "rejected the idea that there was any kind of dialogue between the government and the Muslim community. He said 'They ignored us when we told them that the war on Iraq was wrong. After 7/7 the communication links were breached. We have sent our representatives to the government.'" According to U.K. Labour MP Sidiq Khan, "Muslims still had a 'big gripe' about foreign policy, particularly over the war on terror and Iraq" (Patrick Hennessy & Melissa Kite, "Poll Reveals 40pc of Muslims Want Sharia Law in UK" *The Telegraph* (19 February 2006), online: www.telegraph.co.uk/news/main.jhtml?xml=/news/2006/02/19/nsharia19.xml&sSheet=/portal/2006/02/19/ixportaltop.html).

cism as confidence. Absent an institutional "culture of justification," which comes about "when a political order accepts that all official acts, all exercises of state power, are legal only on condition that they are justified by law, where law is understood in an expansive sense, that is, as including fundamental commitments such as those entailed by the principle of legality and respect for human rights," [37] and a social culture of inclusion and tolerance, legal principles, however coherent and well-crafted, will not make a difference.

If we expand our perspective beyond the legal institutions of North Atlantic states, we may find that other strategies might also prove effective in containing the use of state power—not by directly restraining it, but by redirecting it towards social strategies. Thus we find that in Singapore the instinctive response to 9/11 was not only to reach for the law (although problematically, from a human rights standpoint, Singapore made extensive use of its *Internal Security Act*[38] to effect preventive detention post-9/11[39]), but equally to social strategies intended to address strains on inter-ethnic relations, including inter-racial confidence circles (known as "IRCCs"), and other community-based institutions designed to address the potential social and political fallout of contemporary terrorism. This is not to say that these strategies are all effective, and elsewhere I have been critical of some aspects of Singapore's approach to the extent that it relies on an essentialist understanding of identity.[40] Yet the approach taken in Singapore acknowledges upfront the importance that social strategies play within a broad counter-terrorism strategy. Indeed, social strategies of this sort have belatedly become much more important in Canada and the United Kingdom. The United

---

37 See David Dyzenhaus's discussion of the importance of a "culture of justification" in the counter-terrorism context in "Deference, Security and Human Rights" in Benjamin Goold & Liora Lazarus, eds., *Security and Human Rights* (Oxford: Hart, 2007), referring to the work of Etienne Mureinik.

38 Cap. 143, 1985 Rev. Ed. Sing.

39 Michael Hor places the use of this Act in its broader historical context in "Law and Terror: Singapore Stories and Malaysian Dilemmas" in Ramraj *et al.*, eds., above note 10 at 273–94.

40 See "The Post-September 11 Fallout in Singapore and Malaysia: Prospects for an Accommodative Liberalism" (2003) Sing. J.L.S. 459; see also C.L. Lim's reply in "Race, Multi-cultural Accommodation and the Constitutions of Singapore and Malaysia" (2004) Sing. J.L.S. 117; and my rejoinder in "Multiculturalism and Accommodative Liberalism Revised" (2005) Sing. J.L.S. 159.

Kingdom's counter-terrorism strategy released in July 2006 openly acknowledges the need to address "structural problems in the U.K. and
overseas that may contribute to radicalization, such as inequalities and
discrimination."[41] To a lesser extent, Canada's security strategy acknowledges, in its introduction, the need to "reach out to communities in
Canada" and "engage in a long-term dialogue to improve understanding
on how to manage security interests in a diverse society,"[42] but (somewhat surprisingly given its official commitment to multiculturalism) it
does not articulate a concrete strategy for doing this beyond a passing
mention of a "Cross-Cultural Roundtable on Security."[43]

Also important are efficiency, fairness, and transparency in the delivery of goods and services by the government, and the U.K.'s counter-terrorism strategy stresses the importance of promoting "good governance
and human rights internationally" as key components of its counter-terrorism strategy.[44] Confidence in the efficiency and impartiality of public
institutions is crucial to resolving underlying tensions. The importance
of institutional reform can be seen both in the Belfast Agreement, which
sought to build trust in key public institutions, such as the police, that
were previously tainted by sectarianism during the Northern Ireland conflict,[45] and even in the United States' national security strategy, which acknowledges (although not in the context of the United States itself) the
danger of political alienation and the importance of addressing it through
institutional reform and good governance strategies.[46]

---

41 U.K. Government, *Countering International Terrorism: The United Kingdom's Strategy*,
    Cm. 6888 (July 2006) at para. 6. Online: www.ukresilience.info/publications/coun-
    tering.pdf.

42 Canada, *Securing an Open Society: Canada's National Security Policy* (Canada: Privy
    Council Office, April 2004) at 2. Online: www.pco-bcp.gc.ca/docs/Publications/
    NatSecurnat/natsecurnat_e. pdf.

43 *Ibid.*

44 Above note 41 at paras. 44–45.

45 *Agreement Reached in the Multi-Party Negotiations* (Cm. 3883, 1998), online: www.nio.
    gov.uk/agreement.pdf. See, in particular, the unnumbered section on policing and
    justice. See also Independent Commission on Policing in Northern Ireland, *A New
    Beginning: Policing in Northern Ireland* (1999), online: www.nio.gov.uk/a_new_begin-
    ning_in_policing_in_northern_ireland.pdf.

46 U.S., White House, *The National Security Strategy of the United States of America*
    (16 March 2006) at 33, online: www.whitehouse.gov/nsc/nss/2006/nss2006.pdf:
    "weak and impoverished states and ungoverned areas are not only a threat to their

Arguments of the sort I am advancing here are not, of course, new, and many before me have emphasized the importance of addressing the underlying causes of terrorism.[47] The point I want to emphasize is that addressing these underlying issues also relieves the courts of the exclusive responsibility for preventing abuse of counter-terrorism powers by the state. It is sometimes said, in response to this sort of underlying-causes argument that economic marginalization is not the cause of terrorism.[48] Look, say these skeptics, at the 7 July 2005 London bombers, who hardly came from impoverished backgrounds, or at Osama bin Laden himself, a wealthy construction magnate; these individuals were not the victims of social injustice, so social solutions would not make a difference. But this reply misses the point: alienation results not only from economic deprivation, but equally from social, cultural, and political marginalization, which itself can be experienced vicariously; just as some liberal, middle-class students might be inspired to political activism by the plight of the poor, so too might middle-class Muslims (or non-Muslims) be politicized by their identification with the situation of Muslims in, say, Palestine or Iraq. The importance of economic (and social, political, and cultural) strategies cannot so easily be dismissed.

There is an important contextual element to the sorts of strategies we might adopt to counter both terrorism and state abuses of counter-terrorism powers. Our choice of strategies may well depend on the extent to which legal norms and issues permeate social attitudes. In states that place a great emphasis on law and litigation, human rights

---

people and a burden on regional economies, but are also susceptible to exploitation by terrorists, tyrants, and international criminals."

47 See Simon Tay & Tan Hsien Li, "Southeast Asian Cooperation on Anti-terrorism: The Dynamics and Limits of Regional Responses" in Ramraj et al., eds., above note 10 at 415: "long-term solution to the problem of Islamic extremist militancy in Southeast Asia lies with dealing with its fundamental causes, which has at its root socio-economic issues and grievances"; Tom Hadden, "Human Rights Abuses and the Protection of Democracy during States of Emergency" in E. Cotran & A.O. Sherif, eds., Democracy, the Rule of Law and Islam (London: Kluwer Law International, 1999) 111 at 124: there is "ample evidence from political and ethnic conflicts throughout the world that the resolution of the underlying political or ethnic problems has been a necessary precondition for the elimination of the abuses associated with states of emergency or repression."

48 Terrorism, the United States government insists, is an "inevitable by-product of poverty," above note 46 at 9–10.

strategies might be relatively more important and legal pronouncement by the courts may well have a powerful symbolic role. Although the importance of law in any given society may differ, we can more confidently surmise that, over the longer term, the solution to the problem of terrorism is not a purely legal one; excessive reliance on law, whether to deter or incapacitate potential terrorists, or to restrain the state in exercising particular powers in particular ways, is unlikely to prove sufficient in the long term to address the deeper social and political causes of terrorism.

E. CONCLUSION: THE SCOPE AND LIMITS OF THE *OTTAWA PRINCIPLES*

I must reiterate, lest my argument be misconstrued, that international human rights principles, including the *Ottawa Principles*, have an important role to play in preventing abuse of state power in times of crisis. They can prevent injustice in individual cases, remind governments of the need for a just and proportionate response to emergencies, inspire law reform, and serve as a symbolic reminder to all, including vulnerable minorities, that fundamental values will not be sacrificed in times of crisis. On all of these counts, the *Ottawa Principles* hold great potential. While not resolving, or purporting to resolve, the normative and conceptual tension between idealism and pragmatism, they affirm fundamental values that acknowledge the importance of national security concerns; and, crucially, they confront squarely some of the most troubling aspects of counter-terrorism measures, particularly those invoked in Canada, the United States, and the United Kingdom.

There are also, within the *Ottawa Principles*, specific principles that hint at the importance of social and institutional strategies. For instance, principle 1.1 emphasizes the importance of equality and non-discrimination; how precisely this principle is understood is particularly important. Broadly construed, it might point towards a rethinking of policies that are socially or culturally divisive, prompting reflection on the government's role in promoting cross-cultural dialogue and social cohesion more generally. Similarly, the principles set out in part 6 (consular and diplomatic protection and nationality), part 7 (information disclosure), part 8 (use and exchange of information and intelligence), and part 9 (oversight, review, and control of security intelligence agencies) go beyond simply constraining state conduct and suggest the importance of good governance. These principles aim not simply at restricting state conduct, but at setting out standards of transparency and accountability. In essence, they are very much about institutional reform and good governance.

These specific principles suggest a recognition within the *Ottawa Principles* as a whole of the importance of moving beyond the centrality of human rights, as interpreted by the courts, in containing the state's response to terrorism. This is not to suggest that some recent counter-terrorism measures are unwarranted; the state certainly has a duty to protect those within its borders from violence. The problem is not *that* the state has deployed its resources to prevent terrorist attacks, but *how* it has done so. It may also be that the way forward is not only to restrain coercive state power, but also to channel it in ways that reduce the incidence of terrorism in the longer term, while limiting the role that human rights law—whether in its idealistic or pragmatic form—needs to play, both in preventing terrorism and constraining the power of the state.

Development Policy—The New Anti-terrorism Policy?

Graham Mayeda

A. INTRODUCTION: THE IMPLICATIONS FOR DEVELOPING COUNTRIES OF ANTI-TERRORISM POLICIES IN CANADA, THE U.S., AND THE U.K.

The *Ottawa Principles on Anti-terrorism and Human Rights* and similar documents, such as the *Berlin Declaration*,[1] rightly recognize that an effective anti-terrorism policy is compatible with the protection of human rights. The *Ottawa Principles* set out how a state can both provide security and respect the rights of those accused or convicted of committing terrorist acts. However, the *Ottawa Principles* overlook five aspects of a country's anti-terrorism policy that must be included when evaluating the extent to which a country's anti-terrorism policies protect human rights.

First, the *Ottawa Principles* overlook the role of the state and state policy in *preventing* terrorism. The principles deal primarily with laws that apply once a person is suspected of having committed a terrorist

---

1   See the principles at Part One of this book [*Ottawa Principles*]; and the *Berlin Declaration*, which is the statement of the International Commission of Jurists on how anti-terrorism law should respect human rights and the rule of law: International Commission of Jurists, *The Berlin Declaration: The ICJ Declaration on Upholding Human Rights and the Rule of Law in Combating Terrorism* (Geneva: ICJ, 2004), online: www.icj.org/IMG/pdf/Berlin_Declaration.pdf.

act. And yet, states also legislate and develop policies to prevent terrorist acts. Arguably, these policies should also respect human rights, although political and civil rights are not the only types of rights implicated.

Second, the *Ottawa Principles* do not explicitly consider the causes of terrorism. Of course, a particular view of the causes of terrorism is implicit in the *Ottawa Principles*. Not unreasonably, they presume that the cause of terrorism is terrorists. However, this approach only considers the most immediate and proximate cause of terrorism, namely the people who commit terrorist acts, rather than the ultimate cause, that is, the reasons why terrorists commit terrorist acts. A consideration of causality is important for ensuring that all government policies aimed at terrorism, both before and after it occurs, respect human rights. Only by considering such ultimate causes can we properly determine the range of government policies that must be assessed for rights compliance. If the ultimate causes of terrorism include poverty and underdevelopment, then government policies that target development should also be subject to scrutiny from a human rights perspective.

Third, as a corollary to the second point, although the *Ottawa Principles* deal with domestic policy in a variety of areas, including criminal law, immigration law, and administrative law, they do not examine the role of development policy in anti-terrorism, despite the fact that many of the anti-terrorism policies of developed countries increasingly consider development policy a key element in preventing terrorism. Many terrorists originate from states classified as developing countries, and many of the states that harbour and support terrorism are also considered developing countries.

Fourth, the *Ottawa Principles* aim at ensuring that a state's domestic anti-terrorism legislation respects human rights. However, the principles are based on a limited conception of human rights, since they focus on the protection of civil and political rights. The principles thus overlook a broader conception of human rights that would include social and economic rights—the very rights implicated by development.

Finally, the focus of the principles is on anti-terrorism policies within the borders of a state. The purpose of the principles is to provide guidelines for states to ensure that their domestic laws respect the civil and political rights of citizens and non-citizen civilians in their countries. The principles do not consider the impact of foreign policy, including development policy, on terrorism, and the role of these outward-directed policies in the prevention of terrorism. However, it is important to consider how foreign policy can contribute to eliminating terrorism by addressing some of its root causes.

I argue that principles aimed at reconciling human rights protections with anti-terrorism ought to consider all five of these issues. They ought not to restrict themselves to laws and policies that apply within a state, and that are enacted to deal with terrorism after a terrorist act has been committed. In other words, the principles ought to deal with laws and policies that states adopt to prevent terrorism, including those in the areas of development policy. Policies to prevent terrorism and, in particular, development policy touch upon more than just civil and political rights; they also have an impact on the social and economic rights of individuals beyond the borders of a given state. Finally, to the degree that development is relevant to the prevention of terror, the domestic situation of developing countries cannot be overlooked. Of particular importance are the economic and legal reforms aimed at eradicating poverty and improving the economy, instituting the rule of law, promoting democracy, protecting human rights, and creating effective governance.

The purpose of this chapter will be to look at these additional policy areas, with a particular focus on the impact of anti-terrorism policies on a country's approach to development. Over the last five years, development policies have become increasingly integrated with defence and foreign policy in a number of member-countries of the Organisation for Economic Co-operation and Development (OECD). From the point of view of preventing terrorism, such integration may make sense, although I will also challenge this view. But integration could also have negative consequences for the economic and social rights that development policy seeks to promote. If development policy is focused on supporting the "war on terror," its *raison d'être* may shift from the protection and promotion of the social and economic rights of those in developing countries to the protection and promotion of the security rights of those in developed countries. It is thus important to investigate the potential impact of shifts in development policy on human rights beyond the domestic context of developed countries.

Overall, my argument is that development policy has an important role to play in preventing terrorism that originates in developing countries, or that is supported by developing countries.[2] Terrorism is related to development policy in two ways. First, there is a correlation between underdevelopment and terrorism—although terrorists are not themselves poor, much of the popular support for them results from dissatisfaction with poverty, which is frequently blamed on developed countries and the international economic institutions they dominate. Additionally, studies have demonstrated a link between the lack of protection for political and civil rights in a country and the likelihood of that country being a base of operations for terrorists. Second, there is a correlation between political marginalization and disaffection and terrorism. Ideologically, terrorists are often opposed to what they perceive to be Western decadence and immorality and the negative impact that an increasingly dominant Western culture has on the sustainability of their own moral and political value systems.

Given these two causes of terrorism, development can play an important role in preventing terrorism. First, development is directly focused on poverty reduction, as is clear from the Millennium Development Goals (MDGs).[3] For instance, the first goal of the MDGs focuses on the eradication of extreme poverty and hunger. Second, development can be focused on facilitating good governance and building successful democratic institutions, both of which contribute to the protection of political and civil rights. Both of these foci make development policy helpful for eliminating the support of certain developing countries for terrorists and terrorist-friendly regimes. Third, development can be (although it rarely is) focused on recognizing the role of developed countries in marginalizing developing countries, thereby leading developed countries to take responsibility for this marginalization. Understanding development work in this way, namely, as a responsibility of developed countries to curb their own consumption and to consider the compatibility of their political and moral ideologies with the plurality of polit-

---

2   I will not deal in this article with terrorism within a state, or terrorism sponsored by developed countries. Although these forms of terrorism should not be overlooked, my focus on the role of development policy in preventing terrorism precludes consideration of other forms of terrorism.

3   UN Millennium Project, *Investing in Development: A Practical Plan to Achieve the Millennium Development Goals* (New York: UN Millennium Project, 2005).

ical and moral views that exist in the world, can help to defuse some of the terrorism that is based on ideological and political disaffection.[4]

This chapter is organized in the following way. First, I address the rights that are implicated in development policy, and demonstrate that they touch on far more than civil and political rights, but also social and economic rights. Second, I review some recent literature on the causes of terrorism and examine the link between poverty and terrorism. Third, I describe some of the development policies of Canada, the United States, and the United Kingdom in order to demonstrate a shift towards integrating development policy with areas more traditionally linked to security issues such as defence and diplomacy. Fourth, I examine how this shift has implicated the nature of development policy and limited its capability to protect the social and economic rights of those in developing countries. This will pave the way for the final section of the chapter, in which I examine whether development policy can be an effective tool in preventing terrorism and, if so, what its role should be.

B. DEVELOPMENT POLICY AND SOCIO-ECONOMIC RIGHTS

There is little question that development implicates a broad range of human rights. In *Development as Freedom*, Amartya Sen outlines a capabilities approach to development. He identifies five kinds of freedoms that are implicated in development issues:

1) Political freedoms
2) Economic facilities
3) Social opportunities
4) Transparency guarantees
5) Protective security[5]

It is clear that, in Sen's view, development implicates not just civil and political rights, but also social and economic rights. Likewise, in *The*

---

4   Of course, a progressive development policy cannot be a panacea. Some terrorist groups espouse ideologies and political structures that are incompatible with domestic or global justice. But, changing development policy can nevertheless go a long way towards demonstrating that developed countries accept their historic and continuing role in marginalizing developing countries.

5   Amartya Sen, *Development as Freedom* (New York: Anchor Books, 1999) at 10.

End of Poverty, Jeffrey Sachs addresses development from a "clinical" perspective by "diagnosing" the various factors that are contributing to a country's lack of development. Regardless of what one might think about taking a clinical view (particularly given that it is largely experts from developed countries that perform the diagnosis), the list of factors that Sachs considers clearly implicates a broad palette of social and economic rights. The diagnostic factors are as follows:

1)   The extent of extreme poverty
2)   Economic policy
3)   Fiscal policy
4)   Physical geography and human ecology
5)   Patterns of governance
6)   Cultural barriers to economic development
7)   Geopolitics[6]

In its report, entitled *Our Common Future*, the Brundtland Commission defines sustainable development as "development that meets the needs of the present without compromising the ability of future generations to meet their needs."[7] The commission's report lists nine objectives that flow from this principle:

1)   Reviving growth
2)   Changing the quality of growth
3)   Meeting essential needs for jobs, food, energy, water, and sanitation
4)   Ensuring a sustainable level of population
5)   Conserving and enhancing the resource base
6)   Reorienting technology and managing risk

---

6   Jeffrey Sachs, *The End of Poverty* (New York: Penguin, 2005) at 83–88.

7   World Commission on Environment and Development, *Our Common Future*, UN WCED, 42d Sess., Annex, Agenda Item 83(e), UN Doc. A/42/427 (1987) [Brundtland Commission]. For a criticism of this concept of sustainable development as it relates to international environmental law, see Graham Mayeda, "Where Should Johannesburg Take Us? Ethical and Legal Approaches to Sustainable Development in the Context of International Environmental Law" (2004) 15:1 Colo. J. Int'l Envtl. L. & Pol'y 29. For an important criticism of the concept of development embodied in the Brundtland Report, see Arturo Escobar, *Encountering Development: The Making and Unmaking of the Third World* (Princeton: Princeton University Press, 1995) at 192–99.

7) Merging environment and economics in decision-making[8]
8) Promoting fair and equitable economic relations[9]
9) Ensuring greater participation in development[10]

Again, we see the panoply of social and economic rights that are involved in development work. Although by no means exhaustive, these examples demonstrate that development touches upon more than just civil and political rights; it also implicates social and economic rights. And as development policy becomes an increasingly important element of anti-terrorism policy in developed countries, this policy will have an impact on these rights. It is for this reason that it is important for a human rights analysis of anti-terrorism policy to consider a broader range of human rights.

C. THE LINK BETWEEN TERRORISM AND UNDERDEVELOPMENT

1) The Link between Terrorism and Poverty

Since September 11, 2001, the number of studies examining the causes of terrorism has increased tremendously. Some studies have found no correlation between poverty and terrorism. Claude Berrebi studied two organizations, Hamas and Palestinian Islamic Jihad, and found that the majority of those involved in terrorist acts had relatively higher standards of living and education.[11] These results have been confirmed outside of the Palestinian context by Alan B. Krueger and Jitka Malečková, both of whom find no correlation between terrorism and poverty or low levels of education.[12]

---

8 Brundtland Commission, *ibid.* at 59–60 (these first seven are outlined at 59–60 in the UN document).

9 *Ibid.* at 76–97.

10 *Ibid.* at 25.

11 Claude Berrebi, "Evidence about the Link between Education, Poverty and Terrorism among Palestinians" *Princeton University Industrial Relations Section Working Paper No. 477* (September 2003) at 2–3, online: www.irs.princeton.edu/wpframe. html. See also Jitka Malečková, "Impoverished Terrorists: Stereotype or Reality?" in Tore Bjørgo, ed., *Root Causes of Terrorism: Myths, Reality and Ways Forward* (New York: Routledge, 2005) at 34–36.

12 Alan B. Krueger & Jitka Malečková, "Education, Poverty and Terrorism: Is There a Causal Connection?" (2003) 17:4 Journal of Economic Perspectives 141. See also

However, other studies consider terrorism to be rooted more broadly in poverty and social and political exclusion.[13] This fits with the well-established view that the likelihood of armed conflict increases during economic downturns.[14] S. Brock Blomberg, Gregory D. Hess, and Akila Weerapana provide an analysis focused on domestic terrorist attacks. They find that, in addition to lowering economic growth,[15] terrorism is linked to periods of poor economic performance.[16] They explain that during economic downturns, dissident groups seek to increase their share of shrinking economic resources. In choosing between the two options of overthrowing a government or using terrorist means, dissidents will take into account the degree to which the government is amenable to

Alan B. Krueger & Jitka Malečková, "Does Poverty Cause Terrorism?" *The New Republic* 226:24 (24 June 2002) 27.

13   For a popular view, see Joseph Kahn & Tim Weiner, "World Leaders Rethinking Strategy on Aid to Poor" *The New York Times* (18 March 2002) A3. See also Scott Atran, "Genesis of Suicide Terrorism" (2003) 299:5612 *Science* 1534; Robert J. Barro, "The Myth that Poverty Breeds Terrorism" *Business Week* (10 June 2002) 26.

14   G.D. Hess & A. Orphanides, "Economic Conditions, Elections and the Magnitude of Foreign Conflicts" (2001) 80 Journal of Public Economics 121; Richard J. Stoll, "The Guns of November: Presidential Reelections and the Use of Force, 1947–1982" (1984) 28 J. Confl. Resolution 231; Charles W. Ostrom & Brian L. Job, "The President and the Political Use of Force" (1986) 80 American Political Science Review 541; Bruce Russett, "Economic Decline, Electoral Pressure, and the Initiation of International Conflict" in C.S. Gochman & A.S. Sobrosky, eds., *Prisoners of War: Nation States in the Modern Era* (Lexington, MA: Lexington Books, 1990) 123; Bradley Lian and John R. O'Neal, "Presidents, the Use of Military Force, and Public Opinion" (1990) 37 J. Confl. Resolution 277; Christopher Gelpi, "Democratic Diversions: Governmental Structure and the Externalization of Domestic Conflict" (1997) 41 J. Confl. Resolution 255; and Tilman Brück, "The Macroeconomic Effects of the War on Mozambique," *Queen Elizabeth House Working Paper No. 11* (Oxford: University of Oxford, 1997).

15   S. Brock Blomberg, Gregory D. Hess, & Akila Weerapana, "Economic Conditions and Terrorism" (2004) 20 European Journal of Political Economy 463 at 477.

16   *Ibid*. See also Basel Saleh, "Economic Conditions and Resistance to Occupation in the West Bank and the Gaza Strip: Here Is a Causal Connection" (2004) 6 Topics in Middle Eastern and North African Economics, online: www.luc.edu/orgs/meea/volume6/saleh.pdf; Edward Sayre, "Labor Market Conditions, Political Events and Palestinian Suicide Bombings" (17 January 2005) [unpublished], online: http://economics.agnesscott.edu/~esayre/research.html; and Robert MacCulloch & Silvia Pezzini, "The Role of Freedom, Growth and Religion in the Taste for Revolution," Paper No. DEDPS 36 The Suntory Centre, London School of Economics and Political Science, September 2002 at 26, online: http://sticerd.lse.ac.uk/dps/de/dedps36.pdf.

the dissidents' demands. A state that responds to these demands will encourage terrorism as an outlet for dissidents. As well, dissidents take into account the quality of government institutions, including the effectiveness of security forces. If the costs of rebellion are too high relative to terrorism, then dissidents will seek their portion of the shrinking economic pie through terrorism.[17] Similar results have been found by Sanjeev Gupta *et al.*, who also conclude that terrorism leads governments to spend more on defence measures, thus diverting funds from the economy, resulting in poor economic performance. They also point to empirical evidence that suggests that terrorism leads to lower levels of government funding for health and education programs, which exacerbates the economic downturn.[18]

David Gold also demonstrates that economic motives continue to play an important role in the behaviour of terrorist groups, since they, like criminal organizations and participants in civil wars, often find themselves providing services to the public that governments are unable or unwilling to provide. In Gold's words:

> Terrorist groups, criminal organizations, and participants in civil wars—whatever their original motives—become increasingly concerned with the business of making money and with the provision of social and economic services that governments are either incapable or unwilling to provide.[19]

As well, Jitka Malečková points out that, although her research does not confirm a strong link between poverty and terrorism, there is a link between lack of civil and political rights and terrorism. For a given level of income, countries with poor protection for civil liberties, as indicated

---

17 Blomberg, Hess, & Weerapana, *ibid.* at 467.

18 Sanjeev Gupta *et al.*, *Fiscal Consequences of Armed Conflict and Terrorism in Low- and Middle-Income Countries*, IMF Working Paper 02/142 (1 August 2002) at 18, online: www.imf.org/external/pubs/cat/longres.cfm?sk=16022. See also Alberto Abadie & Javier Gardeazabal, "The Economic Costs of Conflict: A Case-Control Study for the Basque Country," *NBER Working Paper No. 8478* (Cambridge, MA: National Bureau of Economic Research, 2001).

19 David Gold, "Economics of Terrorism" *CIAO* (May 2004) at 11, online: www.ciaonet. org. See also David Gold, "The Costs of Terrorism and the Costs of Countering Terrorism," *International Affairs Working Paper 2005-03* (March 2005) at 14–16, online: www.newschool.edu/internationalaffairs/docs/wkg_papers/Gold_2005-03.pdf ["The Costs of Terrorism"].

by the Freedom House Index of Political Rights and Civil Liberties, produce more international terrorists.[20] Since poor countries tend to have less robust protections for these rights, an indirect link can be made between poverty and terrorism.

In addition, poverty is related to terrorism in another way. States with high incidence of poverty and poor government and rule of law institutions can provide safe havens for terrorists. In her review of state sponsorship of terrorism, Louise Richardson points out that by far the most common form of state support is to provide "training, financing and a safe haven" for terrorists.[21] The reasons why poor states harbour terrorism are sometimes ideological, arising out of sympathy between the marginalization experienced by a developing country and the marginalization that motivates terrorists. Other reasons are pragmatic. As Stewart Patrick contends, these states provide safe havens, conflict experience, settings for training and indoctrination, access to weapons and equipment, financial resources, staging grounds and transit zones, targets for operations, and pools of recruits.[22] These pragmatic reasons explain why poor countries are effective bases for terrorist groups. States with poor institutions provide "ungoverned spaces" that are convenient platforms for transnational terrorist organizations to access global economic institutions, as well as access communication, technology, transportation, and banking systems.[23]

2) Terrorism and Ideology

It is easy to confuse two important questions about the causes of terrorism. One is the question of the identity and background of the in-

---

20 Malečková, above note 11 at 40–41. See also MacCulloch & Pezzini, above note 16 at 26.

21 Louise Richardson, "State Sponsorship—A Root Cause of Terrorism?" in Bjørgo, ed., above note 11, 189 at 196.

22 Stewart Patrick, "Weak States and Global Threats: Fact or Fiction?" (2006) 29:2 Washington Quarterly 27 at 34. See also U.S., Office of the Coordinator for Counterterrorism, *Patterns of Global Terrorism 2003* (Washington, DC: U.S. Department of State, 2004); and U.S., Office of the Coordinator for Counterterrorism, *Country Reports on Terrorism 2005* (Washington, DC: U.S. Department of State, 2006).

23 Patrick, *ibid.* at 35. See also Ken Menkhaus, *Somalia: State Collapse and the Threat of Terrorism*, Adelphi Paper No. 364 (New York: Oxford University Press for the International Institute for Strategic Studies, 2004).

dividuals who carry out terrorist acts. The second is a question about the economic, social, and political conditions that support, encourage, and legitimize terrorism. In my view, it is the latter that is relevant to our discussion about development and anti-terrorism policy, since to be effective, anti-terrorism policy ought to aim, not only at the proximate or immediate causes of terrorism, but at any ultimate causes. In other words, anti-terrorism policy ought to deal with the hopes and goals of those who commit terrorist acts, to the degree that these are rational and identifiable.[24] Ethan Bueno de Mesquita argues that it is in fact possible to account for the apparently conflicting results that poor economic performance is correlated with increased incidence of terrorism, while terrorism is also caused by individuals with relatively high levels of education and means. According to Mesquita, the explanation is that

> as a result of an endogenous choice between economic activity and terrorist mobilization, individuals with low ability or little education (and consequently few economic opportunities) and strong antigovernment dispositions are most likely to volunteer to become terrorists. However, the terrorist organization wants to recruit only the most effective, highly skilled terrorists. This is because higher ability, better educated peopled are more likely to succeed at the demanding tasks required of a terrorist operative. Consequently the terrorist organization screens the volunteers.[25]

In addition to explaining why the better educated and more affluent among terrorist volunteers are chosen by terrorist groups to carry out their plans, this explanation confirms that even those who may not be suffering the most from economic, social, or political marginalization are motivated by this marginalization and disaffection with a government.

---

24 If terrorism is irrational, development policy will have less capability to prevent it. However, terrorism that is based on religious fundamentalism can be dealt with to some degree through development policy. For instance, according to Sen's broad conception of development, it is important to see democratic reform, women's rights, and human rights more broadly as integral parts of a capabilities approach to development. A robust democracy that protects gender equality and supports the protection of generally recognized human rights can serve to prevent extremist views from dominating the political and public spheres. See above note 5.

25 Ethan Bueno de Mesquita, "The Quality of Terror" (2005) 49:3 American Journal of Political Science 515.

This seems to confirm the view that ideology and economic marginalization—what I call "ultimate" causes of terrorism—are both important causal components.

How are underdevelopment and ideology mutually reinforcing causes of terrorism? Poor governance, poverty, and social and political marginalization can cause people to be disaffected with their government and turn to non-governmental institutions, such as terrorist organizations and organized crime, for support and as an outlet for grievances. As Stewart Patrick points out, groups that do not have peaceful outlets for expressing their political views will be more likely to use violent means to express these views. As well, he argues that terrorist organizations provide some of the economic and social services that a weak state fails to provide.[26] Recipients of these essential services will tend to support the radical ideologies of those who provide them.

The ideological causes of terrorism that are related to development are frequently the legacy of colonialism, which has created a "colonial" mentality that Amartya Sen calls a "reactive self-perception."[27] In Sen's view, this mentality has created a mindset or ideology that is at the root of our current global political situation:

> the nature of this "reactive self-perception" has had far-reaching effects on contemporary affairs. This includes (1) the encouragement it has given to needless hostility to many global ideas (such as democracy and personal liberty) under the mistaken impression that these are "Western" ideas, (2) the contribution it has made to a distorted reading of the intellectual and scientific history of the world (including what is quintessentially "Western" and what has mixed heritage), and (3) the support it has tended to give to the growth of religious fundamentalism and even to international terrorism.[28]

According to Sen, this ideology is not a pure fiction, although it does rest on some questionable perceptions about the nature of the "West" and "non-West." For instance, in discussing Africa, Sen points out that the post-colonial ideology is grounded in the fact that developed coun-

---

26 Patrick, above note 22 at 36.

27 Amartya Sen, *Identity and Violence: The Illusion of Destiny* (New York: W.W. Norton, 2006) at 89.

28 *Ibid.*

tries were not only responsible for oppressive colonial regimes but, in modern times, conflicts between developed countries such as the Cold War have had a profound negative impact on African development, since it sustained "dictatorial strongmen who were linked to one side or the other in the militancy of the cold war."[29] Additional modern foundations for this post-colonial ideology in developed country policies are evident in the arms trade, in which the United States sells approximately half of the arms in the world market, with two-thirds of its exports purchased by developing countries.[30]

It seems evident to me that both underdevelopment and ideology play a significant role in sustaining global terrorism. This is confirmed by the literature on the causes of conflict.[31] Ideology plays a role in supporting terrorism to the degree that it allows terrorists to distinguish themselves from the West, which in turn justifies, in its more militant forms, the destruction of Western supremacy. As Sen points out, "[t]o dedicate one's life to undermining the West and to blowing up prominent edifices that have practical or symbolic importance in the West reflects an obsession with the West that overwhelms all other priorities and values."[32] And as we have seen, although there is no firm link between poverty and the recruitment of terrorists, there is some evidence that low levels of economic growth and poor protection of civil rights create conditions favourable to terrorism. Indeed, as de Mesquita points out, there is "some reason to believe that policies that promote economic growth may decrease violence in countries suffering from terrorist conflicts."[33]

D. ANTI-TERRORISM POLICIES AND DEVELOPMENT POLICIES IN CANADA, THE U.S., AND THE U.K.

As a result of the relationship between poverty and terrorism outlined in the previous section, many academics have argued for the use of develop-

---

29   *Ibid.* at 97.
30   *Ibid.*
31   Ted Robert Gurr, *Why Men Rebel* (Princeton: Princeton University Press, 1970); Mark Irving Lichbach, "An Evaluation of 'Does Economic Inequality Breed Political Conflict?' Studies" (1989) 41:4 World Politics 431; Edward N. Muller & Mitchell A. Seligson, "Inequality and Insurgency" (1987) 81:2 American Political Science Review 425.
32   Sen, above note 27 at 101.
33   de Mesquita, above note 25 at 526.

ment budgets to prevent terrorism. Economist David Gold, for instance, observes that "development assistance, both financial and technical, in the form, for example, of improved governance and aid aimed at basic sources of growth, can support political alternatives to violence."[34] As well, the participants in the International Summit on Democracy, Terrorism and Security concluded that to combat terrorism, countries should implement international aid and investment programs that will empower groups that are marginalized by rapid socio-economic change.[35] Karin von Hippel also suggests that development policy be used to prevent developing countries from harbouring terrorists. In her view, developed countries can prevent failed states from supporting or tolerating terrorists within their borders by funding the reform of governance, economic, and security institutions.[36]

A number of developed countries have followed these suggestions. This has led to greater coordination of development initiatives with military and foreign affairs policies in these countries. The Development Assistance Committee (DAC) of the OECD, for instance, suggested as early as 2001 that development policies be used to prevent violent conflict.[37] In DAC's view, supporting sustainable development is essential for eliminating poverty and developing representative government, thereby addressing some of the root causes of terrorism.[38] The OECD issued a new document in 2003 that narrowed the focus from security to terrorism. The DAC identified the following link between development and terrorism that mirrors the connection that I have identified above:

> However, development co-operation does have an important role to play in helping to deprive terrorists of popular support and addressing the conditions that terrorist leaders feed on and exploit. Many conditions that

---

34   Gold, "The Costs of Terrorism," above note 19 at 17.

35   Ted Robert Gurr, "Economic Factors" in *Club de Madrid Series on Democracy and Terrorism Vol. 1: Addressing the Causes of Terrorism* (Madrid: Club de Madrid, 2005) 23, online: www.clubmadrid.org/cmadrid/fileadmin/Juneo5_VOLUMEN_1para_pdf_fh9.pdf.

36   Karin von Hippel, "The Roots of Terrorism: Probing the Myths" (2002) 73:1 Political Quarterly 25 at 34.

37   OECD, Development Assistance Committee, *Helping Prevent Violent Conflict*, DAC Guidelines and Reference Series (Paris: OECD, 2001), online: www.oecd.org/dataoecd/15/54/1886146.pdf.

38   *Ibid.* at 37.

allow terrorists to be politically successful, build and expand constituencies, find recruits, establish and finance terrorist rganizations, and secure safe-havens fall within the realm and primary concerns of development cooperation. Donors can reduce support for terrorism by working towards preventing the conditions that give rise to violent conflict in general and that convince disaffected groups to embrace terrorism in particular.[39]

Out of these initiatives arose the following *Principles for Good International Engagement in Fragile States*, developed by the OECD:

1. Take context as the starting point [an exhortation to consider differences between fragile states];
2. Move from reaction to prevention;
3. Focus on state-building as the central objective;
4. Align with local priorities and/or systems;
5. Recognise the political-security-development nexus;
6. Promote coherence between donor government agencies;
7. Agree on practical coordination mechanisms between international actors;
8. Do no harm;
9. Mix and sequence aid instruments to fit the context;
10. Act fast . . .
11. . . . but stay engaged long enough to give success a chance;
12. Avoid pockets of exclusion.[40]

As well, in his report in 2005, then UN Secretary-General Kofi Annan, again emphasized the link among security, development, and human rights that had been identified in earlier UN documents.[41] The

---

39 OECD, Development Assistance Committee, *A Development Co-operation Lens on Terrorism Prevention: Key Entry Points for Action*, DAC Guidelines and Reference Series (Paris: OECD, 2003), online: www.oecd.org/dataoecd/17/4/16085708.pdf.

40 OECD, Development Assistance Committee, *Principles for Good International Engagement in Fragile States*, Doc. No. DCD(2005)8/Rev2 (Paris: OECD, 7 April 2005), online: www.oecd.org/dataoecd/59/55/34700989.pdf. See also OECD, Development Assistance Committee, *Chair's Summary: Senior Level Forum on Development Effectiveness in Fragile States*, Doc. No. DAC/CHAIR(2005)3 (Paris: OECD, 2005), online: www.oecd.org/dataoecd/60/37/34401185.pdf.

41 See, for example, Commission on Human Security, *Human Security Now* (Washington, DC: Commission on Human Security, 2003), online: www.humansecurity-chs.org/finalreport/English/FinalReport.pdf.

Secretary-General pointed out that, although poverty is not a cause of security threats, it is closely linked to them. He also emphasized the catastrophic effects of terrorism in one country on the global economy and developing countries:

> Not only are development, security and human rights all imperative; they also reinforce each other. This relationship has only been strengthened in our era of rapid technological advances, increasing economic interdependence, globalization and dramatic geopolitical change. While poverty and denial of human rights may not be said to "cause" civil war, terrorism or organized crime, they all greatly increase the risk of instability and violence. Similarly, war and atrocities are far from the only reasons that countries are trapped in poverty, but they undoubtedly set back development. Again, catastrophic terrorism on one side of the globe, for example an attack against a major financial centre in a rich country, could affect the development prospects of millions on the other by causing a major economic downturn and plunging millions into poverty. And countries which are well governed and respect the human rights of their citizens are better placed to avoid the horrors of conflict and to overcome obstacles to development.[42]

This general policy has also been accompanied by Security Council resolutions requiring countries to act to prevent terrorism. These resolutions have often been interpreted by countries as implicating development policy. *Security Council Resolution 1373*, adopted shortly after the attacks of September 11, 2001, required states to take a number of actions to prevent terrorism, including preventing the financing of terrorists, denying support and protection to terrorists on their soil, bringing terrorists to justice, assisting each other in the investigation and prosecution of terrorists, sharing information related to the detection of terrorists, and signing the thirteen international instruments relating to terrorism.[43] As well, Resolution 1373 established the Counter-Terror-

---

42 Report of the Secretary-General, *In Larger Freedom: Towards Development, Security and Human Rights for All*, UN GAOR, 59th Sess., Agenda Items 45 and 55, UN Doc. A/59/2005 (2005). See also United Nations Development Program, *Human Development Report 2005* (Washington, DC: UNDP, 2005), online: http://hdr.undp.org/en/media/hdr05_complete.pdf.

43 *Security Council Resolution 1373*, SC Res. 1373, UN SCOR, 2001, S/RES/1373 [Resolution 1373].

ism Committee. The activities of the committee have been motivated in part by Resolution 1377, which reinforces the call in Resolution 1373 for countries to support each other in preventing terrorism, for instance, in its call "on all States to take urgent steps to implement fully Resolution 1373 (2001), and to assist each other in doing so," and in its reminder of "the obligation on States to deny financial and all other forms of support and safe haven to terrorists and those supporting terrorism."[44] The resolution then goes on to elaborate on the importance of state aid to prevent terrorism. This is evident in the following paragraphs, in which the Security Council

> *Recognizes* that many States will require assistance in implementing all the requirements of resolution 1373 (2001), and *invites* States to inform the Counter-Terrorism Committee of areas in which they require such support,
>
> *In that context*, invites the Counter-Terrorism Committee to explore ways in which States can be assisted, and in particular to explore with international, regional and subregional organizations:
>
> - the promotion of best-practice in the areas covered by resolution 1373 (2001), including the preparation of model laws as appropriate,
> - the availability of existing technical, financial, regulatory, legislative or other assistance programmes which might facilitate the implementation of resolution 1373 (2001),
> - the promotion of possible synergies between these assistance programmes.[45]

Finally, the call to provide assistance to countries in implementing counter-terrorism policies was reinforced in Resolution 1456, in which the Security Council notes that "States should assist each other to improve their capacity to prevent and fight terrorism, and notes that such cooperation will help facilitate the full and timely implementation of resolution 1373."[46]

---

44 UN, *Security Council Resolution 1377*, SC Res. 1377, UN SCOR, 2001, S/RES/1377 [Resolution 1377].
45 *Ibid.* [emphasis in original].
46 UN, *Security Council Resolution 1456*, SC Res. 1456, UN SCOR, 2003, S/RES/1456 [Resolution 1456].

Denmark, for instance, has interpreted the call for assistance in these two resolutions as requiring a coordination of development and security policies. In its document *Building States' Counter-Terrorism Capacity*, it concludes a section on the relationship between development and security policy by stating that it is

> possible to use the assessments of good governance needs promoted within the development community as a starting point in crafting a methodology for assessing wider CT [counter-terrorism] capacity building needs. Such an approach would help identify and promote integrated approaches and better practical relationships between development and security-related issues in the context of improving good governance, with a specific view to furthering States' implementation of resolution 1373.[47]

Canada's Ministry of Foreign Affairs and International Trade has also indicated that the mandate for its Counter-Terrorism Capacity Building Assistance Program is derived from these resolutions.[48] The government announced that this program would be funded through an allocation from the International Assistance Envelope.[49]

Having demonstrated a trend among both international organizations and academics of urging the use of development policy to prevent terrorism, I turn now to a demonstration of how these exhortations have influenced policy in some developed countries. The countries I will

---

47 Danish Ministry of Foreign Affairs, *Building States' Counter-Terrorism Capacity: Development Assistance, Support for Good Governance and Counter Terrorism Capacity Building*, Zero Draft Working Paper (February 2006) at 6 [on file with author].

48 Foreign Affairs and International Trade Canada, Counter-Terrorism Capacity Building Program, *Counter-Terrorism Capacity Building Assistance*, online: www.international.gc.ca/internationalcrime/ctcbp/menu-en.asp: "Much of the impetus driving this assistance stems from the UN Security Council Counter-Terrorism Committee (CTC), which plays a central role in ensuring that states implement UN Security Council Resolution (UNSCR) 1373."

49 See Canada, Privy Council Office, *Securing an Open Society: Canada's National Security Policy* (Ottawa: Privy Council, 2004) at 59, online: www.pco-bcp.gc.ca/docs/Publications/NatSecurnat/natsecurnat_e.pdf: "We are also allocating funds from the International Assistance Envelope towards counter-terrorism capacity building in developing states; these funds will be managed by the Department of Foreign Affairs. We expect to provide additional funding for broader capacity-building programs in failed and failing states in the future."

focus on are the U.S., the U.K., and Canada. In order to limit the scope of this article, I will not discuss the blurring of the line between military and humanitarian aid, which occurs as the military is increasingly used to further humanitarian goals.[50]

Also, although I am arguing that there has been a change in development policy that has modified it for use in the prevention of terrorism, this is not a sea change but, rather, a re-orientation of existing trajectories in development policy. As others have noted, during the Cold War, development policies that focused on governance and poverty alleviation were used by non-Communist countries in order to prevent the spread of Communist influence.[51] The threat of Russian communism may no longer exist, but anti-terrorism policy continues to be motivated by similar political goals.

1) The United States

In the United States, the coordination of development with political and security policy has been an explicit goal of the president. In his announcement in 2002 of the Millennium Challenge Account, a $5 billion plan to help developing countries, George W. Bush made the link between poverty and terrorism, stating:

> Poverty doesn't cause terrorism. Being poor doesn't make you a murderer. Most of the plotters of September 11th were raised in comfort. Yet persistent poverty and oppression can lead to hopelessness and despair. And when governments fail to meet the most basic needs of their people, these failed states can become havens for terror. In Afghanistan, persistent poverty and war and chaos created conditions that allowed a terrorist regime to seize power. And in many other states around the

---

50   See Andrew Cottey & Ted Bikin Kita, "The Military and Humanitarianism: Emerging Patterns of Intervention and Engagement" in Victoria Wheeler & Adele Harmer, eds., *Resetting the Rules of Engagement: Trends and Issues in Military-Humanitarian Relations* (London: Overseas Development Institute, 2006) 21–23; Stuart Gordon, "The Changing Role of the Military in Assistance Strategies" in Wheeler & Harmer, *ibid.* at 39–52.

51   Ngaire Woods, "The Shifting Politics of Foreign Aid" (2005) 81 International Affairs 393 at 394.

world, poverty prevents governments from controlling their borders, policing their territory, and enforcing their laws.[52]

This link was further strengthened when the White House later announced its National Security Strategy, also in 2002. Policy statements
accompanying the announcement made clear that "America is now
threatened less by conquering states than we are by failing ones."[53] This
policy statement was followed in February 2003 by the *National Strategy for Combating Terrorism*, which outlines the U.S.'s policy objectives
known as the "4D strategy":

1.   Defeat global terrorists;
2.   Deny terrorists support;
3.   Diminish the underlying conditions that terrorists exploit; and
4.   Defend U.S. citizens and interests.[54]

The goal of diminishing "the underlying conditions that terrorists
exploit" clearly indicates that development policy is to be integrated
into American security policy. In fact, the two causes of terrorism I identified above, namely underdevelopment and ideology, are to be specifically addressed in U.S. government policy. In regard to the first cause,
underdevelopment, the *National Strategy for Combating Terrorism* identifies the following link between terrorism and development:

> Weak states and failed ones are a source of international instability.
> Often, these states may become a sanctuary for terrorism. Therefore,
> we will ensure that efforts designed to identify and diminish conditions
> contributing to state weakness and failure are a central U.S. foreign pol-
> icy goal.[55]

---

52   U.S., White House, News Release, "President Proposes $5 Billion Plan to Help
     Developing Nations: Remarks by the President on Global Development at the
     Inter-American Development Bank" (14 March 2002), online: www.whitehouse.
     gov/news/releases/2002/03/print/20020314-7.html.

53   U.S., White House, *The National Security Strategy of the United States of America*
     (September 2002) at 1, online: www.whitehouse.gov/nsc/nss.pdf.

54   U.S., White House, *National Strategy for Combating Terrorism* (February 2003) at
     11–12, online: www.whitehouse.gov/news/releases/2003/02/counter_terrorism/
     counter_terrorism_strategy.pdf [National Strategy].

55   *Ibid.* at 23.

In regard to ideology, the National Strategy identifies a "war on ideas" aimed at ensuring "that the conditions and ideologies that promote terrorism do not find fertile ground in any nation, to diminish the underlying conditions that terrorists seek to exploit in areas most at risk, and to kindle the hopes and aspirations of freedom of those in societies ruled by the sponsors of global terrorism."[56]

From an institutional point of view, the 4D strategy has had an impact on existing development institutions, and has also resulted in the creation of development-related bodies within both the military and the state department. The U.S. Agency for International Development (USAID) acknowledges in its policy documents that foreign aid is a foreign policy and national security tool. In its white paper *Foreign Aid in the National Interest*, it stated that "[f]or the first time development has been elevated as the third pillar of U.S. national security, along with defense and diplomacy."[57] As well, the U.S. Department of State has created an office of "Reconstruction and Stabilization." The acting secretary of defense issued directive DODD 3000.05, which explains that one of the purposes of the U.S. military action in failed states will be to create and stabilize many of the developing country institutions that would traditionally have been targeted by foreign aid. The directive stated that the military will, among other things, be charged with the following tasks:

4.3.1. Rebuild indigenous institutions including various types of security forces, correctional facilities, and judicial systems necessary to secure and stabilize the environment;

4.3.2. Revive or build the private sector, including encouraging citizen-driven, bottom-up economic activity and constructing necessary infrastructure; and

4.3.3. Develop representative governmental institutions.[58]

---

56 *Ibid.*

57 U.S. Agency for International Development, *Foreign Aid in the National Interest: Promoting Freedom, Security and Opportunity* (2002) at 1, online: www.usaid.gov/fani/Full_Report--Foreign_Aid_in_the_National_Interest.pdf.

58 U.S., Department of Defense, *Department of Defence Directive Number 3000.05* (DODD No. 3000.05) (28 November 2005) at 2, online: www.dtic.mil/whs/directives/corres/pdf/d300005_112805/d300005p.pdf.

This state department directive was strengthened by National Security Presidential Directive NSPD-44, which expanded the responsibilities of the Office of Reconstruction and Stabilization to include development issues, the promotion of democracy, the development of market economies, and the rule of law. The directive states:

> The United States has a significant stake in enhancing the capacity to assist in stabilizing and reconstructing countries or regions, especially those at risk of, in, or in transition from conflict or civil strife, and to help them establish a *sustainable path toward peaceful societies, democracies, and market economies*. The United States should work with other countries and organizations to anticipate state failure, avoid it whenever possible, and respond quickly and effectively when necessary and appropriate to promote peace, security, *development, democratic practices, market economies, and the rule of law*. Such work should aim to enable governments abroad to exercise sovereignty over their own territories and to prevent those territories from being used as a base of operations or safe haven for extremists, terrorists, organized crime groups, or others who pose a threat to U.S. foreign policy, security, or economic interests.[59]

From an institutional point of view, the Department of State created the position of Director of Foreign Assistance (DFA) in January 2006. The DFA has authority over Department of State foreign assistance programs, while at the same time serving as USAID Administrator.[60]

Overall, there is a shift both in the rhetoric and in institutional structures that indicate that development programs for failing states are an integral part of the United States war on terror.

2) The United Kingdom

The United Kingdom's development policy is similar to the American policy, in that it coordinates development and security goals. The U.K.

---

59 U.S., White House, *National Security Presidential Directive NSPD-44* (7 December 2005), online: www.fas.org/irp/offdocs/nspd/nspd-44.html; [emphasis added]. The term "National Security Presidential Directive" is used to refer to a presidential directive issued after consultation with the National Security Council.

60 See U.S., U.S. Department of State, News Release, 2006/67, "Two Senior State Department Officials on Foreign Assistance" (19 January 2006), online: www.state. gov/r/pa/prs/ps/2006/59426.htm.

was one of the first countries to see the need for coordinating development with security and foreign affairs policies. In 2001, the government
created "Conflict Prevention Pools" (CPPs), which are administered by
three departments: the Foreign and Commonwealth Office (FCO), the
Ministry of Defence (MOD), and the Department for International Development (DFID).[61] However, funding for CPPs is independent of these
three departments, all of which compete for funding in each round of
government spending. The CPPs were created before September 11, 2001
in an effort to coordinate programs in different departments that targeted similar policy areas.[62] Currently, two exist—an African pool and a
global pool. The mandate of CPPs is to ensure

> [i]mproved effectiveness of the UK contribution to conflict preven-
> tion and management, as demonstrated by a reduction in the number
> of people whose lives are affected by violent conflict and a reduction
> in potential sources of conflict, where the UK can make a significant
> contribution.[63]

The CPPs are designed to apply resources to address development
issues, foreign policy, defence and security, law enforcement, and trade.[64]
At present, CPPs are targeted at eleven geographic areas: the Balkans,
Russia and the Commonwealth of Independent States (CIS), Afghan-
istan, the Middle East and North Africa, Central and Eastern Europe,
Indonesia and East Timor, India and Pakistan, Sri Lanka, Nepal, Latin
America (including Belize and Guatemala) and the Caribbean, and Iraq.

---

61 For a recent overview of the role and goals of DFID see U.K., Department for International Development, *DFID Delivery Service Agreement 2003–2006* (2002), online:
www.dfid.gov.uk/pubs/files/servicedeliveryagree03-06.pdf. See also U.K., Department for International Development, *DFID Departmental Report 2005* (Norwich:
The Stationery Office, 2005), online: www.dfid.gov.uk/pubs/files/departmental%2D
report/2005.

62 U.K., Foreign & Commonwealth Office, *The Global Conflict Prevention Pool: A Joint
U.K. Government Approach to Reducing Conflict* (London: Foreign & Commonwealth
Office, 2003) at 6, online: www.fco.gov.uk/Files/kfile/43896_Conflict%20Broc,0.pdf.

63 *Ibid.* at 7.

64 Dan Smith, *Towards a Strategic Framework for Peacebuilding: Getting Their Act
Together. Overview Report of the Joint Utstein Study of Peacebuilding* (Oslo: Royal
Norwegian Ministry of Foreign Affairs, April 2004) at 37, online: www.dep.no/filar-
kiv/210673/rapp104.pdf.

In contrast to the U.S. program that developed as a direct response to terrorism, the U.K. coordination program aims at complementing the existing development program by promoting conflict prevention. This can be seen from the evaluation of the CPPs conducted in 2004:

> Three main considerations appear to have been important in the decision to set up the CPPs: the wish of HMG [Her Majesty's Government] to bring under control, or at least make more practical the management arrangements for its escalating financial commitment to emergency peacekeeping operations; the increased priority given to preventing conflict as a means of enhancing the strategic impact of UK poverty reduction policies, especially under the newly-created DFID; and the belief that conflict prevention was less costly than the sorts of interventions needed once large scale deadly violence had broken out. Underlying this was the conviction that large scale organised violence had become a consistent and recurring risk to UK policies and interests worldwide, requiring a combination of actions from all foreign policy Departments. There was a sense that ad hoc response was no longer adequate.[65]

Initiatives undertaken under the CPP umbrella include both traditional military support and governance and legal reform that has historically been the province of development policy. These initiatives aim to assess conflicts to determine their impact on U.K. programs in conflict areas, promote safety and security by supporting military operations and improve local police and armed forces, demobilize soldiers and reintegrate them into civilian life, help establish "fair and accessible" justice systems, protect human rights and support civil society organizations, and provide support to the UN and the EU in developing their programs for dealing with post-conflict areas.[66]

Two other U.K. initiatives complete the picture on U.K. departmental coordination efforts. In September 2004, the United Kingdom created the Post-Conflict Reconstruction Unit (PCRU) in order to coordinate military and civilian resources in post-conflict areas. The PCRU is locat-

---

65   U.K., Department for International Development, *Evaluation of the Conflict Prevention Pools: Synthesis Report* (Evaluation Report EV 647) by Greg Austin *et al.* (London: DFID, March 2004) at 15–16, online: www.dfid.gov.uk/aboutdfid/performance/files/ev647synthesis.pdf [*DFID Report*].

66   Foreign & Commonwealth Office, above note 62 at 9.

ed within DFID, but it reports to DFID, MOD, and the FCO, as well as to the cabinet. As well, Quick Impact Projects (QIPs) have been instituted by DFID and the MOD in order to provide a rapid response in conflict-ridden areas that are designed to immediately change local perceptions. The goal of QIPs is to "tackle high visibility problems and to try to win 'hearts and minds.' In some cases, they are the precursor to more developmental approaches, centred on community-based reconstruction."[67]

3) Canada

Canadian policy is largely based on the U.K. model. The national security policy statement issued in 2004 announced that the "3Ds," defence, diplomacy, and development, would be integrated in order to combat terrorism.[68] The statement also announced that the government will focus on building anti-terrorism capacity in developing countries.[69] Presumably, this work implicates development work traditionally carried out by the Canadian International Development Agency (CIDA) such as rule of law reform, the development of legal institutions, and improvements in governance. In the policy document titled *Canada's International Policy Statement—A Role of Pride and Influence in the World: Development*,[70] the government also underlined the importance of further integration of the 3Ds, stating:

[a]n important aspect of increasing the effectiveness of Canada's international contribution will be to strengthen coherence among the Gov-

---

67 U.K., Department for International Development, *Approaches to Improving the Delivery of Social Services in Difficult Environments* (PRDE Working Paper #3) by Chris Berry *et al.*, (London: DFID, October, 2004) at 12, online: www.dfid.gov.uk/pubs/files/fragile-states/social-services.pdf.

68 Canada, Privy Council Office, above note 49. The policy states: "Working to prevent [terrorist] attacks . . . requires a more integrated approach to national security—integrated inside the Government of Canada and with key partners" (at 4). It goes on to say: "Canada's national security will be one of the top priorities in our international Policy Review. The international policy that results from this review—particularly in the security realm—will also reflect our increasingly integrated approach to defence, diplomacy and development (the '3Ds')" (at 47).

69 *Ibid.* at 48.

70 Canadian International Development Agency, *Canada's International Policy Statement—A Role of Pride and Influence in the World: Development* (Gatineau, QC: CIDA, 2004).

ernment's aid and non-aid policies and actions, with the objective of reducing global poverty.[71]

The integration of defence, diplomatic, and development policies is evident in the creation of Provincial Reconstruction Teams (PRTs), which are currently working in Afghanistan. These PRTs were created "as a way to integrate diplomats, development officials, military assets and police officers to address the causes of instability: poor governance, weak institutions, insurgency, regional warlords and poverty."[72] The mandate of PRTs as described by CIDA involves both traditional development goals and military goals. According to CIDA, the PRTs are designed to

- promote the extension of the Afghan central and provincial government;
- implement development and reconstruction programs;
- assist in stabilizing the local security environment; and
- support security sector reform.[73]

Funding for PRTs is provided by the Department of National Defence, the Department of Foreign Affairs and International Trade (DFAIT), CIDA, and the Royal Canadian Mounted Police (RCMP),[74] providing further evidence of the integration of the 3Ds.

As well, the October 2006 report of the Senate Committee on National Security and Defence[75] advocated even greater integration of defence and development aid. The report began by advocating a doubling of Canada's foreign aid budget from 0.6 percent of gross national product (equivalent to $2.7 billion CAD in 2003–4[76]) to 0.7

---

71   *Ibid.* at 8.
72   Canada, Standing Senate Committee on National Security and Defence, *Managing Turmoil: The Need to Upgrade Canadian Foreign Aid and Military Strength to Deal with Massive Change* (October 2006) at 150, online: www.parl.gc.ca/39/1/parlbus/commbus/senate/com-e/defe-e/rep-e/RepOct06-e.pdf. See also Canada, *Canada's Provincial Reconstruction Team (PRT) in Kandahar Province* (2005), online: www.canada-afghanistan.gc.ca/prov_reconstruction-en.asp.
73   Standing Senate Committee on National Security and Defence, *ibid.* at 150.
74   *Ibid.* at 151.
75   *Ibid.*
76   Canada, Canadian International Development Agency, "Statistical Report on Official Development Assistance, Fiscal Year 2003–2004" (March 2005), online: www.acdi-cida.gc.ca/INET/IMAGES.NSF/vLUImages/stats/$file/Stat_rep_03-04.pdf.

percent.[77] However, the committee also recommended that aid in Afghanistan, the largest recipient of Canadian foreign aid,[78] be administered by the Canadian Forces. In the view of the committee, "[u]sing Canadian Forces to help deliver . . . aid [in Afghanistan] would bring our Kandahar deployment much closer to the genuine 3D kind of effort that the Government trumpets as the Canadian way."[79] In addition, the committee recommended that most of the aid flowing to Afghanistan be concentrated on Kandahar, where Canadian forces are conducting military operations.[80] The committee listed two rationales for its recommendations. First, it was concerned that foreign aid was being administered by multilateral agencies and the Afghanistan government. In the committee's view, the Afghanistan government is known to be corrupt.[81] As well, allowing aid to be administered by multilateral agencies and foreign governments makes it

> impossible to measure the success of Canadian development projects in Afghanistan [since] Canadian aid funds are being given to third parties to use in a way that may or may not be efficient, may or may not be getting to the people in remote and dangerous areas, and may or may not be in Canada's interests or the interests of Canadian troops serving in Afghanistan.[82]

Note that the emphasis is clearly on the achievement of the Canadian government's objectives rather than on the achievement of Afghan development objectives. Second, the committee stressed that it is important for the military to administer foreign aid, since it will improve the image of the military among the Afghan population. In the committee's words:

> The Committee believes that Canada's aid effort in Afghanistan should be clearly tied to Canada's military effort in Afghanistan, to make a clear impression on the hearts and minds of the residents of Kandahar that

---

77 Standing Senate Committee on National Security and Defence, above note 72 at 24.
78 *Ibid.* at 28. CIDA's budget for Afghanistan is $100 million CAD in each of fiscal years 2006–7 and 2007–8.
79 *Ibid.* at 31.
80 *Ibid.*
81 *Ibid.* at 29.
82 *Ibid.* at 30.

these troops are not bloody-minded occupiers, but rather providing protection for the reconstruction of the country.[83]

In my view the 3D approach, modeled on the British CPPs, and the
use of PRTs, modeled on British CPRUs and QIPs, are evidence of the
similarity between the structure of Canadian aid and that of aid in the
U.K. Both countries have integrated their development assistance with
foreign policy and the military. As well, the Senate Committee appears
to be recommending even greater integration of the military and foreign
aid in Afghanistan.

4) Reflections on Government Policies Integrating Development and Military Agendas

The reasons that the Canadian Senate Committee on National Security and Defence gives for supporting its policy recommendations are,
in my view, not based on sound development policy, but rather rest on
the exigencies of military intervention in Afghanistan. Although the
Canadian policy, like the American and British approaches, recognizes
the link between development and terrorism, the approach of all three
governments reframes development policy as a tool for the military. As
we will see, by allowing development policy to be co-opted to deal with
security concerns, effective development work based on sound principles of development may become impossible as development agencies
lose both the means and the legitimacy necessary to deal with the root
causes of terrorism, namely poverty, political and social marginalization,
and ideological disaffection.[84]

---

83 *Ibid.* at 31.

84 Some Canadian NGOs refuse to be involved in CIDA projects in Afghanistan as
    long as the Canadian military is also involved in the projects. Groups such as Care
    Canada and World Vision Canada felt that the presence of the military would "con-
    taminate the aid workers by association, in the eyes of Afghans, compromis[ing]
    their impartiality and put[ting] relief staff in danger": Rosie DiManno, "Aid Groups
    Wearing out Welcome" *The Toronto Star* (23 April 2007).

E. DEVELOPMENT POLICY AS PART OF A POSITIVE PREVENTATIVE APPROACH

There are a number of different means for preventing terrorist attacks. I address three of the principal means. The first is the "stick" approach, which involves proactive coercive deterrence such as military and police enforcement; the second is the "carrot" approach, which involves providing positive incentives for terrorists to cease their activities;[85] and the third is the defensive approach, which involves protecting likely targets of terrorism by making them less vulnerable.[86] In what follows, I explain why the "carrot" approach—providing positive incentives for terrorists to cease committing terrorist acts—and the defensive approach are superior to a coercive deterrence approach. I then demonstrate that using development policy to achieve military and diplomatic goals supports an ineffective coercive deterrence approach rather than using it for its more traditional purposes. Not only does the use of development policy to support military and security initiatives ignore its important role in protecting social and economic rights, it also uses development in a manner that is likely ineffective in preventing terrorism. In my view, if development policy is used for its traditional purpose of eradicating poverty and addressing social, political, economic, and civil rights, it raises the opportunity costs for a country supporting terrorist acts, and thereby also raises the costs of terrorism for terrorists. Proper funding for development assistance will ultimately be more effective in deterring terrorists than co-opting development policy into security and foreign affairs policy.

Walter Enders and Todd Sandler use game theory to demonstrate that proactive policies are needed alongside defensive ones in order to maximize protection against terrorism at the global level. This is because countries that take merely defensive action domestically, by shor-

---

85 Bruno S. Frey, *Dealing with Terrorism—Stick or Carrot?* (Cheltenham, UK: Edward Elgar, 2004) at 27.

86 *Ibid.* at 85–92 where Frey discusses the possibility of "polycentricity," which means that "[a] target's vulnerability is lower in a society composed of many centres than it is in a centralised society" (at 85). See also Walter Enders & Todd Sandler, *The Political Economy of Terrorism* (Cambridge: Cambridge University Press, 2006) at 90: "Defensive measures protect potential targets either by making attacks more costly for terrorists or by reducing their likelihood of success."

ing up domestic defences, will create externalities in other countries, which will become relatively easier targets for terrorism.[87] For instance, efforts in developed countries to increase security after 9/11 has resulted in more terrorist incidents in countries such as Kenya, Morocco, Malaysia, Indonesia, and Turkey.[88] Enders and Sandler point out that attacks on other countries must be prevented because, in a globalized world, increased terrorism in country A can easily affect the interests of country B.[89] Therefore, in addition to making domestic improvements to prevent terror, developed countries must also invest in increasing the defences of developing countries.[90] This further suggests that a proactive defensive policy in which developed countries help to build the defensive infrastructure of developing countries is superior to a proactive coercive one, in which development policy is relegated to the role of supporting coercive military measures. A coercive military approach may simply shift terrorist activity to other countries if a proactive policy is not in place to build the capacity of developing countries to resist terrorism.

As well, despite the popularity of coercive deterrence, policies based on such deterrence tend not to achieve the desired goal. Frey points out that most leading scholars are of the opinion that the use of force as a primary anti-terrorism policy is ineffective.[91] Jeffrey Sachs points out that a military solution to terrorism will never be entirely successful. In his view, a successful preventative policy must also deal with the root causes of terrorism:

> [T]errorism has complex and varying causes, and cannot be fought by military means alone. To fight terrorism, we will need to fight poverty and deprivation as well. A purely military approach to terrorism is doomed to fail. Just as a doctor fights disease by prescribing not only medication, but also by bolstering a person's immune system through adequate nutrition and by encouraging a healthy lifestyle for his patient, so, too, we need to address the underlying weaknesses of the societies in which terrorism lurks—extreme poverty; mass unmet needs for jobs, incomes,

---

87 Enders & Sandler, *ibid.* at 109.

88 *Ibid.*

89 *Ibid.*

90 *Ibid.*

91 Frey, above note 85 at 35. See also Paul Wilkinson, *Terrorism Versus Democracy: The Liberal State Response* (London: Frank Cass, 2000) at 115.

and dignity; and the political and economic instability that results from degrading human conditions. If societies like Somalia, Afghanistan, and western Pakistan were healthier, terrorists could not operate so readily in their midst.[92]

More success is likely with positive incentives for groups to abandon terrorist activity. Frey points out that providing other means for terrorists to achieve their political, economic, or social goals raises the opportunity costs of terrorism.[93] Of course, the cost to terrorists of committing terrorists acts can be raised either through positive or negative sanctions. However, Frey argues that positive incentives are more likely to be effective for the following reasons: negative sanctions will tend to destroy any possibility of cooperation between terrorists and governments; negative sanctions may induce terrorist acts and escalate violence when terrorist groups become desperate to escape military retaliation; and negative sanctions tend to reduce the willingness of terrorist groups to cooperate on other issues such as the protection of the welfare of local people, the exchange of prisoners and hostages, etc.[94]

Among positive incentives, there are two main kinds: direct incentives and indirect incentives. Direct incentives are incentives that states can provide directly to terrorists in order to obtain compliance. Indirect incentives are those that states can provide to other groups, such as states that harbour terrorists, in order to raise the opportunity costs of terrorist activity. There are a number of difficulties with direct incentives. First, providing such incentives may create domestic political difficulties. Domestic voters may feel that the state, in providing incentives directly to terrorists, is being "soft" on terrorism. Second, these incentives are difficult to enforce. Agreements between states and terrorists may not be public, making it difficult to enforce the agreements or assess compliance. As Frey points out

> A well-defined legal framework would enable contracts to overcome the problems of lacking observability and enforcement. But the situation between the government and the terrorist group is characterised by

---

92 Sachs, above note 6 at 215.
93 Frey, above note 85 at 47: "Providing alternatives to terrorists raises the marginal opportunity costs to terrorists."
94 *Ibid.* at 98–99.

an anarchic system, where neither party can have recourse to a higher power in enforcing the contract.[95]

Third, attempting to directly accommodate terrorists can lead to new terrorist activity on the part of those whose interests are harmed by accommodating the initial terrorists.[96] Fourth, accommodation legitimizes terrorism as a means of achieving the terrorist organization's goal.[97] Fifth, terrorist demands are often difficult to accommodate because they are not well-articulated.[98]

Given some of the difficulties facing direct incentives, indirect incentives can be more effective. These indirect incentives would make it less expensive for groups to pursue non-terrorist means of achieving their goals rather than pursuing terrorist means.[99] Frey gives the following examples of what I have called "indirect" incentives:

> Among the positive sanctions are granting of most-favoured-nation status; tariff reductions; debt relief; favourable taxation; access to advanced technology; military, environmental and social cooperation; security assurances; cultural exchanges; or membership in organisations. Most importantly, many of the funds dispersed as aid to countries in the Third World are given in the expectation that their faster economic development also benefits the givers. Their own export markets expand and a more peaceful world is advantageous to all.[100]

We can see that indirect incentives implicate many aspects of traditional development policy. These incentives do not face the same contractual compliance issues that arise in direct incentives. However, for these incentives to be effective, they must meet real needs in the developing country at which they are targeted. The development paradigms that have evolved over the last fifty years are, in my view, more effective than traditional military or diplomatic paradigms at ensuring that development needs are met.

---

95 *Ibid.* at 101.
96 Enders & Sandler, above note 86 at 109.
97 *Ibid.* at 108.
98 *Ibid.*
99 *Ibid.*
100 Frey, above note 85 at 96.

The U.S., the U.K., and Canadian policies linking development, the military, and foreign diplomacy generally aim at both ineffective coercive deterrence and potentially more effective positive incentives. These policies are intended to target some of the root causes of terrorism by helping to improve governance institutions in the developing country. Little attention is given, however, to some of the more traditional goals of development policy such as poverty alleviation. In this regard, existing government coordination policies seemed to be aimed more at ineffective coercive strategies rather than providing more effective positive incentives. Admittedly, there will be interests within a country such as Afghanistan that attempt to subvert the efforts to change existing incentive structures in the way that I have suggested above. But this suggests the need for a comprehensive anti-corruption strategy, accompanied by investment in domestic security institutions. It does not necessarily follow that subversive forces can only be eliminated through military action.

As well, we have seen that the integrated approaches of the U.S., the U.K., and Canada use development funding to support military and security initiatives. In the Canadian context, we have seen that money from the International Assistance Envelope has expressly been used to support anti-terrorism work.[101] In my view, such approaches divert funds away from traditional development work that is itself an effective indirect incentive for terrorists to give up terrorism. Instead, it diverts funds towards potentially effective policies for building developing-country security-capacity, but it also uses funds for demonstrably ineffective coercive deterrence projects. In my view, development policy should not be co-opted by security and diplomatic policies if the consequence is that money will be diverted from effective to ineffective uses. Of course, there will be hard cases such as Pakistan's support of destabilizing forces in Afghanistan. And yet it is hard to see how Canadian military intervention in Afghanistan has been more effective at dealing with this problem than an effective use of development policy. As David Gold points out, retaliation against terrorist attacks has generally proven to be an ineffective deterrent:

---

101 See section D, above in this chapter, where CIDA funding for provincial recon-
     struction teams operating in Afghanistan is discussed.

Responding in kind to terrorist incidents may be psychologically and politically satisfying, but it is not clear if it is effective. It may, of course, be hard to evaluate effectiveness, since it is difficult to measure the number and size of terrorist operations that are not undertaken because of effective deterrence. However, there is considerable evidence that retaliatory behavior does not, in general, reduce the incidence of terrorist activity. Retaliation may, in fact, stimulate more activity by raising the political stakes, especially in situations where more than one group is competing for the allegiance of a population.[102]

F. RECOMMENDATIONS FOR AN ANTI-TERRORISM POLICY THAT RESPECTS THE GOALS OF DEVELOPMENT

I have identified two main ultimate causes of terrorism, namely underdevelopment (including poverty, which implicates social and economic rights and lack of civil and political rights) and an ideology that rejects what it identifies as corrupt Western values.[103] These causes can be addressed by changes in the development policy of developed countries.[104] As we have seen, developed countries have increasingly integrated development programs into the "war on terror" by ensuring greater coordination between government ministries charged with dealing with development policy and ministries of defence and foreign affairs. The stated goals are to ensure greater efficiency by coordinating activities in post-conflict states, and to provide support to military and diplomatic activities of developed countries in these states. In my view, these coordination efforts present a number of potential problems for the protection of human rights. These potential problems arise for a number of reasons. First, they can arise because of the potential for shaping development programs to support a developed country's security at the expense of meeting the development needs identified by developing countries. Second, emphasizing security goals over the development of

---

102 Gold, *The Costs of Terrorism*, above note 19 at 10. See also Mia Bloom, "Palestinian Suicide Bombing: Public Support, Market Share, and Outbidding" (2004) 119:1 Political Science Quarterly 61.

103 See Sen's discussion of the colonial mentality, above note 27.

104 See, for example, *ibid.* at 98 (Sen points out that "[d]ecolonizing the colonized mind must be supplemented by changes in Western international policy").

civil, political, social, and economic rights fails to provide positive incentives for developing countries to end or eliminate support for terrorism on their soil. Third, it is not clear that the coordination programs are providing effective or efficient coordination of various government ministries. Finally, coordinating development policy with military and diplomatic policy may not address key ideological causes of terrorism.

On the first point, coordination of development with security and diplomatic policies results in the combination of conflicting paradigms. Development programs have tended to be state-based, since each country faces its own unique set of challenges. However, the state-based paradigm is ineffective at combating terrorism. First, as Stewart Patrick points out, not all developing countries are havens for terrorists, and it would be unwise to paint all of them with the same brush, given the vastly different conditions that exist in each country.[105] As a result, it may be harmful to require all development aid to have a security and diplomatic aspect. Most of the U.S., the U.K., and Canadian programs currently appear to be targeted at particular states or regions. However, developed countries may inappropriately lump several developing countries into one bag, given that many terrorist groups have transnational organizations, eschewing bases in a single country.[106] It will be important to monitor these programs in the future to ensure that development aid does not become conditional on the adoption of specific anti-terrorism security policies where a given country is not engaged in supporting terrorism.

As well, the conflict among development, military, and diplomatic paradigms can result in other difficulties. One of the principal problems is, if development is viewed as supportive of military solutions, it reduces development to contributing to ineffective coercive state action against terrorists. Furthermore, when funding for aid is inadequate or programs are cut, for instance in favour of increasing military spending, a backlash can result that will exacerbate rather than alleviate security threats as former recipients react negatively to the withdrawal of funding and return to supporting terrorist groups.[107]

---

105 Patrick, above note 22.

106 *Ibid.* at 35.

107 Gold, "The Costs of Terrorism," above note 19 at 17. See also Kim Cragin & Peter Chalk, *Terrorism and Development: Using Social and Economic Development to Inhibit a Resurgence of Terrorism* (Santa Monica, CA: Rand, 2003).

The second problem outlined above, namely, the failure of current policies to provide incentives for countries to stop supporting terrorism, arises out of the types of development assistance that is provided under coordinated programs. Assistance is restricted to those development programs that support security and the installation of effective government. But social and economic rights, as well as the political and civil rights that have been correlated with increased incidence of support for terrorism, are not pursued to the same degree. Often, development assistance can exacerbate income inequalities within a country, even if it increases overall economic growth or helps alleviate particular targeted harms.[108] The correlation between terrorism and economically disadvantaged groups found by Blomberg, Hess, and Weerapana indicates that exacerbating income discrepancies can lead to further terrorism if marginalized groups are not given a voice in political forums and governments remain unresponsive to their concerns. This means that civil and political rights, which do not appear to be the main goals of current coordination policies in the U.S., the U.K., or Canada, should also be improved, since failure to do so may undermine the effectiveness of poverty reduction programs.

The third reason for coordinating development with security and diplomacy is to achieve more efficient and effective government responses. One of the major advantages of coordinating development, foreign affairs, and military engagement with developing countries is the efficiency of eliminating overlapping programs run by different government departments. However, the political economy of bureaucratic government and the different political orientations and goals of these departments appear to place a limit on the benefits of this efficiency. For instance, a review of the U.K. conflict prevention programs in 2003 suggested the following problems with the U.K. approach. First, it pointed out that bureaucratic interests tend to prevail over the achievement of the Public Sector

---

108 Carol Graham, "Can Foreign Aid Help Stop Terrorism?" (2002) 20:3 The Brookings Review 28 at 30. There is a large literature on the ineffectiveness of development aid in spurring economic growth. See, for example, William Easterly, *The White Man's Burden* (New York: Penguin, 2006), who suggests, among other things, that, contrary to Sachs, aid cannot provide the "big push" that will help developing countries escape poverty traps (see for instance chapter 2: "The Legend of the Big Push"). For the opposite view, see Sachs, above note 6 (in particular chapter 3: "Why Some Countries Fail to Thrive").

Agreement among the three departments,[109] which sets the goal of "improved effectiveness of the UK contribution to conflict prevention and management, as demonstrated by a reduction in the number of people whose lives are affected by violent conflict and a reduction in potential sources of conflict, where the UK can make a significant contribution."[110] Second, it indicated that in many cases, CPPs "are limited by what the three principal Departments can agree."[111] Third, the report expresses concern that decision-making about peacekeeping and other programs (including development-related programs) remain separate. Finally, the report indicates that the CPP "may represent little more than a new accounting mechanism (a new budget line) for pre-existing programs of involved Departments, rather than a way of enhancing UK efforts in conflict prevention."[112] On this last point, David Gold, in reviewing the U.S. experience, points out that the administration of aid programs by various departments can raise administrative costs.[113]

Finally, one of the major characteristics of the shifts in development policy in the developed countries that I have surveyed is the adaptation of the categories used for the purposes of determining development assistance for the ultimate goal of preventing terrorism. The adaptation of categories that are relevant for determining development assistance for the purpose of the "war on terror" risks politicizing categories created to meet distributive justice concerns into categories that can reinforce the "clash of civilizations" that many now identify with the "war on terror," both in the media and in foreign policy. Amartya Sen, in his book *Identity and Violence: The Illusion of Destiny*, speaks about the dangers of categorization:

> There are two distinct difficulties with the theory of civilizational clash. The first, which is perhaps more fundamental, relates to the viability and significance of classifying people according to the civilizations to which they allegedly "belong." This question arises well before problems with the view that people thus classified into cartons of civilizations must be somehow antagonistic—the civilizations to which they be-

---

109 *DFID Report*, above note 65 at para. 22.
110 *Ibid.*
111 *Ibid.*
112 *Ibid.*
113 Gold, "Economics of Terrorism," above note 19 at 18.

long are hostile to each other. Underlying the thesis of a civilizational clash lies a much more general idea of the possibility of seeing people primarily as belonging to one civilization or another. The relations between different persons in the world can be seen, in this reductionist approach, as relations between the respective civilizations to which they allegedly belong.[114]

As part of the battle against identity politics that promote polarized ideological positions, there is a role for reconciliation and renewed commitment to development that targets some of the social, political, and economic marginalization that is at the root of terrorism. As von Hippel points out,

> [r]educing humiliation will be a long-term project, but can be achieved through spreading the benefits of globalisation as widely as possible, especially by enhancing international assistance programmes, opening markets, and making greater diplomatic efforts to achieve peace in conflict zones, whether they be in eastern Congo or the Middle East. President Bush can demonstrate goodwill and positive intentions by fulfilling promises . . . to increase the US foreign aid budget by 50 per cent from 2004, which would contribute to overcoming perceptions of inequity.[115]

If we are going to take seriously the idea that the post-colonial mentality and ideology can support terrorism, then it is essential to disconnect coercive deterrence measures from positive incentives.

G. CONCLUSION

I have already indicated in the previous section that there are a number of problems with adapting development policy in order to achieve a country's anti-terrorism goals. First, such an approach results in the allocation of development funds and the institution of development programs without a guarantee that the factors generally used to ensure the effectiveness of development assistance will be used to allocate funds and direct and evaluate development programs. Second, the use of development programs to achieve security goals may be ineffective if development assistance is used to support coercive state action by developed countries against developing countries, specific terrorists, or

---

114 Sen, above note 27 at 40–41.
115 von Hippel, above note 36 at 37.

terrorist groups. Third, recent reviews of the implementation of coordin-ated security and development policies indicate that the political econ-omy of government may make these coordinating programs inefficient and ineffective. Fourth, there is a danger that development assistance will be infected by security goals that will make development policy seem illegitimate in the eyes of certain recipient countries. Fifth, the coordination of development and security policies risks reinforcing the ideology that supports terrorism by reinforcing the view that develop-ment aid is not about meeting the needs of developing countries, but about meeting the security needs of developed countries.

In addition to these conclusions, there is an important point to be made about the *Ottawa Principles*. If these principles are serious about ensuring that a government's anti-terrorism policy respects human rights, then they should cast their net more broadly and consider the impact of government policies coordinating development assistance with security and diplomatic policies on social, economic, civil, and pol-itical rights. In order to do so, the principles should recognize that

1) Using development assistance to prevent terrorism in developed countries risks sacrificing the social, economic, political, and civil rights of those in developing countries to the achievement of secur-ity in developed countries. Developed countries should continue to use development assistance to ensure protection of these important human rights.

2) Although developing countries have an interest in preventing ter-rorism abroad and in their own territory and are required to do so by *Security Council Resolutions* 1373 and 1377, coordinating development and security policies in developed countries undermines needs-based development assistance because it limits the capability of de-veloping countries to direct development assistance based on the development goals that they have set.

In order to adequately recognize the importance of separating de-velopment from diplomacy and defence, I would suggest the following three principles be added to the *Ottawa Principles*:

1) *Development assistance must be separate from military activity.*
   Commentary: The military may legitimately be involved in ensur-ing the secure delivery of development assistance. But the military

should not make decisions about the allocation of development assistance or about development policy more generally.

2) *Development assistance must be separate from foreign policy.*
   Commentary: The direction of development assistance to countries based on political decisions by developed countries puts at risk the important principle that developing countries must be able to set their own development goals.

3) *An anti-terrorism policy that respects principles of sustainable development must ensure that development assistance*:
   a. *meets developing country needs*: developing countries must have the ability to set their own development agendas based on the needs of the people in their country;
   b. *promotes partnerships*: development assistance must be delivered through meaningful partnerships between developed and developing countries;
   c. *recognizes different needs and responsibilities*: countries at different levels of development will have different needs and, consequently, different obligations and these must be recognized in an effective, contextualized development policy.

The *Ottawa Principles* are an essential first step in helping states to recognize how anti-terrorism policy can both infringe important civil and political human rights and, at the same time, fail to achieve desired security goals. The suggestions that I have made indicate that further work must be done in order to ensure that anti-terrorism policy respects human rights broadly conceived. Over the last five years, states have increasingly used their development assistance programs to protect their national security interests. However, they have not yet recognized the important social and economic dimensions of these security policies.

Civil Remedies for Terrorism and State Immunity

François Larocque

A. INTRODUCTION

The central theme of the *Ottawa Principles* is the protection of human rights in the age of anti-terrorism. Most of the papers presented in the course of the colloquium addressed the many thorny issues surrounding access to information, investigation, arrest, detention, and prosecution of persons suspected of planning acts of terrorism. To be sure, the manner in which our legal system treats the civil liberties of suspected terrorists represents one of the most delicate and pressing questions of our time, challenging as it does our constitutional commitment to human rights and to the rule of law. But quite apart from terror suspects, this paper seeks to provoke a discussion about the rights of another important group: the survivors and victims of terrorism. Though few would dispute that individual victims of terrorism and their families deserve some form of reparation, there has been conspicuously little debate on the nature or scope of such reparation in Canada in general and at the Ottawa colloquium in particular. In fact, aside from the opening address by Susheel Gupta, whose mother was killed in the Air India Flight 182 bombing, and my own short presentation on the topic, there was very little mention of victims or civil remedies during the three-day conference. This is unfortunate. In my view, the exercise of delineating the appropriate scope of criminal law in preventing, deterring, and punishing terrorism should not be undertaken without also considering the prospect of using civil litigation and tort law as a possible part of a comprehensive response to terrorism; a response that sensibly pursues both the societal imperatives of criminal justice and the equally important principle that individual wrongs be righted and compensated.

To be fair, the *Ottawa Principles on Anti-terrorism and Human Rights* are not entirely unmindful of civil remedies. Principle 4.4, for instance, recognizes the right of terror suspects who have been tortured while in detention to sue and obtain adequate compensation.[1] Unimpeachable as that proposition may be, the *Ottawa Principles* unfortunately say nothing about the rights of victims of terrorism to seek civil redress. Nor does the Canadian *Anti-terrorism Act*[2] provide victims of terrorism with a right to sue.[3] Quite simply, both Canadian and international law largely ignore the plight of victims of terrorism who, save for mournful memorials and annual televised tributes, are left alone to cope with their loss.

The aim of this paper is thus to spark a thoughtful and long overdue debate both about the right of victims of terrorism to obtain a civil remedy in Canadian courts and about the procedural obstacles to such redress posed by the doctrine of state immunity. As will be seen, though clearly not the largest impediment to civil actions for terrorism, state immunity is currently at the forefront of the civil redress debate in light of recent legislative and jurisprudential developments, which will be discussed at length below. Section B broaches the general topic of civil remedies for terrorism and discusses the broader social value of responding to terrorism simultaneously through the civil and criminal legal process. The articles that, in my opinion, ought to have been included in the *Ottawa Principles* are set out and explained in section C. Section D describes the international and national legal context in which civil redress for terrorism and state immunity collide, and analyzes relevant legislative and jurisprudential developments both within Canada and abroad. Indeed, when debating whether Parliament should

---

1   See the *Ottawa Principles on Anti-Terrorism and Human Rights* in Part One of this book [*Ottawa Principles*].

2   S.C. 2001, c. 41.

3   F. Larocque & M.C. Power, "Bill C-36 Lacks Civil Remedies" *The Lawyer's Weekly* 21:30 (7 December 2001).

provide victims of terrorism with the right to sue and obtain compensation from terrorist organizations and their state sponsors, it is useful to consider the manner in which other jurisdictions have so legislated. In this connection, the civil remedies provisions of the United States anti-terrorism legislation will be discussed in section E, along with the judicial treatment they have received.

B. GENERAL REMARKS ON CIVIL REMEDIES FOR TERRORISM

It is not uncommon in many legal systems for harmful conduct to attract both criminal and civil liability. In Canada, for instance, a reckless driver can be convicted under section 219 of the *Criminal Code*[4] in addition to being found negligent in tort. Environmental damage, assault, fraud, and unlawful detention are further examples of injurious behaviour capable of attracting both criminal and civil responsibility. The reason for this *dédoublement* of legal means is rooted in the basic proposition that the effects of certain wrongs are felt both publicly and privately. Publicly, the community has a clear and pressing interest in deterring reckless driving or fraud because such crimes are harmful to the community as a whole. Privately, the victim of an automobile accident has an interest in the loss of income and life enjoyment that may result from her injuries. Accordingly, in simultaneous furtherance of these public and private interests, the law employs distinct juridical methods and standards to determine the liability of the offender and to restore the injured parties.

In addition to pursuing compensatory goals, civil litigation serves several other functions. For instance, tort actions have a distributive effect.[5] Indeed, once the injured person has been made whole by the award of damages against the responsible party, it is assumed that the latter will in turn transfer the cost of his responsibility to the wider community, for example, by increasing prices (in case of manufacturers) or taxes

---

4   R.S.C. 1985, c. C-46, s. 219.

5   The "distributive justice" function of civil actions is to be distinguished from the paradigm of "corrective justice." The former seeks to compensate the injured party not by virtue of the injurer's fault, but rather on the basis of the membership of the parties to the community. On corrective and distributive justice generally, see Aristotle, *Éthique à Nicomaque*, trans. by J. Tricot (Paris: Vrin, 1990) at 219–20. See also E. Weinrib, "Aristotle's Forms of Justice" (1989) 2 Ratio Juris 211 at 214.

(where a government body is sued). Another important function of civil actions is deterrence, that is, the discouraging of further repetitions of the injurious behaviour through legal sanctions. It is thought that the award of damages achieves both specific and general deterrence by not only causing the wrongdoer to avoid a reoccurrence of the injury, but also by putting others on notice with regards to the consequences that await them if they too engage in the harmful conduct.[6] Also, tort law is an "ombudsman" insofar as "it can be used to apply pressure upon those who wield political, economic or intellectual power; in short, it empowers the injured."[7] The adverse publicity of a lawsuit is believed to be a powerful weapon against powerful tortfeasors, spurring them to act more responsibly lest they suffer a loss of prestige or esteem in the court of public opinion. Finally, tort law serves a psychological function. Much like criminal law, civil actions bring a substantial measure of relief and vindication to injured parties by providing them with a forum in which to air their grievances and, if they are successful, obtain some official recognition of the wrong they have suffered.[8] In a similar vein, tort actions can help to assuage an injured party's thirst for revenge or to "get even" with the tortfeasor, thus promoting peaceful dispute settlements. As Linden remarked, "It is better to pursue a wrongdoer with a writ than with a rifle."[9]

Criminal law, for its part, is more concerned with punishing the offender, deterring future crimes, and, where possible, rehabilitating the offender and facilitating her eventual reintegration into society. Together, criminal law and tort law collaborate by responding to both public and private interests of the community and the individual, respectively, and by fostering acceptable, safe standards of social behaviour and responsibility. It is more by virtue of their methods and operations than of their goals and functions that criminal prosecutions and civil litigation differ from one another. Civil actions, for instance, are instigated by the plaintiff at his own cost. By contrast, it is the government that controls and funds criminal prosecutions. The evidentiary standards are also different: while

---

6   A. Linden, *Canadian Tort Law*, 7th ed. (Markham, ON: Butterworths, 2001) at 8.

7   *Ibid.* at 22. See also A. Linden, "Tort Law as Ombudsman" (1973) 51 Can. Bar Rev. 155.

8   Linden, above note 6 at 16.

9   *Ibid.* at 17.

civil liability is established on the balance of probabilities, criminal culpability must be proven beyond all reasonable doubt. Finally, while criminal law potentially results in the punishment of the offender through fines or imprisonment, tort law seeks to make the victim whole by way of financial compensation. But even here there is overlap between these two forms of corrective justice. For instance, the award of punitive damages in tort is avowedly aimed at punishing and deterring particularly egregious conduct. Similarly, in criminal trials, a judge, upon sentencing, may order the offender to make restitution.[10] In short, at the national level, criminal law and tort law work hand in hand towards consonant goals of corrective justice, employing their own methods and standards, each one enhancing the other's functions and effects.

With perhaps the exception of investor-state dispute settlement procedures, there is no international equivalent for the complementarity of criminal punishment and individual civil redress at the domestic level, though this state of affairs may one day change. The development of international criminal law and the establishment of the International Criminal Court (ICC) are important steps. International criminal law is aimed at deterring and punishing individuals who commit acts that are contrary to international law, violations that are held to be the concern of all nations and peoples: for example, genocide, war crimes, and crimes against humanity. In this sense, international criminal law, much like its domestic counterpart, is protective of the public interest, that is, the *international* public interest. The elevation of human rights among the organizing principles of international society after World War II helped crystallize the notion that the members of the human family are linked by bonds that transcend nationality and geography. Contemporary transnational society strives to advance with the hard lessons learned from recent history firmly in mind, notably that "the recognition of the inherent dignity and of the equal and inalienable rights of all members of the human family is the foundation of freedom, justice and peace in the world."[11] These opening words of the *Universal Declaration of Hu-*

---

10 See, for example, *Criminal Code*, above note 4, s. 738 and *Rome Statute of the International Criminal Court*, 17 July 1998, 2187 U.N.T.S. 90, 37 I.L.M. 1002, UN Doc. A/CONF.183/9 (1998), Article 75(2) [*Rome Statute*].

11 *Universal Declaration of Human Rights*, GA Res. 217 (III), UN GAOR, 3d Sess., Supp. No. 13, UN Doc. A/810 (1948).

man Rights are not mere grandiloquent cosmopolitan sentimentalism; they express a basic axiom of the United Nations and of the enterprise of international criminal justice. The enforcement of international law, specifically of the prohibitions that strike to the heart and health of all nations, is perhaps an indication that international society is at long-last beginning to conceive of itself as a society and to behave like a society does, that is, by fulfilling its own interest in the fulfilling of the interests of its members.[12] It may be that by purporting to enforce those norms of international law that are said to be the concern of all states and all peoples, transnational human rights litigation, like international criminal law, may contribute in protecting the public interest.

C. THE *OTTAWA PRINCIPLES'* MISSING ARTICLES ON CIVIL REDRESS FOR TERRORISM

1) Principle A: Right of Victims of Terrorism to Civil Redress

A.1 Victims of terrorism have the right to obtain civil redress. In the event of the death of the victim as a result of an act of terrorism, his or her dependents shall be entitled to compensation as well as other forms of appropriate reparation.

A.2 Each State shall ensure in its legal system that victims of terrorism obtain redress and have an enforceable right to fair and adequate compensation, including restitution, rehabilitation, satisfaction, and guarantees of non-repetition.

a) Commentary
1) Principles A.1 and A.2 track the language of Article 14 of the *Convention against Torture or Other Cruel, Inhuman or Degrading Treatment and Punishment*.[13] Together they recognize the right of victims of terrorism to obtain a civil remedy and the obligation of states to make such remedies available.

---

12   See generally P. Allott, *Eunomia: New Order for a New World* (Oxford: Oxford University Press, 1990).

13   *Convention against Torture or Other Cruel, Inhuman or Degrading Treatment and Punishment*, 10 December 1984, 1465 U.N.T.S. 85 [*Convention against Torture*].

2) While principle A.1 focuses on "compensation," principle A.2 points to a broader range of civil redress, including restitution, rehabilitation, satisfaction, and guarantees of non-repetition.[14] Such an approach to civil remedies is apposite, though not identical, to the broad remedial powers of the International Criminal Court (ICC), as provided under Article 75 of the *Rome Statute* with regards to the core international crimes.[15]

3) Compensation should be provided for any economically assessable loss resulting from acts of terrorism, such as: (i) physical or mental harm, including pain, suffering, and emotional distress; (ii) lost opportunities; (iii) material damages and loss of earning potential; and (iv) the cost of legal, medical, psychological, and social services. Rehabilitation, for its part, includes the actual medical, psychological, and social services required by the victims. Finally, satisfaction and guarantees of non-repetition for terrorism could potentially include: (i) the search for the bodies of those killed and assistance in the identification and burial of the bodies in a manner respectful of the cultural and religious practices of the concerned families; (ii) a formal enquiry into the facts of the event; (iii) full and public disclosure of the truth; (iv) an apology from responsible parties and a guarantee of non-repetition; and (v) appropriate commemorations and tributes to the victims.[16]

2) Principle B: Jurisdiction of National Courts to Provide a Civil Remedy

B.1 National courts shall exercise subject-matter jurisdiction over acts of terrorism wherever they occur, provided personal jurisdiction over the defendant or defendants can be properly established.

B.2 In the context of civil proceedings for acts of terrorism, the justiciability doctrines of state immunity, act of state, and forum non conveniens

---

14 See Commission on Human Rights, *Final Report of Special Rapporteur, C. Bassiouni, The Right to Restitution, Compensation and Rehabilitation for Victims of Gross Violations of Human Rights and Fundamental Freedoms*, UN ESCOR, 56th Sess., UN Doc. E/CN.4/2000/62 (2000).

15 *Rome Statute*, above note 10, Article 75.

16 Above note 14.

must be applied in a manner consistent with the peremptory prohibition of terrorism in international law.

a) **Commentary**

1) The first phrase of principle B.1 reflects the position that the prohibition against terrorism is a peremptory norm of international law. Because terrorism threatens world public order, it attracts both criminal and civil universal jurisdiction.[17]

2) The second phrase of principle B.1 mandates a qualified version of universal jurisdiction predicated on the capability of the forum to obtain personal jurisdiction over the defendants in accordance with normal rules of process, including service *ex juris*.

3) Principle B.2 addresses the unwieldiness of traditional rules of justiciability in the context of transnational human rights litigation. The transnational character of terrorism requires traditional rules to be reconceived not in terms of territorial connections, but rather in light of the peremptoriness of the prohibition against terrorism and of the vital interests it protects.

4) Because terrorism is prohibited by a peremptory norm of international law, it cannot be characterized as an act *jure imperii* for state immunity and as an act of state purposes.[18]

---

17 See Alexander Orakhelashvili, *Peremptory Norms in International Law* (Oxford: Oxford University Press, 2006). See also American Law Institute, *Restatement (Third) of the Foreign Relations Law of the United States* (St. Paul, MN: American Law Institute, 1987) at § 404 [*Restatement (Third)*]: "A state has jurisdiction to define and prescribe punishment for certain offenses recognized by the community of nations as of universal concern, such as piracy, slave trade, attacks on or hijacking of aircraft, genocide, war crimes, and perhaps certain acts of terrorism"; *United States v. Yunis*, 288 U.S. App. D.C. 129, 924 F.2d 1086 at 1092 (D.C. Cir. 1991) [*Yunis*]: "Aircraft hijacking may well be one of the few crimes so clearly condemned under the law of nations that states may assert universal jurisdiction to bring offenders to justice, even when the state has no territorial connection to the hijacking and its citizens are not involved."; and *Convention for the Suppression of Unlawful Seizure of Aircraft*, 16 December 1970, 860 U.N.T.S. 105, to which there are currently 182 state parties.

18 See *Ferrini v. Federal Republic of Germany* (2004), Cass. Sez. Un. 5044/04 [*Ferrini*]; *Siderman v. Republic of Argentina* (1992), 965 F.2d 699 (9th Cir.) [*Siderman*]; *Prosecutor v. Furundzija*, IT-95-17/1-T at para. 155 (10 December 1998) (ICTY, Trial Chamber) [*Furundzija*]; Orakhelashvili, *ibid.*; A. Bianchi, "Denying State Immunity to Violators of Human Rights" (1994) 46 Austrian J. Publ. Int'l L. 195; and François Larocque, "*Bouzari v. Iran*: Testing the Limits of State Immunity in Canadian Courts" (2003) 41

D. TRANSNATIONAL HUMAN RIGHTS LITIGATION AND THE ARTICLES ON CIVIL REDRESS FOR TERRORISM

The principles pertaining to civil redress for victims of terrorism set out in the previous section express the basic tenet of transnational human rights litigation, namely, that violations of international human rights may properly give rise to civil redress in addition to criminal sanctions. Indeed, both international and domestic law recognize that human rights victims are entitled to a range of civil remedies including compensation, restitution, rehabilitation, satisfaction, and guarantees of non-repetition.[19] While other, non-adversarial processes exist—such as truth commissions and diplomatic channels—transnational human rights litigation focuses on the obtainment of compensation for victims of grave human rights abuses through civil trials. The *Ottawa Principles* do contain some language in support of civil redress for terror suspects who are tortured while in state custody,[20] but the general thrust of those recommendations is arguably weakened by their failure to extend to the primary victims of terrorism. Nevertheless, it can be said that principle 4.4 is generally aligned with the central goal of transnational human rights litigation.

Transnational human rights litigation, which can broadly be defined as civil proceedings in the courts of one state in relation to violations of international law in another state, raises a number of procedural and substantive problems: For which violations of international law may victims sue? Is there such a thing as common law cause of action for violations of international human rights law? Is there such a thing as universal civil jurisdiction? Can personal jurisdiction over a foreign wrongdoer be established through the normal rules for service *ex juris*? How can a state claim immunity for violations of peremptory norms of international law? In what manner should choice of law issues be resolved? Many more questions surface downstream, in relation to evidence and to the

---

Can. Y.B. Int'l Law 343. But see also *Al-Adsani v. United Kingdom*, [2001] 34 E.H.R.R. 273, aff'g (*sub nom. Al-Adsani v. Kuwait*) (1996), 107 I.L.R. 536 (C.A.), aff'g (1995), 103 I.L.R. 420 (Q.B.) [*Al-Adsani*]; *Bouzari v. Islamic Republic of Iran* (2004), 71 O.R. (3d) 675 (C.A.), aff'g [2002] O.J. No. 1624 (S.C.J.) [*Bouzari*]; *Jones v. Ministry of Interior (Saudi Arabia)*, [2006] UKHL 26 [*Jones*].

19 Above note 14 at 10.

20 See *Ottawa Principles* contained in this volume, principle 4.4.

execution of judgments, for instance, though none of them will be discussed here.[21] Rather, largely because of recent developments in Canadian and English law, the remainder of this paper narrows focus onto the issue of the procedural bar raised by the doctrine of state immunity in the context of transnational civil claims for terrorism.

1) Recent Judicial Developments

On 14 June 2006, the House of Lords released its decision in *Jones v. Ministry of Interior (Saudi Arabia).*[22] In that case, a group of plaintiffs (which included Canadian citizen William Sampson) sued the Kingdom of Saudi Arabia and several named Saudi officials for the physical and psychological torture they endured while in Saudi prisons. The House of Lords dismissed the claims against both the Kingdom and the officials on the basis of the *State Immunity Act 1978,*[23] generally for the same reasons given by the Court of Appeal for Ontario in *Bouzari v. Islamic Republic of Iran*[24] and the European Court of Human Rights in *Al-Adsani v. United Kingdom,*[25] namely, that the rules of state immunity in international law, and as codified in domestic law, admit no exception for torture or violations of peremptory norms.

The implications of this jurisprudence for the argument made in this paper are significant: if courts are not prepared to recognize a new exception to state immunity in proceedings relating to torture, either in common law or as an emerging rule of customary international law, they are not likely to do so in proceedings relating to terrorism. For one thing, the international definition and rules relating to torture are well-established and enjoy near universal assent.[26] Moreover, courts have consistently held the prohibition against torture to be a peremptory

---

21　For a general discussion of many of these issues, see Craig Scott, ed., *Torture as Tort: Comparative Perspectives on the Development of Transnational Human Rights Litigation* (Oxford: Hart, 2001).

22　*Jones*, above note 18.

23　(U.K.), 1978, c. 33.

24　*Bouzari*, above note 18.

25　*Al-Adsani*, above note 18.

26　*Convention against Torture*, above note 13, has 74 signatories and 144 parties. See online: http://untreaty.un.org/ENGLISH/bible/englishinternetbible/partl/chapter IV/treaty14.asp.

norm of international law.[27] The international legal status of terrorism, by contrast, is not quite as clear. Though unquestionably reviled and condemned by the international community—the Security Council has characterized "acts of international terrorism" as threats "to international peace and security"[28]—the prohibition of terrorism suffers from the indeterminacy of the term itself. At the time of writing, there is no comprehensive international legal definition of terrorism. It may be said however that certain acts of violence are generally considered to constitute particular forms of terrorism, such as the taking of hostages; the seizure, diversion, and destruction of civilian aircrafts; and attacks against the life, physical integrity, or liberty of internationally protected persons, including diplomatic agents. These wrongful acts are more readily definable and many of them are said to be prohibited by *jus cogens*. For example, Libya conceded that its participation in the bombing of Pan-AM flight 103 was a violation of *jus cogens*.[29] Similarly, the Institute of International Law notes that the diversion of aircrafts has attracted the "general condemnation" of the international community as being "unlawful under international law" and in violation of "elemental considerations of humanity."[30] In *United States v. Yunis*, the court stated that "Aircraft hijacking may well be one of the few crimes so clearly condemned unde the law of nations that states may assert universal jurisdiction to bring offenders to justice, even when the state has no territorial connection to the hijacking and its citizens are not involved."[31]

Be that as it may, the *Al-Adsani*, *Bouzari*, and *Jones* decisions ultimately turned on strict constructions of the Canadian and U.K. state immunity statutes in proceedings for acts of torture, and their combined

---

27 See *Furundzija*, above note 18 at paras. 153–55; *R. v. Bow Street Metropolitan Stipendiary Magistrate, ex parte Pinochet (No. 3)*, [2000] 1 A.C. 147 at 197–99 (H.L.); *Al-Adsani* above note 18; *Bouzari*, above note 18 at paras. 61 and 88; *A(FC) & Others v. Secretary of State for the Home Department*, [2005] UKHL 71 at para. 34; *Jones*, above note 18 at para. 15.

28 *Security Council Resolution 1373*, SC Res. 1373, UN SCOR, 2001, S/RES/1373 [Resolution 1373].

29 *Smith v. Socialist People's Libyan Arab Jamahiriya*, 101 F.3d 239 at 242 (2d Cir. 1996).

30 Institute of International Law, *Resolution on the Unlawful Diversion of Aircraft* (Zhagreb Session, 3 September 1971), online: www.idi-iil.org/idiE/resolutionsE/1971_zag_04_en.pdf.

31 *Yunis*, above note 17. See also *Restatement (Third)*, above note 17 at § 404, listing attacks and hijacking and "certain acts of terrorism" as crimes of universal jurisdiction.

weight does not permit much optimism for those who argue in favour of the development of transnational human rights litigation writ large outside the United States. That country has legislation in place creating a cause of action for extraterritorial violations of international law[32] and removing immunity of certain states in proceedings for certain transnational human rights proceedings.[33] Canada and the U.K. have no such legislation. The failed attempts in those countries to sue for extraterritorial human rights breaches have been brought on the sole basis of the common law. Ultimately, the English and Canadian transnational human rights litigation jurisprudence disclose a lack of judicial appetite for asserting jurisdiction in civil claims with respect to violations of international law, in the absence of direction from Parliament. As it will be seen below, such direction may come sooner rather than later.

2) Canadian Legislative Developments

There are legislative efforts currently under way in Canada to provide victims of terrorism with a cause of action and to deny state immunity in civil proceedings for acts of terrorism. It should be pointed out that these innovative attempts are private member's bills rather than government initiatives and as such stand a slim chance of being made into law. Nevertheless, at the time of writing, they are still making their way through Parliament.

Bill C-394, entitled *An Act to amend the State Immunity Act and the Criminal Code (terrorist activity)*, was initially tabled on 17 May 2005 in the House of Commons[34] and on 18 May 2005 (as Bill S-35) in the Senate. The bills lapsed when the 38th Parliament dissolved in November 2005. Both bills were then reintroduced without significant modification in

---

32   See *Alien Tort Statute*, 1 Stat. 73 (1789) and *Torture Victim Protection Act of 1991*, Pub. L. 102–256, 106 Stat. 73 (1992) (both codified at 28 U.S.C. §1350).

33   See *Antiterrorism and Effective Death Penalty Act of 1996*, Pub. L. 104-132, 110 Stat. 1214 (1996) (codified at 28 U.S.C. § 1605(a)(7)).

34   The proposed legislation was actually first introduced in the House of Commons as Bill C-367 on 19 April 2005. It was withdrawn and renumbered as Bill C-394 on 17 May 2005.

the House of Commons[35] and the Senate[36] during the opening weeks of the 39th Parliament. Both new bills (S-218 and C-272) are substantially identical to each other and to their previous versions, save, most notably, for a slightly more explicit title and the addition of a preamble in the new Senate bill.[37] The preamble of Bill S-218 reads as follows:

An Act to amend the State Immunity Act and the Criminal Code (civil remedies for victims of terrorism)	Loi modifiant la Loi sur l'immunité des États et le Code criminel (recours civils des victimes d'actes terroristes)
WHEREAS it is desirable to confirm in Canadian law the existing peremptory norms and provisions of international law against terrorism (jus cogens) that are accepted and recognized by the international community of states as a whole;	ATTENDU qu'il est souhaitable de confirmer en droit canadien les normes et les dispositions impératives existantes en droit international contre le terrorisme (jus cogens ou « droit contraignant ») qui sont acceptées et reconnues par l'ensemble de la communauté internationale des États;

35 Oddly, the bill was introduced twice in the House of Commons during the 39th Parliament. First, the Honourable Susan Kadis (Liberal—Thornhill) introduced Bill C-272, *An Act to amend the State Immunity Act and the Criminal Code (terrorist activity)*, 1st Sess., 39th Parl., 2006 (first reading 10 May 2006), online: www2.parl. gc.ca/HousePublications/Publication.aspx?Language=E&Parl=39&Ses=1&Mod e=1&Pub=Bill&Doc=C-272_1&File=19. Then, in June 2006, the Honourable Nina Grewal (Conservative—Fleetwood/Port Kells) introduced Bill C-346, *An Act to amend the State Immunity Act and the Criminal Code (terrorist activity)*, 1st Sess., 39th Parl., 2006, online: http://www2.parl.gc.ca/HousePublications/Publication. aspx?DocId=2493464&Language=e&Mode=1 (accessed 24 April 2007). Bills C-272 and C-346 are essentially identical, save minor wording differences and the presence of a rather lengthy preamble in C-346.

36 Bill S-218, *An Act to amend the State Immunity Act and the Criminal Code (civil remedies for victims of terrorism)*, 1st Sess., 39th Parl., 2006 (first reading 15 June 2006; debates 22 and 27 June 2006; second reading 2 November 2006), sponsored by the Honourable David Tkachuk. See online: www.parl.gc.ca/LEGISINFO/index. asp?Language=E&Chamber=N&StartList=A&EndList=Z&Session=14&Type=0&Sco pe=I&query=4788&List=stat.

37 The following discussion focuses on Bill S-218 because it has a cogent preamble and because it is further along in the legislative process than its House of Commons counterpart, Bill C-272. The full text of Bill S-218 is included in Annex A.

AND WHEREAS state immunity is generally accepted as applying only to sovereign acts of state (*acta jure imperii*);

AND WHEREAS terrorism is a threat to democracy, and the support and financing of terror is a crime under international law and as such is not a sovereign act of state to which a claim of state immunity can apply;

AND WHEREAS it is necessary that judicial awards against persons who engage in terrorist activities be sufficiently large to deter such conduct in the future;

AND WHEREAS the victims of terrorist activities include the individuals as well as their family members who are physically, emotionally or psychologically injured by the terrorist activities,

qu'il est généralement accepté que l'immunité de juridiction s'applique uniquement aux actes de gouvernement (*acta jure imperii*);

que le terrorisme représente une menace pour la démocratie et que le soutien et le financement du terrorisme est un crime en vertu du droit international et qu'en tant que tel, il n'est pas un acte de gouvernement auquel il serait permis d'appliquer l'immunité de juridiction;

qu'il est nécessaire que la portée des décisions des tribunaux défavorables aux personnes qui se livrent à des activités terroristes soit suffisamment large pour décourager cette conduite par la suite;

que les victimes des activités terroristes ne sont pas uniquement les particuliers qui ont été blessés physiquement, émotionnellement ou psychologiquement par les activités terroristes, mais également les membres de leur famille,

The title of the bill explicitly indicates that the draft legislation seeks to amend both the *Criminal Code*[38] and *State Immunity Act*,[39] which may have been deliberately intended to shore up Parliament's constitutional authority to enact the proposed legislation. It could be reasonably objected that the creation of a civil cause of action is usually a matter for the provinces, pursuant to their exclusive jurisdiction to legislate in

---

38   Above note 4.
39   R.S.C. 1985, c. S-18 [*State Immunity Act*].

relation to "property and civil rights."[40] This jurisdiction, as Hogg notes, is typically understood to include "most of the private law of property, contracts and torts, and their many derivatives."[41] On the other hand, the drafters of Bill S-218 could argue that the proposed cause of action is part of a comprehensive federal scheme meant to proscribe, punish, and deter terrorist activity, and that the legislation is valid insofar as the right to sue for terrorism is ancillary to its prohibition in the *Criminal Code*. In *R. v. Zelensky*[42] a majority of the Supreme Court of Canada upheld a provision of the *Criminal Code* that allowed a sentencing judge to order the accused to pay a compensatory award to the victim for his or her loss. The majority agreed that the compensation orders were so closely tied to the judge's sentencing powers that their validity could not be questioned on federalism grounds. Likewise, it could be argued that the Bill S-218 cause of action forms an integral part of Canada's legal response to terrorism under Part II.1 of the *Criminal Code* and, as such, is a valid federal enactment.[43]

The proposed amendments to the *Criminal Code* operate generally by providing victims with a cause of action and recognizing the jurisdiction of superior courts to adjudicate civil claims against persons who engaged in terrorist activity on or after 1 January 1985.[44]

Loss or damage	*Perte ou dommages*
83.34 (1) Any person who has suffered loss or damage, on or after January 1, 1985, as a result of conduct that is contrary to any provision	83.34 (1) Toute personne qui, le 1er janvier 1985 ou après cette date, a subi une perte ou des dommages par suite soit d'un comportement

---

40 *Constitution Act, 1867* (U.K.), 30 & 31 Vict., c. 3, s. 92(13).

41 Peter Hogg, *Constitutional Law of Canada*, 5th ed. supplemented, looseleaf (Toronto: Carswell, 2007–) vol. 1 at 17-2.

42 [1978] 2 S.C.R. 940.

43 But see C. Davidson, "Tort au canadien: A Proposal for Canadian Tort Legislation on Gross Violations of International Human Rights and Humanitarian Law" (2005) 38 Vanderbilt J. Transnat'l L. 1403 at 1431–34 where the author concludes that the legislative authority to create a cause of action for breaches of international human rights more plausibly lies with the provinces.

44 As Senator Tkachuk's speech at first reading suggests, the 1985 temporal threshold appears to be designed to capture the victims of the Air India Flight 182. See Canada, *Senate Debates (Hansard)*, 39th Parliament, vol. 143, issue 27 (22 June 2006) at 1720–40 [*Hansard*].

| of this Part or the failure of any person to comply with an order of a court under this Part may, in any court of competent jurisdiction, sue for and recover from the person who engaged in the conduct or failed to comply with the order an amount equal to the loss or damage proved to have been suffered by the person, together with any additional amount that the court may allow by way of punitive damages or otherwise. | allant à l'encontre d'une disposition de la présente partie, soit du défaut d'une personne d'obtempérer à une ordonnance rendue par un tribunal en vertu de la présente partie peut, devant tout tribunal compétent, réclamer et recouvrer de la personne qui a eu un tel comportement ou n'a pas obtempéré à l'ordonnance une somme égale au montant de la perte ou des dommages qu'elle est reconnue avoir subis, ainsi que toute somme supplémentaire que le tribunal peut fixer, notamment à titre des dommages intérêts punitifs. |

Proposed section 83.34 would be added to the anti-terrorism provisions under Part II.1 of the *Criminal Code* and would make any violation of the offences listed therein civilly actionable. Furthermore, the amendments would prevent the applicable limitations period from running during the time the plaintiff is mentally or physically incapable of bringing the claim or while the identity of the defendant is not known (proposed section 83.34(2)). Finally, Canadian courts would be required under proposed section 83.34(3) to give full faith and credit to foreign judgments in civil proceedings for terrorism to facilitate their enforcement in Canadian law.

The Bill S-218 cause of action appears to be predicated on something not entirely removed from universal civil jurisdiction, the only significant restrictions being the limitations period (which may still run after the section 83.34(2) suspension expires)[45] and the court's ability to assert personal jurisdiction over the defendant ("a court of competent jurisdiction"). Significantly, the Bill S-218 cause of action would be available to "any person," a far more expansive category of potential plaintiffs

---

45 Indeed, universal jurisdiction is generally understood to extend to international wrongs that "are by their nature imprescriptible." See Commission on Human Rights, *Updated Set of Principles for the Protection and Promotion of Human Rights through Action to Combat Impunity*, UN ESCOR, 61st Sess., Addendum, Item 17, E/CN.4/2005/102/Add.1 (2005) 14.

than that contemplated by the U.S. anti-terrorism legislation.[46] Furthermore, to broaden the personal jurisdiction of Canadian courts, proposed section 83.34(4) makes clear that the civil proceedings contemplated by section 83.34(1) may be initiated against "a foreign state and an agency of a foreign state as defined in the *State Immunity Act.*"

Bill S-218 then goes on to amend the *State Immunity Act* to allow plaintiffs to bring claims against states for terrorism. The first three preambular paragraphs of the bill are ground-breaking as they set out the syllogism that English and Canadian courts have thus far declined to accept with regards to the interaction of peremptory (*jus cogens*) and ordinary norms of international law, namely, (1) that the prohibition against terrorism is a peremptory norm of international law; (2) that state immunity applies only to sovereign acts of state (*acta jure imperii*); and (3) that terrorism cannot be characterized as *jure imperii* as it is a wrongful act that threatens world public order. It is in this manner that the preamble explicates the legal basis for denying immunity in civil proceedings against states who are alleged to have engaged in terrorist activity.

While the courts in *Al-Adsani*, *Bouzari*, and *Jones* rejected similar normative hierarchy arguments, the Italian Corte di Cassazione applied it in *Ferrini*.[47] The U.S. Court of Appeal for the Ninth Circuit also considered the *jus cogens*-trumps-state-immunity argument in *Siderman*, a civil suit for torture.[48] The court stated that the argument held "much force," but ultimately found itself to be bound by the U.S. Supreme Court's prior characterization of the *Foreign Sovereign Immunities Act*[49] as an exhaustive codification and the sole basis for determining immunities in the United States.[50] Indeed, however persuasive and weighty the argument may be, international normative hierarchy cannot displace the unequivocal wording of domestic jurisdictional statutes. As Goudge J.A. noted in *Bouzari* with regards to the Canadian *State Immunity Act*, "s. 3(1) could not be clearer. [I]t says: . . . *Except as provided by this Act*, a foreign state is immune from the jurisdiction of any court in Canada. The plain and

---

46 See discussion of the U.S. legislation in section E, below in this chapter.

47 *Ferrini*, above note 18.

48 *Siderman*, above note 18.

49 28 U.S.C. § 1602–1611 [*FSIA*].

50 *Amerada Hess Shipping Corp. v. Republic of Argentina*, 488 U.S. 428 (1989).

ordinary meaning of these words is that they codify the law of sovereign immunity."[51] Bill S-218 accordingly amends the *State Immunity Act* to permit plaintiffs to bring civil claims against states and their agencies for acts of terrorism. The salient provisions of the proposed amendment read as follows:

6.1 (1) In this section, subsection 11(4), paragraph 12(1)(*d*), and subsection 13(3), "terrorist activity" means any transaction, act or conduct that involves or relates to the support of any terrorist group that is a listed entity as defined in subsection 83.01(1) of the *Criminal Code*.

6.1 (1) Au présent article, au paragraphe 11(4), à l'alinéa 12(1)*d*) et au paragraphe 13(3), « activité terroriste » s'entend de tout acte, comportement ou opération qui comporte l'appui d'un groupe terroriste qui est une entité inscrite au sens du paragraphe 83.01(1) du *Code criminel*, ou qui se rapporte à l'appui d'un tel groupe.

6.1 (2) A foreign state is not immune from the jurisdiction of a court in any proceedings that relate to any terrorist activity that the foreign state conducted on or after January 1, 1985.

6.1 (2) L'État étranger ne bénéficie pas de l'immunité de juridiction dans les actions portant sur des activités terroristes auxquelles il s'est livré le 1er janvier 1985 ou après cette date.

In short, following the paradigm of restrictive immunity enacted in the *State Immunity Act*, the amendment creates a new exception to the general rule by adding terrorism to the list of subject-matters that do not attract state immunity.

According to Senator Tkachuk, if adopted, Bill S-218 would contribute to implement some of Canada's international commitments under the 1999 *International Convention for the Suppression of the Financing of Terrorism*[52] and Resolution 1373.[53] In the senator's words:

51 *Bouzari* (2004) above note 18 at paras. 57–58 (C.A.) [emphasis in original].
52 10 January 2000, 39 I.L.M. 270, 2002 Can. T.S. 9, [*Financing Convention*]. Canada signed the *Financing Convention* on 10 February 2000 and ratified it on 15 February 2002.
53 Acting under Chapter VII of the UN *Charter*, the Security Council called on all states to "become parties as soon as possible to the relevant international conventions and protocols relating to terrorism, including the *International Convention for*

This proposed legislation is driven by the fact that Article 5 of the UN convention states that liability under the convention may be criminal, civil or administrative. In addition, Article 5 states that each state party shall ensure that legal entities liable in accordance with provisions of the convention are subject to effective, proportionate and dissuasive criminal, civil or administrative sanctions that may include monetary sanctions. Bill S-218 takes Canada's commitment and enacts it within our legal system.[54]

For its part, Article 5 of the *Financing Convention* provides:

Article 5

1. Each State Party, in accordance with its domestic legal principles, shall take the necessary measures to enable a legal entity located in its territory or organized under its laws to be held liable when a person responsible for the management or control of that legal entity has, in that capacity, committed an offence set forth in article 2. Such liability may be criminal, civil or administrative.

2. Such liability is incurred without prejudice to the criminal liability of individuals having committed the offences.

3. Each State Party shall ensure, in particular, that legal entities liable in accordance with paragraph 1 above are subject to effective, proportionate and dissuasive criminal, civil or administrative sanctions. Such sanctions may include monetary sanctions.

Though Bill S-218 could be more explicit about its relationship to the *Financing Convention*, in its preamble for instance,[55] its provisions would certainly give substantial effect to the obligations contained in Article 5 of the convention. Indeed, even if one rejects the argument that the prohibition against terrorism is a peremptory norm, it can at least be asserted that the obligation to provide victims with a remedy is treaty-based.

---

the *Suppression of the Financing of Terrorism of 9 December 1999*." See Resolution 1373, above note 28, s. 3(d).

54 *Hansard*, above 44 at 1730.

55 The Supreme Court of Canada has directed that implementing statutes should contain some explicit recital or reference to the international treaties they seek to implement, such that "the Courts should be able to say, on the basis of the expression of the legislation, that it is implementing legislation": *MacDonald v. Vapor Canada Ltd.*, [1977] 2 S.C.R. 134 at 171.

As the parliamentary activity with regards to Bill S-218 indicates, the question of civil remedies for terrorism is a live issue, though it remains to be seen whether the bill will ever become law. The *Ottawa Principles'* silence on this front is unfortunate, especially when one considers that the bill had been tabled a few days prior to the colloquium and debated immediately after. It is in this general context of judicial abstention and legislative enterprise that the principles on civil redress were written and must now be read.

E. THE UNITED STATES EXPERIENCE

An informed discussion about the suitability of Bill S-218 and its wider policy objectives is required. To this end, Canadian lawmakers and academics would be well-advised to examine the particular features of the United States anti-terrorism legislative package, which has included civil remedies since the early 1990s.[56] In addition to criminalizing domestic and international terrorism, Congress has provided U.S. nationals and their families with a right to sue and obtain compensation equal to three times the damages sustained as a result of terrorist activity, as well as court costs and legal fees. The civil remedies provisions of the U.S. anti-terrorism legislative package are codified at §§2333–2338 of the *United States Code*, which set out (1) the cause of action of the plaintiffs,[57] (2) the jurisdiction of the Federal District courts over civil claims for terrorism,[58] (3) a four-year limitations period,[59] (4) as well as other procedural bars relating to immunity, limits on discovery, and suits relating to acts of war.[60]

Section 2333 creates the cause of action by allowing U.S. victims or their estates to sue for acts of international terrorism. The term "international terrorism," for its part, is defined at §2331 as activities that in-

---

56 See Annex B. The civil remedies provisions were adopted by Pub. L. 102-572, title X, s. 1003(a)(4), 29 October 1992, 106 Stat. 4522; amended Pub. L. 103-429, s. 2(1), 31 October 1994, 108 Stat. 4377.

57 18 U.S.C. §2333.

58 18 U.S.C. §2334.

59 18 U.S.C. §2335.

60 18 U.S.C. § 2336. The immunity of the U.S. government and its officials from suit is provided for at § 2337, while § 2338 specifies that jurisdiction over civil proceedings for terrorism lie exclusively with the federal district courts.

volve violent acts or acts dangerous to human life that are a violation of U.S. or international criminal laws and that appear to be intended to intimidate or coerce a civilian population or a government. Moreover, the impugned acts must occur primarily outside the United States, or be of such a character that they transcend national boundaries in terms of their participants, planning, or execution. The definition of "terrorism" in the *Ottawa Principles* captures most of these elements, but appears ultimately to be wider than the §2331 definition in that it has no territorial constraints, much like the definition of "terrorist activity" at section 83.01(1) of the *Criminal Code*. By contrast, the U.S. cause of action appears to be limited to acts of terrorism that contain some element of extraterritoriality.

It is also noteworthy that the cause of action is made available only to U.S. nationals and estates. Foreign nationals cannot sue under §2333. Of course, on the other hand, foreign nationals have no need for the civil remedies provisions of the U.S. anti-terrorism legislation since they can avail themselves of the wider jurisdiction provided by the *Alien Tort Statute*.[61] In this respect, §2333 extends to U.S. nationals the same benefit that foreign nationals enjoy under the *ATS* by allowing them to sue for terrorism, much like the *Torture Victim Protection Act*[62] extended to U.S. nationals the right to sue for torture and other violations of international law in federal courts, a right that foreign nationals already had under the *ATS*. That statute succinctly provides that "the district courts shall have original jurisdiction of any civil action by an alien for a tort only, committed in violation of the law of nations or a treaty of the United States." Thus, in the ongoing litigation in *Burnett et al. v. Al Baraka Investment et al.*,[63] the class action arising from the attacks on the World Trade Center on September 11, 2001, U.S. plaintiffs are basing their claim on §2333, while foreign plaintiffs (some of whom are Canadian) are suing under the *ATS*.

Following the landmark 2004 decision in *Sosa v. Alvarez-Machain*,[64] in which the U.S. Supreme Court set a high threshold of definitional and normative specificity in order for international offences to be actionable

---

61   28 U.S.C. §1350 [*ATS*].

62   Annotation to 28 U.S.C. §1350, added by Pub. L. 102-256, 106 Stat. 73 (1992).

63   392 F. Supp. 2d 539 (S.D.N.Y. 2005).

64   542 U.S. 692 (2004) [*Sosa*].

under the *ATS*, using as benchmarks the eighteenth-century paradigms of piracy, assaults against diplomatic personnel, and passport violations, there was some question as to whether terrorism possessed the required degree of international recognition to give rise to *ATS* jurisdiction. The answer to that question came in 2005 in *Mutaka Mwani v. Bin Laden*, where the Court of Appeal for the District of Columbia, overturning the district court's dismissal for lack of jurisdiction, held that a terrorist car bomb attack more than likely fell in the narrow class of actionable offences described in *Sosa*.[65] Specifically, the plaintiffs were suing in relation to a car bomb attack outside the U.S. embassy in Kenya allegedly orchestrated by Osama bin Laden and Al-Qaeda, thus falling well within the eighteenth-century paradigmatic crime against ambassadors and diplomatic envoys. Accordingly, it is difficult to say how far the holding in *Mutaka Mwani* can be taken and whether the court would have asserted *ATS* jurisdiction had the car bomb been detonated in a market square or near a military base. Would such a terrorist attack suffice to trigger *ATS'* jurisdiction? Given the lack of international consensus as to the definition of terrorism, it is difficult to imagine that this broad category could, in itself, meet the high definitional requirement articulated in *Sosa*. U.S. courts will have to proceed on a case-by-case basis, examining the specificity of relevant international norms proscribing individual terrorist acts, rather than of terrorism writ large, in exercising *ATS* jurisdiction. For example, in a pre-*Sosa* case, the D.C. District Court stated that terrorist aircraft hijacking "may well be one of the few crimes so clearly condemned under the law of nations that states may assert universal jurisdiction to bring offenders to justice, even when the state has no territorial connection to the hijacking and its citizens are not involved."[66]

A distinctive feature of the U.S. anti-terrorism legislative package is the selective removal of immunity with regards to states that have been designated as "state sponsors of terrorism." Responding to growing pressure from families of victims and survivors of the Pan AM Flight 103 bombing in 1988, Congress amended the *FSIA* in 1996 by creating a new exception to state immunity for serious human rights violations. The *Antiterrorism and Effective Death Penalty Act*,[67] codified as part of the *For-*

---

65   417 F.3d 1 at 32 (D.C. Cir. 2005) [*Mutaka Mwani*].

66   *Yunis*, above note 17 at 1092 (F.2d).

67   Above note 33, § 221.

eign Sovereign Immunities Act,[68] at 28 U.S.C. §1605(a)(7), allows U.S. citizens to bring a claim for compensatory and punitive damages[69] against certain designated state sponsors of terrorism[70] for death or personal injury arising from an act of torture, extrajudicial killing, aircraft sabotage, hostage-taking, or for supporting such activities, provided the plaintiff afforded the foreign state with a reasonable opportunity to resolve the matter through arbitration. The U.S. manner of selectively removing immunity pursuant to executive determinations is reminiscent of the policy outlined in the so-called Tate Letter[71] of 1952, whereby the restrictive doctrine of state immunity was formally adopted (at least with regards to *acta jure gestionis*) and courts subsequently granted or denied immunity following a mix application of principle and directions from the executive branch.[72] With the enactment of the *FSIA* in 1976, the determination of immunities became an exclusive judicial matter, that is, until §1605(a)(7) was enacted in 1996. In civil proceedings for certain acts of terrorism, U.S. courts must follow the directions of the executive branch and its determinations as to which foreign state is entitled to immunity, and which is not. At the time of writing, Cuba, Iran, North Korea, Syria, and Sudan are not immune from civil actions under §1605(a)(7).[73] Such an approach is

---

68 Above note 49, § 1605(a)(7).

69 In its initial form, the *FSIA* amendment only permitted the recovery of compensatory damages. Five months after its enactment, however, Congress returned with the *Omnibus Consolidated and Emergency Supplemental Appropriations Act, 1999,* Pub. L. 105-277, § 117, 112 Stat. 2681, 21 October 1998, which authorizes the award of punitive damages [*OCESA*].

70 The designation is made pursuant to § 6(j) of the *Export Administration Act of 1979,* 50 U.S.C. App. §2405(j) and § 620A of the *Foreign Assistance Act of 1961,* 22 U.S.C. § 2371.

71 Letter to U.S. Acting Attorney-General, "Changing Policy Concerning the Granting of Sovereign Immunity to Foreign Governments" (19 May 1952), 26 U.S. Department of State Bulletin 984 [Tate Letter].

72 International Law Commission, *Mr. Sompong Sucharitkul, Special Rapporteur,* "*Fourth Report on Jurisdictional Immunities of States and Their Property,*" UN Doc. A/CN.4/357 and Corr. 1 in *Yearbook of the International Law Commission 1982,* vol. 2, part 1 (New York: United Nations, 1982) at 219. See also *Republic of Mexico v. Hoffman,* 324 U.S. 30 at 35–36 (1945).

73 Iraq and Libya were originally designated as state sponsors of terrorism for *FSIA* purposes. Iraq was removed from the list in 2003 by Presidential Determination (see 69 Fed. Reg. 18,810 (9 April 2004)), and its designation was officially rescinded in October of 2004 (see 69 Fed. Reg. 61,702 (20 October 2004)). Moreover, by

reflective of policy, not principle. By contrast, section 6.1(2) of Bill S-218 proposes to deny the immunity of any state that is alleged to have participated in or supported acts of terrorism after 1 January 1985 on the theory that terrorism can never be a valid and internationally recognized act *jure imperii*. This approach, unprecedented as it may be, at least has the merit of treating immunities as a question of law rather than politics.

Though §1605(a)(7) is often referred to as the "Flatow Amendment" in memory of the deceased student in *Flatow v. Islamic Republic of Iran*,[74] the first judicial application of the torture and terrorism exception is *Alejandre v. Cuba*.[75] In *Alejandre*, plaintiffs sued the government of Cuba after fighter jets shot down two civilian planes in international airspace over the Florida straights, killing four people. The plaintiffs were awarded $49.9 million in compensatory damages and $137.7 million in punitive damages. In *Flatow*, parents of a student killed in a suicide bombing in Israel sued Iran for financially supporting the terrorist group that claimed responsibility for the attack, the Palestine Islamic Jihad. The Flatow family was awarded $22.5 million in compensatory damages and $225 million in punitive damages.[76] In both cases, however, indeed as in most transnational human rights cases,[77] plaintiffs hardly ever collect on their judgments since most foreign state assets located in the United States are consular or diplomatic in nature and thus protected under international law.[78] To overcome this difficulty, Congress returned with further amendments to the *FSIA*, controversially allowing plaintiffs to access frozen assets and even certain diplomatic property to satisfy judgments obtained under §1605(a)(7).[79]

Presidential Determination dated 12 May 2006, President G.W. Bush certified the rescission of Libya's designation as a state sponsor of terrorism (see 71 Fed. Reg. 31, 907 (1 June 2006)) pursuant to his administration's move to restore diplomatic relations with that country.

74   999 F. Supp. 1 (D.D.C. 1998) [*Flatow*].

75   996 F. Supp. 1239 (S.D. Fla. 1997) [*Alejandre*].

76   See also *Cicippio v. Islamic Republic of Iran*, 18 F. Supp.2d 62, 70 (D.D.C. 1998), decided shortly after *Flatow*, above note 74. In that case, the court awarded three men $65 million after having been kidnapped and held hostage by Hezbollah in Beirut.

77   R.B. Lillich, "Damages for Gross Violations of International Human Rights Awarded by U.S. Courts" (1993) 15 Hum. Rts. Q. 207.

78   Most notably under the *Vienna Convention on Diplomatic Relations*, 18 April 1961, 500 U.N.T.S. 95, to which the United States became a party on 13 December 1972.

79   OCESA, above note 69: permits the attachment of frozen and diplomatic assets of foreign states to satisfy judgments under § 1605(7); *Victims of Trafficking and Vio-*

As a matter of international law, it is irrelevant whether international crimes are committed in Cuba, Iran, or, indeed, Canada. Individual acts of terrorism are outlawed wherever they occur. Under United States law however, the *locus* of the offence and nationality of the offender are determinative of legal consequences. Clearly, the distinction created by the *FSIA* between friendly states and so-called state sponsors of terrorism is a political decision, not a legal one. Be that as it may, despite certain objectionable features, it can be fairly acknowledged that the *FSIA*, *ATS*, and *TVPA* together constitute an ambitious and innovative legislative framework, which has produced an equally ambitious and innovative jurisprudence, ostensibly aimed at enforcing international law and providing victims of human rights violations with some form of redress. On the other hand, ambitious and innovative does not necessarily mean effective and desirable. Indeed, while meeting with the general approval of the national judiciary and academia, U.S. transnational human rights litigation has its share of detractors.[80] Judges Higgins, Kooijmans, and Buergenthal noted in their concurring opinion in the *Case Concerning the Arrest Warrant of 11 April 2000*: "while this unilateral exercise of the function of guardian of international values has been much commented on, it has not attracted the approbation of States generally."[81] Clearly, a broader discussion of the policy objectives of concurrently pursuing civil redress and criminal sanctions for terrorism is warranted. It is argued in the final section of this paper that civil remedies may properly consti-

---

lence Protection Act, 2000, Pub. L. 106-386, § 2002, 114 Stat. 1464, 28 October 2000 [*TVPA*]: permits specified successful § 1605 claimants against Cuba and Iran to be paid the compensatory portion of their awards out of frozen assets. For analysis of the *FSIA* amendments, see A. Taylor, "Another Front in the War on Terrorism? Problems with Recent Changes to the *Foreign Sovereign Immunities Act*" (2003) 45 Ariz. L. Rev. 533; and M. Reisman & M. Hakimi, "Illusion and Reality in the Compensation of Victims of International Terrorism" (2003) 54 Ala. L. Rev. 561.

80 Among the most prolific supporters of transnational human rights litigation are, for example, Michael Ratner, Beth Stephens, Anthony D'Amato, Harold Koh, Anne-Marie Slaughter, and Ralph Steinhardt. The most notable critics include Curtis Bradley and Jack Goldsmith. See also the judgments of Judge Bork in *Tel Oren v. Libyan Arab Republic*, 726 F.2d 774 (D.C. Cir. 1984) and Judge Randolph in *Al-Odah et al. v. United States*, 321 F.3d 1134 (D.C. Cir. 2003).

81 *Case Concerning the Arrest Warrant of 11 April 2000 (Democratic Republic of Congo v. Belgium)*, I.C.J. General List No. 121 at § 48 (14 February 2002), Concurrent Opinion of Judges Higgins, Kooijmans, and Buergenthal.

tute a significant component of a comprehensive national response to the international challenges posed by terrorism.

F. CONCLUSION

Insofar as the *Ottawa Principles* seek to delineate the salient issues and imperatives that ought to guide anti-terrorism policy, their virtual silence on the question of civil remedies for the primary victims of terrorism is regrettable. The effects of terrorism are felt both publicly and privately, by national communities and by the individuals that compose them. Advanced democracies must strike an appropriate balance between the need to protect their populations from the threat of terrorism and the constitutional undertaking to protect individual rights. The rights of persons suspected of planning or facilitating acts of terrorism clearly must be upheld, but so too must the rights of the families that have suffered great loss in the wake of terrorist attacks. Criminal law alone cannot shoulder the task of preventing, punishing, and deterring terrorism. Other concurrent means should be explored.

The time has come for lawmakers and legal scholars to engage in a full and frank debate on the upsides and downsides of permitting victims of terrorism to seek civil redress in Canadian courts. Of course, this debate should not be restricted to terrorism, but should also extend to other breaches of international law such as torture, war crimes, and crimes against humanity, and to the general propriety of enforcing international norms in national courts. The recent English and Canadian transnational human rights cases have shown, first, that national courts are reluctant to exercise their jurisdiction over such cases in the absence of a clear legislative mandate and, second, in the context of suits against states, that existing state immunity legislation poorly countenances the particular exigencies of civil proceedings with respect to extraterritorial violations of international law. The proposed amendments to the *Criminal Code* and the *State Immunity Act* contained in Bill S-218 should go some way in addressing these issues and, it is hoped, in generating meaningful debate both inside and outside Parliament.

ANNEX A

<table>
<tr>
<td>

1st Session, 39th Parliament,
55 Elizabeth II, 2006

BILL S-218

An Act to amend the State Immunity Act and the Criminal Code (civil remedies for victims of terrorism)

WHEREAS it is desirable to confirm in Canadian law the existing peremptory norms and provisions of international law against terrorism (*jus cogens*) that are accepted and recognized by the international community of states as a whole;

AND WHEREAS state immunity is generally accepted as applying only to sovereign acts of state (*acta jure imperii*);

AND WHEREAS terrorism is a threat to democracy, and the support and financing of terror is a crime under international law and as such is not a sovereign act of state to which a claim of state immunity can apply;

AND WHEREAS it is necessary that judicial awards against persons who engage in terrorist activities be sufficiently large to deter such conduct in the future;

AND WHEREAS the victims of terrorist activities include the individuals as well as their family members who are physically, emotionally or psychologically injured by the terrorist activities,

</td>
<td>

1re session, 39e législature,
55 Elizabeth II, 2006

PROJET DE LOI S-218

Loi modifiant la Loi sur l'immunité des États et le Code criminel (recours civils des victimes d'actes terroristes)

ATTENDU qu'il est souhaitable de confirmer en droit canadien les normes et les dispositions impératives existantes en droit international contre le terrorisme (*jus cogens* ou "droit contraignant") qui sont acceptées et reconnues par l'ensemble de la communauté internationale des États;

qu'il est généralement accepté que l'immunité de juridiction s'applique uniquement aux actes de gouvernement (*acta jure imperii*);

que le terrorisme représente une menace pour la démocratie et que le soutien et le financement du terrorisme est un crime en vertu du droit international et qu'en tant que tel, il n'est pas un acte de gouvernement auquel il serait permis d'appliquer l'immunité de juridiction;

qu'il est nécessaire que la portée des décisions des tribunaux défavorables aux personnes qui se livrent à des activités terroristes soit suffisamment large pour décourager cette conduite par la suite;

que les victimes des activités terroristes ne sont pas uniquement les

</td>
</tr>
</table>

NOW, THEREFORE, Her Majesty, by and with the advice and consent of the Senate and House of Commons of Canada, enacts as follows:

State Immunity Act

1. The *State Immunity Act* is amended by adding the following after section 6:

6.1 (1) In this section, subsection 11(4), paragraph 12(1)(*d*), and subsection 13(3), "terrorist activity" means any transaction, act or conduct that involves or relates to the support of any terrorist group that is a listed entity as defined in subsection 83.01(1) of the *Criminal Code*.

(2) A foreign state is not immune from the jurisdiction of a court in any proceedings that relate to any terrorist activity that the foreign state conducted on or after January 1, 1985.

2. Section 11 of the Act is amended by adding the following after subsection (3):

(4) This section does not apply to a foreign state that engages in terrorist activity.

3. Subsection 12(1) of the Act is amended by striking out the word "or" at the end of paragraph (*b*), by adding the word "or" at the end of paragraph (*c*) and by adding the following after paragraph (*c*):

particuliers qui ont été blessés physiquement, émotionnellement ou psychologiquement par les activités terroristes, mais également les membres de leur famille,

Sa Majesté, sur l'avis et avec le consentement du Sénat et de la Chambre des communes du Canada, édicte :

Loi sur l'immunité des États

1. La *Loi sur l'immunité des États* est modifiée par adjonction, après l'article 6, de ce qui suit :

6.1 (1) Au présent article, au paragraphe 11(4), à l'alinéa 12(1)*d*) et au paragraphe 13(3), « activité terroriste » s'entend de tout acte, comportement ou opération qui comporte l'appui d'un groupe terroriste qui est une entité inscrite au sens du paragraphe 83.01(1) du *Code criminel*, ou qui se rapporte à l'appui d'un tel groupe.

(2) L'État étranger ne bénéficie pas de l'immunité de juridiction dans les actions portant sur des activités terroristes auxquelles il s'est livré le 1er janvier 1985 ou après cette date.

2. L'article 11 de la même loi est modifié par adjonction, après le paragraphe (3), de ce qui suit :

(4) Le présent article ne s'applique pas à un État étranger qui se livre à des activités terroristes.

3. Le paragraphe 12(1) de la même loi est modifié par adjonction, après l'alinéa *c*), de ce qui suit :

(d) the attachment or execution relates to a judgment rendered in connection with terrorist activity.

4. Section 13 of the Act is amended by adding the following after subsection (2):

(3) Subsection (1) does not apply to a foreign state that engages in terrorist activity.

Criminal Code

5. The *Criminal Code* is amended by adding the following after section 83.33:

Loss or damage

83.34 (1) Any person who has suffered loss or damage, on or after January 1, 1985, as a result of conduct that is contrary to any provision of this Part or the failure of any person to comply with an order of a court under this Part may, in any court of competent jurisdiction, sue for and recover from the person who engaged in the conduct or failed to comply with the order an amount equal to the loss or damage proved to have been suffered by the person, together with any additional amount that the court may allow by way of punitive damages or otherwise.

(2) Any limitation period in relation to a claim under subsection (1) shall not run while the person with the claim

(d) la saisie ou l'éxecution à trait à un jugement rendu à l'égard d'activités terroristes.

4. L'article 13 de la même loi est modifié par adjonction par ce qui suit :

(3) Le paragraphe (1) ne s'applique pas à un État étranger qui se livre à des activités terroristes.

Code criminel

5. Le *Code criminel* est modifié par adjonction, après l'article 83.33, de ce qui suit :

Perte ou dommages

83.34 (1) Toute personne qui, le 1er janvier 1985 ou après cette date, a subi une perte ou des dommages par suite soit d'un comportement allant à l'encontre d'une disposition de la présente partie, soit du défaut d'une personne d'obtempérer à une ordonnance rendue par un tribunal en vertu de la présente partie peut, devant tout tribunal compétent, réclamer et recouvrer de la personne qui a eu un tel comportement ou n'a pas obtempéré à l'ordonnance une somme égale au montant de la perte ou des dommages qu'elle est reconnue avoir subis, ainsi que toute somme supplémentaire que le tribunal peut fixer, notamment à titre des dommages intérêts punitifs.

(2) Le délai de prescription applicable à la cause d'action visée au paragraphe (1) ne court pas pendant la période au cours de laquelle la per-

(*a*) is incapable of commencing a proceeding in respect of the claim because of his or her physical, mental or psychological condition; or

(*b*) is unaware of the identity of the person who engaged in the conduct that resulted in the loss or damage.

Judgments of foreign courts

(3) Any court of competent jurisdiction shall give full faith and credit to a judgment of any foreign court in favour of a person who has suffered loss or damage as a result of conduct contrary to any provision of this Article.

(4) In this section, "person" includes a foreign state and an agency of a foreign state as defined in the *State Immunity Act*.

sonne ayant subi la perte ou les dommages :

(*a*) soit est incapable d'intenter une action en raison de son état physique, mental ou psychologique;

(*b*) soit ne connaît pas l'identité de la personne dont le comportement a entraîné la perte ou les dommages.

Jugement d'un tribunal étranger

(3) Tout tribunal compétent est tenu d'accorder pleine foi et crédit au jugement d'un tribunal étranger rendu en faveur d'une personne ayant subi une perte ou des dommages par suite d'un comportement allant à l'encontre d'une disposition de la présente partie.

(4) Au présent article, « personne » désigne en outre un État étranger et un organisme d'un État étranger au sens de la *Loi sur l'immunité des États*.

ANNEX B

The Civil Remedies Provisions of the United States Antiterrorism Act of 1991, 18 U.S.C §2333–2338

Sec. 2333. Civil remedies

(a) **Action and Jurisdiction**—Any national of the United States injured in his or her person, property, or business by reason of an act of international terrorism, or his or her estate, survivors, or heirs, may sue therefor in any appropriate district court of the United States and shall recover threefold the damages he or she sustains and the cost of the suit, including attorney's fees.

(b) **Estoppel Under United States Law**—A final judgment or decree rendered in favor of the United States in any criminal proceeding under section 1116, 1201, 1203, or 2332 of this title or section 46314, 46502, 46505, or 46506 of title 49 shall estop the defendant from denying the essential allegations of the criminal offense in any subsequent civil proceeding under this section.

(c) **Estoppel Under Foreign Law**—A final judgment or decree rendered in favor of any foreign state in any criminal proceeding shall, to the extent that such judgment or decree may be accorded full faith and credit under the law of the United States, estop the defendant from denying the essential allegations of the criminal offense in any subsequent civil proceeding under this section.

Sec. 2334. Jurisdiction and venue

(a) **General Venue**—Any civil action under section 2333 of this title against any person may be instituted in the district court of the United States for any district where any plaintiff resides or where any defendant resides or is served, or has an agent. Process in such a civil action may be served in any district where the defendant resides, is found, or has an agent.

(b) **Special Maritime or Territorial Jurisdiction**—If the actions giving rise to the claim occurred within the special maritime and territorial jurisdiction of the United States, as defined in section 7 of this title, then any civil action under section 2333 of this title against any person may be instituted in the district court of the United States for any district in which any plaintiff resides or the defendant resides, is served, or has an agent.

(c) **Service on Witnesses**—A witness in a civil action brought under section 2333 of this title may be served in any other district where the defendant resides, is found, or has an agent.

(d) **Convenience of the Forum**—The district court shall not dismiss any action brought under section 2333 of this title on the grounds of the inconvenience or inappropriateness of the forum chosen, unless—

1)   the action may be maintained in a foreign court that has jurisdiction over the subject matter and over all the defendants;

2)   that foreign court is significantly more convenient and appropriate; and

3)   that foreign court offers a remedy which is substantially the same as the one available in the courts of the United States.

Sec. 2335. Limitation of actions

(a) **In General**—Subject to subsection (b), a suit for recovery of damages under section 2333 of this title shall not be maintained unless commenced within 4 years after the date the cause of action accrued.

(b) **Calculation of Period**—The time of the absence of the defendant from the United States or from any jurisdiction in which the same or a similar action arising from the same facts may be maintained by the plaintiff, or of any concealment of the defendant's whereabouts, shall not be included in the 4-year period set forth in subsection (a).

Sec. 2336. Other limitations

(a) **Acts of War**—No action shall be maintained under section 2333 of this title for injury or loss by reason of an act of war.

(b) **Limitation on Discovery**—If a party to an action under section 2333 seeks to discover the investigative files of the Department of Justice, the Assistant Attorney General, Deputy Attorney General, or Attorney General may object on the ground that compliance will interfere with a criminal investigation or prosecution of the incident, or a national security operation related to the incident, which is the subject of the civil litigation. The court shall evaluate any such objections in camera and shall stay the discovery if the court finds that granting the discovery request will substantially interfere with a criminal investigation or prosecution of the incident or a national security operation related to the incident. The court shall consider the likelihood of criminal prosecution by the Government and other factors it deems to be appropriate. A stay of discovery under this subsection shall constitute a bar to the granting of a motion to dismiss under rules 12(b)(6) and 56 of the Federal Rules of Civil Procedure. If the court grants a stay of discovery under this subsection, it may stay the action in the interests of justice.

(c) **Stay of Action for Civil Remedies**—(1) The Attorney General may intervene in any civil action brought under section 2333 for the purpose of seeking a stay of the civil action. A stay shall be granted if the court finds that the continuation of the civil action will substantially interfere with a criminal prosecution which involves the same subject matter and in which an indictment has been returned, or interfere with national security operations related to the terrorist incident that is the subject of the civil action. A stay may be granted for up to 6 months. The Attorney General may petition the court for an extension of the stay for additional 6-month periods until the criminal prosecution is completed or dismissed.

(2) In a proceeding under this subsection, the Attorney General may request that any order issued by the court for release to the parties and the public omit any reference to the basis on which the stay was sought.

Sec. 2337. Suits against Government officials

No action shall be maintained under section 2333 of this title against—

(1) the United States, an agency of the United States, or an officer or employee of the United States or any agency thereof acting within his or her official capacity or under color of legal authority; or

(2) a foreign state, an agency of a foreign state, or an officer or employee of a foreign state or an agency thereof acting within his or her official capacity or under color of legal authority.

Sec. 2338. Exclusive Federal jurisdiction

The district courts of the United States shall have exclusive jurisdiction over an action brought under this chapter.

About the Editors and Authors

Nicole LaViolette

Nicole LaViolette is Associate Professor of Law at the University of Ottawa where she teaches public international law, international humanitarian law, conflicts of laws, and family law. Her research is devoted mainly to international human rights, international humanitarian law, and the rights of refugees. She has authored several articles and studies relating to refugee law, war crimes, international human rights, and the rights of sexual minorities. She has several years of experience working as a legislative assistant in the House of Commons of Canada and she has worked extensively with both governmental and non-governmental organizations specializing in human rights. She is a graduate of the University of Ottawa's Faculty of Law and Carleton University. She was a law clerk at the Federal Court of Appeal of Canada before completing a graduate degree at Cambridge University in 1998.

Craig Forcese

Craig Forcese joined the Faculty of Law at the University of Ottawa in 2003. He teaches public international law, national security law, administrative law, and public law/legislation. Much of his present research and writing relates to national security, human rights, and democratic accountability. Prior to joining the law school faculty, Professor Forcese practised law with the Washington, D.C. office of Hughes Hubbard & Reed LLP, specializing in international trade law. He has a B.A. from Mc-Gill, an M.A. in international affairs from Carleton University, an LL.B. from the University of Ottawa, and an LL.M. from Yale University. He is a member of the bars of Ontario, New York, and the District of Columbia.

François Larocque

François Larocque is an Assistant Professor of Law at the University of Ottawa where he teaches, among other things, constitutional law and tort law. His doctoral research at the University of Cambridge and his subsequent publications focus on adjudicative jurisdiction in transnational human rights litigation. In 2004, he intervened on behalf of Canadian Lawyers for International Human Rights in *Bouzari v. Islamic Republic of Iran* at the Court of Appeal of Ontario, where an Iranian national sued Iran in relation to acts of torture.

Graham Mayeda

Graham Mayeda joined the Faculty of Law at the University of Ottawa in 2005. His current research focuses on law and development, criminal law, and the nature of common law reasoning. His legal career began at the University of Toronto, where he completed his J.D. in 2004. He has been a law clerk to the Hon. Madam Justice Louise Charron at the Supreme Court of Canada in 2004–5, and he was called to the Bar of Ontario in July of 2005. Since switching fields to law from philosophy, he has continued to explore the importance of difference in various legal contexts. His recent work has focused on the impact of international trade regimes and development policy on developing countries. He is also interested in the impact of cultural, socio-economic, racial, and gender difference in Canadian criminal law.

David M. Paciocco

Professor Paciocco has taught at the Faculty of Law of the University of Ottawa since 1982. He taught at the University of Windsor in 1981–82 and was a Visiting Lecturer at the University of Auckland, New Zealand in 1989–90. He has worked as an Assistant Crown Attorney, and as a criminal defence counsel, doing appellate advocacy. He is the author of *Charter Principle and Proof in Criminal Cases* (1987); co-author, with Professor Lee Stuesser of the University of Manitoba, of *The Law of Evi-*

dence (1995); *Jury Selection in Criminal Cases: Skills, Science and the Law* (1997) with David M. Tanovich and Steven Skurka, and author of *Getting Away with Murder: The Canadian Criminal Justice System* (1998). He has published extensively in the law of evidence, criminal law, as well as on the *Charter* and the law of trusts. He teaches criminal law, evidence, and the law of trusts.

Gar Pardy

Gar Pardy is the former Director General of the Consular Affairs Bureau of the Canadian Department of Foreign Affairs. He retired from the Canadian Foreign Service in 2003. Previously he was the Ambassador of Canada for Costa Rica, El Salvador, Honduras, Nicaragua, and Panama and served in Canadian missions in New Delhi, India, Nairobi, Kenya, and Washington, D.C.

Cathleen Powell

Cathleen Powell obtained her B.A. and LL.B. degrees at the University of Cape Town and was then awarded a scholarship by the *Deutscher Akademischer Austauschdienst* to read for an LL.M. at the Humboldt University in Berlin, Germany. After carrying out further legal research at this institution and at the *Wissenschafts-zentrum zu Berlin,* she returned to UCT in 1999. She teaches constitutional, international, and international criminal law. In addition to these areas, her research interests include aboriginal title. Her recent publications focus on terrorism and its relationship with other legal disciplines, notably criminal, constitutional, and human rights law, together with the law of international organizations. She served on a panel of foreign experts to advise the Chinese government on its proposed emergency law.

Victor V. Ramraj

Victor V. Ramraj is an Associate Professor and Vice-Dean (Academic Affairs) in the Faculty of Law, National University of Singapore. He has qualifications in law (LL.B, Toronto; LL.M, Queen's University Belfast) and philosophy (B.A., McGill; M.A., Ph.D., Toronto) and was called to the bar of Ontario in 1995. Before joining the Faculty, he served as a judicial law clerk at the Federal Court of Appeal in Ottawa and as a litigation lawyer in Toronto. His main areas of teaching and research are legal theory, criminal law, constitutional law, and counter-terrorism policy. He is the co-author/co-editor of three books, including *Global Anti-Terrorism Law and Policy* (2005); and *Fundamental Principles of Criminal Law* (2005). His scholarly work has been published in leading international law journals. He has held visiting appointments in the Faculty of Law, University of Toronto, and at Kyushu University, Japan, and has presented academic papers to audiences in Canada, Hong Kong, India, Iran, Ireland, the Philippines, Singapore, South Africa, Sweden, Taiwan, the United Kingdom, and the United States.

Kent Roach

Kent Roach is a Professor of criminal law at the Faculty of Law of the University of Toronto. He works actively in the area of criminal law and anti-terrorism. He has served on the advisory board for the Commission of Inquiry into the Actions of Canadian Officials in Relation to Maher Arar and as a consultant to the Economic Law, Institutional and Professional Strengthening Project on Indonesia's Proposed Anti-terrorism Law. Recent publications include *Global Anti-terrorism Law and Policy* (Victor Ramraj, Michael Hor, and Kent Roach, eds., Cambridge: Cambridge University Press, 2005); and *September 11: Consequences for Canada* (Montreal: McGill-Queen's University Press, 2003).

Lorne Waldman

Lorne Waldman is one of Canada's top litigation lawyers, specializing in immigration and refugee cases. He graduated from Osgoode Hall Law School in 1977 and obtained his LL.M from University of Toronto in 2000. He has practised in Toronto since 1979 exclusively in the area of refugee and immigration law. He has appeared at all levels of court in Canada, including the Supreme Court of Canada. He has written and spoken extensively about the use of immigration proceedings as a vehicle for dealing with persons who are perceived to be threats to national security. He was one of the senior counsel representing Canadian citizen Maher Arar at the commission of inquiry into the circumstances behind his deportation from the United States to Syria where he was brutally tortured.

Andrea Wright

Andrea Wright is a solicitor with the Department of Constitutional Affairs in London, U.K., presently working on a bill to reform the oversight and regulatory system for the legal profession. From April 2004 to January 2006, she was counsel to the Arar Commission of Inquiry, where she assisted Justice Dennis O'Connor with his policy security activities. Andrea has also been a lawyer with the Canadian Human Rights Commission and with McCarthy Tetrault LLP, and has published and delivered papers in the areas of human rights and administrative law. She is a graduate of McGill University's Faculty of Law and Dalhousie University.

List of Participants, The Human Rights of Anti-terrorism: A Colloquium, Ottawa, 15–17 June 2006

PART 1: The following experts participated in their individual capacities in the colloquium held at the Law Faculty of the University of Ottawa to draft the *Ottawa Principles on Anti-terrorism and Human Rights*. Organizations and affiliations are listed strictly for purposes of identification and not as an indication of organizational endorsement of these principles:

- Sharryn Aiken, Faculty of Law, Queen's University, Canada
- Warren Allmand, former Solicitor General of Canada
- Ron Atkey Q.C., Osler, Hoskin and Harcourt LLP, Canada
- Michael Byers, University of British Columbia, Canada
- Sandra Coliver, Open Society Justice Initiative, United States
- John Currie, Faculty of Law, University of Ottawa, Canada

PARTIE 1 : Les spécialistes suivants ont participé en leur capacité personnelle au colloque tenu à la faculté de droit de l'Université d'Ottawa pour élaborer les *Principes d'Ottawa relatifs à la lutte au terrorisme et aux droits de l'homme*. Les organisations et les affiliations ne sont mentionnées que pour permettre l'identification (des participants). Nul ne peut inférer que ces organisations ou affiliations endossent ces principes :

- Sharryn Aiken, Faculty of Law, Queen's University, Canada
- Warren Allmand, ancien solliciteur général du Canada
- Ron Atkey c.r., Osler, Hoskin and Harcourt S.E.N.C.R.L., Canada
- Michael Byers, University of British Columbia, Canada
- Sandra Coliver, Open Society Justice Initiative, États-Unis
- John Currie, Faculté de droit, Université d'Ottawa, Canada

- Carla Ferstman, REDRESS, United Kingdom
- Edward J. Flynn, Human Rights Advisor, United Nations
- Craig Forcese, Faculty of Law, University of Ottawa, Canada
- Vera Gowlland-Debbas, Graduate Institute of International Studies, Switzerland
- Susheel Gupta, Lawyer and Air India victim family member, Canada
- Julia Hall, Human Rights Watch, United States
- Ben Hayes, Statewatch, United Kingdom
- Barbara Jackman, Jackman & Associates, Canada
- François Larocque, Faculty of Law, University of Ottawa, Canada
- Nicole LaViolette, Faculty of Law, University of Ottawa, Canada
- Graham Mayeda, Faculty of Law, University of Ottawa, Canada
- Alex Neve, Secretary General, Amnesty International, Canada
- Lisa Oldring, Rule of Law and Democracy Unit, UN Office of the High Commissioner for Human Rights
- Juliet O'Neill, Journalist, *Ottawa Citizen*, Canada
- David Paccioco, Faculty of Law, University of Ottawa, Canada
- Gar Pardy, Former Director General, Consular Affairs Bureau, Canadian Department of Foreign Affairs, Canada
- Cathleen Powell, Faculty of Law, University of Cape Town, South Africa

- Carla Ferstman, REDRESS, R.-U.
- Edward J. Flynn, conseiller en matière de droits de l'homme, Nations-Unies
- Craig Forcese, Faculté de droit, Université d'Ottawa, Canada
- Vera Gowlland-Debbas, Institut universitaire de hautes études internationales, Suisse
- Susheel Gupta, avocat et membre de la famille d'une victime de l'attentat à la bombe du vol Air India, Canada
- Julia Hall, Human Rights Watch, États-Unis
- Ben Hayes, Statewatch, R.-U.
- Barbara Jackman, Jackman & Associates, Canada
- François Larocque, Faculté de droit, Université d'Ottawa, Canada
- Nicole LaViolette, Faculté de droit, Université d'Ottawa, Canada
- Graham Mayeda, Faculté de droit, Université d'Ottawa, Canada
- Alex Neve, secrétaire général, Amnistie Internationale, Canada
- Lisa Oldring, Rule of Law and Democracy Unit, Bureau du haut commissaire des Nations Unies aux droits de l'homme
- Juliet O'Neill, journaliste, *Ottawa Citizen*, Canada
- David Paccioco, Faculté de droit, Université d'Ottawa, Canada
- Gar Pardy, ancien directeur général, Bureau des Affaires consulaires, ministère des Affaires étrangères, Canada
- Cathleen Powell, Faculty of Law, University of Cape Town, Afrique du Sud

- Victor V. Ramraj, Faculty of Law, National University of Singapore
- Kent Roach, Faculty of Law, University of Toronto, Canada
- Alasdair Roberts, Maxwell School, Syracuse University, United States
- Margaret Satterthwaite, NYU School of Law, United States
- Craig Scott, Osgoode Hall Law School, York University, Canada
- Roch Tasse, International Civil Liberties Monitoring Group, Canada
- Lorne Waldman, Waldman & Associates, Canada
- Stephen Watt, American Civil Liberties Union, United States
- Maureen Webb, Legal Counsel, Canadian Association of University Teachers, Canada
- Rick Wilson, Washington College of Law, American University, United States
- Andrea Wright, Former Legal Counsel, Policy Review, Commission of Inquiry into the Actions of Canadian Officials in Relation to Maher Arar, Canada

PART 2: The following people were present and participated in the discussions but are not able to take a position on the principles because of their organizational affiliations or for other reasons:

- Ian Seiderman, Senior Legal Advisor, Amnesty International, International Secretariat, U.K.

- Victor Ramraj, Faculty of Law, National University of Singapore
- Kent Roach, Faculty of Law, University of Toronto, Canada
- Alasdair Roberts, Maxwell School, Syracuse University, États-Unis
- Margaret Satterthwaite, NYU School of Law, États-Unis
- Craig Scott, Osgoode Hall Law School, York University, Canada
- Roch Tasse, International Civil Liberties Monitoring Group, Canada
- Lorne Waldman, Waldman & Associates, Canada
- Stephen Watt, American Civil Liberties Union, États-Unis
- Maureen Webb, conseillère juridique, Association canadienne des professeures et professeurs d'université, Canada
- Rick Wilson, Washington College of Law, American University, États-Unis
- Andrea Wright, ancienne conseillère juridique, Examen de la politique, Commission d'enquête sur les actions des responsables canadiens relativement à Maher Arar, Canada

PARTIE 2 : La personne suivante a assisté aux discussions et y a participé, mais elle n'a pu se prononcer sur la teneur des principes en raison de son appartenance ou affiliation à une organisation, ou pour d'autres motifs :

- Ian Seiderman, conseilleur juridique principal, Secrétariat d'Amnistie Internationale, R.-U.

Table of Authorities

NATIONAL CASELAW

NATIONAL LEGISLATION

INTERNATIONAL CASELAW

INTERNATIONAL TREATIES

SECURITY COUNCIL RESOLUTIONS

GENERAL ASSEMBLY RESOLUTIONS

INTERNATIONAL LAW COMMISSION TEXTS

OTHER INSTRUMENTS

SECONDARY SOURCES

Index